Industrial Society and Social Welfare

HAROLD L. WILENSKY
and
CHARLES N. LEBEAUX

Industrial Society
and
Social Welfare

*The impact of industrialization on
the supply and organization of social
welfare services in the United States*

WITH A NEW INTRODUCTION
BY HAROLD L. WILENSKY

This Study was
Originally Supported and Published
by Russell Sage Foundation

THE FREE PRESS, *New York*
COLLIER-MACMILLAN LIMITED, *London*

Collier-Macmillan Canada, Ltd., Toronto, Ontario

Library of Congress Catalog Card Number: 58-8637

FIRST FREE PRESS PAPERBACK EDITION 1965

printing number
7 8 9 10

Introduction to the Paperbound Edition

THE PROBLEMS AND PROSPECTS
OF THE WELFARE STATE

by

HAROLD L. WILENSKY

Each profession makes progress, but it is progress in its own groove.
. . . The dangers arising from this aspect of professionalism are great,
particularly in our democratic societies. . . . The rate of progress is
such that an individual human being . . . will be called upon to face
novel situations which find no parallel in his past. The fixed person
for the fixed duties, who in older societies was such a godsend, in the
future will be a public danger. . . . In short, the specialised functions
of the community are performed better . . . but the generalised direction lacks vision. The progressiveness in detail only adds to the
danger produced by the feebleness of coordination. . . . We are left
with no expansion of wisdom and with greater need of it.
              —A. N. WHITEHEAD, *Science and the Modern World*[1]

ALL MAJOR POLITICAL PARTIES in the rich countries of the free world
claim the maintenance of the "Welfare State" as an article of faith.
But everywhere there is great reluctance to accept its main implications: the redistribution of income from the middle majority to
the minority poor; the financing and manning of a vast apparatus
of social agencies in the fields of education, health, and welfare;
the need to study the actual operation of such agencies; the necessity of welfare planning and a rational delineation of welfare priorities so that the total effort moves us toward widely shared goals.

During the seven-year period since this book was first published,
several trends discussed in it have become a matter of public concern. Certain welfare expenditures have increased sharply; debate

---

[1] Whitehead, Alfred North, *Science and the Modern World*. Macmillan Co.,
New York, 1926, pp. 282–284.

TABLE 13

SOCIAL WELFARE EXPENDITURES UNDER PUBLIC PROGRAMS FOR FISCAL YEARS 1954–1955 AND 1963–1964

Program	Total expenditures				Federal expenditures		State-local expenditures	
	1954–1955		1963–1964[a]		1954–1955	1963–1964	1954–1955	1963–1964
	Amount	% of total	Amount	% of total	% of total	% of total	% of total	% of total
	(In millions)		(In millions)					
Social insurance	$9,854	30.5	$26,846	37.8	45.0	58.5	19.1	17.6
Old-age, survivors, disability	4,436	13.7	16,161	22.8	31.2	46.0	….	….
Railroad retirement, unemployment and temporary disability	788	2.4	1,245	1.8	5.5	3.5	….	….
Public employment retirement	1,388	4.3	4,000	5.6	5.7	6.9	3.2	4.4
Unemployment insurance and employment service	2,081	6.4	3,280	4.6	2.3	1.8	9.7	7.4
State temporary disability	218	0.7	480	0.7	….	….	1.2	1.3
Workmen's compensation	943	2.9	1,680	2.4	0.4	0.2	4.9	4.5
Public aid	3,003	9.3	5,565	7.8	10.6	9.0	8.3	6.7
Health and medical except veterans'	3,054	9.4	6,078	8.6	8.2	7.8	10.4	9.3
Other welfare[b]	647	2.0	1,935	2.7	1.7	1.7	2.2	3.7
Veterans' programs, including health and education	4,370	13.5	5,667	8.0	30.3	16.0	0.3	0.1
Education, except veterans'	11,299	35.0	24,647	34.7	3.7	6.3	59.6	62.5
Public housing	89	0.3	271	0.4	0.5	0.6	0.1	0.2
Total	$32,317	100.0	$71,009	100.0	100.0 (14,233)	99.9 (35,096)	100.0 (18,084)	100.1 (35,912)
Total, excluding all education	$20,318	62.9	$46,298	65.2	96.3 (13,712)	93.7 (32,888)	40.4 (7,308)	37.5 (13,473)

a. Preliminary estimate for 1963–1964.
b. Vocational rehabilitation, institutional care, school lunch, child welfare.

SOURCE: Merriam, Ida C., "Social Welfare Expenditures, 1963–1964," Social Security Bulletin, vol. 27, October, 1964, Table I,

about the balance between the public and private sectors has been
renewed; more national attention is now devoted to domestic issues,
symbolized in the civil rights movement and the "war on poverty";
the question of whether the continued push for equality threatens
the security and freedom of middle strata has been taken seriously
(the managers of the Goldwater and Johnson campaigns of 1964
had to calculate not only the "white backlash" but also a kind of
"welfare backlash"); the shortage of manpower in social welfare
has grown worse, and the possibilities and dilemmas of new programs of community action have become clear. If we examine these
recent developments, we can underscore the main conclusions of the
book and learn more of the problems and prospects of the welfare
state.

The Direction of Recent Welfare Expenditures

In the decade from 1954–1955 to 1964–1965, government expenditures for social welfare, excluding education, jumped from
about $20.3 billion to more than $46.3 billion.[2] As we noted for
the early 1950's (page 157), the most rapid rise is occurring in the
social insurances (about $10 billion to about $27 billion), and this
added effort continues to be much more a matter of federal expenditures ($13.7 to $32.9 billion) than state and local ($7.3 to $13.5
billion). The trend toward the institutionalization of welfare services, noted in Chapter VI, is clear; these social insurance programs
cover a vast majority of the population; they are increasingly taken
for granted.

Recent increases in welfare expenditures reflect not only population expansion and price inflation; they represent a solid rise in the
proportion of our gross national product devoted to social welfare
programs—from about 5 per cent in the early 1950's to 7.7 per cent
in the early 1960's.

Taking account of population growth and inflation, what welfare
programs are making most rapid strides? Table 14 shows increases
from 1954–1955 to 1963–1964 in public civilian social welfare expenditures per capita adjusted for inflation. The most impressive
real gains were in social insurance (107 per cent) and education
(66 per cent)—both of which would be greater if the figures reflected the passage in 1965 of "Medicare" financed from Old Age,
Survivors, and Disability Insurance and a federal aid to education

[2] See Table 13, which brings Table 4 on p. 154 up-to-date. The minor discrepancies in the 1954–1955 figures are due to slight changes in definition
designed to improve the estimates and their comparability with 1964–1965.

TABLE 14. SOCIAL WELFARE EXPENDITURES PER CAPITA UNDER PUBLIC PROGRAMS, ACTUAL PRICES AND PERCENTAGE DIFFERENCE FOR FISCAL YEARS 1954–1955 AND 1963–1964

Program	Annual per capita expenditures in actual prices		Percentage difference 1963–1964 — 1954–1955 (adjusted for inflation)[a]
	1954–1955	1963–1964	
Social insurance	$ 58.84	$ 138.61	107
Public aid	17.98	28.86	41
Health and medical services	18.29	31.52	51
Other welfare[b]	3.87	10.03	127
Veterans' programs	25.83	29.13	−1
Education	67.65	127.72	66
Public housing	.54	1.42	131
Total	$ 192.99	$ 367.26	67
Per capita income	1831.00	2502.00	20

a. Difference in prices, adjusted for inflation, expressed as a percentage of 1954–1955 amounts. Positive percentage differences indicate a gain in per capita expenditure in the fiscal year 1963–1964 over per capita expenditure in 1954–1955. Per capita income for the United States is included for comparison with per capita expenditures.
b. Vocational rehabilitation, institutional care, school lunch, child welfare.
SOURCE: Merriam, Ida C., "Social Welfare Expenditures, 1963–1964," *Social Security Bulletin*, vol. 27, October, 1964, Table 3, p. 9. Adjustments for inflation employ the implicit price deflator for consumption expenditures prepared by the National Income Division, Office of Business Economics, Department of Commerce.

bill. In both level and rate of growth, social insurance again dwarfed the other public programs. That fact, however, does not signify a great expansion of welfare consciousness or a marked liberalization of benefits; it is rather a matter of the maturing of the OASDI program—more of the covered persons are now reaching retirement age, experiencing disability or the death of a breadwinner—and of the higher rates of unemployment of the early 1960's, which brought an increased number of claims. Nevertheless the real per capita gains are more impressive for social insurance than for health and medical services (51 per cent) and public aid (41 per cent). And with the decline in beneficiaries of programs rooted in World Wars I and II, veterans' pensions and compensation actually decreased (−1 per cent). "Other welfare" programs such as vocational rehabilitation, institutional care, school lunch, and child welfare increased most rapidly (127 per cent), but in the absolute terms of Table 13 they remain small ($647 million to $1.9 billion). In actual dollar outlays we continue to do almost nothing about public housing (from $89 million to $271 million), representing a shift from a meager per capita expenditure of 54 cents a year in the mid-fifties to the lavish figure of $1.42 in the mid-sixties.

The gains of the past decade must be cast against both the increase in the wealth of the nation and the greater efforts of other rich countries to tackle problems of income maintenance. During those years the gross national product climbed 62 per cent from about \$373 billion in 1954–1955 to about \$604 billion in 1963–1964; adjusted for inflation, the increase is 42 per cent. Thus welfare expenditures in almost every general field, except public aid and veterans' benefits, climbed faster than our ability to pay. However, the American achievement (or what some critics call "creeping socialism") looks weak compared to the performance of our sister "welfare states." America continues to lag in its income maintenance and social security programs. For instance, in 1957 when the United States was spending 5.5 per cent of its national income on social security benefits and "other current transfers," France was spending a roughly comparable 17.3 per cent; West Germany, 17.3 per cent; Austria, 14.6 per cent; Italy, 13.2 per cent; Belgium, 11.2 per cent; Canada, 8.8 per cent; the Netherlands, 8.6 per cent; and the United Kingdom, 6.9 per cent. If we include health programs, the disparity would be even greater.[3] (Similar comparisons for earlier years appear on our pages 156 ff.)

Until now, and for the reasons spelled out in this book, the more

[3] See Gordon, Margaret S., *The Economics of Welfare Policies*, Columbia University Press, New York, 1963, chap. 2, the best recent summary of the international evidence. Of the 15 countries surveyed by the Organization for European Economic Cooperation, only Portugal performed worse than the United States. Of the 30 countries for which the International Labour Office reported data on social security expenditures, including health insurance and health service programs, not one Western European country fell below the United States. We surpassed only a handful of poor countries in Asia (Ceylon, Taiwan, India) and Africa (The Union of South Africa); we were about even with Japan and Tunisia. Or consider another measure: the per cent of "general government current expenditure" going to "social security and assistance" in the United States in 1960 was 15 compared to 29 in Denmark, 22 in Australia, 18 in the United Kingdom. The per cent spent on "health and special welfare services" was 7 in the United States, 16 in the United Kingdom, 16 in Australia, and 14 in Denmark. (United Nations, *Compendium of Social Statistics: 1963*, New York, 1963, Table 102.) Such comparisons must take account of national differences in the size of private welfare expenditures, in administrative costs, and in housing supplies in relation to housing programs. The addition of private welfare expenditures, in which America leads, would not significantly change the picture. If we focus not on welfare costs but on what people receive in benefits, the spending figures mentioned above may be slightly exaggerated measures of service since they include administrative overhead, and administrative costs are perhaps higher in the better developed welfare states. A final qualification applies to housing programs. Here it is difficult to make meaningful comparisons between the United States and rich countries where much housing was destroyed in World War II. In free Europe, housing supplies, both public and private, are so limited that even the middle class struggles for space and subsidy. And Communist countries, notably the Soviet Union, have put housing so low in their planning priorities that everyone shares in a colossal shortage.

industrialized the nation, the larger the slice of its national income spent on welfare services. Whether this trend will continue is uncertain. There may be a stage of affluence when the rate of dependency drops so much, when the population can buy so much on the market or bargain for so much privately, that the percentage of national income spent by very rich countries on welfare services will drop. On the other hand, should we arrive at that opulent stage, the remaining social problems (for example, the "clinical poor," manpower upgrading) may be so formidable and the demand that they be solved so urgent, that increased effort will be required. Meanwhile, in relation to their ability to pay, rich countries have been boosting their welfare expenditures, but the United States, the richest of them all, has moved only slowly with the general tendency.

More important than trends in the size of welfare expenditures are the purposes and effects of specific programs—the meaning of all this money for various populations. And the import of welfare budgets is best understood in relation to the distribution of American abundance generally. The paradoxes, well stated by J. K. Galbraith, are now clear to everyone: the cars pour out of the Detroit factories at a great rate, but the supply of streets, highways, parking space, traffic control (and hospitals to accommodate the annual massacre) lags far behind. The greater the wealth, the thicker the dirt—the smog of Los Angeles is only a taste of things to come. Our children may be a bit crowded in schools, but on the outside they will be generously supplied with TV, motor bikes, and narcotics. In Galbraith's words,

> The family which takes its mauve and cerise, air-conditioned, power-steered, and power-braked automobile out for a tour passes through cities that are badly paved, made hideous by litter, blighted buildings, billboards, and posts for wires that should long since have been put underground. They pass on into a countryside that has been rendered largely invisible by commercial art. . . . They picnic on exquisitely packaged food from a portable icebox by a polluted stream and go on to spend the night at a park which is a menace to public health and morals. Just before dozing off on an air mattress, beneath a nylon tent, amid the stench of decaying refuse, they may reflect vaguely on the curious unevenness of their blessings. Is this, indeed, the American genius?[4]

[4] Galbraith, John Kenneth, *The Affluent Society*. Houghton Mifflin Co., Boston, 1958, p. 253.

The argument is that a society preoccupied with private production and aggressive sale of consumer goods, however magnificent, is a society that starves its public sector. Yet the problem is not merely one of "balance" between public and private effort; the fraction of our gross national product spent by government at all levels for all purposes is, in fact, over one-fifth—by Western standards very large. The problem is instead what we emphasize in our public sector, with what effect on the security, freedom, and equality of our people: How much for improving the technology of missiles, how much for improving techniques of community organization and welfare administration? How much for the further training of scientists and engineers, how much for the staffing of mental hospitals? How much for reaching the moon, how much for reaching the unreached poor? In short, the balance between public and private may be less fateful than the balance between public civilian and public military. Despite heroic economy drives in the defense establishment, despite renewed concern with the quality of American domestic life, our defense budget in 1964 remained about 56 per cent of the total federal budget.[5] So long as we pursue our national interests as a world power, so long as we accent military means in that pursuit, we will lag in the most civilizing of our public expenditures.

Still, the sum left over for the welfare state after deductions for the garrison state is not inconsiderable. The small annual welfare fraction of 7.7 per cent of a huge gross national product of $604 billion is more than $46 billion. Surely such a sum should substantially increase equality and economic security, that is, move us toward the major goals of the welfare state; unfortunately, the net outcome is in doubt.

[5] Fifty-five billion of the $98 billion budgeted. *Statistical Abstract of the United States,* Government Printing Office, Washington, 1964, p. 254, preliminary estimate. Even expenditures by private industry can represent the "public sector," for they are often dominated by national military considerations. We must not overlook some incidental benefits beyond the mixed blessings of military power and responsibility. When the war on poverty is over, the training and health programs of the armed forces will deserve their share of the credit. An army that draws heavily on the working class and civilian misfits for its enlisted men is an agency engaged in literacy training and manpower upgrading. It not only teaches some of its recruits to read and write and orients them toward disciplined work, thereby enhancing their future employment possibilities; in its rejection of millions for military service it also dramatizes the need for public action to make "unemployables" employable. In the context of the billions spent to channel already trained manpower to purely military purposes, however, this incidental salvage operation is a minor qualification. For further discussion of defense vs. welfare budgets, see page 267.

The Reluctant Welfare State

Critics of the welfare state complain that it impoverishes the professional and middle classes, undermines the virtues of thrift and self-reliance among the poor, discourages charity (the voluntary giving of unrewarded services) among the rich, rewards the idle and improvident at every level, and increases the power of the state, thereby threatening the property rights and freedom of the individual. The liberal defenders of the welfare state say that it softens the risks of modern life, provides a measure of security for all, enhances equality of opportunity, thereby dampening class conflict and promoting greater social justice.

This clash of high principle obscures an underlying consensus. Critics and enthusiasts alike agree not only that the welfare state exists but that its essence is *government-protected minimum standards of income, nutrition, health, housing, and education for every citizen, assured to him as a political right, not as charity.* Two implications for public policy are also widely recognized: first, the welfare state means a redistribution of income; second, it means an emphasis on equality of opportunity for the young.[6] If everyone is to have a floor below which he is not to sink, income must be transferred from those able to provide for themselves to those not so well off. To limit the burden and maximize the benefit of such transfer payments it is prudent to concentrate on the young. There is usually less resistance to investment in youth; even those hostile to the general idea of income redistribution perceive that the main handicap of the children of the poor is that they chose the wrong parents. And the chance of salvaging the child of the slum is perhaps greater than that of rescuing his parents. In any case everyone acknowledges that if all children are to have anything like an equal start, the children of culturally and economically impoverished families must somehow receive special attention, although there is little agreement about methods.

The promise of the welfare state—minimum living standards brought about by government action to redistribute income and make opportunity equal—is nowhere fulfilled. In fact, it is doubtful

---

[6] Cf. Myrdal, Gunnar, *Beyond the Welfare State.* Yale University Press, New Haven, 1960; Titmuss, Richard M., *Essays on "The Welfare State,"* George Allen and Unwin, London, 1958, chaps. 1 and 2, and "The Welfare State: Images and Realities," *Social Service Review,* vol. 37, March, 1963, pp. 1–11; Hacker, Andrew, "Again the Issue of 'the Welfare State,'" *New York Times Magazine,* March 22, 1964.

that state-administered, tax-financed social services have significantly
redistributed wealth in the United States or even in Britain, presumably the epitome of a successful welfare state. The fears of the
critics, like the claims of the advocates, are only weakly related to
reality. As we argue on pages 159–160, "welfare programs have
had a small income-equalizing effect within the lower strata and a
still smaller effect on the income distribution as a whole." Recent
trends that give the point more force are useful to elaborate here.

The Impact on Equality.   Leaving education aside, the distributional effect of welfare programs varies with the type of program,
the condition of the economy, and the size of dependent populations
(for example, how many young people, how many old). There are
reasons to believe, however, that in the United States, Britain, and
possibly some other rich countries, the total effect of all welfare
programs on equality is negligible.[7]

 1. The largest, fastest-growing programs in the United States—
the social insurances—are the least egalitarian. When unemployment is low and the ratio of labor force participants to nonpartici-
pants is not greatly different from the present ratio, social insurance
may actually be regressive. Insurance taxes at every level of government take a larger proportion of the income of the poor than of the
well off;[8] and more money is collected from these regressive taxes
on wages and salaries than is paid out in benefits. When unemployment goes much beyond the already unacceptable levels of recent
years and the ratio of dependents to the self-supporting increases
(that is, when the payout of benefits markedly increases), the main
effect of social insurance programs is not a shift of income from rich
to poor but from average families to families at the bottom; most
of the redistribution occurs within the population having annual
family incomes below $5,000 or $6,000.

 2. If we did not have welfare payments, many beneficiaries
would be partly or wholly supported by relatives or others; the real
benefits of many transfer payments thus flow *upward* to self-supporting persons who would otherwise be forced to share their income

---

 [7] Gordon, Margaret S., *op. cit.*; Titmuss, Richard M., *op. cit.*, and *Income
Distribution and Social Change,* George Allen and Unwin, London, 1962.
 [8] Including federal, state, and local levels, the estimated effective rates of
taxes for social insurance in 1954, as a percentage of spending unit income,
were as follows: for spending units with incomes of 0–$1,000, the total tax was
4.1 per cent; $2–3,000, 4.8 per cent; $3–5,000, 5.1 per cent; $5–7,500, 3.9 per
cent; $7,500–10,000, 3.1 per cent; over $10,000, 1.4 per cent. Gordon, Margaret S., *op. cit.*, p. 27.

with present beneficiaries.[9] This possibility was perhaps the major political appeal of "Medicare": shift the burden either of guilt or of financial responsibility from the children of aging, sick parents to the government via a small social security tax.

3. The most egalitarian programs are those financed from general, federal tax revenues—public assistance, public housing, and that medical aid not based on social security. Benefits here go largely to the lowest-income families while revenues derive heavily from progressive income and corporation taxes. As we have shown, these are the very services we continue to starve; they are becoming a smaller fraction of the total welfare effort.[10] Our reluctance to expand those programs most effective in income equalization is expressed in the miserly benefits we allow. When unemployment is widespread, unemployment compensation doubtless shifts income to poor families; but one in four of wage and salary workers is not covered at all, uncertain proportions of the remainder are excluded by numerous and sometimes severe qualifying requirements, and the weekly check for the average unemployed American who actually receives benefits is $36. The duration of payment is so short that in 1962 1.6 million unemployed exhausted their benefits, a figure that climbs during recessions.[11] A striking clue to the lag in this program is that average weekly benefits for those fortunate enough to collect unemployment insurance declined from 42 per cent of average weekly wages in 1939 to 35 per cent in 1959.[12] Similarly, the pro-

[9] Gordon, Margaret S., op. cit., p. 25. The quantitative effect of this fact, because it is perhaps impossible to estimate, is not thereby trivial.

[10] The lag in one of these categories, public aid, is to be expected as social insurance covers more people and benefits expand. For instance, if OASDI had not extended its coverage, public aid spending would doubtless have increased faster than Table 14 shows; and if we now raised pensions and survivors' benefits substantially, fewer old people would have to apply for supplementary old-age assistance. The discussion above, however, addresses only the question, "Which welfare programs growing at what rate have an income equalizing effect?" Whatever our present level of benefits (and we keep them low both in OASDI and in public aid), the fast-growing social insurances are regressive while the slowly-growing public aid programs are not.

[11] Benenson, Louis, "Research in UI Coverage," Unemployment Insurance Review, vol. 1, April, 1964, p. 26; and Becker, Joseph M., "The Adequacy of Benefits in Unemployment Insurance" in Insurance Aid of the Unemployed, edited by J. S. Becker, John Hopkins University Press, Baltimore, 1965, chap. 5; Murray, Merrill G., "Unemployment Insurance: Risks Covered and Their Financing," in ibid., chap. 4; and U.S. Department of Labor, Bureau of Employment Security, Unemployment Insurance Statistics, March, 1965, p. 8.

[12] "Unemployment Insurance in the USA, 1956–60," Employment Security Review, vol. 27, August, 1960, p. 12. For some sensible recommendations, see Becker, J. M., W. Haber and S. A. Levitan, Programs to Aid the Unemployed in the 1960's. W. E. Upjohn Institute for Employment Research, Kalamazoo, Mich., January, 1965.

gram of aid to dependent children, mainly financed from federal funds, clearly favors the poor; but the average payment for an AFDC beneficiary is about $23 a week for a fatherless family of three. Finally, programs for public housing, which again favor the poor, are so tiny that they scarcely touch the slum. In short, for the entire range of welfare programs, and especially for programs with a strong potential for reducing inequality, benefits provide little more than subsistence, and the beneficiaries have little reason to believe that they have a continuing right to services, welfare state style.

4. A final force subverts the aims of the welfare state. In every rich country, a proliferation of private welfare measures that tend to increase inequality accompanies the expansion of public welfare measures ostensibly aimed at reducing inequality. Consider the vast array of "occupational welfare benefits" employers have adopted: pensions, death benefits, cash sickness benefits, sick leave, medical care, travel expenses, meals, cars, houses, credit cards, cheap loans, school fees, season tickets, holiday expenses, education and training grants. Most of these benefits are types of untaxed or lightly taxed "income"; their ultimate cost is thus borne by the government. For instance, Titmuss estimates that private, tax-exempt pension schemes alone cost the British government far more in uncollected taxes than the entire Exchequer cost of national insurance pensions.[13] Most important for the issue of equality, these fringe benefits are typically tied to employment, seniority, and occupational achievement; employees already well off receive a disproportionate share of both hard cash and subtle amenities—the stably employed more than the unemployed, the executive more than the factory worker, the professional more than the clerk. Of all social welfare measures these are the most regressive.

Although comparative data on private benefit plans are weak, it is likely that (1) there is a tendency common to industrial societies for an increasing proportion of total wages and salaries to be paid in the form of fringe benefits; and, less surely, (2) the greater the employer contributions to nonstatutory social security schemes, the less the fraction of national income devoted to public welfare programs. It appears that the United States has traveled farthest down this anti-egalitarian path: our contributions to employee benefit plans in relation to national income are larger than those in other rich countries, but our expenditure on social security and private plans combined is nevertheless lower. Apparently, lush private bene-

[13] Titmuss, Richard M., Essays . . . , p. 69.

fits foster the cheerful illusion that stingy public programs are adequate.[14] What the welfare state seeks to achieve, private welfare measures tend to negate.

In sum: if we take account of the increasing dominance of public welfare programs that are regressive or neutral in their effects on income distribution, and the growth of private welfare programs (any "collective" assumption of responsibility for any sort of dependence), the advantaged appear to gain as much if not more than the needy. This is not to say that social security and other programs that do little to increase equality are not justified on other grounds—OASDI and Unemployment Insurance on the grounds of family security and humanitarianism, UI as an anti-recession weapon. And it is not to deny a major thesis of this book: that the correlates of industrialization—mass education, a shift into higher-paid occupations and industries and more efficient workplaces, increased labor force participation by women—tend in the long run to reduce inequality of income (see Chapters IV and V). Finally, the welfare state can become more of a reality if we recognize that it is now largely an illusion and adopt policies that assure a decent minimum standard of life for every citizen.

The Roots of Reluctance.   In countries both rich and free the welfare state presents an opportunity to be generous and yet not lose anything. The redistribution of income it implies is less of a loss to the affluent than the high cost of perpetuating poverty and dependency in the slum. Yet, the theme of the Appendix and Chapter II ("Capitalism and American Culture") still holds: the United States is more reluctant than any rich democratic country to make a wel-

---

[14] Gordon, Margaret S., *op. cit.*, pp. 21–23. As Titmuss argues, whatever the aims of these "occupational social services" their whole tendency thus far has been "to divide loyalties, to nourish privilege, and to narrow the social conscience." (*Essays* . . . , p. 52.) This seems especially true for the United States, the United Kingdom, and Western Germany. (Cf. *The Cost of Social Security 1947–1957*, International Labor Organization, Geneva, 1961, pp. 233–238.) Voters lodged in a comfortable *private* welfare state do not support the real thing with enthusiasm. Employers already paying princely fringe benefits vigorously resist the expansion of competing public services. A possible exception is the case of private pension negotiations in 1949. Aiming to give employers incentive to press for government action, some unions, notably the UAW-CIO, negotiated plans under which the employer's costs were to be reduced if the government program were liberalized. This may have been a factor in the raising of old age benefits under OASDI in the early 1950's. But other factors, especially a steep increase in the cost of living, played a part and, in any case, this tie-in strategy lasted only a few years; employer contributions are no longer tied to government benefits. For a discussion of the entire range of voluntary welfare efforts in the United States, see our pages 160–167.

fare effort appropriate to its affluence. Our support of national welfare programs is halting; our administration of services for the less privileged is mean. We move toward the welfare state but we do it with ill grace, carping and complaining all the way. This is understandable when we review the sources of resistance to the welfare state. First, there are cultural values that set us apart from other nations—our economic individualism, our unusual emphasis on private property, the free market, and minimum government (see Chapter II). One expression of these values is the great accent on private welfare services; private expenditures, including the budgets of all local agencies (church, secular, fund-raising and central administrative) and all private benefit plans (pensions, and so forth), are only about one-sixth of the annual public welfare expenditure, but they generate many times the public interest and involvement, both reflecting and reinforcing a philosophy of voluntarism (see pages 169 ff.). Second, there are solid structural props for these values: a lush standard of living for the majority; great expansion of educational opportunity; a rapid growth of the new middle class and with it increased chances for occupational mobility; a slow drift toward income equalization, welfare state aside; reduced discrimination against minorities; a modest diffusion of power—in short, reasons for the self-serving optimism that denies the need for social action on behalf of the least successful (see Chapters III, IV, V, IX, and X). Finally, there are our worldwide military commitments, which use up resources that could otherwise finance the welfare state and improve the quality of American civilization (see above).

Two structural roots of the reluctant welfare state, only briefly discussed later in this book, deserve more attention here: (1) racial, ethnic, and religious heterogeneity; and (2) political decentralization.

Gunnar Myrdal, long a perceptive and sympathetic observer of the American scene, believes that the puzzling lag in our welfare effort is mainly due to the great variety of competing minority groups. "In spite of the very rapid advances made toward national integration, heterogeneous elements still linger everywhere in the population, and with them remnants of separatistic allegiances."[15] Racial, ethnic, and religious diversity, he argues, blocks meaningful participation in the less parochial voluntary associations that flourish

[15] Myrdal, Gunnar, op. cit., p. 54. Cf. pp. 54 ff., 87, 100 passim. For background on American immigration, see below, pp. 51–55.

in Europe and especially in Scandinavia—unions, "co-ops," political parties and their women's and youth auxiliaries, institutions for adult education and cultural uplift. A wider civic virtue cannot fully develop when ties to minority groups are strong.

In America minority groups do retain a tenacious hold. A network of cliques, clubs, and voluntary associations comprises three broad subcommunities of Protestant, Catholic, and Jew; they are social worlds within which courtship and marriage take place and informal social life is centered. While economic growth undermines minority group ties (see pages 63 ff.), assimilation proceeds faster among some ethnic groups (for example, Greeks, Romanians, Swedes) than others (third-generation Italian Catholic neighborhoods in Boston attest to the persistence of ethnic variants of the religious community); assimilation is generally slower among the broad minorities of Catholic and Jew than among national groups; and it is painfully slow and uncertain among racial minorities, whose exclusion from the mainstream of American life is assured by segregation in the ghetto. Moreover, religious cleavages have had a direct effect in slowing down expansion of school facilities; touchy problems of state-church relations plague every step toward federal aid to education. The doctrine of separation of church and state has also fostered a large welfare structure under religious auspices. And racial conflict is at the heart of resistance to a serious program of public housing. But these cleavages are not unique to the United States. For instance, bitter religious controversy has not prevented progress toward the welfare state in Belgium, the Netherlands, and Canada that exceeds our own. Further, we simply do not have the evidence to say that the vitality of participation in communal life is significantly less in the United States than in Europe, whether we attribute our level of participation to minority attachments or not.

Racial, ethnic, and religious conflict could not count so much in the determination of public policy if it were not for our extraordinary degree of political decentralization. The dogma of local self-government is enshrined in our constitution and laws; a federal system divides powers among the central government and 50 sovereign states, which, in turn, divide powers among thousands of counties, townships, municipalities, and other local units. Of course, these arbitrary geographical boundaries, drawn before the rise of industrialism and urbanism, have little relation to economic, demographic, cultural, and social realities, little connection with the loyalties, interests, and styles of life of the people bound by them. In order to survive, the modern metropolis is thus forced to create a staggering number of special district governments—school districts, water districts, fire districts, sanitation districts, park and port districts, rapid transit authorities—each concentrating on a limited area-wide task, each competing for budget, tax base, or subsidy, all adding to the maze of overlapping and duplicating units. It is free enterprise in government—with every municipality, every district for itself. The almost total failure of the "metropolitan government" movement in recent years is testimony to the will of such local units to survive.[16] If there is a political explanation of why we fail to come to grips with the problems of community welfare and metropolitan planning, it is here, in the tyranny of locality, made possible by federalism. No other rich country of the Free West has kept its central government so weak.

The effect of political fragmentation on the welfare state is not hard to see. The lack of federal standards in unemployment compensation accounts for the meager benefits paid under unemployment insurance. For years, southern Democrats, crying "states' rights," blocked passage of effective civil rights legislation; we can assume that for masses of Negroes of the Southeast the exercise of political rights will be a major step toward economic advance. The accent on state prerogatives has not only kept many welfare benefits too low to implement program goals and prevented the enactment of still other programs; it has also given welfare financing a regressive cast. The more we rely on the states to meet our health, education, and welfare needs, the more we subvert the aims of the welfare state, for state taxes (for example, on sales) tax the poor proportionately more than the rich (see pages 154 ff.). As Table 13 shows, the state and local shares of welfare expenditures have recently declined but are still large.

Most important, in such a system the problem of what government unit is to finance and administer what service becomes formidable. Locality, class, and minority origin have converged to create powerful social cleavages, reflected in the political life of the metropolis and affecting every effort to serve its needs. With only a little exaggeration, this is the picture:[17] The middle-class native whites

---

[16] Cf. Greer, Scott, *Governing the Metropolis*, John Wiley and Sons, New York, 1962.
[17] Cf. *Ibid.*; Dobriner, William, editor, *The Suburban Community*, G. P. Putnam's Sons, New York, 1958; and our discussion of suburbia, pages 125 ff. and Chapter VIII.

who have fled to the suburbs pay property taxes where they live; they typically pay nothing to the central city (or to an "employing suburb") where they work, where they use streets and sidewalks, and where they demand police and fire protection and the usual amenities. Among the suburbanites are the prosperous owners and managers of most of the department stores, banks, utilities, and factories in the city. Although a few of these business leaders identify with the city and use their influence to restore its magnetism, most are commuters from the periphery with no official power in the center and a strong desire to stay out of its troubles (see pages 269 ff.). Meanwhile, left behind in the center is the poorest, least educated segment of the working class—low-income blue-collar and service workers, the aged, the broken families, and such minorities as nonwhites, foreign-born, and Catholics. Their capacity to pay for an increasing load of welfare and other public services is limited. Left behind, too, are area-wide facilities—the parks, museums, and zoos, the concert halls, theaters, and universities, the hospitals and medical centers. They, too, demand service, but the land which they occupy usually cannot be taxed, for they are nonprofit enterprises.[18] The social distance between majority men and minority men, the free-riding commuter, the manager with no roots in the city, and the discouraging combination of dwindling tax bases and mounting needs for service—all make it difficult for anyone to act for the metropolis as a whole.

The suburbs are really in no better shape; no one can act for them either. Consider two little suburban villages standing side-by-side. A large industrial plant locates in the first; a tax bonanza flows to the village. The plant draws its labor force, however, from the whole area; school enrollment triples in the adjacent village, the

---

[18] That liberals concerned about urban poverty underestimate the importance of this tax-base problem is suggested by their increasing disaffection from the urban renewal program. "Urban renewal," they say, "is Negro removal." It is painfully true that the immediate effect of transforming blighted areas into sites for expensive high-rise apartments and modern office buildings is to redistribute the displaced poor in other slums. At the same time, the new land uses yield great gains in tax revenues, which for the most part support city agencies and services for everyone, especially for minorities and the poor, who are increasingly the dominant residents of the city. A possible strategy is to combine a more selective urban renewal effort—one which clears only really harmful slums and accommodates the displaced poor in decent places they can afford—with a rehousing scheme using vacant land in and out of the city. The case for the latter is persuasively stated in Herbert J. Gans' "The Failure of Urban Renewal: A Critique and Some Proposals," *Commentary,* vol. 39, April, 1965, pp. 29–37.

demand for welfare services doubles in several nearby municipalities. Unfortunately, these neighboring suburbs can collect no taxes from the corporation to meet the needs it has created; it belongs to the village across the line. As Robert Wood puts it, suburban fragmentation results in "the segregation of resources and needs," especially in the smaller suburbs. "Historical caprice . . . the location of a single industrial plant, the decision of a developer to build one hundred homes, the construction of one express highway—insignificant elements in the total urban complex . . . drastically affect the public fortunes of the jurisdiction . . . local governments [are like] players at a roulette wheel, waiting to see what number will come up. . . ."[19] The result is that residents of some suburbs pay high taxes and receive desperately poor services; the lucky residents of others pay little and reap a steady harvest of excellent services.

Short of regional political integration, some solutions to the metropolitan problem seem inevitable: in financing, massive federal aid to cope with the most pressing issues of education, housing, transportation, sanitation, and the like; in planning and administration, more area-wide special governments such as the Bay Area Rapid Transit Authority (San Francisco), a model of bold experimentation. Before we accept the inevitable, however, we may allow a dangerous deterioration of many a metropolis. And whatever reforms we accomplish, the accompanying rhetoric will be heavily rural and Jacksonian, accenting the referendum, the sacred right of local self-rule, and the joys of life in the open country, the small town, the "suburblet."

In considering "urbanism as a way of life" (Chapter V), in examining the problem of financing and distributing welfare services (Part Three), it is important to understand that the political context is a home-grown American product, a welfare state effort aimed mainly at a population concentrated in a dozen metropolitan regions but channeled obliquely through a labyrinth of local government units, each more reluctant than its neighbor to yield a fraction of its autonomy.

The American lag in welfare expenditures would not be so serious if we allocated more of what we do spend to the lagging programs. Given the roots of the reluctant welfare state, however—affluence

[19] Wood, Robert, *1400 Governments, the Political Economy of the New York Metropolitan Region.* Harvard University Press, Cambridge, Mass., 1961, pp. 50, 60–62.

and its correlates, a decentralized political system which gives expression to racial, religious, class, and other community divisions and to every local barrier to change—it takes unusual political courage to fight for programs at the core of the welfare state.

Business, political, and educational elites do not lack the wisdom to see the potential gains. It is widely known that education, health, and welfare programs improve the utilization of manpower, save wasted lives, and serve the ends of social justice and economic efficiency. Nor do these elites lack understanding of the social costs of poverty and slum conditions; it is widely known that the whole community, including those who have escaped to the suburbs, bears the costs of dependency, crime, delinquency, and disease; the "good citizens" pay not only for relief but also for the clean-up specialists required—relief investigators, police, health officers, probation and truant officers, scores of others; and the total bill comes to far more than the investment required for poverty prevention. Further, everyone knows that polluted air and water do not respect divided jurisdictions. There is even some recognition that the political explosiveness of a densely packed, racially segregated slum cannot be confined to its borders.

The political pressures generated by welfare programs, however, render wisdom difficult to apply. Hard-pressed community leaders, invoking the idea that politics is the "art of the possible," adopt mediocre expectations and succumb to the line of least resistance. For instance, compare the response to social insurance with that to public housing. Vested interests abound in both cases: expansion of OASDI is vigorously opposed by private insurance companies, medical insurance by the American Medical Association, public housing by real estate and construction firms. But it is easier to fight for OASDI, which is deducted painlessly from the pay and received later routinely in the mail in the form of a noncontroversial check. It is not so easy to fight for public housing, which is financed from general taxes, which comes to the people in the form of controversy over site location ("An integrated housing project in *my* ward?"), demolition ("Where do I move to?"), eligibility ("They're discriminating against Negroes and Puerto Ricans," "only Negroes and Puerto Ricans can get in"), planning and management ("The place is hideous," "urine stains in the elevators," "potted plants in the bathtubs"). If these allegations are not entirely groundless, they simply reflect the Spartan budgets for the buildings or the pitifully small scale of the operation (the new units are so few that for every tenant accommodated there are a hundred made bitter). But a monumental fuss is certain.

Or consider the mild controversy potential of a highway program compared to the political dynamite of a TVA. The need for transportation is clear to all. And everyone loves the highway. The average American is attached to his suburban location, the single-family dwelling, and the private automobile; he is willing to commute long distances in heavy traffic ("Once you get into the car it doesn't matter how far you go"). He may be restive about the rush-hour crush, but he is delighted by the $41 billion plan to build nonstop, limited access, high-speed freeways that will permit him to go anywhere just by hopping into the car—that is, if not too many others have the same idea at the same time. Mobilizing these sentiments is a potent nationwide highway lobby with roots in every local community: auto manufacturers and their 64,000 local car dealers, gasoline companies, tire producers, the state motor clubs, highway contractors and highway department officials in city halls and state capitols, the trucking industry, the cement and asphalt companies, and the many businesses and industries that profit from cars and roads. In 1956 this formidable combination led to a fateful choice—the adoption of the Interstate Highway System embracing both rural and urban areas, the line of least resistance. Described as "old fashioned" were plans to rebuild rapid transit facilities; ignored was the unwritten law that added roads demand added parking space and the two together merely invite a new overflow of automobiles.[20] In the early 1960's our weekly per capita expenditure on roads climbed to more than $1.00, a figure whose import we can grasp by comparing it to the 55 cents we spend for all public aid programs or to the $4.60 bill for the entire welfare state (weekly per capita cost of all the public welfare programs listed in Table 14 except education).

Now contrast the problem of a federal or state agency that wants to put down not a network of integrated highways but a network of integrated services designed to foster the economic growth of a depressed area. The people of the area, after years of futility and

[20] Ignored, too, was the likelihood that in the next few years this highway program will displace more people from slum (and nonslum) areas than will the housing program, without providing the new sources of city tax revenues that urban renewal provides, and certainly without providing new housing. Cf. Meyerson, Martin, Barbara Terrett, and William L. C. Wheaton, *Housing, People, and Cities,* McGraw-Hill Book Co., New York, 1962, p. 16—a book which offers a constructive program for public and private action to increase the housing supply.

failure, are apathetic; the population not directly involved is indifferent. Congressmen representing less depressed areas are reluctant to let aid flow exclusively to areas of greatest need and insist on relaxed eligibility standards to spread the spending, thereby spreading it too thin. Or if a "growth center" idea is applied—promoting the development not of the most run-down towns but of the most prosperous and hopeful communities in the area, thus creating opportunities for the surrounding population—congressmen representing the bypassed communities set up a howl. Any effort to provide venture capital for new businesses willing to locate in the area brings cries of unfair competition from unsubsidized local entrepreneurs. Retraining programs outside the existing vocational training, apprenticeship, and school systems are resented by men running the latter. Even more passionate debate would be aroused by a regional development approach, such as the TVA, which combined extensive federal aid, an overview of regional needs in power and water supply, flood control, conservation, industrial research, navigation and recreation, and grass roots administration by a semi-autonomous federal agency with undivided responsibility. Today's agencies (for example, the Area Redevelopment Administration), more limited in finances, finely slicing up responsibility by both level and function, are inclined to leave to local initiative the major responsibility for rehabilitation. Their success has been less than resounding.

Where we try to approximate a regional approach, we find the principle of least resistance at work. In 1965 President Johnson signed into law the Appalachia Development Program, an anti-poverty measure covering an 11-state area from Pennsylvania to Alabama, costing almost $1.1 billion. Although for the first two years $162 million is allocated for health centers, vocational education, soil conservation projects, mine area restoration, the development of timber and water resources, and the like, and another $90 million to supplement funds available to local communities under existing federal grant-in-aid programs, the lion's share ($840 million for five years) will be applied to the least controversial feature of the Appalachia program—again the building of roads. The roads are labeled "development highways" and "access roads" and are designed to "open the region for industry and tourism and widen the horizons of the population."[21] While this program is obviously

[21] *Economic Report of the President,* January, 1965, Government Printing Office, Washington, pp. 141–142; and *Congressional Quarterly Weekly Report,* vol. 23, March 5 and 12, 1965, pp. 327–328.

better than the meager efforts of the 1950's, we must ask, "For combating poverty, is the heavy accent on highways wise? Would not a somewhat reduced highway program coupled with much greater support of education, out-migration, and birth control hold more promise?"

The roots of our reluctant welfare state are evident in our present preoccupation with noncontroversial programs, epitomized by social insurance and highways, and the least innovative aspects of controversial programs, epitomized by the Appalachia road building plan. Despite formidable barriers to progress, however, the general level of welfare-state spending will continue to rise and services will continue to expand in coverage. There is increasing recognition that expenditures aimed at income maintenance, continuing education, rehabilitation, and poverty prevention are part of the cost of doing business in modern society. There is increased understanding of three facts: (1) Those most exposed to the risks of modern life (see Part One) are least able to protect themselves through private means (savings, insurance). (2) Private welfare expenditures, one-sixth of the public expenditure, cannot carry the burden, cannot meet urgent demands for greater equality for Negroes, for aid to culturally and economically impoverished families in every category, in general, for the eradication of slums and poverty. (3) Rehabilitation of the dependent where possible and an emphasis on dependency-prevention among their children is cheaper than even our present begrudging support.[22] In short, there is a relaxation of fixed positions and hard political lines, a willingness to experiment, to be more pragmatic and less ideological, in the best American tradition.

The Rediscovery of Poverty

In less than a decade popular social science has moved from *The Affluent Society* to *The Other America*. Aware that fads and fashions are as characteristic of intellectual life and public opinion as they are of styles of dress, we tried, in the first edition of this book,

[22] The cost of poverty prevention, relative to the cost of present levels of support of dependent families, is a matter of conjecture. Edward W. Brice, chief of adult education in the U.S. Office of Education, guesses that the economic drag caused by illiteracy and under-education is about $100 billion a year—the difference between what illiterates or semi-illiterates earn and what they could earn with a minimum of basic education. The direct costs are enormous; most adults supported by public assistance programs are illiterate. The indirect costs cannot be calculated; they involve not only that portion of the cost of physical and mental illness, crime, delinquency, illegitimacy, and urban blight attributable to poverty, but also the cost of the intergenerational transfer of patterns of opportunity, motivation, information, and ability that perpetuate poverty.

to avoid the competing myths of the affluent worker and of the persistence of poverty. Our arguments in Chapter IV that continued economic growth in the rich countries implies long-run income equalization, and an expanding middle mass (lower-middle and upper-working classes), and that casework responds to such changes (Chapter VIII) are not vitiated by short-run reversals in equality or by the recent rediscovery of poverty. That every stratum has made real gains, that the stratification order has become more complex, the classes more diversified in structure and culture is the central story in the rise of industrialism. These long-term trends should not be exaggerated by the myth of proletarian affluence, nor obscured by the myth of the "Other America," uniform in its culture of poverty. Although these myths contain partial truths and they are at the core of recent debate about equality and the welfare state, they should be seen in the context of the major social trends discussed in this book.

The Affluent Worker and Middle-Class Culture

By world standards many skilled workers are indeed rich, having family income of eight or ten thousand dollars a year.[23] But in millions of homes it takes two jobs and often many overtime hours (for which workers are generally eager) to put their families in the middle brackets, and when they arrive their affluence is typically unsteady; over a lifetime affluent workers, like most workers, typically shift about, moving from job to job, occupation to occupation, with periods of unemployment or retraining punctuating a cycle of ups and downs. For this and other reasons we must be cautious when we hear that American workers are adopting "middle-class" styles of life, or—more broadly—that on both sides of the iron curtain, a culture peculiar to the "working class" is all but dead. The lines between upper-working class and lower-middle class—between the mass of foremen, craftsmen, and high-paid operatives, on the one hand, and the mass of·clerks, salesmen, small entrepreneurs, managers with few subordinates, semi-professional, semi-technical people,

[23] The median annual income of male "craftsmen, foremen, and kindred" 25–64 years old in the civilian labor force in 1959 was $5,444, more than the $5,216 of "clerical and kindred workers," the $4,645 of "operatives and kindred," or the $3,504 of "laborers, except farm and mine." Comparable figures for three or four person families with two or more earners were: $7,206 for households headed by craftsmen and operatives combined, $5,164 for those headed by laborers. U.S. Bureau of the Census, *Census of Population 1960*, Final Report PC(2)–7B; "Occupation by Earnings and Education," U.S. Department of Commerce, Government Printing Office, Washington, 1964.

on the other—these lines are blurring. But much of working-class culture persists.[24]

Mass education has made at least high school available to all; manual workers, like white-collar workers, commonly want a college education for their children. But education means something different for each stratum. For his daughters, the worker less often counts on college, and for his sons, he tends to see it in strictly vocational terms. Middle-class parents in contrast are more egalitarian, broader in their aspirations; they expect education to pay off at once in a better job, a more enjoyable life, and skills in "getting along with other people." And, although the proportion of working-class children in college is rising, it is still lower than that in the lower middle class. Further, the type of college—community or junior college, or a mass state university—is typically both less desirable and less costly.

It is the same with housing. A satirical song[25] by Malvina Reynolds spoofs suburbia in these phrases:

> Little boxes on the hillside,
> Little boxes made of ticky-tacky,
> Little boxes on the hillside,
> Little boxes all the same,
>
> There's a green one and a pink one
> A blue one and a yellow one
> And they're all made out of ticky-tacky
> And they all look just the same.

The idea is that suburban tract-housing is uniform and depressing as are the people in it. Although we lack solid data on this matter, it is likely that the working-class couple, more than their middle-class counterpart, is moved to buy one of the "boxes" because of previous subordination to a landlord or previous experience with racial conflict in the central city. For workers, suburban home-ownership is a flight to freedom; for middle strata, more a routine validation of status. (For both, of course, it is mainly a search for more space and better schools for their children. Nor is the uniformity of appearances confined to the suburbs.)

[24] The next three paragraphs rely, in part on essays by G. Handel and L. Rainwater, S. M. Miller, and F. Riessman in *Blue-Collar World: Studies of the American Worker,* edited by A. B. Shostak and W. Gomberg, Prentice-Hall, Inc., Englewood Cliffs, N.J., 1964; in part on Wilensky's observations and data in *Work, Leisure, and Freedom,* The Free Press, New York, forthcoming.

[25] Words and music by Malvina Reynolds. © Copyright 1962 by Schroder Music Company, Berkeley, Calif. Used by permission.

Differences in the quality and meaning of education and houses lead to differences in how these strata spend their money. They buy similar homes, the same automobiles and other consumer durables, but workers spend far less for services than their middle-class colleagues. The carpenter, in contrast to the bank teller, doesn't hire other craftsmen to fix up his home, car-washers and mechanics to clean and repair his car; he tends to do it himself. And as his wife confronts the family washing, she is unlikely to use a commercial laundry or diaper service; she does it at home. For outings, the worker falls easily into an aimless Sunday drive culminating in a park or a "drive-in" with food or film rather than dinner in a downtown restaurant. For vacations, he is more likely to stay at home, or visit relatives than to travel long distances for a planned adventure.

The Affluent Worker and Lower-Class Culture. Differences that divide the upper working class from the lower middle class—differences in career prospects, in the quality and meaning of housing, in the uses of money and leisure—are not as great as the contrasts between the stable upper half of the working class and the depressed lower half. Unemployment rates are far higher among semi-skilled operatives, unskilled laborers, and service workers than among other manual workers.[26] Their work histories are more chaotic. They face more obstacles to upward escape. They lack sophistication in shopping, are susceptible to "easy credit," and are therefore entangled in debt and victimized in the market place. The natural title for a recent study of the consumption patterns of low-income families in New York City was *The Poor Pay More*.[27] Like the lower class everywhere, they receive less of every reward modern society offers— economic security, physical safety and health, living space, and opportunity for education and interesting work. The major response to this unyielding and unpredictable environment is retreat. The lower class is more apathetic politically, more isolated socially (their ties to kin and friends are few and weak). Their leisure is more privatized (they often eat and drink and watch television alone). Their family lives are unstable and impoverished (broken homes among

[26] In November, 1963, the unemployment rate for craftsmen, foremen, and kindred was only 3.9 per cent compared to 11.9 per cent for laborers, 7.2 per cent for operatives, 5.8 per cent for service workers (excluding private household). U.S. Department of Labor, Bureau of Labor Statistics, *Monthly Report on the Labor Force,* November, 1964, p. 30.
[27] Caplovitz, David, *The Poor Pay More.* The Free Press, New York, 1963.

some lower-class groups constitute a majority).[28] Exposed to sustained stress and lacking strong primary group support to cushion anxiety, their rate of mental illness is startlingly higher than that of majority America. Divide the population into five strata, by income and occupational prestige, and you will see only small differences in rates of treated psychiatric illness as you move from the top through the upper-working class. Pass to the bottom fifth and the rate leaps up to almost three times that of any other stratum.[29]

The theme that the upper working class is closer to the lower middle class than either is to the poor is at first blush contradicted by some research reporting behavior and attitudes of skilled workers similar to those of the less skilled. Such findings usually result from weak classifications. For instance, a detailed study based on two nationwide surveys comparing "clerical, sales"; "craftsmen, foremen"; and "operatives" shows that the latter two are similar in level of organizational affiliation, types of affiliation, union membership, religious involvement, media behavior, politics, home ownership, and attitudes toward education and foreign affairs.[30] Such studies not only fail to control for education (which is often the only distinction that matters when the "classes" are compared), they also lump stably employed, high-income operatives with the rest to form the lowest stratum, thereby obscuring crucial differences between the two halves of the working class. Where the similarities are not due to spurious classification but are real, they are found most often in politics and the uses of the mass media and mass entertainment —sources of cultural standardization powerful in every modern state.[31]

Great diversity within each stratum matches persistent differences in structure and culture between the upper-working and lower-middle classes and the even greater gulf between both of these and the

[28] One of the best reviews of evidence is that by Genevieve Knupfer, "Portrait of the Underdog" in *Class, Status, and Power,* edited by R. Bendix and S. M. Lipset. The Free Press, New York, 1953, pp. 255–263. Cf. Harrington, Michael, *The Other America: Poverty in the United States,* Macmillan Co., New York, 1962.

[29] Hollingshead, A. B., and F. C. Redlich, *Social Class and Mental Illness,* John Wiley and Sons, New York, 1958. The neurotic and psychotic poor rarely rest on the analyst's couch; instead, they ignore symptoms or take pills or find themselves incarcerated in custodial mental institutions.

[30] Hamilton, Richard F., "The Behavior and Values of Skilled Workers" in *Blue-Collar World: Studies of the American Worker,* edited by A. B. Shostak and W. Gomberg, *op. cit.,* pp. 42–57.

[31] Wilensky, H. L., "Mass Society and Mass Culture," *American Sociological Review,* vol. 29, April, 1964, pp. 173–197.

depressed lower class. The characteristics of the American poor illustrate this point.

The Many Faces of Poverty

Most Americans consider Mississippi a national disgrace. The median annual personal income of Negroes in Jackson, Mississippi in 1959 was only $944 a year. Yet that same year, per capita income in Puerto Rico—a model of an underdeveloped area that has achieved economic success, an island whose prosperity puts it in the upper quarter of the world's nations—was $819, less than that of the mainland's most deprived urban citizens.[32]

Or consider possessions. A study of 464 families in four low-income housing projects in Manhattan, New York City, whose median annual income in 1960 was $3,300, reported that, in spite of their weak economic position and shaky credit ratings, all but 5 per cent owned at least one television set, three in five owned a phonograph, two in five a sewing machine, two in five an automatic washing machine, one in four a vacuum cleaner, and one in seven an automobile.[33]

Plainly, American poverty is not like the grinding poverty of two-thirds of the world's population. It is poverty relative to the comfortable life of the vast majority of Americans. It is not thereby less poignant, less miserable. A minority poor, surrounded by affluence, can feel their deprivation more deeply than the majority poor of Asia, Africa, and Latin America, whose poverty is traditional. And a minority poor may be more of a drag on the conscience of the rich, as we can see when a moderately conservative President feels compelled to declare "war on poverty."

In the current debate about poverty in the midst of plenty, it is generally agreed that one-fifth to one-fourth of the population of the United States lives below a culturally and politically defined poverty line. Their social composition has not changed from that described on page 106: a heavy concentration of persons over sixty-five, women

[32] U.S. Bureau of the Census in the *Census of Population: 1960* (Washington, 1963, pp. 26–159) reports nonwhite personal income in the Jackson Standard Metropolitan Area; volume 1 (pp. 53–130) reports income of persons 14 years of age and older in Puerto Rico. The annual per capita income in India in the early 1960's was about $70. (Central Statistical Organization, Department of Statistics, Government of India, "Estimates of National Income 1948–49 to 1962–63," February, 1964, Table 1, p. 1—counting one rupee as 21 cents, 339.4 rupees would be $71.27.) Cf. Studensky, Paul, *The Income of Nations*, New York University Press, New York, 1958, pp. 228–233, especially Table 16–3.

[33] Caplovitz, David, *op. cit.*

heading broken homes, and nonwhites.[34] Nor are the poor less heterogeneous in economic position and prospects than they were in the 1950's. Some live on welfare checks, some on pensions; some are unemployed, others not; some are sick, others well; some are refugees from rural poverty, others are veterans of the urban slums; some are migratory workers following the seasons and the crops, others are fixed in low-paid jobs as watchmen and housemaids.

In short, when you hear of the "working class," you should ask yourself, "Is it the underdog, down and out, going nowhere in a disorganized way, or the factory worker, getting by despite some ups and downs?" When you hear of "skilled craftsmen and foremen," ask, were they reared on a farm or not; did they follow their fathers' footsteps in a guild-like craft; did they move up from the bottom or down from the middle? Have their work histories been full of ups and downs, with intermittent attempts to set up a business of their own, or do they display an orderly job progression? Are they young strivers who expect steady moves to a high-income peak or men in their forties who have given up the race? Finally, when you hear of the "lower class," it helps to know whether they are the welfare poor, the aged poor, or the deserted-woman poor; whether they are militant young Negroes or apathetic old men on skid row.

Given the fragmentation of the working class suggested by these examples, we should not expect American workers or the American poor to display a strong community of values and interests. Generally we find such solidarity only where "class" in economic terms is combined with race, religious-ethnic origins, and locality. The Negro ghetto, the Polish-Catholic factory workers' neighborhood, the metropolitan police department dominated by Irish Catholics, the craft union dominated by second- or third-generation German-American Lutherans, the succession of minority groups in the needle trades, with the early Jewish and Italian garment workers giving way to Negroes and Puerto Ricans—these are ready examples of the convergence of occupation, minority origin, and locality. This is

[34] If we say that an annual income of less than $3,000 for a family of four makes them poor, then one in three of the household heads is over sixty-five, one in four a woman heading a broken home, one in five a nonwhite. Half the heads of poor households, compared to a fifth of the general population, have one or more of these three characteristics. For recent data, see Committee on Education and Labor, House of Representatives, 88th Congress, 2d Sess., *Economic Opportunity Act of 1964*, March, 1964, Part I pp. 33-34, 38, 41; and Lampman, Robert J., "The Low Income Population and Economic Growth," *Study Paper Number 12*, Joint Economic Committee of Congress, December 16, 1959.

where we can expect to find some uniformity of values and beliefs, "subcultures" that count.

What distinguishes the heterogeneous American poor, aside from their relative poverty, is their invisibility.[35] They are segregated in the valleys of Pennsylvania, the coal patches of West Virginia and other area-wide "pockets" of poverty; segregated in the core of the metropolis in racial slums; or driven from slum-cleared tenements to double up in new slums on the margin of the old. If they are aged or sick, they stay close to a rented room, often alone; if they are young, they stay close to the block or neighborhood. When they appear in public, their slacks and white shirts are virtually indistinguishable from the similar dress of better-off workers; as Harrington observes, it is easier to be decently clothed in the affluent society than to be housed, fed, or doctored. With the possible exception of the Negroes, whatever their social characteristics they are politically invisible. Far more than their predecessors, the new poor are segregated and isolated—socially, residentially, culturally, politically—out of sight and out of mind. But they are invisible for yet another reason: the contrasting work situation of those who cannot or will not see. Long-hours men whose work is steady, moonlighters whose work is unstable but sufficient, double-earner families who put together enough to manage—this relatively comfortable majority are predisposed to the self-serving myth that the new poor do not exist or, if they exist, are rapidly dwindling or, at least, not really trying.[36] Paradoxically, our long-run gain in income equalization, which may be common to all rich countries, increases public indifference to the remaining poor.

The War on Poverty and the "Welfare Backlash"

Given a stratification system predisposing the majority to embrace the myth of the affluent worker and ignore the poor, a political system accenting local autonomy, and a culture strong in economic individualism, how can the United States best tackle the problems of the welfare state? What can be done to reduce dependency and relative poverty?

The first line of attack is federal action to maintain full employ-

[35] Harrington, Michael, op. cit.
[36] Wilensky, H. L., "The Uneven Distribution of Leisure: The Impact of Economic Growth on 'Free Time,' " Social Problems, vol. 9, Summer, 1961, pp. 32–56; and Work, Leisure . . . , op. cit. For a history of the discovery of American poverty in the nineteenth century, see Bremner, Robert H., From the Depths, New York University Press, New York, 1956.

ment and a high rate of economic growth. When the demand for labor is heavy, employers try harder to find and train people for existing jobs and, in fact, they often remake the jobs to fit the limitations of the human beings on hand. There is nothing like a brisk labor market to make a grammar school dropout look useful, an old man look strong, an unskilled woman skilled, a Negro acceptable, an "unemployable" a good bet for the next opening. As we suggest on page 105, the list of anti-depression weapons available to an alert administration today is long (from variable taxes to actions of the Federal Reserve System, from unemployment compensation to deficit spending)—none of them alien to the American tradition. While discussion of full employment policy is beyond the scope of this book, it should be mentioned that each of the two main ideas in current debate about the jobless contains truth; there is a problem of "aggregate demand" (many employers will not do what has to be done unless they are short of help), and there is a problem of "structural unemployment" (even with sharply increased demand, millions of the unemployed will not fit job requirements in an age of automation). Both problems yield to sensible public policy.

The second answer to poverty is an administration committed to mobilizing the resources of government and of public opinion to act, occasionally crossing the line of least resistance. In the early 1960's the nation began to confront its major domestic problems. Although support for core programs of the welfare state lagged by international standards or by the standard of our ability to pay, a vast array of plans was announced, and some got off the ground. Under the omnibus Economic Opportunity Act of 1964, several federal agencies and hundreds of private and public local agencies converged on out-of-school, out-of-work youth to recruit them for job-training camps (the Job Corps). Supplementing this effort were Labor Department "Youth Opportunity Centers" offering work-training programs for youth who do not qualify for existing vocational training and who will learn work habits (punctuality, how to dress, how to take supervision) on public service projects in libraries, hospitals, playgrounds, parks, settlement houses and similar non-profit agencies; a small domestic peace corps (Volunteers in Service to America) which supplies semi-professional talent to local projects in poverty areas; and a variety of community action, work-study, and adult education programs. The 1962 Manpower Development and Training Act and later amendments provided for labor-mobility demonstration projects, training allowances to unemployed household heads, and the like. Under various acts, the Bureau of Employment Security in the Department of Labor was given the responsibility of going beyond its operation of local employment offices and working with other federal and state agencies in manpower planning, for example, selection of trainees. The 1962 Welfare Amendments made it possible for states to give Aid to Families with Dependent Children even if an unemployed father is present (thereby discouraging the farce in which public assistance workers conduct dawn raids on AFDC mothers to uncover disqualifying husbands or lovers); they also encouraged training for the adults in such families, day care centers for the mothers, and part-time public service employment for their teenagers attending school.

Perhaps the law with the greatest potential for poverty-prevention, and surely the one with the best federal financing, is the Vocational Education Act of 1963. Enacted swiftly after the assassination of President Kennedy as a sort of memorial to the education-minded President, it plainly states that any disadvantaged person—in school or out, old or young, urban or rural, employed or not—can be given vocational education in any type of school, covering a broad range of subjects. This hardly sounds radical, but against a background of decades of support to high schools and traditional extension programs heavily accenting home economics and agriculture, it is a great stride toward modernization.[37] The act strengthened the hand of the Commissioner of Education, authorizing him to establish residential vocational schools to remove boys from slum environments, area vocational schools, work-study programs, and other pilot projects.

By mid-1965, over 150 separate programs had been developed in the war on poverty. The administration was groping for a viable legislative and administrative framework for that war, but it was still succumbing to the principle of least resistance. All of these programs require an extraordinary amount of interagency cooperation at a federal level; almost all demand elaborate clearance at local levels. Few decisions can be implemented without passing them through a maze of overlapping federal, state, municipal, private, and public jurisdictions. It is especially difficult to gear vocational education and manpower development programs (for example, the

[37] Cf. U.S. Office of Education, *Education for a Changing World of Work,* Report of the Panel of Consultation on Vocational Education, Government Printing Office, Washington, 1963; and Levitan, Sar A., *Vocational Education and Federal Policy,* W. E. Upjohn Institute for Employment Research, Kalamazoo, Mich., May, 1963.

MDTA) to the needs of a changing labor market because certification and training are done by state agencies and local educational bodies; it means shaking up or bypassing entrenched political bureaucracies whose ideas are often as obsolete as the hardware in the vocational schools they serve.[38]

While many a weary planner was tempted to bet on the least controversial programs, by the mid-1960's the urge to act was clear, and the legislative log jam was breaking up. Some social critics, in fact, fear that if these programs are successful, they will create new and more explosive inequities. They note that the Job Corps removes school dropouts from a hostile slum environment and gives them intensive training in a pleasant camp. Some of the camp contractors are industrial corporations which have a stake in successful placement of their trainees. If the dropouts are trained well and placed in good jobs, how will less fortunate youths who finish high school and make out less well feel? Already one successful salvage operation in New York City, has been picketed by eight youngsters who complained, "Why are you doing all this for those bums?" Other similar paradoxes come to mind: Lower-class school children are overgraded because school officials want to move them along; upper-middle-class school children are overgraded because their parents, seized by the college panic, pressure the teachers; the children of the middle mass meanwhile get the grades they deserve.[39] Some poor families receive better medical service from free clinics than the self-supporting middle mass can afford. More dramatic is the insistent demand among more militant race leaders that Negroes receive not merely compensatory education but preference in jobs. Here is the specter of a Great Society in which the poor will be placed in decent jobs and houses while the middle mass will scrape along, barely getting by. And the latter's response, it is argued, will be like white backlash voting.

The possibility of a "welfare backlash" should not worry us. The target populations in the war on poverty are large; they start with extremely limited resources of motivation, information, and skill;

[38] Similarly, the employment service will not become a "community manpower center," linking people to jobs through appropriate training and counseling pointed toward projected regional and national needs, until federal performance standards can be imposed, financing and staffing greatly improved, stronger ties with public school counselors formed, and wider employer acceptance achieved.

[39] Based on a study of grade averages in relation to expected achievement measured by aptitude scores among Nashville junior high school students. Reiss, Albert J., Jr., and A. Lewis Rhodes, *Youth Conformity and Deviation*, The Free Press, New York, forthcoming.

the proportions touched by the entire effort are small; and the rate of success will not be overwhelming. Some rescued young men, and a few retrained older workers will doubtless obtain somewhat better jobs than high school graduates, Negroes and whites alike, who made it without special help. But relative to the gross inequities in American life—the great gulf that divides the poor from majority America—the problem is hardly worth mentioning. Even if we doubled our present efforts, we would find that there are powerful forces in economy and community as well as in the welfare programs themselves that slow down the push for equality.

The general tendency toward income equalization (see pages 100–105) was virtually halted in the 1950's, mainly because of slack in the economy (defense expenditures tapered off).[40] Unemployment rates for the lower working class continue to be three times that of the upper working class; Negro rates continue to be twice as high as white rates. Finally, as we have seen above, the distributional effects of welfare services are, to say the least, uncertain.

Community resistances to equality are equally formidable. Racial discrimination gives way only slowly. In local job markets, Negroes made modest but very selective gains during 1950–1960 in middling jobs, most of them highly vulnerable to the displacement effects of automation, and no gain (relative to whites) in professional and technical jobs. Using an "index of occupational change," which directly compares shifts in the occupational distribution of Negroes and whites between two time periods, Daniel O. Price finds that Negro gains in all regions of the United States were greater in 1940–1950 than in 1950–1960, greater for Negro females than for males; that the relative occupational position of Negro males in the Northeast and North Central Regions "probably deteriorated" in the 1950's; that the main exceptions were occupations serving segregated clientele such as ministers and teachers (who constitute 40 per cent of the Negro males in "professional, technical, and kindred"), musicians, music teachers, social welfare and recreation workers; and that most of the gains for the two decades have been in occupations in which a large proportion of the nonwhites are hired by government (a product of vigorous nondiscrimination policies of government agencies). For instance, almost two in five of the nonwhite medical and dental technicians are government

---

[40] There is some evidence this was happening in other rich countries, too, although the equalization trend continued longer in the United Kingdom, the Netherlands, and Sweden.

employees. The more favorable picture for the 1940's and for the West is due largely to defense booms.[41]

In the absence of massive federal intervention, local patterns of discrimination against Negroes tend to remain firm. Only the action of federal executive and judicial agencies threatening force and the withdrawal of federal funds has made school desegregation more than a promise. And virtually no progress has been made in housing: studies of housing segregation show that from 1910 to 1950 the segregation of immigrant groups declined but the segregation of Negroes actually increased.[42]

Finally, there are strong resistances built into the anti-poverty agencies and programs themselves. Just as vocational training until 1963 reached only the already literate, the already work-oriented youngsters, so the Job Corps program avoids seriously delinquent or disturbed youths. In early 1965, the Office of Economic Opportunity was criticized for barring parolees and probationers from the Job Corps—the very ones who need training most. Similarly, in selecting tenants for public housing, project managers for many years displayed a natural tendency to favor the steadier, more reliable, less troublesome families. Especially in new programs and in areas of controversy, welfare administrators, afraid of recalcitrant clientele and anxious to minimize risk of failure, concentrate on salvaging the almost saved. In view of these obstacles, the likelihood that help for the poor will move them beyond the self-starting workers of the middle mass is slight; we should not be diverted by the rare paradoxes of success, the occasional case of reverse discrimination where we invest heavily in a poor family less deserving than one we fail to notice. Insofar as the resentment of the overlooked family is a problem, a solution can sometimes be found by including them as helpers or beneficiaries. When Mobilization for Youth was picketed in 1962, it invited the pickets to join the work program.

Ideology, Politics, and Manpower in Welfare Planning

The more numerous and specialized the welfare services, the less intelligible they are to laymen and politicians. As welfare expendi-

[41] Price, D. O., "Changes in Occupational Distribution of the Negro Population, Chapter 5 of an unpublished manuscript, 1964.

[42] Leiberson, Stanley, *Ethnic Patterns in American Cities,* The Free Press, New York, 1963, p. 16. Moreover, the most recent immigrants—Puerto Ricans and Mexicans—although economically worse off than Negroes, already show less residential segregation. Taeuber, K. E., and A. F. Taeuber, "The Negro as an Immigrant Group: Recent Trends in Racial and Ethnic Segregation in Chicago," *American Journal of Sociology,* vol. 69, January, 1964, pp. 374–382.

tures increase, the criticisms of the welfare state and its administration described in Chapter II and Part Three (especially pages 250 ff.) will mount. Hostile critics will cry "welfare scandals" and insist that "welfare chiselers" are driving about in second-hand Cadillacs. More important, friendly critics will underline the undeniable difficulties of planning and administering the great variety of services comprising an up-to-date welfare state. While the civil rights movement and the warriors against poverty promise new political support for the push toward equality, they ensure more criticism of the welfare establishment from the left. The appetite for action is whetted; expectations that something will be done about the multi-problem family soar. It therefore becomes urgent to cope with the problems of specialization and coordination, to organize professional services effectively—to overcome the bureaucratic pathologies described in Chapter X. We must grasp the implications of a shortage of personnel to man the apparatus of the welfare state, consider new sources of manpower, and devise new roles to meet new needs. Once an alert administration mobilizes our national resources for full employment and community action, a final campaign in the war on poverty remains—the neglected campaign to improve the efficiency and quality of welfare service.

The Shortage of Professional Social Workers. The demand for professional services continues to rise and, as this book argues, the supply is not likely to be adequate. In contrast to accounting, such professions as medicine and social work do not lend themselves to rapid computerization, for they combine science and insight, systematic knowledge and intuition. Few of the caseworker's or group worker's tasks can be turned over to machines. Thus, in the next decade, while social work will continue to expand rapidly, the ratio of professionals to nonprofessionals in many welfare fields will decrease (part of a general trend described on page 91). To make better use of scarce skills and to meet increased demand for service, especially in government programs, social work professionals will either share their tasks with less-trained semi-professionals and nonprofessionals or they will find that persons trained outside the schools of social work will pre-empt the major fields of social welfare.

That a major shortage of welfare workers has developed in the past decade is suggested by two facts: (1) salaries have gone up rapidly;[43] (2) the proportion of male recruits has climbed.[44] That we have not yet faced up to the manpower needs of the emerging welfare state is suggested by the heavy concentration of professional social workers in private agencies and the grave recruitment problems of the agencies engaged in the war on poverty.

The Uses of Amateurs.   This book ends with a plea for tolerance for the aims and claims of the diverse groups, lay and professional, working for social welfare. The need is to maintain fluid lines of jurisdiction in the welfare industry, in keeping with the changing base of knowledge and technique, and to devise ways to tap the service motives of amateurs, thereby lessening the shortage of welfare manpower, and increasing the chances of victory in the war on poverty.

The various federal agencies involved in anti-poverty programs (discussed above), the neighborhood and city-wide "opportunity

[43] The following table compares the income distribution of all social welfare workers in 1950 and 1960 in constant (1960) dollars:

	Per Cent of All Workers	
	1950	*1960*
Under $4,000	62	17
$4,000 and under 6,000	30	49
6,000 and under 8,000	5	24
8,000 and over	3	10
Total	100	100

The figures for graduate social workers are, of course, higher; with recreation workers excluded, the median annual salary for male social welfare workers with a degree or two-year certificate was $7,020 in 1960, for comparable females it was $6,340.
SOURCES: U.S. Department of Labor, Bureau of Labor Statistics, Division of Wages and Industrial Relations, *Social Workers in 1950,* A Report on the Study of Salaries and Working Conditions in Social Work—Spring 1950, American Association of Social Workers, New York, 1952, Table D-31, p. 59; U.S. Department of Labor, Bureau of Labor Statistics, *Salaries and Working Conditions of Social Welfare Manpower in 1960,* National Social Welfare Assembly, New York, n.d., Table 37, p. 74. Adjusted for inflation based on consumer prices for all commodities as computed by the Department of Commerce, Office of Business Economics.
[44] In 1950, men constituted 31 per cent of the 74,240 social workers; in 1960, they were 57 per cent of 115,799. In the second century of the industrial revolution and despite the spread of emancipation ideologies and feminist movements, women have entered low status men's occupations (bookkeeper, bank teller) but do not control them, while men have entered and are gaining control of the more attractive female occupations (secondary school teaching, social work, librarianship, hospital and perhaps nursing administration). The better the prospects of an occupation, the more men we find in it. The case of social work is explained on pages 322–324, and that argument is applied to other occupations and countries in Wilensky, H. L., *Work, Leisure* . . . , chap. 5.

mobilizations" sponsored by the President's Committee on Delinquency and Youth Crime, The Ford Foundation "gray areas" projects—all recognize that social problems are rooted in social structure; all accent political skills and the uses of "indigenous nonprofessionals" to break cultural barriers between helping agents and the poor; all involve the efforts of public as well as private agencies; and all assume that substantial change will not occur unless the target people themselves are involved in the action. These new programs are not exactly new in their strategy (see Chapter IX, especially pages 210 ff. on "Area Projects and Group Work for Neighborhood and Gang"), but their rapid expansion in the 1960's promises a unique blend of the institutional approach of this book and traditional casework and community organization approaches. At the same time, these programs generate romanticism about the joys of life in the ethnic slum and optimism about the effects of local initiative on welfare planning and the "opportunity structure." They also pose new dilemmas of financing, coordination, and control.

Consider two of these experiments in community self-help—Mobilization for Youth on New York's lower East Side, and Community Progress, Inc., in New Haven—as samples of the range of strategies and difficulties.[45]

Mobilization for Youth is a three-year demonstration project begun in 1962 with a $13.5 million budget provided by the federal government, New York City, and The Ford Foundation. It aims to saturate a small area with social services, most of them new, designed to reshape the "opportunity structure" by changing education, work, and neighborhood organization.[46] Services are channeled both through traditional agencies such as settlement houses and through formal and informal neighborhood leaders, often placed on the staff as part-time organizers. A key element in the strategy is to encourage social action on issues the local people regard as critical—juvenile behavior, housing, government service, and discrimination. Although community groups are at first guided by Mobilization for Youth,

---

[45] For details on these and other programs, see Kahn, Alfred J., "Trends and Problems in Community Organization" in *Social Work Practice, 1964,* Selected Papers, 91st Annual Forum, National Conference on Social Welfare, Los Angeles, May 24–29, 1964, Columbia University Press, New York, 1964, pp. 3–27, a balanced overview; *American Community Development,* The Ford Foundation, New York, 1963; *A Proposal for the Prevention and Control of Delinquency by Expanding Opportunities,* Mobilization for Youth, Inc., New York, 1961; *New Haven Youth Development Program,* Community Progress, Inc., New Haven, 1963, 4 vols.

[46] Cloward, Richard A., and Lloyd E. Ohlin, *Delinquency and Opportunity.* The Free Press, New York, 1960.

they are expected to move on their own eventually. MFY is an intensive effort to organize an area for self-help on a broad range of interrelated problems, using both social casework adapted to the special needs of low-income families and a variety of other professional specialists in employment counseling, education, group work, and community organization.

The New Haven Community Progress program, in contrast, is citywide; it aims to develop plans for education, counseling, job training, and placement covering seven neighborhoods, which includes almost two-thirds of the city's residents. Like other "gray areas" programs (Boston, Oakland, Philadelphia, Washington, and a statewide project in North Carolina), New Haven emphasizes the involvement of the government establishment and the city fathers, the achievement of consensus, and the use of existing channels for planning and administration. For instance, the program seeks to make the public school a kind of resocialization agency—a base for general and adult education, civic, cultural and recreational activity, and family life education, a neighborhood outlet for health clinics, family counseling, legal aid, job counseling, as well as for local action on community problems. The Youth Development program is placed in the context of an ambitious Program for Community Progress, led by the mayor; planning took place against a backdrop of five large-scale renewal projects and a housing and school building program; youth employment proposals were part of a long-range manpower training program submitted to the Office of Manpower, Automation, and Training.

One promising development in these new programs is the creation of new roles for indigenous nonprofessionals and for semiprofessional social service workers, a new army of helpers in education and social welfare.[47] The first group are people who come originally from the disadvantaged areas they serve and who have personal understanding of the kinds of people and problems they serve. They fill a crucial gap in welfare manpower: social work professionals are scarce and they are often reluctant to work with the poor; the new indigenous welfare workers serve as a bridge between agencies or schools and the poor. Their backgrounds match

---

[47] See Rieff, Robert, and Frank Riessman, *The Indigenous Nonprofessional,* National Institute of Labor Education, Mental Health Program, Report No. 3, November, 1964. Labor unions and veterans' organizations have long had rank-and-file counselors who link the citizen to the social services. More recently, Arthur Pearl and Leonard Duhl have worked to create such roles among the poor.

their functions: Youth for Service in San Francisco trains older gang leaders to become streetworkers; the New York State Division for Youth uses former juvenile offenders in interviewing delinquents and in related research tasks; Howard University's Community Apprentice Program trains delinquent youth to be recreation, child welfare, and research aides; Puerto Rican informal leaders act as liaison between the schools and the Spanish-speaking community; Mobilization for Youth employs such nonprofessionals as community action organizers, case aides, parent education aides, homework helpers. To transform the welfare case into a homemaker, the delinquent into a research assistant, the impoverished student into a teacher is to make welfare services more effective and at the same time provide employment for the poor.

These examples represent the kind of imaginative reorganization of welfare services necessary to "reach the unreached" and overcome the disadvantages of interagency specialization discussed on pages 250–257. With the expansion of the anti-poverty program, the indigenous nonprofessional becomes indispensable as a guide through the bureaucratic jungle. The referral who never gets there, the relief recipient frightened by the formalities, the AFDC mother perplexed by the snoopers constantly checking on violations, the discouraging waiting list, the frustrating clinic delay—this red tape is only partly inevitable; it can be unsnarled by expediters.

Perhaps expediting has been the most impressive function of Mobilization for Youth. During the first few months of the program, each Parent Education Aide cared for about 35 families, escorting parents to schools, welfare agencies, clinics, legal aid, Consumers' Bureau—even locating apartments and mediating family quarrels; homemakers used their know-how to help poor families negotiate life in the slum, showing them how to use the thrift shop, the remnant pile, free recreation facilities, free public clinics, the barber school (for free haircuts), how to get surplus food. In Scandinavia, where the welfare state has attained its most humane development, the expediter has been institutionalized in the role of public *ombudsman,* a government official to whom citizens can submit complaints about injustice or negligence involving service functionaries.[48] In the reluctant welfare state of America, a more aggressive matching of agency to clientele than that afforded by a grievance commissioner may be necessary.

The recruitment and training of indigenous nonprofessionals is

[48] *News of Norway,* vol. 22, May 6, 1965, p. 68.

not easy. Many of these people are serious, enthusiastic, and dedicated. But more is required. As Rieff and Reissman suggest,[49] they must be similar to their neighbors in education or economic standing, they must neither have turned their backs on the less successful in achieving a more stable way of life for themselves nor have become defeatist about the possible success of others. Yet they must be able to work comfortably with middle-class functionaries in school and agency, to accept supervision, to carry on conversation across class lines. Such talent, extremely hard to locate, is only moderately hard to train. A combination of field work and on-the-job service, like social work training but more circumscribed in classroom content, is typical. How to retain roots in the community, avoid cynicism, combine authority and warmth, avoid throwing your weight around (a common temptation for new recruits in community organization), and maintain confidentiality (some of the potential recruits are neighborhood gossips) are attitudes and skills that can be discussed; but the indigenous nonprofessional best learns them in action. While the extended use of these workers is too recent to evaluate, they may yet constitute an answer to the high "mortality" (turnover and "burn out") of the streetworkers described on page 223.

Women with some college training or a degree who want to go beyond child rearing provide a second major source of untapped manpower. Because women are marrying earlier and spacing children closer together, many millions will reach their forties with the will to work and nothing to do. An obvious way to tap this pool of energy and good will is to offer them short training programs in social service, to use them as "team mothers," "parent education coordinators," and paper graders in the schools—in general, to create roles that fit their talents and motives.

A final source of manpower for the welfare state is clergymen, young college activists, and Negro militants of the civil rights movement. Just as the Army has not always been given credit for its vocational training achievements, so the troops commanded by Martin Luther King have not been recognized as welfare workers in the anti-poverty drive. In their efforts to encourage voter registration, Negro churches have become centers for literacy training; the message, "What kind of Negro are you that you can't read?" has penetrated where all the outside exhortation has not.

These amateurs are neither the intelligent, kind, "friendly visitor"

[49] *Op. cit.,* pp. 23–43.

of the charity organization societies of seventy years ago, whose approach to the pauper was one of moral superiority, nor the objective professional of today, whose relation to the modern poor is that of the expert. Neither condescending nor expert, they are something new. They represent a flood of idealism and good sense waiting to be channeled. Minor problems in mobilizing these resources—for instance, the nonprofessionals may take up too much of the time of their social worker supervisors—need not prevent progress. A profession already devoted to close supervision should not shy away from the challenge of training. The obvious limitation of more orthodox approaches to the poor justify more experimentation. And the political climate of the early 1960's was right for a new attack.

Romanticism and Reality in the New Programs

The attack on poverty, with its revival of "grass roots" programs for social action and community development is hopeful, but it sharply poses three familiar dilemmas of centralization and decentralization: (1) infiltration vs. cooptation, (2) federal financing and control vs. private financing and local autonomy, (3) efficiency vs. privacy in the context of centralized welfare information and data processing.

Infiltration vs. Cooptation. Grass roots organizations with social action aims and a strong political line are open either to infiltration by activists whose aims diverge from those of the organization or integration into the political establishment with a concomitant loss of reform purposes. Minority defense organizations and neighborhood self help groups alike are vulnerable to these traps. Many a CORE or SNCC chapter has come to see fighting as an end in itself, losing sight of its main aim—the elimination of racial discrimination. Such groups can also come under the control not of militants who divert their aims to international politics, utopian demands, or irresponsible attacks on the wrong targets, but of status-seekers busy escaping the people they represent. Like board members in welfare agencies whose vested interests clash with agency interests (see pages 269–277), they are alienated from the values and practices of their constituency. Self-selection of the least representative residents into leadership positions is especially characteristic of slum-based organizations. Since targets of pressure are often outside the area— building inspectors, health inspectors, the school board, the housing authority, the mayor's office—the upwardly mobile leaders who

apply it may bask in the reflected glory of the powerful, rest content
with symbolic appointments to the Youth Commission, the Urban
Redevelopment Commission, and similar committees, and forget
their mission. In short, these programs can be victims of their greatest virtue, their accent on rank-and-file participation and control.

On the other hand, some programs avoid subversion from below
by accenting professional leadership and conventional channels of
action and protest, only to find that they reach few of the clients
they aim to help. Moreover, they open themselves to charges of
"paternalism" and "welfare colonialism"—epithets critics have
applied to The Ford Foundation's "gray areas" projects. For instance, a typical critic asks, ". . . who is to do the planning for
whom? The answer is all too plain. 'The composition of the Board
of Directors [of Community Progress, Inc., in New Haven, its executive director said], is a reflection of the basic communitywide
consensus which has been achieved. Represented on the Board is the
Community Council, the United Fund, the Board of Education,
The Redevelopment Agency, the Citizens Action Committee, Yale
University, the New Haven Foundation, and the Mayor's Office.'
Everybody, in short, except the people being planned for." The result, it is claimed, is that the issues that divide tenants and landlords,
Negroes who want jobs and white unionists afraid of giving up
theirs—the hard issues—are avoided.[50]

[50] Silberman, Charles E., *Crisis in Black and White,* Random House, New
York, 1964, p. 352. In the case of Mobilization for Youth, Silberman comments, large-scale financing from government and domination by "representatives of the old-line settlement houses and social work agencies" make it difficult
for it to act according to its stated principles. Silberman reserves his uncritical
applause for Saul Alinsky's Industrial Areas Foundation, especially The Woodlawn Organization in Chicago, which he sees as "real democracy." It is difficult to see how T.W.O. is any less a matter of "welfare colonialism" than its
rivals. Full-time organizers fan through the community hunting for issues with the
maximum potential for arousing the citizens, which inevitably means accenting
conflict and hate. In the language of a T.W.O. memorandum, Alinsky aims to
"rub raw the sores of discontent." Silberman quotes and answers a critic of this
approach: " 'The fact that a community may be stirred and organized by
sharpening dormant hostilities and rubbing raw the sores of discontent is not
new,' says Julian Levi, executive director of the South East Chicago Commission. . . . As an example of the methods to which he objects, Levi cites a
T.W.O. leaflet naming a local food store and warning people to 'watch out'
for short weights, spoiled food, and short-changing. 'If this is what this merchant is really doing,' Levi says, 'he should be punished by the court—but with
all the safeguards the law provides.' " Similarly, Levi argues, people should be
taught to register complaints with the Department of Health (about spoiled
food), the Department of Weights and Measures (about short weights), and
the Police Department (about short change). If landlords were violating the
building code, T.W.O. should have brought action through the Building Department instead of launching rent strikes. Silberman finds this argument weak:
"slum dwellers . . . have been complaining to the Building Department and to

In the search for means of protest at once nonviolent and effective, the direct action techniques of the civil rights movement—rent
strikes, boycotts, picketing—are increasingly popular. If a grass
roots agency financed largely by government encourages the use of
such tactics against City Hall, however, it invites political attack.
In 1964, 23 school principals in the area organized by Mobilization
for Youth demanded publicly that The Ford Foundation investigate
the program; in their view groups of parents demanding that the
schools be more responsive to their needs had been disrupting the
orderly conduct of school business. More serious, some city officials,
faced with urgent demands for action on slum problems and a push
for wider participation in party politics, launched an all-out coun-
ter-attack on Mobilization for Youth, using demagogic accusations
of political disloyalty—labeling "Communist" those involved in a
suspect organization decades ago, asserting "Communist takeover"
without proof that the small number of alleged subversives had any
authority, and so on. If direct action techniques are used by a privately financed grass roots agency like The Woodlawn Organization,
less open to public scrutiny or professional influence, the problem is
not so much political attack as the vulnerability to private manipulation and outside subversion. In either case the grass roots ideology
and direct action tactics, although at times appropriate, will not
suffice to solve the problems of the slum.

The urge for grass roots participation should not blind us to the
limits of local community action; the desire to avoid cooptation
should not tempt us to romanticize life in an ethnic slum. Decentralization, like patent medicine, is not really good for what ails you.
The logic underlying any self-help program designed to expand the
opportunities of the poor implies a merger with urban renewal and
rehousing strategies, and ultimately with political pressures for federal action to improve education, training, and placement, and to
increase aggregate demand (one year after the tax cut of 1964, the
unemployment rate had dropped one per cent). There is no use
whetting the appetite for action—that is, overcoming apathy, increasing motivation, even increasing skill—unless jobs are opened,
houses made livable, and income assured.

Many of the advocates of indigenous organization, repelled by the

other city agencies for years, to no avail. . . ." And ". . . Levi's criticisms miss
the point—that the tactics he deplores are designed to serve more than one
end . . . the most urgent need was to persuade the local population that it
could solve some of its problems through organization"—to overcome apathy.
Ibid., pp. 331–333.

"middle class bias" of the welfare establishment, deny that any accommodation of the slum to the existing power structure and prevailing success ideology is desirable. Some of these critics even view Mobilization for Youth as just another misguided effort to transform the poor into pale imitations of the bourgeois status striver. While an earlier generation of social uplifters saw the poor as evil, mean, sordid, insolent, and criminal, these new students of the slum find a "subculture of poverty" with "an integrity of its own" worth preserving. Do the poor lack the ability to plan ahead? "Living immersed in the present may develop a capacity for spontaneity, for the enjoyment of the sensual, the indulgence of impulse, which is too often blunted in our middle class future-oriented man." Do parents beat their children savagely? Is weak school performance a block to subsequent employment? The poor are freer in physical than in verbal expression; they are not "word bound." Is family life unstable, are the children unsupervised? No, that is really a "peer group orientation," informality and good humor, freedom from sibling rivalry, "freedom from self-blame and over-protection."[51]

Not only do these new stereotypes miss the "Many Faces of Poverty" (see above), not only do they idealize life in the ethnic slum (see pages 183–207), they also ignore the fact that "education for mobility," which provokes the scorn of romantic sociologists, is the main hope for most of the poor, unless they are the aged poor. Even if the virtues of "lower-class culture" were uniform, a strategy that seeks to reinforce them would freeze the least promising limitations of information, motivation, and abilities which block opportunity and perpetuate poverty through the generations. To have enough money, health, a decent home, a neighborhood without rats and garbage in the alleys, requires both political organization and steady employment, which in turn require the "middle-class" skills of reliability, literacy, and self-control. This is not to advocate an oppressive uniformity; a strategy stressing education, the exploitation of existing opportunities, and the creation of new opportunities does not prevent the poor from the full expression of diverse traditions of ethnic-religious group, class, and locality. Nor is it to say that helping institutions need not understand and respect the special characteristics of their clientele.

To blend the requisite parts of "middle class" culture with viable local traditions demands the great empathic skill of the mediators

[51] For references to such literature, see Herbert J. Gans' *The Urban Villagers,* The Free Press, New York, 1962, chaps. 11 and 12.

and expediters discussed above. The dilemma of infiltration vs. cooptation can be overcome by linking self-helping groups of the poor to the system through officials assigned to represent them (we could use a variety of *ombudsmenn*), indigenous nonprofessionals, semi-professional social service workers, and professional social workers. The place of casework in this emerging welfare structure is plain: traditional social work skills can be adapted to briefing and supervising the new helping agents; more emphasis can be given to case-finding and evaluation, to teaching, planning, and administration. Moreover, no amount of political organization, no amount of steam in the anti-poverty drive will change those poor families enmeshed in self-defeating adaptations; the usual personalized therapeutic and rehabilitation efforts must accompany institutional change, in a general effort to improve the quality and impact of social services.

Federal Control vs. Local Autonomy.   The merits of grass roots programs should not obscure the costs of political decentralization and fragmentation discussed above. The answer to poverty may be blowing in the wind, the civil rights movement may provide the necessary political courage, but until federal welfare standards and strong federal intervention develop, the wind will have little force and no direction. Our previous polemic against decentralization is a complaint about the decentralization that keeps the welfare state reluctant, the financing weak (as in state welfare legislation), programs timid (as in metropolitan planning, housing, and transportation). Obviously, to be effective, large-scale federal aid and metropolitan and area-wide administration must link up with the cities and local neighborhoods. The liveliest local participation, however, is futile without the resources and coordination appropriate to the problem.

Centralized Welfare Information: The Social Worker as Policeman. The issue of the proper place of the federal government in the financing or control of local community welfare effort should not be confused with two other issues harassing every level of government: (1) outdated laws reflecting a "charity" approach to welfare administration; (2) a new issue of centralization posed by the availability of electronic data processing (EDP).

The specter of a centralized welfare bureaucracy with files on the private lives of everyone, speedily accessible to a variety of officials, investigations, and researchers, is not a pretty one. A society already plagued by wire-tappers and other electronic snoopers, crisis journalism with its exposé spirit, and professional informers can ill afford more invasions of privacy. Yet the most horrendous examples of violations of civil rights and of invasion of privacy in the welfare field occur not at the federal but at the state and local levels.

The problem is partly one of antiquated and repressive laws, some of dubious constitutionality. Deriving from the Elizabethan Poor Law, rooted in an age of autocracy and aristocracy when the poor were a separate, degraded class, these state statutes overemphasize the personal causes of poverty and seek to overcome them by excessive doses of criminal law. In California nearly 500,000 men, women, and children are carried as family cases under the Welfare and Institutions Code. Under the Code the "adult male assuming the role of spouse" must contribute to the upkeep of whatever children live in the household. The outcomes include the following: county investigators conduct "night raids" or "bed checks" to catch men sleeping with mothers receiving dependent-children aid; social workers are in effect empowered to create an ad hoc marriage merely by discovering a "man in the house" and designating him as the husband (a distinctive type of common law marriage, which presumes the man to be legally both incompetent and irresponsible) ;[52] and, in the course of gathering information about applicants for Aid to Needy Children (ANC), welfare officials use the threat of withholding support to force applicants to inform on their boy friends regarding such crimes as nonsupport, adultery, and statutory rape (any nonmarital act of coitus with a girl under eighteen years of age). That social workers function literally as detectives is shown by a study of 134 statutory rape cases handled

[52] Ten Broek, Jacobus, "California's Dual System of Family Law: Its Origin, Development, and Present Status," *Stanford Law Review*, vol. 16, March, July, 1964, pp. 257–317, 900–982; vol. 17, April, 1965, pp. 614–682. In the family law of the poor the man is considered to have "assumed the role of spouse" and is therefore legally obliged to support both needy children and mother if in the words of the AFDC manual: "(a) He is in or around the home and is maintaining an intimate relationship with the mother, or is the father of one or more of the children, and (b) He has assumed substantial financial responsibility for the ongoing expenses of the ANC family, and/or (c) He has represented himself to the community in such a way as to appear in the relationship of husband and/or father." *Ibid.*, p. 620. In civil family law, applied to cases where the children are not declared needy, no such obligation of support is imposed on the comparable de facto spouse. The legislature and welfare administration make and apply the family rules for the poor; the courts make and apply them for those in more comfortable circumstances. The main aim of the former is to keep welfare costs at a minimum; the main effect is to force the wider sharing of poverty.

by the morals detail of one metropolitan police department between January and October, 1963. The Family Support Division of the County Welfare Department requires its interviewers to question unmarried ANC mothers about the paternity of each child. If the applicant is under eighteen, she must go to the police department and charge the father with statutory rape as a condition of receiving aid; about half of all cases that came to police attention were welfare referrals, the complaining witness almost always acting under duress. Six in 10 cases were initiated by public agencies, including welfare and probation agencies, as by-products of their official business.[53]

The problem is general and it goes beyond unconstitutional invasions of privacy; it involves the protection of the legal rights of every category of the poor. As several students of justice have observed, citizens' rights under social insurance and public assistance, unemployment compensation and workmen's compensation programs, job rights and related retirement and fringe benefits, legal protections against the debtors' spiral, the rights of tenants to heat, water, and electricity as well as more celebrated civil rights—these are characteristic forms of wealth and security for the poor.[54] The view of public agencies that the welfare services are a privilege leads to routine violations of welfare rights.

The spread of more sophisticated uses of high-speed computers at every level of government will make such violations easier at the same time that it improves service. The school, the police, the court, the welfare agency, the hospital, and workplace could all usefully draw on a centralized file on the entire population. This would reduce the need for repeated taking of life histories and speed the processing of applications of all kinds. Better records more speedily processed could increase the efficiency of the welfare services. Significantly, the Office of Economic Opportunity has already adopted the "cost effectiveness" techniques of the Pentagon. A computer-controlled information system will store and analyze data on the nation's poor to highlight the impact of various anti-poverty programs on specific social categories—to discover, for instance, which of several teaching techniques in preschool programs such as "Project Head Start" produce best results at least cost.

[53] Woodworth, J. Richard, "The Administration of Statutory Rape Complaints: A Sociological Study." Unpublished Master's thesis, University of California, Berkeley, 1964.
[54] Carlin, Jerome E., and Jan Howard, "Legal Representation and Class Justice," *UCLA Law Review*, vol. 12, January, 1965, pp. 381–437.

Within the framework of a "Poor Law" approach to income maintenance, and without better safeguards of welfare rights and civil rights, gains in efficiency can mean a loss in individual privacy and dignity. Welfare planners must be alert to the danger that in the name of improved coordination of the welfare services, in pursuit of the humane purposes of the welfare state, we may simply subject the underlying population to more efficient surveillance.

Conclusion

Between the social surveys of the turn of the century and the rediscovery of poverty in the early 1960's came a long period of professional growth, the proliferation of welfare services and new welfare occupations; the refinement of casework methods; and efforts to fund and coordinate largely private welfare agencies. More reluctantly than other rich countries, the United States moved toward the welfare state—government-protected minimum standards of income, nutrition, health, housing, and education for every citizen, assured as a political right, not as a charity; the aversion for that move is evident in the growth of the social insurances and private occupational welfare benefits, regressive in economic effect, and in the lag in programs with a strong potential for reducing inequality. To the roots of the reluctant welfare state discussed in Part One of this book, we must add the persistence of racial, ethnic, and religious divisions, and, above all, a great degree of political decentralization which sometimes paralyzes the will to act, makes planning difficult, and tempts planners to accent the least controversial programs—for example, highway building. Yet, the civil rights movement, together with intellectual ferment about the quality of American life in general, has produced promising beginnings, including the war on poverty. Community resistances to equality and a natural tendency for welfare programs to salvage the almost saved, educate the already literate, bypassing those most in need, are slowly being overcome.

In the future we can expect an emphasis on the interrelation of various social problems (see pages 215–228), already an official line of the "gray areas" and other community action programs; an accent on the uses of indigenous amateurs and of semi-professional helpers to meet manpower shortages, to improve the quality and impact of services, and generally to soften contact with an impersonal welfare state; the expansion of public programs and increasing attention to the tortuous process of coordinating them with private effort; the recognition of local political and organizational realities and the need to protect the citizen against administrative abuse; more serious planning and evaluation, making use of social sciences and reflecting federal and foundation guidelines based on a national view of social trends. We hope that this book will continue to provide a historical and sociological perspective useful in understanding and solving the problems of the welfare state.

University of California, Berkeley
May 26, 1965

Contents

PART ONE
THE DEVELOPMENT OF URBAN-INDUSTRIAL SOCIETY AND THE EMERGENCE OF SOCIAL PROBLEMS

3

PART TWO

SOCIAL PROBLEMS AND THE SUPPLY OF WELFARE
SERVICES IN THE UNITED STATES

PART THREE

THE ORGANIZATION OF WELFARE SERVICES
IN THE UNITED STATES

Tables

7

Charts

Foreword

IN JANUARY, 1955, the United States Committee of the International Conference of Social Work asked Russell Sage Foundation for assistance in the preparation of a summary account of industrialization in this country and its effects on social work for family and community welfare. The following month the Trustees of the Foundation authorized the requested cooperation and appropriated the necessary funds. Work on the project was begun shortly thereafter.

The desired manuscript, in the words of the Committee, should include "A definition and description of industrialization in its several phases in the development of our economy; an account of the effects of industrialization on our social institutions, including the community and the family (with focus on the resulting social problems); an account of the way the United States has coped with the adverse effects of industrialization, including the development of governmental and voluntary social services; and an appraisal of today's situation and outlook." A "fairly brief volume" of 200 pages was suggested, and October, 1955, was set as the time for completion. Almost unbelievably, a manuscript of just a little over the prescribed length was completed and distribution begun in processed form only one month late, in November, 1955.

The rare efficiency and speed with which a manuscript amply satisfying the requirements of the Committee was prepared is a tribute to the professional skill and devoted hard work which the authors applied to the task. It was unusual good fortune that the services of so well-balanced a team as Dr. Harold L. Wilensky and Dr. Charles N. Lebeaux were secured, first on a part-time basis during the latter part of the academic year and then full-time for the summer. Dr. Wilensky, associate professor of sociology at the University of Michigan, was exceptionally well suited for the assignment both by his training as an industrial sociologist and by his interests and experience. His central concern has been with theories of social organization and change as applied to industrial relations, occupations and professions, and politics. His nonacademic experience has ranged from factory work to social research and labor union staff jobs.

Dr. Lebeaux, associate professor of social work in the Wayne State University School of Social Work, holds advanced degrees in social work and sociology. His teaching career includes appointments in both fields. At present he is responsible at Wayne for those areas of the social work curriculum concerned with research and with the societal setting of social work.

David G. French, executive secretary of the Coordinating Committee on Social Welfare Research, University of Michigan School of Social Work, deserves credit not only for finding persons so well equipped for the collaborative preparation of the manuscript, but also for facilitating their work both as an adviser and by assuming the burden of administration in all its multitudinous details. Dean Fedele F. Fauri of the University of Michigan School of Social Work and Professor Amos G. Hawley, chairman of the Department of Sociology, served with Mr. French as members of an efficient administrative committee.

Only 800 copies were made of the manuscript prepared by Dr. Wilensky and Dr. Lebeaux in the spring and summer of 1955, just a few more than enough for use as a point of departure in making local studies in various parts of the country preparatory to United States participation in the Eighth International Conference of Social Work and for use at the August, 1956, meetings at Munich. The report was titled *Industrialization and Social Welfare*, and carried the subtitle *An Analysis of the Impact of Industrialization on the Supply and Organization of Social Welfare Services in the United States*. It was marked "Preliminary Draft—Not for Publication," and no copies were sold. Since the manuscript was prepared for a special purpose which was well served, it was thought that that would be the end of the matter. It was soon obvious, however, that this was not to be the case.

The report aroused so much interest both in this country and abroad that its limited original objective clearly required extension. The chairman of the United States Committee of the International Conference of Social Work, Lester B. Granger, in a letter to the Foundation said that he did not know "of any social work document produced in recent years that has stirred more energetic discussion than the monograph *Industrialization and Social Welfare*. It has been responsible," he continued, "for a degree of professional self-analysis that is as remarkable as it is healthy. . . ." As Mr. Granger's well-deserved words of praise make plain, the monograph was received with mixed reactions by the profession for which it was prepared. This was expected and regarded as encouraging by those concerned with its production. Bland acceptance would have been as dismaying as blind rejection, for such a response could only have meant that the crucial issues in the development of American social welfare practice had either been avoided or weakly compromised. They were in fact presented as vital problems requiring continuous effort for resolution.

When it became evident that both the scope and circulation of the monograph should be extended, it was also evident that the authors should be given the opportunity to revise their manuscript with more time at their disposal than had been available for the preparation of the original draft. It was a happy circumstance that they were able and willing to undertake its revision and expansion into the present publication, *Industrial Society and Social Welfare*. Their approach and basic point of view has not been materially altered but they have reorganized, revised, and added to their original monograph to a much greater extent than might be suggested by the very slight change in title from *Industrialization and Social Welfare* to *Industrial Society and Social Welfare*. No less than half entirely new, the present volume is in fact a new book written for a broader purpose and wider audience than was the antecedent draft out of which it grew.

The expansion of industrialization and the increasing importance of welfare programs and institutions are well-documented and well-known phenomena in western society. The present authors have not attempted a compressed summary of what is known about these subjects. They have not written a short factual history of social problems in the light of technological developments in the United States. Rather they have utilized the tools of social science, especially but not exclusively of sociology, to deepen the understanding of the impact of industrialization on the demand for social welfare services, both public and voluntary, and on the nature of the response to this demand. The authors' purpose in studying the past is always to gain better understanding both of present problems of social welfare and also of those most likely to gain importance in the near future.

Industrial Society and Social Welfare could properly carry the subtitle "A Study of the Origin and Development of a Profession." What the authors have done is to demonstrate how and why welfare institutions and the profession of social work have achieved their present roles in the United States. It would be interesting and instructive to make comparisons between the development of welfare institutions and personnel and that of other institutions and their professional staff, for example, schools and teachers, hospitals and nurses, or churches and the clergy. Studies of professions too often are thought to be of value only to members of the profession under examination. All professions, however, should be able to find something of value in a study of any one. Certainly Dr. Wilensky and Dr. Lebeaux have made a contribution to the understanding not only of welfare agencies and personnel but also of institutional and professional development in general.

DONALD YOUNG
President
Russell Sage Foundation

Preface

THIS IS A BOOK about social order and social change. It is also a book about the people who staff a set of institutions devoted to social welfare. Our problem is the impact of industrialization on the demand for, and supply and organization of, social welfare services in the United States. The analysis tries as systematically as theory and research permit to spell out the links between changes in technology; changes in social structure; the social problems those changes create in the setting of American culture; and the nation's response in the form of welfare expenditures, social agencies, and welfare occupations, including the social work profession. The task is twofold: (1) to report what the social sciences, especially sociology, have to say about the main drift of urban-industrial society, and (2) to suggest the implications of industrialization for the development and practice of social work in the United States in the short-run future.

The massive changes wrought by industrialization in the western world are now spreading at accelerated pace to the most isolated parts of the globe. The machine and the factory—from the eighteenth century English textile mill to the latest push-button marvel—these are the symbols both of progress and of problems in human living. Urban-industrial society is the central stage for more and more of the human drama.

American social work is part and product of the larger social and cultural setting in which it lives. While it helps to shape the larger society, social work reflects more than it determines the nature of the whole. It cannot be understood apart from its social context. And the more we understand its links to society and culture, the better we will see opportunities to influence the development of welfare services and the profession of social work.

We assume throughout that what people speak of as the "larger context," or the "sociocultural environment," deserves to be made specific. For major changes in these big units (societies, communities) deeply affect what goes on in the smaller ones (families, clubs, friendship groups, workgroups in social agencies). As a preview of the argument, there are six main links between the effects of industrialization on the structure of American society, on the one hand, and the nature of welfare services and the practice of social work, on the other:

1. The problems the social worker deals with would not be matters for organized public attention if it were not for industrialization. Some of them—old age, unemployment, leisure time—have increased in importance with economic growth. Others, whether they have increased or decreased in frequency (and this is something we often do not know), are now visible, urgent subjects for public action—family breakup, delinquency, mental and physical illness, poverty, and so on. No social problems—no welfare services, no profession of social work.

2. Welfare expenditures on a scale which evokes the label "welfare state" could not be made if the resources were lacking. Industrialization so vastly increases the income of a society that it makes such expenditures possible. No industrialization —few welfare services, and few specialists to dispense them.

3. A major function of social work, its liaison function, derives from a major effect of industrialization: the specialization of modern life. The social worker is, among other things, a guide through a kind of civilized jungle, made up of specialized agencies and service functionaries the citizen can hardly name, let alone locate. From this fact stems another function many social workers and agency administrators perform: the planning and coordination of specialized services.

4. Changes in the clientele of social agencies derive from another major effect of industrialization: shifts in stratification. On the casework rolls the people of poverty and low status are dwindling and those from the middle class growing—with lasting effects on the services demanded, relations with clients, and the status of social work.

5. All industrial societies develop large numbers of "bureaucracies"—large-scale formal organizations; all move toward central controls over many spheres of community life, including the welfare services. The specialized social agency and the central fund-raising body, both professionally staffed, are part of this general tendency—with important consequences for social service. The business elite, coupled with high-status lawyers and doctors, play a prominent role in the control of these bureaucracies. Working out a satisfactory relationship with these men in the formulation of welfare policy is a major problem for welfare professionals. Another major problem is that of resolving the conflict between professionalism and technique, on the one hand, and social reform, on the other.

6. American culture (especially those values shaping economic action—our individualism, our ideas about private property, the free market, and the role of government) affects not only the amount of cash we spend for welfare services, but also the kinds of services we assign to private versus public agencies, local and state versus federal agencies. In America alone among advanced societies has the voluntary, private welfare effort remained so large a part of the total; the very ambiguities of the term "social welfare" reflect these values in our culture.

All chapters in this book aim to spell out these ideas about the social and cultural context of welfare practice. Detailed application to social work is avoided, however, until after we deal with the complex relationships between industrialization[1] and the

[1] Industrialization is a matter of degree. Throughout this book we will consider a society industrialized to the extent that in the production and distribution of goods and services it uses: (1) tools that multiply the effects of their applications of energy, and (2) inanimate sources of energy (energy is the ability to do work—i.e., to bring about a change in physical relationships, as when a weight is lifted or a bomb exploded). (207: p. 115; and 66) "Nonindustrial" will be used to mean industrialized to a very low degree. "Industrialized" ("industrial," "industrialism," "highly industrialized," "mature" or "advanced" industrialism) will be used to mean industrialized to a very high degree, and can be translated "makes much use of high-energy technology." This includes high-energy technology used on the farm as well as in the factory. The social changes that accompany advanced industrialism always include among other things large-scale organization and urban employment. Such changes in social structure, along with related changes in values discussed in this book, do *not* appear automatically with passing time; they *do* appear in varied form *if* with passing time a society adopts high-energy technology.

NOTE: Parenthetical numbers in the text indicate references cited in full in the bibliography and, when appropriate, pages. For example, (19: II, pp. 245-246) indicates bibliography entry number 19, volume II, pages 245-246.

structure of American society—for in order to understand the effect of something we must first describe what the something is. And if we are to speak of the impact of industrialization, we cannot ignore the question "Which are the universal character-istics and consequences of industrialism and which are unique to America?"

Thus, the major chapters of Part I (II to V) deal first with the culture of capitalism (those American values and beliefs which concern economic life); then with the impact of industrialization on social structure—on the work people do and where they do it, the position and outlook of different groups and strata in the community, and the effect of all this on the family system.

We will not attempt a comprehensive description of American society and culture. Rather we will describe changes in a few basic features of American society and suggest how in the context of the relevant values they affect both the social problems social workers deal with and the welfare services they man. Our choice of what is "basic" for discussion in Chapters III to V will be guided by certain necessary conditions for societal survival—needs any society must meet if it is to continue. These include: (1) population; (2) specialization and stratification (including the division of labor, the allocation of authority, and assignment of persons to child-rearing); (3) solidarity or "integration"; (4) perpetuation of the social system (which involves the socialization of new members). A good way to grasp the impact of industrial-ization on urban-industrial America is to focus on each of these major problems which all societies face. (The Appendix defines these terms and gives reasons for saying that the problems re-ferred to are "universal.")

Industrialization brings the emergence of a "new middle class" of salaried white-collar and professional workers (a change in specialization). This affects income and power distribution (a change in stratification). These changes in turn affect the ways in which American children are brought up (a change in social-ization). All such shifts affect the birth rate. Since everything cannot be said at once we will deal with these things one by one, as though they were not in fact intertwined. In Chapters III and

IV we will accent the initial and the later impact of modern industry on mobility, specialization, and stratification as these affect the family system and the problem of the newcomer to industry. Treatment of shifts in the income and social composition of social welfare clientele is found both in Chapter IV (Distribution of Income) and in Chapter VIII (Family Services). The rise of the city will be considered when we discuss the problem of social integration in America in Chapter V. Since urbanism intensifies and channels the effects of industrialism, this discussion of it will serve as a convenient summary for Part I.

Throughout, using American examples, we will concentrate on the universal effects of advanced industrialism: a large and mobile labor supply; complex specialization, stratification, and large-scale organization; the concentration of people in metropolitan centers. These massive changes in American society are the major determinants of the social problems which create the demand for social welfare services.

Given the social-problem challenge posed by industrialization, what is the social welfare response?[1] Part II links the types of services to the features of industrialism and the social changes and problems described in Part I. What is considered social welfare and what is not? What is the cost of welfare services and who takes responsibility for their administration? Chapter VI attempts to spell out the American concept of welfare; while Chapter VII briefly lays out the *scope* of existing welfare programs in terms of *auspices* and *expenditures*. In Chapters VIII and IX, using family problems and juvenile delinquency as illustrative fields, we try to show how changes in social organization, themselves induced by industrialization, have, in the context of American values, called forth our characteristic welfare services. As we shall see, predictions of what family life will be like ten or twenty years from now must rest on predictions of what an advanced

---

[1] *Social welfare* will refer to those formally organized and socially sponsored institutions, agencies, and programs, exclusive of the family and private enterprise, which function to maintain or improve the economic conditions, health, or interpersonal competence of some parts or all of a population. *Social work* will refer to an occupation or profession, a group of people with more or less specified training and skills, who occupy key positions, along with other groups, in the provision of welfare services.

industrial society will demand from its members in the way of
obligations and offer in opportunities. And the work of such
agencies as the Family Service Association will reflect these
changing patterns of family life.

In Part III we turn from the connections between social
problems and social services to the *internal organization* of the
services (whatever problems they aim to meet) and how this
affects their operation. Welfare is no longer much a matter of
"a friend in need," or of neighborhood mutual aid. Specialized
agencies, many of them large and the majority manned by
specialized, self-conscious occupational groups, now administer
the supply of welfare services. We focus here on the structure and
control of the social agency.

Finally, all occupations in America with any opportunity to do
so strive to become professional. Social work is no exception.
There are reasons for the striving, obstacles in the path of professionalization, and consequences for the provision of welfare
service which we will try to describe.

For the reader impatient for the story to unfold we have
provided on page 230 a chart that summarizes the main theme
of the book.

Uses of This Book

The book aims to be useful to four groups: (1) students now in
or planning to go into Graduate Schools of Social Work; (2)
students of sociology and social problems, especially those interested in industrial sociology, occupations and professions, the
family, deviant behavior, and, more generally, economic development, urbanism, and social change; (3) the U.S. welfare public,
especially social work practitioners—teachers, workers, agency
administrators, and researchers; (4) welfare workers abroad who
want a short guide to urban-industrial America and the problems of welfare administration in a highly developed economy.

In existing curricula for social work, much of what should be
included from sociology, anthropology, economics, and history is
found scattered about various departments of the university. We
feel there is no real substitute for basic courses taught by people

competent in those disciplines. But we agree with many teachers and students in social work who complain that most of the content of such courses falls short of their needs in two ways. First, the burden of integrating scattered texts in separate social science courses is too much for most students in and out of social work, graduate or undergraduate. Second, even where most students enrolled in social science courses are headed toward social work, the available readings either are not oriented to the experience and career interests of the students, or, if so oriented, they are typically light in social science content.

The experience of teachers who used an earlier draft of Part I suggests that the first five chapters especially can be integrated into such specialized courses as Social Welfare Organization, Social Work and Social Backgrounds, Sociocultural Elements in Social Work Practice, The Field of Social Work—in short, the "social services area" of the social work curriculum—as well as general courses in sociology and social problems.

When confronting professional issues in their training, students in social work, like all students (and whatever their teachers intend), quickly learn the difference between the official word and what is alleged outside the classroom to be "the inside story." If they do not get what they think is candid information from self-critical professional journals or the School grapevine, they seek it from the more sensational popular press—which finds articles on the professions increasingly salable.

We believe that direct and responsible discussion of touchy problems of social policy and social work practice can be stimulating and appropriate not only to the mature professional but also to the fledgling student. What is food for thought to the one is often good training for the other. For instance, in Part III we raise questions about the consequences of different types of social agency specialization, and the implications of social work professionalism for welfare service. Or in Chapter IX on juvenile delinquency we devote a section to problems for research and another to problems of social policy—and provide enough context so that the beginning student, as well as the experienced practitioner or researcher, may find the analysis useful. The chapter on delinquency, like chapters on the family services, agency structure, and the professions, can be used separately to open up an area for class discussion, term papers, student research, or professional debate.

Sociologists interested in the study of professions and bureaucracy should find Part III especially relevant; those interested in urbanism and deviant behavior should look at Chapters V, VIII, and IX. People in community organization may find in Chapter X a suggestive approach to the problems they are struggling with.

Social Science and Social Practice

For all social workers or administrators who find anything here worth reading, we want to record three observations regarding the relation of social science to social practice that have guided our effort.

1. *The practitioner wants answers to practical problems and the surer the answers the better. But only a little of social science is immediately practical and less is sure.* Only a small portion of the data turned up in social research reaches a high level of reliability, validity, adequacy, and representativeness. Some of the generalizations we make are therefore speculative; some rest on inferences from several studies of uncertain or uneven quality; others are better supported by systematic evidence. We try throughout to make clear by context and phrasing the differences between opinion, established fact, and fact less established. Thus, when we say, "in our opinion" we do not mean "these studies demonstrate . . ."; and when we say the latter, we do not mean "from this one study one might infer. . . ." We ask the reader to be alert to the cues that warn him, however crudely, of the degree of uncertainty involved. This is especially important in Part III, which deals with the agency and the profession, where empirical research has hardly begun.

2. *What the social scientist thinks of as "objective investigation" the practitioner often takes as "hostile attack."* To some, our analysis in Parts II and III may seem too coldly critical. Three reasons help to explain this. First, we have tried to avoid repetition of what has already been said well by others and is firmly embedded in the social work literature; this tends to minimize in our treatment that portion of the truth which

is familiar and favorable. Second, we think it is not the role of the social scientist to be as innocuous as possible and it is not wise for the practitioner to consider only the positive side of welfare developments.

Finally, the relation of science to social practice is different from the relation of science to nonsocial practice: the pathologist does not study the social organization of medicine, the physicist does not study the ideologies of engineering societies; but it is part of the job of the sociologist to study the social organization of occupations, among them social work. The social scientist, in short, must be a bit of a snooper—and this leads to conflict between him and the professions that draw upon his work for their daily practice. We think that social workers, who, more than other professionals, tend to be self-analytical, will more than others understand a spirit of objectivity, despite its inevitable product, a critical tone.

3. *The practitioner often puts high value on practical experience and common sense as guides to truth; the social scientist is suspicious of both.* We do not believe that understanding and knowledge are denied to those whose experience is vicarious (had through books, interviewing, observation from the outside). Nor do we believe that to be of practical value, experience has to be firsthand, direct—had by the man who is going to make use of it. In fact, in grasping the truth about social life the informed stranger has many advantages over the man of affairs immersed in the details of a demanding job routine.

Thus, although one of us has had some years of experience as a social worker and the other in adult education and social action, we prefer to view our efforts as those of foreign visitors making incursions into provinces whose terrain is a bit strange. We are more sure of our equipment and passports (as sociologists) than of the customs of the host. We hope that our conversation with those more native to social work than we are, will thereby be rendered more, not less, useful.

Acknowledgments

The authors exchanged comment and criticism on all chapters. Major responsibility for Chapters I to V, IX, and the Appendix was taken by Wilensky; for Chapters VI and VII by Lebeaux— with joint responsibility for Chapters VIII, X, and XI.

If the book has any merit, we must share credit with those social scientists and social workers who gave so generously of their time and ideas.

When in 1955 we prepared a monograph for the International Conference of Social Work out of which this book has developed, it was fortunate that David G. French, executive secretary of the Coordinating Committee on Social Welfare Research, University of Michigan, was available. He oriented us toward the audience, persuaded us that the task might be feasible, and carried major administrative responsibility during the early phase of the project. Equally great were his intellectual contributions—specific comment on both the first and last drafts.

Professors Guy E. Swanson of the University of Michigan Department of Sociology and Ernest Greenwood of the University of California (Berkeley) School of Social Welfare read an early draft; their characteristically penetrating comments have vastly improved the book. Professor Kingsley Davis of the University of California (Berkeley) Department of Sociology and Social Institutions gave us the benefit of a gloves-off critique that was in every way constructive. His keen sense of sociological relevance and his impatience with vagueness made us sit up and revise one last time. A careful, perceptive reading by Professor Eveline M. Burns of the New York School of Social Work was similarly fruitful.

Professors Harold M. Levinson of the Department of Economics and Wilbur J. Cohen of the School of Social Work, and Dr. Robert N. McLarty of the Department of History, University of Michigan, and Professor Carl Bridenbaugh, University of California (Berkeley), helped to clarify some points of fact and interpretation in economics, social welfare, and history. Dr. Helen Witmer of the U.S. Children's Bureau provided useful comment on Chapter IX. Professors David F. Aberle, Robert C. Angell, Robert O. Blood, Arthur Dunham, F. F. Fauri, Ralph C. Fletcher, William Haber, Amos H. Hawley, and Guy E. Swanson of the University of Michigan, who consulted with us in the planning stages, did much to formulate the structure of the analysis.

Malcolm W. Roemer, as chief research assistant and editor of the manuscript, made a creative contribution without which clarity would have suffered. Hugh Edwards and Richard Curtis, former teaching fellows in the Department of Sociology, University of Michigan, Kenneth Ives, student in the School of Social Work of Wayne State University, and Miriam Gallaher, research assistant, Center for Advanced Study in the Behavioral Sciences, gave further research aid.

Generous financial aid from Russell Sage Foundation coupled with the time and uniquely stimulating intellectual climate provided by the Center for Advanced Study in the Behavioral Sciences, under the direction of Dr. Ralph W. Tyler, made research and writing possible.

The extent of our indebtedness to our wives, Jeanne and Lillian, only we can fully appreciate.

The International Conference of Social Work at its 1956 meeting in Munich used a working draft of about half the material contained in this book. Because of its wide distribution we have had the benefit of an amount of friendly criticism seldom available to an author before publication. We hope that our complete revision of Parts II and III reflects the spirit in which that criticism was welcomed. We wish especially to acknowledge the help given by Dr. Grace Coyle, Jack Fasteau, Lester B. Granger, Dr. Hertha Kraus, George W. Rabinoff, and Herman Stein.

It is taken for granted that all those mentioned above, with the possible exception of our wives, are absolved from the authors' sins.

HAROLD L. WILENSKY
CHARLES N. LEBEAUX

Ann Arbor, Michigan
Detroit, Michigan
November, 1957

PART ONE

THE DEVELOPMENT OF URBAN-INDUSTRIAL SOCIETY
AND THE EMERGENCE OF SOCIAL PROBLEMS

I. The Industrial Revolution: Traditional Indictment and Defense

"EVERY ADVANCE OF INDUSTRY," wrote T. N. Whitehead, "has so far been accompanied by a corresponding impoverishment in social living"—for industrialization means unsatisfying work, purposeless activity after hours, class distinctions and class conflict, and a disorganized and disintegrating community life. (403: pp. 165, 231–237) This indictment of industrialism[1] is typical of an army of modern writers, popular and scientific, American and European. It reechoes old complaints. During the past 150 years, liberals, humanitarians, Marxists, communists, and conservatives alike have greeted the human effects of the machine with dismay.

Much of the early complaint was prompted by the belief that the emergence of the factory system in late eighteenth century England had led to the dehumanization of labor and an actual *worsening* of the condition of the poor. Engels, collaborator of Karl Marx, was not alone when he charged that industrial capitalism shaped the propertyless proletariat into machine slaves, made their work meaningless, and forced them to seek substitute gratifications in pub and brothel. (101: especially pp. 118–119, 128–129) The theme was a common one: under the yoke of private property and factory organization, man had been cut off not only from the product of his toil but also from his fellow man. Parliamentary commissions had earlier made similar charges—and modern scholars like the Hammonds and the Webbs have repeated their reports. What emerges is a uniform

[1] The rise of industrialism (i.e., the increasing use of high-energy technology) in the eighteenth and nineteenth centuries so unsettled the traditional routines of family and community life that the term "industrial revolution" is commonly used to describe it.

27

picture of cruelty, misery, disease, and deformity among factory children, and of slum-crowding, poverty, insecurity, and moral degradation among their parents.

Describing what they saw as the random, formless factory towns of the nineteenth century, devoid of beauty, without parks or pure water supply, public lighting or drainage, the Hammonds comment:

> . . . England asked for profits and received profits. Everything turned to profit. The towns had their profitable smoke, their profitable slums, their profitable disorder, their profitable ignorance, their profitable despair. The curse of Midas was on this society: on its corporate life, on its common mind, on the decisive and impatient step it had taken from the peasant to the industrial age. . . . The new factories and the new furnaces were like the Pyramids, telling of man's enslavement, rather than of his power; casting their long shadow over the society that took such pride in them. (135: p. 232)

In America, where industrialism triumphed later, it evoked a similar commentary. As early as 1776 Adam Smith, while he praised the marvelous economies resulting from increased specialization, had seen this feature of economic development as a producer of idiots. (334: pp. 734 ff.) By the end of the nineteenth century, in a period of unprecedented industrial expansion, Jane Addams was telling the story of tens of thousands of Chicagoans working in cheap basement sweatshops and living in poverty in squalid and crowded tenements, with grossly inadequate sanitary provisions and a shortage of relief facilities. (2: pp. 98–100) And recently a leading scientist-philosopher, Bertrand Russell, summed up the case:

> The industrial revolution caused unspeakable misery both in England and in America. I do not think any student of economic history can doubt that the average happiness in England in the early nineteenth century was lower than it had been a hundred years earlier; and this was due almost entirely to scientific technique. (311: p. 22)

This view of the industrial revolution as a catastrophe has not been restricted to its early impact. Conceding that, with time, industrialization lifted the material well-being even of the workers, modern critics have continued the indictment along other familiar lines. The price of economic progress, they say, has been too high—the split of society into economic classes, exploitation (reflecting the loss of a sense of obligation among the rich, of contentment among the poor), the piling up of huge fortunes by evil means, the vulgarization of taste, the loss of pride in work, the burden of "freedom" to be unemployed, the psychological strains of urban-industrial living which have brought alarming increases in mental disease and crime. The notion, both in popular and scientific literature, that an industrial society is a "sick society" shows no loss of vitality in midcentury American and British thought.[1]

The dismay of the critics has been countered by the undiluted optimism of the enthusiasts. The sweeping pronouncement of the National Association of Manufacturers that "mechanization of industry, or technological progress . . . brings about such a reduction of prices for thousands of articles that it may be said that the luxuries of one generation become the necessities of the next" (261: I, pp. 40–41) has its early counterpart in the claim that the initial impact of the industrial revolution on living standards of the poor was favorable, not unfavorable. The Society for the Diffusion of Useful Knowledge announced in England in 1831: " 'Two centuries ago not one person in a thousand wore stockings; one century ago not one person in five hundred wore them; now not one person in a thousand is without them.' " (*The Results of Machinery*, quoted in 135: p. 210.) Not only were the poor of this time said to be better off than the rich of other times, but the capitalist's desire for profit was seen as the best guarantee of benefit to consumer and worker. The belief was strong that men in pursuing their self-interest would inevitably contribute to the general good. There might be temporary depressions "to which so

---

[1] See, for example, three widely influential interpretations of the impact of industrialization: Beard, *The Rise of American Civilization* (19), especially Chapter 25, The Gilded Age, and Chapter 31, The Machine Age; Mumford, *Technics and Civilization* (258); Tawney, *The Sickness of an Acquisitive Society* (357). See also Frank, *Society as the Patient* (113). In contrast were the favorable ideological responses to industrialism described in Reinhard Bendix's recently published *Work and Authority in Industry.* (23)

complicated a system of commerce and manufacture must always be liable," explained Lord Grenville to the House of Lords in 1819. But "the capital of every civilized country, especially if permitted to find for itself its most profitable employment, tends naturally to increase in a more rapid proportion than the population: and the effect of this . . . is felt in the correspondent increase of all which constitutes national prosperity. But it operates most immediately and visibly to the benefit of the lower classes of Society." (127: pp. 9–10) Not only to their material advantage, but also to their intellectual enlightenment. A prize-winning essay on "The Operative Classes of Great Britain" rejoiced in 1851: "The lessons of science . . . are now popularized. . . . Knowledge now accommodates her voice and manner to almost every order and grade of intellect. . . . In this respect . . . the workman and his employer are placed very much on the same level." (275: p. 35)

Applied to the American scene, and in the retrospect of a century and a half, the favorable appraisal was as enthusiastic as the denunciations were indignant. A modern scholar, writing of "The Triumph of American Capitalism," argues that the industrial revolution, under the auspices of private enterprise, had in the nineteenth century "created the potentialities of physical abundance and left behind the legacy of political freedom." It "conquered (wastefully it is true) and harnessed the natural resources of a great land, and filled that land with efficient agencies for turning out consumer goods in a vast flood. . . . it wove the idea of egalitarianism into the warp and woof of our tradition." It shaped other important features of the American way of life: "The natural rights of the individual to his life, liberty and the pursuit of his happiness. Representative, republican government. The separation of the church and state. The public school. Universal suffrage. A free associational life. Equality before the law. The hatred of a privileged caste. The right to challenge oppressive public authority." (130: pp. 434–435)

Thus, two broad ideological themes recur: the industrial revolution as a catastrophe; the industrial revolution as an unmitigated blessing. The tendency of the critics is to single out urban poverty in the initial phase of industrialization in early nineteenth century England and late nineteenth century America; and to picture moral degradation and social disintegration throughout. The tendency of the enthusiasts is to point to material abundance (relative abundance even in the early phase, even in the nineteenth century), and political freedoms—sometimes identifying them with the concomitant rise of capitalism, sometimes not.

To appraise any of this objectively requires more precision than the parties to the moral debate have evidenced. "Does mechanization mean the dehumanization of labor?" Questions such as this are unanswerable without translation into questions about whether specific changes in work and leisure among groups of people variously situated can be traced to specific changes in technology and social organization. "Do the rich get richer and the poor get poorer with advancing industrialism?" As we shall see, even so specific a question turns out to be too vague in this form to answer, and the problem of amassing data to answer the several more precise questions implied is formidable (see pages 100–106).

Our task for the rest of Part I is to assess both the indictment and the applause that greeted the industrial revolution.

Many features of American society singled out in the debate about Man and Machine arose not because our society was becoming urban and industrial but because it was northwest European in culture. America developed certain values in its heritage from Europe to a high degree. This is especially true of those values which affected our economic behavior and which by a quirk of usage became known as "capitalistic." America is said to be the last stronghold of capitalism. Its people, held together by a money tie, are said to epitomize the acquisitive urge of a business civilization. The spirit of free enterprise is nowhere else so highly developed.

Thus, in making our appraisal we must distinguish the *culture of capitalism*—a system of ideas undergirding the factory system in the modern West—from *industrialism* and its effects on social and economic organization. We must try to sort out some major features of American life which can be traced more or less directly to the extensive use of high-energy technology from those features due mainly to the values of "capitalism." The focus throughout will be on what is necessary to the development of industrialism everywhere and what is unique to American culture. Those features of American society that lead to its major social problems will receive special attention.

II. Capitalism and American Culture

IT IS USEFUL to think of the culture of capitalism as centered around two big ideas: the interrelated concepts of "individualism" and "the free market." These summary labels get at much that is distinct about the American approach to industrialization. They point to features of industrial organization in America which either by differences in degree or kind mark us off from other industrial societies. They also provide a clue to some social problems that do not stem from industrialization, but are a product of, or are intensified by, the culture of American capitalism. Although these ideas grip us less firmly than they did in the late nineteenth century, they still shape the size and organization of our welfare effort.

Individualism

Of basic importance to American capitalism is its great emphasis on the rational, acquisitive, self-interested individual. "In-

---

[1] Both modern capitalism and the factory system came to full flower in the nineteenth century, though each is the product of long previous development and the features of each have some antecedents in the premodern era. Sometimes the long evolution of capitalism is divided into stages: mercantile, industrial, finance, and state capitalism. See, for example, 130: pp. 19–24; and 319: pp. 93–95. Economic historian T. S. Ashton gives us warning about this procedure: ". . . to suggest that commerce, industry, finance and state control are *successive* dominant forces [in the thousand years over which man became especially rational and acquisitive] . . . is to hide . . . the interaction and interdependence of all these at every period of time." (144: p. 59; cf. 287.) We shall confine our initial discussion to the *values that sustain and reflect the economic organization of modern western capitalism as they developed in America.* Many features of economic organization labeled "capitalistic" are clearly intrinsic to any industrial society—for example, a monetary system, extensive use of capital and rational capital accounting, mechanization, a working class, etc. At the end of this chapter we will point to these elements of culture and of economic organization which have been called "capitalistic" but which are not unique to western capitalist countries. Our discussion relies heavily on Max Weber's *General Economic History* (397: pp. 275–369); and Talcott Parsons' Introduction to Weber's *Theory of Social and Economic Organization* (399). Cf. Wilbert E. Moore's *Industrial Relations and the Social Order* (255), chaps. 18, 24, 25.

dividual initiative"—an acquisitive spirit, highly developed, widely diffused—is the mark of a society where labor is a commodity, sold on a more or less competitive market. It is not the "wage system" as such that distinguishes American capitalism, for all highly industrialized societies are "employee societies" where most people work for wages or salaries under a boss; it is instead the fact that all labor—salaried or wage-roll, managerial or manual—is formally free to compete for better jobs, better pay, for the best possible place in the economic world.

Individualism is both a theory of human behavior and a doctrine in justification of laissez faire. As theory, it tries to explain man's conduct in terms of a pleasure-pain calculus. Man, it is assumed, pursues his self-interest because of an acquisitive instinct or biological needs. Self-interest is seen in economic terms: he acquires and consumes material goods (pleasure); he avoids economic loss (pain). As a theory of human motivation, it is easily disposed of and will not concern us.

As doctrine, individualism states that the good of all will best be served if each individual pursues his self-interest with minimal interference. As articulated by American business leaders, this doctrine sometimes has a more concrete and restricted meaning: individualism becomes freedom for acquisitive enterprise, unhampered by government restriction, unchallenged by labor organizations. It is, of course, more complex than the after-dinner speeches at the Rotary Club would have it. And it is so important as an ideology which grips American hearts and shapes American behavior that it must be spelled out.

The doctrine of American individualism can best be grasped as a set of beliefs about what *should be* and another set of beliefs about what *is*. Large and influential segments of the American people (not just businessmen) believe strongly that:

1. The individual should strive to be successful in competition with others, under the rules of the game.
2. These rules involve "fair play":
   (a) everyone should start with equal opportunity; (b) no one should take unfair advantage through force, fraud, "pull."

3. The test of reward should be ability (especially ability to contribute to the productive and other purposes of the enterprise). There should be unequal reward for unequal talents and unequal contributions.

They also believe strongly that:

1. Those who work hard and have ability will be rewarded with success. (Success is a tangible package which mainly includes income and wealth, possessions, occupational prestige, and power—along with the style of life these permit.)

2. Success is the reward also of virtue; virtue will bring success. Failure (if it is not a temporary way-station to success) is sin and reveals lack of virtue.

3. Where the lazy, incompetent, and unvirtuous attain success it is purely a matter of luck; it could happen to anybody. Besides, it does not happen too often.[1]

If there is any formula summing up these beliefs, it is the one repeated in the American home and school: Everyone has equal *opportunity* to get ahead; everyone has the moral *duty* to *try* to get ahead ("make the most of himself"); if a man fails, it is his own fault and he should feel guilty (and, some would add, his children and his parents should feel ashamed). (411; 84; 236, chap. 4)

This accent on achievement in a competitive struggle is carried into the bosom of the family, down into crib and cradle, for many parents make their aspirations for high performance clear by word and gesture before the child enrolls in school. Margaret Mead even suggests that there is an "initial condition, inserted into the mother's simplest kiss, that 'I will love you only if you achieve as much as other people's babies. I can't love you if you don't'. . . ." (229: p. 109)

So while the child is learning that his whole place in the world, his name, his right to the respect of other children—everything—de-

[1] Of course, many Americans believe that "some people get all the breaks," that job ascent is through pull, so "don't knock yourself out." We are here concentrating, however, on what we see as the guiding ideas of a dominant segment of the population in the period from the Civil War to the Great Crash—the values of nineteenth century liberalism, still important in characterizing the American approach to social welfare, though now joined with the values of twentieth century social democracy.

pends upon his parents and on what kind of a house they have been able to build or buy or rent, what kind of a car they are able to drive, what kind of toys they are able to buy him, he also learns that his own acceptance by these parents, who are his only support, is conditional upon his achievements, upon the way in which he shows up against other children and against their idea of other children. To the anxiety with which small boys in many if not all cultures of the world view grown men and wonder if they will ever be as tall and strong, is added in America, for both boys and girls, the anxiety as to whether they will be successful in keeping their parents' love as children. (229: p. 90)

This lurid picture may be exaggerated; the evidence for it is lacking; and it is our hunch that it applies more to the rearing of male children in the most ambitious urban middle-class free-enterprising families than to other segments of American society (see Chapter V). But it does underscore the fact that economic individualism—the accent on dollar success—is linked to individualism in other, noneconomic spheres of life. It is this link between economic individualism and the broader framework of American values to which we now turn.

Economic individualism in America is reinforced by more general democratic values, especially the doctrine of "inalienable rights." In American tradition the individual is felt to have a value of his own, to be entitled therefore to uniqueness. It is felt he should have the right to enjoy a wide range of choice—within broad social limits (for example, clear and present danger to society) and his personal limits (from prejudice to everything else he has or has not learned). His choices of occupation, of mate, of religious and political belief, of purchases at the store—these are considered to be "his own business." Just as in the economic sphere the accent is on free enterprise and the self-reliant individual, so in education the "elective system" is common and the recommended teaching techniques aim at individual expression in classroom and competitive participation outside. A grading system ranks each on the basis of rivalry with all. In the sphere of politics and government, despite many limits and much quick intolerance, there is still important emphasis on individual liberty—freedom of association, freedom of expression, freedom from the heavy hand of censorship. Even in the sphere of the family it is felt "each must live his own life"—and the young man and woman typically move out on their own, to their own jobs, their own families, their own homes—chosen pretty much on their own.

This is not to say that the individual is free from control by custom and authority. He is not. Nor is he anywhere. But in America such control tends to be more indirect, voluntary, and limited than in the primitive or peasant society or in the totalitarian industrial society (for example, Nazi Germany or the U.S.S.R.). In America the traditional ways are treated less tenderly, surrendered with more ease, and the individual's range of choice in all areas of life is relatively broad.

The presence of a democratic value system which emphasizes individualism in the noneconomic spheres of life is thus a powerful support for the doctrine of laissez faire, so central to the culture of capitalism.[1]

Private Property, the Free Market, and Minimum Government

Related to economic individualism is a second idea basic to American capitalism: private ownership of the means of production and their operation for profit by private enterprisers competing in a free market. Two terms to keep straight here are private ownership and the free market.

Property is a system of rights and duties, socially recognized and sanctioned, of persons or other social units (for example, a

---

[1] Weber's analysis of "ascetic Protestantism" suggests that the dominant religion of western capitalist countries has also lent support to economic individualism. The Protestant concept of the "calling," reflecting a basic attitude toward worldly activity—a positive approval of active, rational mastery over worldly things and ideas, the treatment of all men by the same impersonal standards; its view of hard work as a virtue, profit-making as obeisance to God—these ideas fit neatly the economic organization and spirit of capitalism. (398; 399; 281) Weber's argument has been criticized on the grounds that the ideas he labeled "ascetic Protestant" are not specifically religious, are not unique to Protestantism, and reflect more than they influence economic conditions and institutions. (301; 356) Moreover, a recent historical analysis suggests that the most enterprising of the seventeenth century merchants in England and the American colonies were the *least* committed to Puritan norms. (14) Whether the "Protestant Ethic" was the adaptation of a religion to changing economic conditions or was a causal factor in the rise of capitalism is still an open question.

corporation) with respect to valued objects (tangible, like a house, or intangible, like an idea). Property defines the relations of persons to these scarce objects and hence to one another. Any economic system has to allocate property rights—decide who controls what (and whom). *Private* property involves two principles: (1) unlimited rights under unitary control (the owner should be a specific person or other social unit and should be able to buy, use, sell, trade, transfer, destroy, bequeath the valued object as he sees fit); (2) individual, not group ownership. (254; 133) The American emphasis on private property in capital goods (machines, materials, factories) is both rare and recent in human history. It is linked to the emphasis on the acquisitive individual. If the ambitious and talented individual is to have access to the wealth of the community, that wealth must be in a form he can get at and put to use for gain. It also means that there must be certain favorable conditions under which he can compete with others for the rights and privileges of ownership. Such conditions are present in a free market system.

The ideology has been strong in America that demand, supply, and price should work themselves out—with no interference by any political or social agency. Public regulation of economic activity, government control of the production and distribution of goods, is seen to be justified only if it aims to keep the market free.

A free market implies not only minimum government regulation, it also requires competition and freedom of contract. It requires competition so that the individual's efficiency can be weighed impersonally within the economic order—so that hard work, talent, and virtue will pay off. It requires freedom of contract so that the individual can sell his goods or services to anyone he chooses, that is, to his best advantage. Where there is freedom of contract, the individual presumably acts as a free agent. He agrees only to rights and obligations which are voluntarily undertaken, specific and limited, as well as advantageous to all parties. Here we come full circle, for such contractual relations are possible only where bargaining is free and equality of opportunity exists—so no one has an unfair advantage. Here again lies theoretical justification for economic individualism and a minimum of interference with market operations.

Every schoolboy can list some limits to individual acquisitiveness and a free market. The ideals expressed in the doctrine of laissez faire do not always work out in practice. No society in the name of protecting free choice and enterprise can let a man choose to burn down his store to collect the insurance, corner a market in blood plasma to make a big profit, kill his neighbor because the neighbor used "connections" to beat him out of a job he wanted. Nor is there any such thing as a system of completely private property; all societies impose some limits on the individual use of wealth (for example, the private citizen is not allowed to buy a private army). The realities of modern industrial life often contradict the doctrines we have discussed: the large corporation is not an "individual," the corporation executive is typically not "running his own business." Thus, corporate ownership is as much a violation of traditional notions of private property as state ownership. The "owners" no longer control, and in the case of participants in retirement, annuity, and insurance programs, they do not even know in what operations their claims are invested. Government interference goes far beyond the maintenance of a free market—witness parity prices for farmers, minimum wages for workers, and loans, tariffs, and other subsidies for business. Private enterprise itself interferes with the free market—as congressional investigation of business lobbies or the history of antitrust legislative and administrative hearings will attest. Labor unions join in the general tendency: like professional associations, they carve out job territories and protect jurisdictions—so the enterprising worker may have to wait his turn on the seniority list for a better job or pay an initiation fee to get one in the first place.

It would be easy to conclude that the doctrines of economic individualism and a free market are irrelevant for an understanding of urban-industrial America. Indeed, William H. Whyte's popular interpretation of American culture, *Organization Man*, seems to argue that the "Protestant Ethic" has already given way to the "Social Ethic," that nineteenth century liberalism has all but disappeared. Whyte paints this picture of organization man: At work, he plays it safe, seeks security, cultivates smooth human relations, minimizes competition, seldom makes an independent decision, preferring to immerse himself and his responsibilities in a network of committees, whose collective solutions are pedestrian and conformist. In the community, he puts down only shallow roots, but while waiting for the next move onward and upward, he participates vigorously and conforms compulsively. Both at work and at home he is guided by the Social Ethic; that is, he believes in the group as the source of creativity, in "belonging-ness" as the ultimate need of the individual, and in the application of science to achieve the belongingness (for instance, by use of personality tests).

This is too easy. And for our problem it is misleading. The culture of capitalism is far from dead. The ideas Whyte calls the "Social Ethic" are emerging only slowly and in those economic organizations which are very large, embrace scores of plants, producing a wide variety of products and services, with a very high ratio of managers to managed and extraordinarily fast expansion. Within such organizations, the Social Ethic is cherished mainly among those members of the younger generation who have moved from college through an executive training program to middle management jobs. As yet these organizations and men represent a modest minority of the labor force—even if we go beyond big business to include with Whyte the spheres of education, science, the military, religion, and mass communications.

Whyte's portrait of organization man is sufficiently sensitive to provide within its own frame the chief qualifications and counter-arguments. Even in the vanguard companies and strata we learn that competition is not sharply reduced in the new era; it merely becomes more subtle and gentlemanly. The plateau of safety, security, and good fellowship sought by organization man turns out to be elusive in practice (among other things, organizations as always have fewer posts at the top than at the bottom). Most important, the men now at the top do not seem to fit the portrait, though the administrative structures they head and problems they face are much the same as those coming to their organization-minded successors.[1]

In short, the doctrines of economic individualism and the free market are quite relevant. First, they enable us to put the scene before us in proper historical perspective. Cultural traditions such as these do not disappear in a generation or two. Second, these doctrines, in some degree, in some areas, *do* describe the workings of American society. To what degree and in what areas will be suggested in subsequent chapters. Third, men's ideas of what is real, even if they do violence to the facts, even if they are unrealistic, are real in their consequences if men believe them. Ideology or sober fact, the culture of capitalism has shaped the American approach to social welfare services in significant ways.

The Culture of Capitalism and Social Problems

The two features of capitalist culture we have discussed—its accent on individualism and the free market—are surely not the whole of American culture. Nor are they any longer shared by large segments of the population. But they are of special significance both in the development of the stresses and strains, instabilities, and social problems encountered by practicing social workers in America, and in the nation's strategy of adjustment to them.

The most general and most obvious effect of the laissez-faire ideology has been first to delay and then to restrict the scope of social legislation dealing with the risks of industry. Whether one looks at old problems that no longer generate heated debate—the employment of women and children, the unsanitary conditions, low wages and blood-curdling schedules of the "sweatshops" (the early textile mills and clothing factories)—or whether one considers current issues of unemployment, old age insecurity, indus-

[1] Whyte, William H., Jr., *The Organization Man.* Doubleday Anchor Books, Garden City, N. Y., 1957, chaps. 9–11. It may be suggested that the disparity of viewpoint between old and young managers reflects not only the coming rise of better-educated men whose careers are more bureaucratic, and the shifts in organizational structure and problems still going on, but also the less effective socialization of the young, who, with increasing authority and responsibility will in time experience the limitations of the Social Ethic for the purposes of getting the organization's work done, and creating a satisfying style of leisure.

trial accidents, and occupational disease (as well as illness and nonindustrial accidents), one sees the hold of individualistic ideas on American society. This is clear both in the late recognition of these risks as social problems and in the choice of ways to deal with them. Unlike other industrial countries in the nineteenth century, the United States undertook no social insurance programs to cover the hazards of industrial life. It relied instead on public assistance programs and voluntary agencies (see Part II). The ancestors of modern American social work—the charity organization society, the county poorhouse, and outdoor relief programs—were themselves products of a "self-reliance" philosophy. Social work practice and policy were derived from the old English Poor Laws, which associated poverty with personal inadequacy, and kept relief to the needy aged, injured, sick, or unemployed below subsistence. (152: p. 21) The U.S. approach to welfare services even today cannot be understood apart from the culture of capitalism.

America's response to the human problems of industrialism represents a constantly moving compromise between the values of security and humanitarianism (whether in the form of paternalism or unionism), on the one hand, and individual initiative and self-reliance in the competitive order on the other. The conflict between these values and the groups supporting them comes clear in our reaction to each of the risks of industry. Most Americans have long seen child labor and the insecurities of unemployment and old age as evils. But the historic policy of American governments in all major depressions before 1929 was almost complete laissez faire.[1] And important segments of American society still view unemployment as a necessary and useful consequence of competition in a free market for labor—just as bankruptcy is the necessary and useful consequence of competition for the consumer's dollar in a product market. Presumably the best men and the best firms survive; some are bound to get hurt. Similarly, in one of the first court cases heard under child labor

[1] In December, 1930, President Hoover approved congressional appropriation of $45 million to feed the livestock of stricken Arkansas farmers. At the same time he opposed an additional $25 million to feed the farmers. The Red Cross, he insisted, could take care of them. (150: p. 307)

legislation, a Michigan judge defended the labor of a newsboy on the grounds that when he was a boy such work was excellent training in initiative and self-discipline. And some religious groups have frowned on government control of child labor as unjustified invasion of the family and home. (202: p. 14)

That a laissez-faire ideology has had a uniquely strong hold on American life is suggested by the fact that no industrializing country today has adopted or is likely to adopt a deliberate policy of neglecting its indigent aged on the grounds that they have failed to save during their productive years and do not now contribute to production. Yet as recently as twenty-five years ago these were major arguments of the groups opposing social insurance in America.[1] That this same laissez-faire ideology still has its true believers among influential Americans is illustrated in two spontaneous remarks of long-time members of the Eisenhower cabinet. Secretary of Defense Charles E. Wilson comments on one aspect of the unemployment situation in 1954: "The idea that a 19 year old boy could be drafted and sent to Korea to be shot at and he didn't have enough gumption to go 100 miles and get himself a job—I don't go for that . . . I've always liked bird dogs better than kennel-fed dogs myself—you know, one who'll get out and hunt for food rather than sit on his haunches and yell." (265: p. 13) And Secretary of the Treasury George Humphrey, commenting on Hemingway's *The Old Man and the Sea*, wonders: "Why would anybody be interested in some old man who was a failure?" (123: p. 140)

There are some less obvious but equally important effects of the doctrines of individualism and the free market. Rules for conduct in one area of life have a way of spilling over into other areas; and in modern society an area so pervasive in its influence as the economic is bound to affect the family system. Individualism and the free market in the economic order produce men who are ambitious for themselves—and their wives and children— who tend to rate occupational or business advancement high in

[1] Many of the underdeveloped countries "appear to be more active in the social field [via welfare programs] than were [highly developed countries] when at a comparable level of economic development and national income." (366: p. 16)

their scheme of life. The mobility this requires (place-to-place, job-to-job) shapes our family system: it is one reason for romantic courtship, "companionate marriage," easy divorce, a declining sense of obligation for aging parents and other, more distant kinfolk. These connections between the economic and the family systems are common to all industrial societies, as we shall see in Chapter III, but the doctrines of individualism in America reinforce them.

A second less obvious link between laissez faire and a set of social problems is this: individualism represents a culturally fostered discontent, a socially approved dissatisfaction. "Every Man a King," we tell ourselves, and "If at first you don't succeed, try, try again." Two things are inevitable where this philosophy is widely shared: much disruptive rivalry, and frustration for capable but unsuccessful or disadvantaged competitors. Chapter IX will suggest that these are not unrelated to such problems as juvenile delinquency.

Capitalist Organization and Capitalist Culture: Some General Elements in Industrial Societies

Before we leave the cultural context which has shaped American experience with industrialization, two cautions are in order: (1) much of what is called "capitalism" turns out to be features of economic organization common to all highly industrialized countries, whatever their culture; (2) the uniqueness of the culture of capitalism is often a matter of degree—for something resembling the doctrines of economic individualism if not the free market is found in noncapitalist societies as well.

Scholars have assigned many meanings to the word "capitalism" and have seen diverse features of modern life as its essence or its prerequisites. Let us consider this list:

1. "An economic system significantly characterized by the *predominance of 'capital'* " (337: p. 196)—capital being the accumulation of that part of current output which is diverted from current consumption to the increase of future output. Such a system is typically seen to involve:

2. *Mechanization* or "the application of technology to production and exchange." (130: p. 18; 144: p. 58)

3. *"A money economy* . . . buying and selling in a market." (227: pp. 82–83)

4. *Rational capital accounting*—the use of "systematic bookkeeping" and the striking of a balance (397: p. 276; 338) and with this

5. The *commercialization and transferability of all property.* (397: pp. 276–278)

6. A reasonably *predictable political order*, including a calculable (not capricious) legal system and a reasonably stable state. (397)

7. A *proletariat* that sells its labor (not the product of its labor), "the wage system"—a working class separated from the means of production and paid wages. (130: p. 16; 227: p. 84; 144: p. 58)

These institutions, however, do not appear to be unique to western capitalism as it emerged in the last 150 years. Capital, mechanization, a monetary system of exchange, double-entry bookkeeping, the conversion of property rights into monetary terms, stable nation-states, the emergence of a working class—these are universal features of highly developed economies. They are all present in the more recent development of Germany, Japan, and the Soviet Union, countries which could hardly be lumped together as capitalist.

For instance, all industrial societies are characterized by a high degree of specialization; a monetary system of exchange is a necessary counterpart. Money makes it possible for one specialized producer to claim the product of another—so the man who digs coal in West Virginia or Prokopievsk can buy working clothes made in Massachusetts or Leninabad. Or, again, all industrial societies are characterized by mechanization, extensive use of capital, and frequent changes in technology: new ways of producing old products (from hand-knit sweaters to machine-knit sweaters); and changes in the products themselves (from horseless carriage to automobile). This means constant changes in operating conditions and output goals of each enterprise.

Capital must therefore be transferable from one use to another—
so shifts in consumer demand or national plan, due to changing
technology as well as changing taste, can be reflected in the expansion of one enterprise and the contraction of another.
Whether the capital gets shifted by state officials in a Commis-
sariat of Finance, by private investors in a stock market or by
boards of directors of large corporations, there must be an effective and accountable control of the productive resources of the
enterprise—machinery, tools, transportation facilities, raw material, cash, and so on. Rational capital accounting makes this
possible. Similarly, without an area of political stability, an
industrial society could neither enforce contracts between enterprises—a necessity in both the American and Soviet economies—
nor ensure the production and distribution of raw materials.

Just as many features of the economic organization of "capitalism" are not unique to the modern West, so the values of economic individualism seem to develop in some degree, whatever
the cultural context in which industrialism appears. Take, for
instance, this characterization of the industrial executive:

> . . . There are "no limits" to what [is expected of him] by way of
> expenditure of energy and time, and he has therefore no excuse for
> failure. To [him] all things are possible. . . . [He is supposed] to
> display qualities of leadership, initiative, and improvisation. . . .
> [There is] ceaseless, compulsive, painstaking toil, entailing the sacri-
> fice of all leisure and private life. . . . The top leaders . . . work
> "day and night," so lesser men hope to show themselves worthy by
> copying them.
>
> . . . Great stress is laid on the virtues of sobriety, punctuality, and
> discipline, avoidance of waste, and on cheerfulness. . . . The need
> to mould and master material, including human vagaries, to impose
> rigid control, to be rational, contained, and orderly, are part of this
> pattern. [There is a] drive to achieve . . . "output" of "production"
> in subordinates. . . . [One] variety of this personality-type is felt
> to be just; as severe and demanding towards himself as to others,
> earnest and sincere like a puritan, and usually competent and hard-
> working. (90: pp. 120, 132, 130, 141)

A description of the hard-driving American capitalist entrepreneurs who carved out industrial empires in the early 1900's?

No, this is a description of the Soviet managerial elite at mid-century—in a noncapitalist country undergoing even more rapidly the industrialization America experienced fifty years ago—a description generally confirmed by recent work of the Harvard University Russian Research Center. (18)

Or consider this statement about the problem of work motivation:

> In a number of factories wage scales are drawn up in such a way as to practically wipe out the difference between skilled labor and unskilled labor, between heavy work and light work. The consequence of wage equalization is that the unskilled worker lacks the incentive to become a skilled worker and is thus deprived of the prospect of advancement. (385: p. 29)

An American factory manager complaining about the union's tendency to reduce the distance between top and bottom wage rates? No, this is Joseph Stalin suggesting in 1931 that the U.S.S.R. should appeal more to the Soviet worker's ambition, or, as he put it, his desire to "seek his fortune." The policies adopted were: creation of vertical gradations, increased wage differentials, and the gradual substitution of individual piecework for group piecework. Stalin's successors, administering an ever-more complex industrial economy, felt compelled in 1956 to relax some of their punitive factory rules and to allow freer occupational choice at home, whatever their varied use of repression in the satellites outside.

We do not mean to imply that there is a rigid mold imposed on a culture by the demands of industry and that economic life in the Soviet Union is just like that in the U.S.A. All we want to note is that all industrial societies face similar problems; and their solutions to these problems, while varied, are often prescribed more by industrialism as such than by other cultural elements. For instance, every industrial system requires some competition for occupational position on the basis of skills relevant to the task, as well as some system of special reward for scarce talents and skills. (255: pp. 426–427; 256) It is probable, too, that industrialization requires an enterprising and innovating leadership group, which, if the initial growth is rapid, resembles the

Soviet managerial elite of today and the American business elite of yesterday.

What is there about the industrial society as such that provokes these similarities in culture? Recognizing great differences in degree, what accounts for the presence of elements of individualism in industrial societies so varied as Japan, the Soviet Union, and the United States? What features of industrialization are *not* unique to the modern West, or the American scene, which have had major impact on the demand for, and supply and organization of, welfare services? With an eye to cross-country comparison, in the next chapters we will examine some of the massive changes that have occurred in American society because of industrialization and the social problems that accompanied these changes.

The social impact of high-energy technology may be conveniently examined in two parts: (1) the early phase (especially post-Civil War); and (2) the advanced phase (the era of the "new technology" of the atom and automation, of which we have hints in the years following World War II).

III. The Early Impact of Industrialization on Society

MANY OF THE PROBLEMS that underdeveloped areas are facing today are the problems America faced in the decades following the Civil War. These were the years of mushroom growth in population—31 million in 1860 to 92 million in 1910; of the development of a vast railroad system and a national market; of mass immigration, old and new. With the settlement of the national domain went the transformation of rural peoples into urban. On the day of Lincoln's first election four in five of the population lived on farms; by the end of the century the proportion was less than two in five. The population of New York City jumped from 814,000 in 1860 to 3,437,000 in 1900; that of Chicago from 109,000 to 1,700,000.

More people, more urbanites, many of them new types of men: the landless proletarian; the "captain of industry," a wealthy owner-manager; and in between a middle order of small entrepreneurs—merchants and independent professionals. It was the time, too, of violent business fluctuations; the great depressions of the seventies and nineties and the crisis of the mid-eighties brought poverty and insecurity to many. Darwinian biology and Spencerian philosophy combined to tell Americans that life is a fierce competitive struggle which only the fittest survive. Industrial strife, poverty, insecurity could thus be seen as signs of the working of immutable laws of evolution, and evolution could be seen as progress. The century closed with Andrew Carnegie declaring, " 'The millionaires who are in active control started as poor boys and were trained in the sternest but most efficient of all schools—poverty.' " (Quoted in 150: p. 166.) And: " 'There is not one shred of privilege to be met with anywhere in all the laws. One man's right is every other man's right. The flag is the guarantor and symbol of equality.' " (19: II, p. 209) About the same time and with equal enthusiasm a million voters put their stamp of approval on a Populist platform which declared that America was ruled by a plutocracy, that the press was a tool of wealth, that labor was impoverished, " 'that the fruits of the toil of millions are boldly stolen to build up colossal fortunes for a few unprecedented in the history of mankind; and possessors of these in turn despise the republic and endanger liberty.' " (19: II, p. 210)

There is no other period in American history when the needs and demands of industry so dominated the nation's political and social life. If the industrial entrepreneur ever had free reign it was then. This era—roughly from the Civil War to World War I— is therefore a good one for highlighting the needs of industry as they shape its initial social impact.

The Supply of Labor, Worker Mobility, and Worker Motivation

Modern industry demands a large, flexible, mobile, and motivated labor supply. In the early stages of economic development, this manpower is typically recruited from peoples accustomed to rural life. The overriding question from the point of view of the industrial entrepreneur, once he has a market and a source of capital, is, "How can I recruit and maintain an appropriate labor supply?" In America, as elsewhere, the problem was how to get peasant peoples into industry, and then how to get them to stay and perform.

Recruiting the Peasant. It is not an exaggeration to say that in the early period of economic development coercion has everywhere played the main role in labor recruitment. People have been *pushed* into the factories and the plantations, more than they have been *pulled* by the great opportunity before them. The coercion has been both direct and indirect, open and concealed.

The enclosure movement of the eighteenth and early nineteenth centuries in England, though its extent has been popularly exaggerated, is an example of both types of coercion. Here, generally by act of Parliament, small strips of peasant-held land producing varied crops for subsistence were consolidated into large units run by a landlord producing corn for a city market. This helped to destroy the medieval village and pushed the peasant into wage labor on the new commercial farms or in the rising industries in the new cities. Under the Poor Law of 1834 the many destitute people wandering about the country were thrust into the workhouse if they did not take a job voluntarily, and anyone who left a job without a certificate from the employer was treated as a vagabond. (397: pp. 306–307) To get and keep workers, the colonial powers in southeast Asia used long-term indenture contracts supported by penal sanction—for example, work without pay—for nonfulfillment. (33) This device is still used to get natives into mines in Portuguese West Africa. Both long-term indenture and peonage (debt servitude) are used widely today in Latin America. (256: pp. 60 ff.)

More indirect forms of coercion appear in British Africa, where a head tax or "hut tax" payable only in cash is a common technique. The natives can get cash only through wage employment. This has been very effective in recruiting mine and agricultural labor in Uganda and Northern Rhodesia, as well as in New Guinea. (256: p. 67) Other indirect pressures that push the native or the peasant into wage employment include: population pressure (food supplies do not keep pace with growing population); social pressure (for example, a man who intermarries in an Indian village becomes an outcaste and escapes to an urban factory); military draft and the like.

Use of direct coercion to recruit a labor supply—political pressure, for instance—has also been common. American commercial agriculture, which in some cases expanded into industrial production, flourished under a system of slavery. In the U.S.S.R. forced collectivization of agricultural production, which was designed in part to increase the urban labor supply, or slave labor camps in the lumber industry furnish ready examples from the modern scene. (27: pp. 150–151; 146; 72: pp. 197–199)

To some extent American industry followed the general pattern of initial recruitment by coercion. It is true that force, in the sense of the use of government police power to drive people

into wage work, was absent. It is also true that in many places
in the 1820's and 1830's factory workers were hardly a depressed
lot. In southern New England they were drawn from artisans'
families; north of Boston from respectable young girls of reasonably high status. (137: p. 71) Child labor was frequent—and the
main coercion here came from the parents who put their children to work beside them in the factory. (185: pp. 314 ff.) The
only immigrants who found a place in manufacturing were a few
skilled operatives and foremen, chiefly from Great Britain, who
worked in textile and iron works. Others, less skilled, were used
to build canals and the early railroads—especially the Irish who
had been pushed out of the homeland by the potato famine and
political and religious persecution. (353: p. 372)

A succession of new inventions, however, brought the growth
of manufacturing in textiles, clothing, shoes, furniture, steel and
machinery, and expansion in the mining of coal and industrial
metals. This meant a large demand for labor; a cheap supply
awaited among the depressed peasantry of Europe. So strong was
this demand that the anti-foreign protests of the Know-Nothing
movement were swamped and those native Americans who in the
1850's noisily resented the flood of German "radicals" and Irish
Catholics soon found themselves to be a weak political fringe. The
surge of immigrants reached an annual total of almost half a
million by 1880; within a quarter of a century it passed the
million-a-year mark.

Of course, both motive and opportunity played a part in the
drama of labor recruitment—but elements of coercion were not
absent on either score. The "push" out of the Old Country—
celebrated in our literature, our ceremonial speeches, our immigrant "Days," our periodic reminders that America was a haven
for the oppressed—is where the story begins. Famine and depression in the run-down agricultural areas of eastern and southern
Europe, peasant land holdings too small to be divided among
many sons, burdensome demands for military service, pogroms
in Poland and Russia, political and religious persecution of the
rebels and sectarians of various places—these supplied ample
incentive for the move. On the receiving end, in addition to plen-

tiful land for farming, there was the great growth in industrial employment. Most of this involved merely the matching of labor supply to labor demand in a free market. Word of the new opportunities, sometimes true, sometimes exaggerated, spread throughout Europe—by letters from relatives already arrived, by advertisements in the foreign press, in some cases by agents of steamship companies drumming up steerage passengers. Even on the opportunity side, however, pressure was felt. Wittke describes the interests promoting the image in Europe of an America whose streets were paved with gold:

> Ship companies and organizations interested in land speculation did their part to keep the America fever burning at the proper temperature. Advertisements in American newspapers reveal a veritable flock of emigration agents; immigrant bankers dealing in remittances, steamship, and railroad tickets; and dealers in foreign exchange, each of whom had his special reasons for keeping the immigrant tide flowing in a steady, unbroken stream to the United States. (420: p. 104)

When he got off the ship, the immigrant was likely to be taken in hand by "runners" who would lead him unsuspecting, sometimes by force, into the hands of the hotelkeeper or baggage agent. (420: p. 119) Wittke also describes the "padrone" system among Italian and Greek immigrants, under which "boys were imported illegally to work for their employers under conditions suggesting feudal serfdom. . . ." (420: pp. 440, 447) And at the beginning of the great industrial expansion, in 1864, Congress enacted the contract labor law which authorized the importation of laborers under terms similar to the indenture contracts of colonial days or of modern Africa and Latin America. The law was repealed in 1868, but the practice continued without legal mandate, though its extent is unknown. Companies which promised to supply employers with European labor in any amount, anywhere, anytime were organized in this period. (Cf. 19: II, pp. 245–246.) The contract labor system in particular and the eagerness to increase the supply of labor in general brought sharp protest from the unions, and an equally vigorous defense from employers, who argued that this was a means of providing liberty and opportunity to the poor who could not otherwise pay their passage. (420: pp. 512–513) The proportion of the total flow of labor to our expanding factories which was brought in under the contract system or the padrone system was probably small. Still, these events must be mentioned to complete the picture of a coercive push out of agriculture into manufacturing, mining, and transportation characterizing the initial development of industrial America.

In the "old immigration" (1830 to 1882) about three-fifths were Irish, German, and Scandinavian; a large proportion were skilled, very few were illiterate. There was only a small excess of males. These immigrants and their families quickly established themselves in industry, agriculture, and politics. Contrast the "new immigration" (1883 to 1917) in a period of great industrial growth: conservatively estimated, about seven in ten were unskilled, one in three illiterate. There was a large excess of males. They were chiefly Roman Catholic, Greek Orthodox, or Jewish in religion; Italian, Greek, Croat, Czech, Slovak, Slovene, Polish, Hungarian, Rumanian, and Russian by nationality. While the German or Swedish peasant who came to America right after the Civil War could take advantage of the Homestead Act and become a farmer, the new immigrants had to settle in cities, in the ghetto and the slum. (353: pp. 372 ff., 454 ff.; 286) They had to adjust simultaneously to urban-industrial ways of life and to American culture. They had much in common with the peasant peoples who today are entering urban industry and commercial agriculture in the rapidly developing economies of other continents.

The pathos of the new immigrants' "adjustment," "acculturation," "Americanization" is too well known to discuss here. Much of the indictment of the industrial revolution in America (see Chapter I) stems from this early period when alien peasant peoples were being recruited to man the new and simplified machines. The immigrant emerged as a social problem about the time that industry's appetite for cheap unskilled labor grew large; his problem of adjustment at that same time created a demand for welfare services—and we see the establishment of immigrant-oriented settlement houses, legal aid societies, adult education movements, and the like.[1]

Transforming the Peasant. We have pointed to the large element of coercion used everywhere to recruit labor in the early phases of economic development. Rural men and women are typically pushed off the land and into wage employment by social, economic, or political pressures. The landless, the hungry, the politically powerless, the socially disaffected—these are the first industrial recruits.

Although coercion may yield a large initial labor supply, it is a highly inefficient way of keeping people at work. Laborers recruited by coercion require too much supervision in the workplace; and their resentment often contributes to political instability in the society (as the experience of colonial powers in Africa and Asia has in our time shown). Above all, it takes more than coercion to develop habits of industrial work and discipline.

The problem of transforming the peasant into an industrial worker with a minimum of social and psychological pain also goes beyond the "acculturation" of the immigrant. It is a matter of overcoming a deep feeling of insecurity induced by the factory system—a feeling widespread among industrial populations but especially strong among the newcomers. To get an idea of the sources of this insecurity and the social problems engendered by it, let us contrast work in a peasant society with work in the urban-industrial setting. The differences have to do with the nature of the discipline imposed; the source of the individual's security; the basis, extent, and kinds of specialization; and the criteria of stratification.

[1] The flow of newcomers to urban industry has not ceased since the restrictive immigration laws of 1924 and 1952—and neither has the pain of their adjustment. Today's "immigrant" is a Mexican or a Puerto Rican or a southern Negro or white. From 1940 to 1950, *e.g.*, the nonwhite population of urban America increased by 44 per cent and in many cities doubled; much of this represents migration from farm to factory. (34: p. 128) Like the European peasants before them, these groups come in at the bottom of the social ladder to feed our growing industrial machine. Three contrasts are worth noting, however. The Puerto Ricans who have moved to New York City are predominantly of urban origin, are in larger part women, and tend to have been squeezed less at home than the depressed European peasants before them. (249: pp. 25, 43–60) Many of the Negroes move from southern agriculture to southern cities before striking out for urban areas in the North. And the Mexican immigration reflects not industrial expansion but a demand for migratory workers in agriculture (about half of the estimated one million active in 1951 were Mexicans). (353: p. 383)

The Factory System: Discipline, Insecurity, Specialization, and Mobility

"Scarcely any evil associated with the factory system was entirely a new evil in kind." (136: I, p. 31) This concession comes from the Hammonds, in their classic indictment of the industrial revolution (see Chapter I). In many home industries preceding the factory system the hours were long, the pay was poor, children were sweated, and both home and workshop were overcrowded and unattractive by virtue of their combination under a single roof. The same can be said of the agriculturalist of peasant village, whose long hours of backbreaking labor and low levels of living were matched by his dependence on the labor of his women and children.

It is not that the American worker of 1870 was still on an eleven-hour day and sometimes a seven-day week, nor that his women and children often worked that accounts for his grievances. Nor is the evidence good that the peasants who were transformed into industrial workers—in America *or* in Britain—experienced any drastic decline in material standard-of-living (even initially).[1] When we think of the transition from European peasant to American industrial worker we are often comparing a run-down rural economy with an expanding industrial economy. It is surprising that life in the urban-industrial setting did not seem wonderful by contrast.

The charge that the machine has enslaved man seems to be based on four major changes that the factory system brought about: (1) Work in modern industry must be regular, workers punctual. (2) The modern worker is dependent for his livelihood on a corporation or an employer who owns the machines and controls the conditions of work (the peasant or the homeworker often owned his own tools and usually set his own conditions of work). (3) The machine often is in direct competition with the worker: mechanization means continual change in jobs; both the number of workmen and the skills needed in the workplace are in constant flux. (4) The modern worker must often move his resi-

[1] See pp. 84–86.

dence in response to the demands of changing technology and opportunity (accelerating technological changes affect the competitive position of companies and even whole industries, which in turn makes for shifts in demand for numbers and kinds of workers). The following sections consider these effects of the factory system one at a time.

The New Discipline. Specialized machine processes must be coordinated with flawless timing; for the worker this means subjection to schedule and disciplined routine. The time clock, the plant rules, the presence of a host of supervisors and other control specialists, the close attention to quantity and quality of output—these add up to a demand for discipline on the job, and acceptance of individual responsibility for performance of the job.

We half forget the sustained regularity insisted upon in office, store, and factory—we are so used to it. But the difficulties of adapting to industrial routines are experienced afresh in each area invaded by modern industry and by each new recruit. It may be a Bemba tribesman who has come to work in a North Rhodesia mine or a Mississippi sharecropper newly arrived at the plant gates of a Chicago steel mill; it may be a Soviet farm youth drafted into a factory training center in Leningrad or an American farm girl now employed in a large typing pool in Hartford. Newcomers to industry everywhere resist a full commitment to industrial ways of life. This is clear in all underdeveloped countries, where absenteeism is the major labor problem of the managers of mines, factories, and plantations. (Many Indian factories have had to hire a group of substitutes who take the place of workers who have run away without giving notice.) It is clear, too, in the more developed countries—including both the Soviet Union and the U.S.A.—where absenteeism and labor turnover are also high among the rural newcomers. (385: p. 33; 154: p. 91; 181; 406; 256: pp. 38–39, 114 ff.; 33: p. 95)

Dependence on Employers and the Labor Market. The peasant newcomer may have worked long hours in the Old Country, but they were his own hours. His wife and children may have worked, but they worked beside him and they were not confined to jobs considered degrading (as maid, laundress, shoeshine boy). The weather and war made life seem full of risks in the Old Country; but the high rate of industrial accidents in the New World seemed to be within the employer's control, a sign of his callousness. The peasant may have been a slave of tradition and the daily round a fixed and monotonous one requiring considerable self-control; but the disciplines of factory life did not permit even the illusion of independence, for the supervisor was always there, personal embodiment of an impersonal system of control. The peasant or the homeworker may have experienced crop failure or unemployment—but in the Old Country a man was his own boss or was hired for the year or the season; and in time of crisis, he had some comforting (if not very effective) insurance policies to fall back on—land ownership or personal ties with landlords, or moral ties with kinsmen. In industry he had nothing to sell but his labor and the employer bought it by the hour or the day. Should the workings of an impersonal market cast him in the role of unemployed, he had to hunt out another job (if there was one), which often meant another neighborhood or community. Should illness cut off his income, the family and community supports were no longer as strong.

In short, the risks of an agricultural existence (even on a narrow margin above starvation) were spread widely among the extended family or whole village; they seemed more like "acts of God." The risks of an industrial existence were his: they were not so easily shared; and they seemed unreasonable, inflicted on him by evil men. It takes even the willing peasant a while to get used to the idea that responsibility for adversity lies with the law of supply and demand. It takes him even longer to realize that security may be had if he shifts from job to job, community to community; acquires some skill; forms a union; becomes active in a political party—if, in short, he adopts the ways by which experienced industrial workers in the early years of industrialization achieve some stability of income and some improvement of conditions.

Early Changes in Specialization. It is a commonplace to say that industrialization brings increased complexity in the division of labor, more specialized jobs. The extent, the kinds, and the trends in specialization and their precise impact on social life are not so obvious.

It has been estimated that there are 30,000 different occupations in the United States today (325: p. 24); the *Dictionary of Occupational Titles* gives definitions of more than 22,000 (378). These lists show astonishing specialization. In the baking industry one can make a living as a cracker breaker, meringue spreader, a pie stripper, or pan dumper. In the slaughter and meat-packing industry one can specialize as: a large stock scalper, belly shaver, crotch buster, gut snatcher, gut sorter, snout puller, ear cutter, eyelid remover, stomach washer (sometimes called belly pumper), hindlegs toenail puller, frontlegs toenail puller, and oxtail washer.

The kind of specialization suggested by these bizarre titles is typical of manufacturing in the early phases of industrialization; it is the specialization that results from the subdivision and simplification of tasks. The writers who complained that the industrial revolution would make automatons of men, turn them into machine slaves, dehumanize them (see Chapter I) were preoccupied with this type of specialization. What they had in mind was an old phenomenon first described in Adam Smith's story of the pinmakers: one drew out the wire, another straightened it, a third cut it, a fourth pointed it, a fifth ground it at the top, two or three others did the necessary operations to make the head. All of this resulted in marvelous economies, but, as Adam Smith saw at that early date, work simplification could also result in a kind of mental stupor for the worker.[1]

The dilution of skills, then, is one effect of this type of specialization. By this we mean that complex operations are broken down

---

[1] Some modern occupational analysis also points toward this conclusion. Shartle reports data on 7,955 occupations in 87 industries as compiled by the USES, 1935-1941. They were grouped by work performed and materials used. Almost all required working under supervision; about half required the worker to adjust to a machine (over half the machine occupations had an on-the-job training period of one week or less, less than half required previous experience); about a third of all occupations were repetitive in nature; more than half had no special educational requirement as stated by the employer and a "high degree of intelligence" was estimated to be necessary only in about one in ten. (325: pp. 185 ff.) Note, however, that occupations in the administrative and professional areas were underrepresented in this study.

into easily learned components. (257) Processes formerly handled by one person are torn apart. The separate components or tasks are then mechanized and/or assigned to unskilled workers. The results: Workers suffer a "loss of workmanship" or "pride of craft." They lose socially recognized skills (even the wives of many machine-tenders have only the vaguest notion of what their semi-skilled husbands do). They also lose independence and individual self-reliance. When we hear protests about these things, it is typically the dilution of skills due to work simplification that is at issue.

The auto-assembly plant—featuring a conveyor system that grips the worker bodily to the line—has been since 1914 the epitome of this type of specialization, though by no means its first example.[1] Mechanically controlled workpace, repetitiveness, minimum skill, predetermination of tools and techniques, minute subdivision of product, surface mental attention—these characteristics of production-line jobs in auto-assembly have, indeed, taken the joy out of work. A careful study by Walker and Guest of one auto plant, where few of the workers had previously been exposed to an assembly line, reports that: (1) the workers' feelings about their work were overwhelmingly negative; (2) the technology of the line kept workgroups weak; (3) worse than either the boredom or the tension that arose from repetitive and machine-paced work was the sense of becoming depersonalized, of becoming anonymous as against remaining oneself; (4) simplified and standardized jobs had reduced wage spreads and all but wiped out job progression—thereby striking at the heart of America's free mobility ideology. (386: pp. 116–117; 59) This case study is given broader significance by the fact that in 1953, at a time when jobs were plentiful, the automobile industry had the fifth highest quit rate for 52 durable goods manufacturing industries for which data are reported. The average voluntary quits per month per 100 employees for auto was 3.0; the average rate for the 52 industries was 2.3. (376)[2]

[1] Long before, Chicago meatpackers had applied the principle of a continuous "disassembly line" to cut up carcasses.

[2] Low job satisfaction and high labor turnover seem to have characterized mass production plants from the first: In the early years of the century, for example,

While there is little evidence on this point, it seems possible that the frustrations of the work routine on the assembly line place a heavy hand on the worker's off-the-job thought and feeling, that the deadening rhythms of the factory tend to be repeated in his leisure time. Lacking satisfaction on the job, he may seek synthetic substitutes in passive consumption of the standardized products of "mass culture" off the job. If this passive exposure to TV, film, comics, and sports arena itself offers insufficient release of tension, it may help to explain the explosiveness of life in a factory city like Detroit—the race riots and bar brawls, the passionate hostility to management shown in workplace and union meeting. (156: pp. 42–43) In what circumstances frustrating job routines and disciplines lead to explosive activity off work, when they lead to dull passivity, when they produce other patterns of leisure use, and when they have little or no effect, are questions only now beginning to interest social researchers. Observations about the links between occupational roles and nonoccupational roles are therefore more speculative than our analysis of the impact of technological change on job satisfaction.

The dilution of skills for those who had experienced the craft life before meant a drastic decline of job satisfaction and self-esteem. For those fresh from the farm it meant an intensification of the industrial disciplines which in any case were hard for them to take. In so far as industrialization brings increased specialization involving work simplification, the evidence suggests a large class of "de-humanized" workers, men who are alienated from their work and from the industrial way of life.[1]

"Ford's radical technology was in a constant state of flux. . . . To give the new machine processes a tryout, men had to be commandeered, uprooted, shunted from job to job at a moment's notice. As early as 1910 the man on the bottom at Ford's had come to feel . . . he had no work he could call his own from one day to the next. . . . A certain factory process at Highland Park which had once required the skills of a craftsman . . . by 1914 had been split up into thirty-four separate operations. . . ." Ford later wrote that turnover of his working force had run to 380 per cent for the year 1913 alone. (352: pp. 49, 47)

[1] At any given time, the extent of such subservience to the machine depends on what proportion of jobs is organized on these lines. Recent technological changes suggest that these jobs may be the model of the past, not for the future. See pp. 97–99.

While work simplification spells dilution of skills for some, it spells *obsolescence* of skills for others. By this we mean a decline or disappearance of demand for certain skills. (257) This may be due to falling demand for certain products (when horse-drawn vehicles were replaced by cars, skilled carriage makers were no longer needed); or it may be due to changes in production methods (as in the mechanization of shoe production just after the Civil War). (392: p. 60) In 1910, to cite a case of mechanization recent enough to furnish accurate data, about half the workers in the tobacco industry were craftsmen, foremen, and other skilled workers—mainly hand cigarmakers. By 1930, after new mass production methods had been introduced, only one in ten was a skilled worker. Some students of labor took the trouble to find out what happened to the displaced skilled workers. Very few of the cigarmakers were converted to machine operators (the latter were usually recruited directly from the ranks of the un-skilled). (163: pp. 265–266) A study of one group of skilled cigarmakers in the Manchester, New Hampshire, area (mechan-ized around 1931) showed that the average length of unemploy-ment was about one year; one in five remained unemployed more than five years. During the seven-year period studied, over half the workers had experienced a minimum of three years of jobless-ness. Only about half of those who got jobs between 1931 and 1937 stayed in the cigar-manufacturing industry. The skilled older workers were especially hard hit. (68: pp. 36–38) A study of displaced textile workers in New England in 1953–1954 suggests that lack of information, opportunity, and motive spells much difficulty even where new industries and other areas offer the dis-placed worker alternative possibilities. (241)

Technological unemployment, then, is the most dramatic effect of this sort of specialization; and the problems of adjust-ment are greatest for the oldest and most skilled. Even in years of prosperity men who have invested their time, their money, their very selves in their work are reluctant to accept downgrad-ing or begin new occupational ventures.

In sum: specialization based on mechanization in the early years of industrial development can mean robotization for some workers, technological unemployment for others. Both have a drastic impact on life in the family and community. (156; 15; 9; 186) Some implications for Family Service Agencies are explored in Chapter VIII.

Who You Are to What You Can Do: Changes in the Basis of Specialization.[1] Work in the primitive tribe or peasant village is traditional; the division of labor is simple. This means several things. Work does not change much from generation to generation; the son can do what his father did. There are only a few special roles to fill (for example, hunting, fishing, gardening, fighting, and religious ceremony); practically anyone can learn all of them. Work can be assigned on the basis of traditional criteria, criteria often irrelevant to the performance of the role—age, sex, and perhaps, as in the Indian caste system, family origin. The elders of the tribe or village may occasionally look for promising young men and in some kinship systems, as among the Manus and the Chukchi, "adopt" them, and sponsor their progress. But generally, even in these cases, little competition need accompany the "placement" of the individual in the economic order.

Contrast the industrial society. Work changes with changing technology and the pace of change accelerates; the division of labor is complex; and work is assigned more often on the basis of ability. Industrialization makes the shift away from traditional criteria of work assignment inevitable. Large portions of the population cannot do what their fathers did, cannot inherit occupations because the occupations change too rapidly. (If occupations were assigned by family origin, we would have too many of one thing and not enough of another.) There are not enough age and sex differences to represent the vast number of specialized roles that need to be filled. For example, we cannot expect all American males to learn to be carpenters, barbers, doctors, lawyers, research chemists, labor leaders, corporation executives, and so on. Some of these roles are so complex that they cannot be left to the accidents of inheritance. Despite the great plasticity of

[1] The following discussion draws upon Linton, *Study of Man* (211); Parsons, *Essays on Sociological Theory*, pp. 189 ff. (280); Moore, *Industrialization and Labor* (256); Levy, *The Family Revolution in Modern China* (206); and Levy, article in Hoselitz, *The Progress of Underdeveloped Areas* (154).

human nature, some individuals are born without the capacity to
fill some roles; and modern society cannot afford an idiot as
President. In fact, industrialization, by creating complex and
important occupational roles, accents the importance of even
small differences in ability. For these small differences may mean
enormous differences in output. Compare, for example, the difference in amounts that can be accomplished by two machine-
shovel operators of different degrees of skill. Or think of the
amount of damage that can be done by a relatively less able (that
is, responsible) stillman in an oil refinery. This is an operator who
has heavy responsibility for expensive processes and equipment.
If he goes to sleep on the job he can ruin thousands of dollars in
machinery and material, as can many semi-skilled machine
operators.

In short, the number, complexity, importance, and frequency
of change of occupational roles in industrial society have meant a
shift in the basis of role assignment. "Who you are" becomes less
important; "what you can do or learn to do" becomes more
important.

The fact that work roles in modern society tend to be achieved,
assigned on the basis of ability, intensifies competition for these
roles. If no one is excluded from consideration, then everyone is
potentially a competitor. This is why there is less chance for the
development of a hereditary elite. This is, moreover, why modern
industry everywhere is such a sifter, sorter, and above all *mixer* of
diverse racial and ethnic groups. (157; 159)[1] It is a major reason,
too, for the increased proportion of women who work. Everywhere industrialization, by challenging traditional criteria of
work assignment, by accenting ability instead of sex, invites

[1] Discrimination in American industry, of course, still exists; and in the underdeveloped areas it is one of the great blocks to rapid economic development. For
instance, where persons of west European origin are in control and treat the natives
as inferior, the possibilities of developing aspirations, motives, and work habits
appropriate to industry are reduced; and caste exclusiveness in India still survives
as a block to industrialization. Even after the rigor of caste law had decayed, attempts to introduce factory organization in the jute industry in the nineteenth
century encountered the difficulty that every caste had a different ritual and different
rest pauses and demanded different holidays. (397: p. 176) What is argued here is
that advancing industrialization inevitably brings a decline in racial discrimination,
and the American experience seems to bear this out. (54; 26; 362)

women to participate as occupational equals. Although there are limits in the extent to which this goes, there is no doubt that industrial societies offer marked contrast to nonindustrial societies in the degree to which women are released from the home. Underscoring this shift is the fact that industrialization has everywhere been accompanied by agitation for the emancipation of women both within the family and within the society—often taking the form of feminist movements. (206: p. 12)

More competition, more mixing of minority groups, more women at work—these are three of the main consequences of the shift in the basis of specialization, the new accent on ability. How this affects the family will be discussed below.

Status to Contract: The Shift from Diffuse to Specific Obligations. Along with the new emphasis on ability as the main criterion for role assignment has gone a shift in the quality of work relations.

In the primitive tribe or peasant village work is hardly distinguished from the rest of life, from one's duties and rights as husband, son, father, clansman. A man's work obligations, which come to him by virtue of his age, sex, and birth, are, like his kinship obligations, broad and diffuse. Both output and consumption are traditionally confined to needs appropriate to his age, sex, and membership in clan or family. When a crisis or dispute arises in the allocation of goods and services, traditional patterns of mutual aid come into play. Help is not likely to be refused on the grounds that the asker has not proved his right to "something extra"; rights and obligations covered by clan and family relations are not so clearly defined and delimited. Loosely put, the formula for preindustrial living is this: the family equals the community equals the insurance against disaster—and none of the rights and duties need be specified in advance.

Contrast the situation in industrial society. Work relations tend to be functionally specific. That means that the rights and obligations and activities covered by economic relationships are clearly defined and delimited—as in a business contract. In the case of dispute over what is due, the burden of proof lies with the one who asks for "something extra." Moreover, work tends to be sharply separated from home and family. Physically, place of work is located some distance from place of residence; socially, family relations remain personal and diffuse, work relations (and increasingly other nonfamilial relations) tend to become impersonal and contractual.

There are good reasons for expecting this to happen in all industrial societies. If there is an inevitable emphasis on ability to perform the role as a basis for role assignment, the rights and duties that make up the role must be spelled out. Otherwise, how could the individual's ability to fill the role be judged? The change in the basis of specialization discussed above, then, means that relationships must become increasingly contractual.

A second reason for the decline in the number and range of diffuse (family-type) relationships is the problem of employing people and disposing of goods in a complex economy with complex specialization. Personalized, familial relations between employer and employee in a large steel mill are obviously impossible. (See discussion of the growth in the Scale of Organization, Chapter IV). And the auto manufacturer can hardly dispose of goods through personal friends; he does it through dealers, people with whom he has specific and delimited relations. If the steelworker should break a leg, or the car dealer should receive damaged cars, neither can invoke any tradition of mutual aid. The employee might appeal to the Workmen's Compensation Claims Board, the dealer might go to the insurance company; both would have to prove a claim.

Industrialization and Mobility. Much of what we have said adds up to this: industrialization represents a multi-front attack on tradition, an attack symbolized by the words "change" and "movement." In the early decades of America's industrial development, and this is matched in the economic growth of other countries, families by the millions were uprooted and pushed into industry. Everywhere advancing industrialization makes the worker dependent on the employer and the labor market (whose changing demands necessitate frequent job shifts), and the nature of his work changes with changing technology (which brings the dilution and obsolescence of skills). The basis of assignment of individuals to work roles changes. In competition with others, the individual can thus move from one job to another with changes in his own ability or the abilities demanded by jobs. Place of work is separated from place of residence; the industrial way of life includes a journey to work. In other words, all of these changes that accompany industrialization make for a *vastly increased mobility* of the population—movement within a single career from job to job, company to company, neighborhood to neighborhood, community to community; movement between generations from father's occupation down, up or across to a new occupation. In addition to these moves to which all are exposed, industrialism has also established a seasonal flow which carries a portion of the population from winter tasks to summer and back again.[1]

How do these trends affect the family? How can we link these massive changes wrought by industrialization—worker dependence on the state of the labor market, the changes in the nature and bases of specialization, and the vastly increased mobility these impose—to the family system? Much of social welfare service in America can be seen as a response to the impact of industrialization on family life. An understanding of this impact can help us see the welfare services (see Chapter VII) in broader context and understand the form they take.

Industrialism and the Family System

Popular discussion reveals two dominant views as to what is happening to the American family. Family expert Carle C. Zimmerman (426), a proponent of one view, says the family is dissolving. Divorce is on the increase; more wives are working and

---

[1] Since the work of Turner, many have argued that America in the years before 1890 was uniquely shaped by its expanding frontier, which permitted the underprivileged industrial worker and the unsuccessful small trader to pick up stakes and move West. We hear much about the sense of expanding opportunity, the self-reliant willingness to move. As Hacker points out, however, "The free farmers of the American West, beginning with the 1820's, were not recruited from the industrial workers of the East, for these simply could not afford the . . . long journey . . . [and] a family farm." (130: p. 9) Moreover, while the expanding frontier may have intensified the mobility of Americans in the period under discussion, it is not at all clear that this mobility lessened when the frontier closed. It is not just America's empty spaces that gave its social life its fluid character (contrast Manchuria, Siberia, Canada); it is also industrialization. The frontier and the impetus to change and mobility it symbolizes, exist not only in land but in industry; and the high degree of geographical and social mobility is rooted in the demands industry makes wherever it develops rapidly and far.

therefore spend less time with the family; the marriage contract is becoming less sacred and more secular; parents are losing authority over children (a fact seen in the "revolt of youth"). Above all, an "unbridled individualism" and a decline in the spirit of self-sacrifice have led to a decline in the birth rate; women are now less willing to bear the large broods of children who form the basis of familism. The decay of the family, our most important primary group, heralds the further decay of civilization itself.

The second view—early stated by another family expert, Joseph K. Folsom (107)—holds that the family is simply changing its organization, and will emerge strengthened, better adapted to a democratic society. The double standard in sex is declining; choice of mate is more voluntary; mechanization of the smaller home plus a flood of goods and services have reduced the drudgery of housework; males are less dominant, wives have more equality in law and in daily living (liberalization of divorce and decline of church authority make it easier to get rid of a cruel husband). Above all, there is a partial shift of traditional family functions—protective, educational, economic—to the state, school, and industry. This makes family members more independent of one another. It thereby strengthens the family as an adaptable emotional unit. Love, freed from economic compulsion and parental authority, may become more loyal and permanent. Companionship and satisfying affection in the family will create men who are less inclined to sabotage democracy in the community. (Cf. 44.)

The interpretations of each proponent stem from different value premises. Both, however, are correct in their facts. Our task in this section is to link these facts to the features of industrial society discussed above.

A student of industrialization suggests that "modern industry and the 'traditional' family are mutually subversive." Commercial agriculture and the factory system everywhere, if they are to develop, must force the breakup of the economically self-sufficient extended family. What has happened to the American family since the Civil War is just one example of this. (206: p. 354; 208: pp. 11–14) A good way to get at this process is to contrast kinship systems of nonindustrial society with the family system prevailing in the American urban middle class. We choose the urban middle-class family because it most closely fits the needs of modern industry and also it is fast becoming a model for the rest of the population.[1]

Main Features of American Kinship. "Family" for midcentury Americans generally means the nuclear (or "conjugal") family of parents and nonadult children living at home. Other kinsmen are all "relatives," who are regarded as far less important. Each of us is a member of two families: (1) the initial or parental "family of orientation" into which one is born as a child; and (2) the "family of procreation," which is founded by one's marriage.

The marriage bond is the key; a man's or woman's first kinship loyalty is unequivocally to spouse and children. Both the interests and the place of residence of this nuclear family tend to be independent of both pairs of parents. It is often hundreds of miles from both. An attitude of impartiality toward the husband's compared with the wife's relatives is the norm. The many extended kin groups, patrilineal or matrilineal clans, so prevalent among nonindustrial peoples have all but disappeared. The nuclear family acts together on matters economic, social, and (if we can take studies of voting behavior as a clue) political. It is the normal household unit.

If the marriage bond is central, how are marriages made? In nonindustrial societies courtship, if it exists at all, typically is closely and formally supervised by the extended family clan, while marriages are typically "arranged" (a child may be betrothed before he is born). "Relatives" are typically in a close and delicate state of interdependence; it is expected that the newly married couple will be incorporated into the larger kin group. Choice of mate is therefore everybody's concern, and a good match is judged in terms of its effect on the economic and

[1] The structural analysis offered here is indebted to the work of Davis (82; 79) and Davis and others (84); Parsons (280: pp. 233–250); Levy (206); Miller and Swanson (242); and Waller (387). The picture of the American kinship system below is desperately oversimplified. For instance, it leaves out many variations that exist among ethnic groups, social strata, and regions. When we say "nonindustrial" we mean "so much less industrialized than the U.S. that traditional agricultural patterns of life remain dominant."

social position of the whole clan. The extended family not only chooses the mate and determines the residence; it controls the property, watches the morals, and in general manages the affairs of the young couple.

In America, by contrast, casual dating and competitive courtship is the rule and personal choice is emphasized. The choice of mate is no major threat either to the parental family or to the relatives. They will not have to live with the newly married couple; generally they will neither support them nor depend upon them. No great harm is done, then, if personal feelings are given free play. Compared to the primitive tribe or peasant village, the courting couple is thus drastically emancipated from ties to parents, siblings, and "relatives." And because economic and kinship pressures to stay married are not so strong, there is an expectation that love will hold; if it does not, the parties may be thought "maladjusted" or "immature." Marriage is idealized as a total intimacy. The belief is strong that romance should play a part in courtship and people should marry for love.

The system also favors equal rights and obligations for both parties in a marriage. Since love cannot be forced, the contract is voluntary and each side is supposed to be a fully responsible partner.

What about having children? In 1790 the average number of persons per family in the United States was 5.2 (excluding relatives, lodgers, servants, and others). In 1950 it was down to about 3.2. (274: pp. 98 ff.) Most of the drop had taken place in the preceding fifty years. The more industrialized we became, the greater the rate of decline in family size.[1]

Does the bumper crop of babies making news after World War II herald a new and lasting pattern? Postwar baby booms have continued in the fifties in the countries with the most rapid rates of economic expansion—Canada, Australia, the U.S. The booms have slacked off, however, in older, more densely popu-

---

[1] It seems likely that in the long run, a low *level* of economic development, whatever the *rate* of growth, is associated with a high fertility rate, but that high levels of economic development coupled with high rates of growth lead to medium fertility rates, and high levels of economic development coupled with low rates of growth lead to low fertility rates.

lated industrial societies where expansion is slow—for example, England. Moreover, despite higher birth rates in the United States, small families are still the fashion. (During the boom the number of fifth children has not increased and the number of sixth, or more, children has continued to fall.) (81) Studies in the Detroit area suggest the emergence of overwhelming consensus among all strata of the urban population that two, three, or four children are "ideal"—and the achievement continues to be lower than the ideal. (115) We seem to have moved to a two- or three-child system—to a medium-small family not to a large one.

Many reasons for this can be cited. Two seem to apply universally to highly industrialized countries, though different rates of economic growth bring variations on the main theme.

First, the shift from self-sufficient agriculture to the factory system makes children less valuable economically. Complex occupational specialization requires long preparation (the spread of universal and compulsory education is correlated with the spread of industry); the child is therefore usually a drain on the family income until he establishes his own family. If children are allowed to work as they were in the initial period of industrialization, they become competitors of adults. Instead of adding to family income as extra hands on the farm, they displace adults at the machine. Child labor laws seem to be the natural outcome, again fixing the child as an economic liability at the same time that they protect his chances for an education.

Second, large-scale industrialization at once presupposes and strengthens rising levels of aspiration for self and children. Some individualization of motives and rewards, while intensified by the culture of capitalism (see Chapter II), may be a universal accompaniment of advanced economic growth; it stems from the necessary accent on ability in assignment of work roles, especially in the recruitment and development of skilled technicians and managers. Large families hinder both generations in the scramble for status. Mobility aspirations for self and children are a major factor in the willingness of Americans to limit family size by using rational birth control.

A final feature of the American kinship system is this: the accent on the nuclear family may increase emotional intensity among its members. There is little evidence for it, but the argument seems plausible: If family size is smaller, if "relatives" become more distant, if the husband's and wife's contacts outside the family are "functionally specific" (more businesslike), and the child's relations in school and play group are more competitive, then the family becomes the main source of psychological security and emotional ties among its members are intensified.

In short, production has been removed from the home, and extended kin sheared away; family size has been reduced, and at the same time a great deal of family sentiment has probably been fostered and directed toward the few persons left.

Mobility and Emancipation. The great emphasis on the nuclear family in the American kinship system is made necessary by industrialization, especially by the occupational and residential mobility it necessitates.

In March of each of the years from 1950 to 1955, almost one in five of all people in the labor force lived in houses other than those they had lived in twelve months earlier; about one in 20 lived in a different county. If conditions for this time of high-level employment are typical, then the average worker under present conditions may be expected to change his residence about eight times in his working life; two or three of these would involve a change of community. (36: p. 145) We change our houses almost as often as we change our cars.

Most of this migration is in response to changing economic opportunity.[1] Job changes also go with changes in family size. About the time the young couple need more room because of children, they also need more money, and they hunt both for better jobs and for better housing. Most of such shifts occur in the first ten years of marriage. (Cf. 309: p. 9.) Note, too, that

---

[1] And most of it involves more than a change of employer. A study of labor mobility in all Census-classified industries and occupations in six cities, 1940–1949, showed that three in five of the people studied had worked for more than one employer in the decade. More than half of all job shifts involved changes in occupations and industry as well as employer. "Roughly three-fourths . . . involved shifts between industries, and nearly three-fifths . . . between occupations." (260: pp. 156–157)

"migration is generally more frequent among the better-educated, higher-income, professional members of a society than among workers of the same age but lower in the socioeconomic scale." (36: p. 151) In other words, geographical mobility is very high for the whole population but it is highest among those who conform most to the kinship pattern dominant in the urban middle class.

The connection between such mobility and the accent on the nuclear family is easy to see. If on the average one picks up and moves every few years, one cannot bring along 10 or 20 in-laws, brothers, sisters, uncles, aunts, cousins—especially if they, too, are moving about at a great rate. Moreover, if one is oriented toward "success" and success is won by investing one's money and energy so they are readily available for transfer to more profitable commitments, by job shifts within and between careers, then one thinks twice before undertaking lasting obligations—financial, emotional, or otherwise—to extended kin of varied social status. A man who moves up in the world from a traditional Chinese family buys his *father* a house that fits his new position; the whole clan comes along. A man who moves up in the world from a poor American home would surely buy *himself* the house, though he might also visit his father once a year or so—or even help him get into a home for the aged.[1] Industrialization (largely through moving people about geographically and socially) has emancipated the married couple.

Such mobility and the emancipation it brings can, of course, be disruptive. The emancipation of women, of youth, of the aged has involved difficult adjustments—and has led to the label "social problem" for each of these categories in the population.

Women: Searching for Identity. About a third of all people at work or seeking work in the United States are women. (129: p. 133) Advancing industrialization not only puts an increasing per-

[1] The extended family system, of course, may also operate to retard the development of motives conducive to industrialization. Fong reports that a large employer of skilled workers in China " 'was moved by the obvious physical inefficiency of many of his employees and the large incidence of sickness among them to raise wages of his own accord. The only result . . . was that each of these men was now supporting an even larger number of relatives than a person in his position was expected to look after.' " Job preference given to relatives and reluctance to fire inefficient kinsmen are cited as reasons for enterprise failure in Greece, China, and Japan. (230: pp. 245–246)

centage of the whole population in the labor force; it not only changes the proportions between employed men and women, but it also gives the edge to *married* women. At midcentury, the number of married women at work exceeded for the first time the number of single women at work, a trend that seems to be continuing. Women work to supplement family income (an aspect of rising levels of aspiration for self and children), to support their families (a necessity, for an increasing number head broken families), to achieve "self-fulfillment" (a reflection of the changing definition of woman's role), and because the opportunities have increased (an aspect of the shift toward work assignment on the basis of "what you can do" and the fact that women can do an increasing portion of the jobs available).

More women, especially married women, work; and more and more of them come to believe they should have "a life of their own." At the same time it is thought that their work should not put them in competition with their husbands; that their careers, if they have careers, should be subordinate to their husbands'; that the demands of a job are in conflict with the demands of the home in an era of "scientific" child-rearing. One of the strains imposed on the newly emancipated nuclear family, then, is the conflict between a rising insistence on equality with men in competitive occupational achievement, on the one hand, and continued blocks to equal competition and the new demands for expertness in home and family management, on the other. Women have become disaffected from traditional marital and family roles without getting released from housewifery; they have achieved new privileges, more equal with men's, but are uncertain of what contribution they ought to make to the new partnership. (187) The old patterns and the new exist side by side: a husband may assist his wife in washing dishes and dressing children to conform to the new norms of equality but resent it when he sees his neighbor getting away with less; or, in a time of change, both parties may find they are not equally "modern" in their notions of their proper "place."

Youth: Temporarily Rebellious. It is often said that youth, in many other societies docile, is rebellious and unmanageable in our own.

Again, the accent on the nuclear family, coupled with the changes in the nature and basis of specialization, can help us understand the drama of parent-youth conflict.

At the same time that family feeling is intensified (for child as well as parent) so is the necessity for youth to become emancipated. To prepare for open competition in the world of work, the child is subjected to the authority of parents during a period of long training (which may not cease until his twenties). But upon its termination—after the intimate association of years among the few members of the immediate family—he moves out on his own, generally with a sharp break in family and other kinship ties. Few societies demand the combination of dependence in a prolonged youth with so much independence in adulthood. Youth culture—its rebelliousness, its studied irresponsibility, its capriciousness, its compulsive rejection of adult standards and conformity to peer-group standards—can be seen as an attempt to ease the passage from heightened emotion and dependency in childhood to necessary emancipation as young adult.

The strain of this transition is further intensified by three features of industrial America: (1) how choices are made in the occupational system; (2) the sex mores; (3) the rapidity of social change.

Industrialism presents both parents and youth with a changing occupational structure (see page 92). Partly because of the rapidity of change, it settles few choices beforehand. The accent is on individual initiative and free occupational choice and there is neither tradition nor chance for a boy to grow into his father's occupation. Should he pursue the college, general, or trade curriculum in high school? Should he quit high school and go to work? What about college? What major subject, what job should he take? When should he go into the armed forces—and in what program? More choices to make, the necessity of making them early coupled with the difficulty of knowing the complex and changing occupational structure for which choice is made— these inevitably bring more confusion as to where the adolescent's best interests lie and more chance for parent-youth conflict over the choices. The problem of emancipation from parents is made still more difficult because it occurs at the time of intensified sexual desire—this in a culture that prescribes both premarital chastity and postponed marriage.

Finally, the pace of technological change accelerates with advancing industrialization (invention breeds invention), and the pace of social change in our society is similarly swift. Standards that fit twenty-five years ago no longer fit. The parent does not catch up with his child's viewpoint, not only because their social experiences vary (things are no longer the way they were when the parent was a child), but also because as a responsible adult he is supposed to dominate, not follow. Moreover, he is filled with doubts—doubts about how to apply discipline and when, doubts about what behavior is proper. Meanwhile, increased specialization has brought not only the "hindlegs toenail puller" in meat packing, the chiropodist in medicine, but also a host of family experts. Competing authorities on child rearing and family life further confuse the parent. A less complete acceptance by child of parental authority is a consequence of these changes.

In subsequent chapters (especially IV, V, VIII, and IX), we will point to some changes in our social structure which may lessen the conflict between generations. In order to caution against generalizing the parent-youth conflict described above to the long-run future or to all segments of our population, however, a few facts should be mentioned as warnings here: average age of marriage is going down (so rigid sex mores, to the extent they survive at all, may become less of a problem), occupationally relevant choices made by adolescents, while complicated, must increasingly be pointed toward clusters of occupations and general status levels (for example, aiming at the professions, aiming at the physical sciences), which should make such choices less of a strain upon parent-youth relations; the leisure activities of teenagers and parents may be more alike and less sharply segregated in the suburban family of the future; and so on.

Existing research on adolescent subcultures in different places and times does not permit much solid generalization. But as one study suggests, the picture of adolescence as a period of unusual storm and stress, and youth culture as rebellious, may apply less well to the new middle class than to any other segment of our society: it "neither explains the correlation between adolescent class position, choice of school courses, and subsequent occupational goals; nor the acceptance by adolescents of adult guidance of many of their activities; nor does it make allowance for deferred gratification patterns, the internalization of adult values, solidary family relationships, or positive relationships with authority figures; all of which are found in studies of middle-class groups." (99: p. 684) More will be said about these class differences later.

The Aged: Left Stranded. Of all the social problems created by the impact of industrialism on the family, none is more certain to increase in importance than the problem of the aged. First, there are more older people than before. Second, the emancipation of the married couple, of women, and the accent on youth, leave the old folk stranded. Here again the conflict between generations may be intensified, because the changes are not complete—the old ways and the new co-exist, and the generations therefore have conflicting expectations.

In nonindustrial society, membership in an extended kinship unit is continuous throughout life: increased age typically brings increased power, prestige, and security. It is the oldest members of the clan who are treated with most respect and have most authority. Parenthood here is a kind of old-age insurance.[1]

The nuclear family of industrial society, as we have seen, changes all this. Here, children have the duty to build their own careers, and set up their own households—with a corresponding right to independence. They leave one by one until the older couple is finally left alone—with "no one left to respect them, for them to have responsibility for or have authority over." (280: p. 247)

At this point, all of the things that happen to old people become much more tragic. If the spouse should die, the widow or

[1] There are variations in degree: in industrial Japan, for example, the traditional authority of the elders is still strong; it is actually used to push the younger generation into the factories. Textile employers are reported to make contracts with the father for the labor of his sons and daughters. (256: p. 74) In industrial France the continued identity of family and firm affords another illustration of such variations. (197)

widower is not generally expected to move in with the married child. If he does, it occasions much strain on both sides. We have already seen that the older worker with heavy investment in a job is the hardest hit by the continual dilution and obsolescence of skills characteristic of industrialism. If the older worker is displaced, or if he is retired, he has no clear claim to support from his children. (91) Should he be subject to disabling illness or debilitation, the same emancipation from the children becomes an even more difficult load to bear. In this system, parenthood in retrospect becomes for many not old-age insurance, but a sacrificial duty, a thankless task.

Millions of Americans are not many years off the land—rural people used to a comfortably extended kinship system. In fact, almost one in three of our urban residents grew up on farms. The generations are thus bound to clash; and the dismay of the old, who hold to the old ways, the guilty consciences of the young who are moving to the new, are painful evidence of the clash.

At the same time that the industrial emphasis on the nuclear family leaves aged parents stranded, their proportion in the population increases. The main reason for this aging of the population is the decline in birth rates that goes with industrialization.[1] Thus, in the United States, since 1900 the population has doubled, but the number of persons 45 to 64 years has tripled, while the number 65 and over has quadrupled. (415) This picture holds, in so far as the data are comparable, for the entire world: the less developed areas show a smaller percentage of old people than the industrial areas. Or, comparing their own past, the industrial societies show a steady increase in percentage of aged. (255: pp. 519–537)

[1] The decline in death rates that occurs with the advance of industrialism is not a significant factor in the aging of the population. True, in the early period of economic growth, mortality declines sharply owing to control of epidemic diseases, improved sanitation and nutrition, increased agricultural productivity. But this does *not* mean that a larger proportion of the population lives to a ripe old age. The main drop in death rates comes among children below fifteen years of age, especially in the age bracket one to four. This can actually increase the proportion of young people. However, if in the long run these babies and youngsters saved by the advance of industrialism are not followed by equally large crops of babies, they grow up to become an ever-larger, aging slice of the total population. (Cf. 381: pp. 79–83.)

The fact that so much of America's welfare spending goes to the aged (see Chapter VII) must be seen, then, as the by-product of an increased emphasis on the nuclear family, the rapidity of social change, and the aging of population. These in turn are the inevitable results of industrialization.

Divorce: The Consequences Are Weightier. A family can be broken in many ways: divorce, desertion, annulment, informal separation, premature death of one of the parents. Except for the last named, all these types of family disruption have probably been on the upgrade.[1] There are no official statistics on desertion and separation. The evidence is better on divorce, and the studies unanimously show an almost uninterrupted increase in the divorce rate for the period known. In 1867 the rate was perhaps less than two per 1,000 married females. In 1900 it was four; in 1920 it was eight; and after World War II, in 1946, it reached an all-time high, 17.8. In fact, in 1946 there was more than one divorce for each four marriages made that same year. The peak reflects both the typical breakup of hasty and ill-advised wartime marriages and the wartime backlog of delayed divorces. (31: p. 278, chart) There has been a slight decline since; but it is our guess that the long-term trend of divorce will not be sharply downward, and divorce will remain far more frequent than it was before America's industrialization.

These trends in divorce rates are very similar for all western nations permitting divorce. (274: p. 219) They accord with our picture of kinship in industrial society. With extended kin sliced away, with deep lifelong friendships outside the family thwarted by great mobility, a heavy load is put upon the small nuclear family. Confusion in the role of women, the strain between youth and parents, feelings of guilt about aid to aging parents—these add to the load. At the same time that the strain on family life

---

[1] Aid to Dependent Children statistics show that many families are "broken" before they are even formed. In November, 1953, "father not married to mother" was the reason for dependency of 19.6 per cent (106,000) of all families receiving ADC. Among Negro families on ADC the figure is much higher—34.6 per cent. (371: pp. 15–17) Official statistics on totals and trends of illegitimacy in the country are lacking. Dublin and Spiegelman found official records for a count of 131,900 illegitimate births in 1947 (95: p. 20), but Kinsey says this figure should be "multiplied several times." (184: p. 326)

increases, the economic and kinship pressures to stay married become weaker. The increased divorce rate and the shift in popular attitude from severe disapproval to mild disapproval of divorce are reflections of the basic changes in the kinship system, changes that come with rapid industrialization.

Divorce is not new. It is not peculiar to our time or our society. Among both modern nations and primitive tribes there are cases where divorce rates are probably higher than ours (for example, in modern Egypt or among the Hopi Indians of North America). But in these societies divorce is not a social problem; in ours it is. The explanation lies in the different consequences for the children where the kinship system rests on the immediate family and where it rests on wider kin groups, which can act as shock absorbers.

Among the Hopi, the married couple lives with the wife's parents and her sisters and their husbands (a "matrilocal" system). Everyone traces descent through the female line (a "matrilineal" system). Each household is practically an independent economic unit. The house plus its children, the food, seeds, springs and gardens, are considered to belong collectively to the women who live in it, in charge of the female head. The core of the clan is a close-knit group of females. The married men of the lineage, though they live in their wives' households, look upon the households of their mothers and sisters and mother's sisters as their real homes. (98: pp. 31 ff.; 359: pp. 34 ff.; 294: pp. 23–43)

Hopi divorce has little significance either to the participants or to their society. If a man's wife does not bother to thank her husband for the grain he brings home one day—a sign she is "fed up" with him—the man simply packs up his personal effects and tools and moves back to his mother's home. Generally the economic adjustments are minor—enough men are left among the wife's unmarried brothers or brothers-in-law to continue farming as before. Little emotional shock attends the break because husband-wife intimacy is only slightly greater than that among all the adults in the household. The children, bound to their mother's kin, also remain much as before, with many substitute "parents" available. The Hopi divorce rate of one in three or four marriages, like that in many primitive societies, is no social problem.

Compare the situation in our own society, with its heavy emphasis on the immediate family. Davis sums up the contrast:

> . . . Any marital discord not only affects the mates acutely but also involves the children. Husband and wife, as a compensation for marital unhappiness, unconsciously seek consolation, revenge, release, prestige, security, or whatnot in the children. . . . [In case of divorce] the child's future must be decided in each case by the discretion of the court, with few principles other than the vague "welfare of the child" to guide it. The parents often use the child as an instrument of mutual conflict. They also compete for his custody, though not for his support. The public exaggerates the disadvantages of the child's situation, and seeks to prove by this means that divorce itself is an evil. In our culture, therefore, the child of divorce is a social problem in the sense that societal machinery for dealing with him does not operate automatically or satisfactorily. Though he is really better off than the child whose parent has died, he is more of a problem because his condition is felt to be somebody's fault, with all that this implies. (84: pp. 673, 686)

The social welfare response to the family disruption industrialization brings is described in Chapter VIII.

Variations in the American Family System. The factory system creates a family system that best fits its needs, especially its need for a large, mobile, and motivated labor supply. At the same time, industrialism creates the social problems of the aged, of youth, of the role of women. It creates more broken families (though fewer are broken by early death of the family head). The incidence of these problems and the form they take, however, vary greatly by social class, ethnicity, race, and degree of urbanization of the community.

What we have described in our discussion of industrialism and the family applies best to the urban middle-class family of the recent past. It is not the family of the lower-class Negro, the Tennessee hillbilly, the recent Italian immigrant. Nor is it the family of the Boston Brahmin or the prosperous Kansas wheat farmer. And it may change somewhat as industrialization proceeds in the age of the atom and automation.

The long arm of the city reaches out to shape the lives of the most rural of our people; and American agriculture has become to a great extent commercialized and mechanized. Despite these facts, rural life still affords more continuity of occupation and status from generation to generation than is possible in the city. Similar continuity is found in some segments of the upper class—where kinship solidarity remains intact, where a kind of loose aristocracy remains (with a tendency to occupational inheritance, patrilineal lines of descent, primogeniture, and the maintenance of an ancestral home). (280) In both cases the problems of divorce, the role of women, and youth and the aged are less acute.

The greatest deviation occurs in the case of the American lower class, which in some ways epitomizes the early impact of industrialization, in other respects does not. Here, the problem of the broken family is much more prevalent. The evidence suggests that the rate of divorce, desertion, and premature death of partner is on the whole inversely correlated with economic and occupational status. (415: p. 530) In his study of "Elmtown," Hollingshead found that in 1941–1942 one-third of working-class families were broken because of one of these factors before the children were reared. (151: p. 106) Of the 6.3 million urban families with incomes below $2,000 in 1948, about 1.5 million were headed by a woman. (370: p. 5) Frazier (in 415) reports that in nearly a third of the Negro families in the cities of the South a woman is head of the family. Two studies of small communities found that from 50 to 60 per cent of lower-class families were broken at least once. (75; 151)

Some effects of early industrialism—the mobility of the population, the instability of their employment, the increasing employment of women, the strain of transition from peasant to proletarian—are intensified for the lower strata, with disruptive effects on the family. The fact that immigrant families come in at the bottom of the class ladder may also further tendencies to disruption at the bottom, for the young become assimilated faster than their parents, which intensifies the conflict between generations. On the other hand, there is less of an equalitarian urge among lower-class women (and hence less husband-wife strain on

this score), and sometimes less rejection of rights claimed by kin—
more of a tradition of mutual aid—than in the middle class,
where what aid there is tends to flow in one direction, from
parents to children. (351) While extended kinship obligations
may be felt more than in the middle class, the cash to contribute,
or with which to visit distant parents, is less abundant. On balance, the disruptive forces carry the day in the lower classes, and
family instability, especially in the early period of industrialization, remains highest for them.

There is a seeming paradox: high-status, college-educated professionals have a lower divorce rate, yet they are more mobile
socially and residentially than manual workers. They are also
more tolerant of liberal divorce, intermarriage, women at work,
and equal authority for husband and wife. As we shall see in
Chapter V, there is reason to believe that mobility (in houses,
jobs, income) among professionals becomes a regular pattern of
urban life, and does not have the disruptive effect that even a
much smaller amount of mobility has on working-class families.

These class variations in family life suggest the necessity of considering the stratification dimension. The future of the lower-
class family will rest in part on changes in the "working class"—
its position, the chances for mobility out of it, and its relation to
the other classes. Already, the changes in the character of the
middle class seem to be shaping family life in a new mold,
different from our description above. To understand both the
early and the late impact of industrialization we must consider its
impact on social stratification. Do the rich become richer and the
poor poorer? Does it become easier or harder to get ahead? Does
social and residential mobility increase or decrease? As industrialization proceeds what changes in the class structure occur?

The Factory System and Stratification

Part of the early indictment of the industrial revolution (see
Chapter I) was that it made the rich richer and the poor poorer;
that it gave interesting and varied work to the few, and boring,
repetitive and physically exhausting work to the many; that
"democratic rights" for the great laboring masses meant the right

to sleep on park benches, to be out of a job or feel insecure in one. In general, it was said, the industrial revolution brought a polarization of social classes and intensified class conflict. An American quotation spells out the theme:

> . . . We find the wealth and luxury of our cities mingled with poverty and wretchedness and unremunerative toil. A crowded and constantly increasing urban population suggests the impoverishment of rural sections, and discontent with agricultural pursuits. . . .
>
> We discover that the fortunes realized by our manufacturers are no longer solely the reward of sturdy industry and enlightened foresight, but that they result from the discriminating favor of the government, and are largely built upon undue exactions from the masses of our people. The gulf between employers and the employed is constantly widening, and classes are rapidly forming, one comprising the very rich and powerful, while in another are found the toiling poor.
>
> . . . We discover the existence of trusts, combinations, and monopolies, while the citizen is struggling far in the rear, or is trampled to death beneath an iron heel. Corporations . . . are fast becoming the people's masters. (Quoted in 150: p. 183.)

This was no Populist soapboxer, no Marxist agitator speaking. This was President Grover Cleveland, hardly a radical fellow, in an annual message to Congress, written in December, 1888. Increasing inequality of income, declining opportunity to rise to fortune, the concentration of power in the hands of a few corporations—Cleveland was articulating charges widespread in that decade, when industrialism was making its most rapid strides. There was much in the decades following the Civil War to give such complaints plausibility. A brief look at the evidence on distribution of income and the facts of labor protest may give us a hint of what was going on.

Initial Polarization of Social Classes. The decade of the 1880's was a period in which our national income (adjusted to 1950 prices) increased by 73 per cent—its biggest jump upward in all the decades between 1850 and 1950. (Based on 89: p. 40.) But did the rich and the poor share equally in the gains? Usable data on income distribution in the United States before 1900 are scarce. S. Kuznets, the leading expert on the matter, suggests, however, that there is an early phase of industrialization in which income inequality may widen. He places this phase in the United States from about 1840 to 1890, especially after 1870, but warns that this is "conjecture." (192: p. 19)[1] One early study suggests that of the 12½ million families in the country in 1890, 11 million had an income of under $1,200 with an average annual income from labor of $380. (343: p. 128) Industrial employment tended to be irregular. (73: p. 19) Whatever the precise figures, it seems very probable that large numbers of American workers in the late nineteenth century lived below the poverty line even by the standards of that day.

Whatever picture of economic misery one can draw for the working class of the 1880's, it cannot explain the bitter militancy of labor protest in that decade, or the willingness of conservative Presidents to speak on behalf of the underdog. Wages rose in the period. (377; 185: p. 494) Many of the workers described as living in poverty had experienced worse poverty on the farms they fled from (where a series of bad harvests could create suffering to match that caused by urban unemployment). Others had experienced worse poverty in industrial jobs the previous decade. There is no evidence that it was more difficult to rise out of the working class than it had been in earlier decades; and what data we have indicate that the men who in the 1880's were at the top of the heap—the business elite—were in larger proportion from the "lower" or "lower middle" classes than were their counterparts in any generation in history. Forty-three per cent of business leaders born in the period 1820–1849 and listed in the *Dictionary of American Biography* had fathers in these categories. (245: p. 30)

---

[1] The evidence for the initial decades of industrialization in Britain is similarly inconclusive. Economic historian T. S. Ashton, considering "The Standard of Life of the Worker in England, 1790–1830," concludes: "A greater proportion of the people came to benefit from [the factory system] both as producers and as consumers. . . . There were, however, masses of unskilled or poorly skilled workers—seasonally employed agricultural workers and hand-loom weavers in particular—whose incomes were almost wholly absorbed in paying for the bare necessities of life. . . ." While he concedes that the relative position of the worker in the decade 1810–1820 "almost certainly worsened," he implies that a reversal took place after 1821. (144: pp. 158–159, 133–136) Kuznets, on the other hand, ventures the guess that "in England during the first half of the 19th century . . . income inequality may have widened." (192: p. 27)

What pained the working class was the perception that the wealth around them was increasing rapidly (on the farm, poverty had been traditional); that it was visibly powerful (this was the age of the "spoilsmen," when many businessmen in politics took their cues from businessmen in industry without shame); and that the worker's lot did not seem to improve at so great a pace. The insecurities of industrial life described above—the new dependence on the employer, the obsolescence and dilution of skills, the difficult adaptation to factory disciplines, the new insecurity of old age—these added to the unrest. At the same time, the very increase of wealth that had been achieved raised the people's hopes and aspirations. Even if the poor were not getting poorer, even if they had shared equally in the great gains of the decade, economic suffering might have seemed more conspicuous and less justified.

Early Labor Protest. The creation of an industrial labor force everywhere brings forth labor protest. Such protest takes many forms: absenteeism, loafing, passive or active insubordination, sabotage, strikes, political protest movements. As industrialization proceeds, various people contend for control over this labor protest, for the right to channel it and direct it: employers, union leaders, politicians, government administrators, religious leaders, military cliques. (178) The protest is channeled in varied directions: a combination of trade unions and labor parties in Great Britain and the Scandinavian countries; revolutionary syndicalist, Catholic, or Communist organizations in France and Italy; state-managed "labor fronts" in Nazi Germany and the Soviet Union; "business unions" in the U.S.; paternalistic "company unions" or government "captives" in Nehru's India. (120; 264; 293)

Labor protest in the early phases of economic development seems typically to be sporadic and loosely organized (labor movements come and go, showing wild fluctuations in membership). Such protest encounters tenacious employer opposition, which generally involves use of the police power. It is often treated as illegal, sometimes goes underground in the form of the secret society. It is easily shaped to political ends by outside intellectuals who assume early labor leadership. (285; 410) (In nonwestern underdeveloped areas labor movements have generally been meshed with nationalist movements and anti-imperialist agitation.)

America is no exception to these generalizations. Until just before the turn of the century, labor protest was intermittently tame and violent, economic and political; labor organizations were unsteady, easily diverted to elaborate political programs (from greenbackism to the Single Tax, from revolutionary anarchism to Marxian socialism, from Owen's "state guardianship" to producers' and consumers' coöperation). Obstinate employers used private armies, the courts declared unions to be criminal conspiracies (even after the Civil War until use of the injunction gave them a better weapon), and the government broke strikes by use of local, state, and federal troops.

The decade of the 1880's is worth special attention both as an instance typifying labor protest in a free society in the early years of rapid industrialization, and as the turning point which led to the emergence of the contemporary American labor movement and the dominance of collective bargaining as the main form of industrial conflict today. That decade produced a near-revolutionary upheaval.

The 1870's had seen a long and devastating panic. The accelerated tempo of industrialization, depression unemployment, and wage cuts had precipitated a nationwide railway strike accompanied by pitched battles of workers against vigilante committees and militia. Conditions peculiar to the coalfields (after the defeat of the strong anthracite miners' union in 1869) had produced a secret organization known as the Molly Maguires, which disposed of its opposition by terrorism and assassination. But it was in the 1880's, especially during and just after the depression of 1884–1885, that labor protest began to sweep the land. Skilled and unskilled, women and men, native and foreign-born—never before (and not again until the 1930's) had American labor displayed such a rush to organize. The peak of immigration was reached that decade, and streams of newcomers captured the enthusiasm. "Labor organizations assumed the nature of a real class movement. . . . General strikes, sympathetic strikes . . . nationwide political movements became the order of the day." (284: p. 84) Employer associations quickly counteracted with lockouts, blacklists, armed guards, and detectives. When the wave of strikes failed, a consumer boycott movement of epidemic proportions got under way. This was the time of the great upheaval of the Knights of Labor, an inclusive labor organization espousing the ideal of producers' cooperation. The Knights spearheaded a mid-eighties mass movement culminating in an unsuccessful nationwide strike for the eight-hour day. It was the time, too, of the famous bomb explosion on Haymarket Square, which touched off a period of hysteria and police terror in Chicago, and resulted in the unjust conviction and execution of some innocent men. (284: pp. 68–105; 19: II, pp. 220 ff.; 73) The strength of employer opposition and the unwieldiness of the Knights' own organization threw the labor movement into decline. The defeat of Henry George in a spirited campaign for mayor of New York City marked the end of its political reverberations. As the movement broke up, the American Federation of Labor (AFL) was established to organize workers on straight trade union lines, for better wages, hours, and working conditions through collective bargaining—foreshadowing the form in which labor protest was to be cast during the next century. The last gasp of working-class militancy came in the form of the Homestead strike of 1892 (which involved a violent battle between an army of 300 Pinkerton detectives hired by Carnegie and armed strikers, including women and boys, who were finally overcome by the militia), and the great Pullman strike of 1894 which was broken with the aid of federal troops, a federal injunction, and the imprisonment of its leaders.

This period represents an enormous thrust upward from the people of poverty and low status—not again repeated until the early days of the New Deal and provoking much the same militant fear on the part of the wealthy and well-born. The mass movement of the 1880's and the big strikes of the early 1890's were the fruit of the sweeping industrialization that followed the Civil War. They had their historical counterpart in the Luddite movement of 1811–1817 in England (in which workers rioted and smashed the new machines that confronted them), and their contemporary counterpart in the social movements of under-developed lands today. The ferment of labor and radical movements of this period provided impetus to parallel movements for social reform and social welfare (see Chapter XI). The enactment by World War I of factory codes requiring proper ventilation and sanitary appliances, workmen's compensation laws, bars on contract labor, child labor laws, the regulation of prison labor, the creation of a Department of Labor and many state labor bureaus, the achievement of first the ten, then the eight-hour day (railroad workers in 1916, nationwide in 1938)—these reforms must be seen in the context of late nineteenth century agitation, epitomized by the great upheaval of the 1880's.

IV. The Later Impact of Industrialization on Society

IN SHIFTING from the "early" impact of industrialization to the more recent, much of what we shall say will seem contradictory to what has gone before. That is as it should be. Business domination and militantly ineffective labor protest, the polarization of social classes (with poverty and insecurity at the bottom, where peasants make the painful adjustment to the Machine and the new family system it imposes)—against this picture must be put another, perhaps more rosy one. For as the industrialization package is opened wide, and the population becomes accustomed to using its contents, some drastic changes take place.

Along with the dilution and obsolescence of skills, which continue to present problems, go a massive development of new occupations and new skills and a general upgrading of the skill level of all. These changes in specialization are accompanied by a redistribution of income and important changes in stratification. Changing technology and increased specialization continue to push the big organizations to the center of the stage. Labor protest if allowed to express itself, becomes regularized and ordered. All these developments, as we shall see in Chapters V and VIII, are reflected in family life. This chapter aims to describe briefly some of these trends as they seem to be taking shape in midcentury America and as they affect the social problems created by early industrialization.

Specialization and Stratification Effects

While the big corporations and the trusts were piling up wealth and power on one side and the labor and populist movements were massing on the other, an uneasy urban middle class was quietly growing. In time it came to dominate the scene, moving American life increasingly toward a middle mold.

The accompanying chart tells the story of the basic shifts in the occupational composition of the labor force from 1910 to 1956, using roughly comparable data. The drastic decline in farm people—owners, managers, and laborers—is most obvious. But note who were taking their place. While farm owners and managers, small businessmen, and independent professionals—the free enterprisers of the old middle class—were slipping into history, a "new middle class" of white-collar and professional and administrative employees was expanding steadily.

The gains in clerical, sales, and professional occupations have been most rapid—a white-collar mass of schoolteachers, salespeople, and office workers (overwhelmingly urban) comprising the present core. (163; 248) Within the "professional, technical, and kindred" category most of the growth has come from the *newer* professions—engineers, scientists, and a host of semi-professional specialties. In 1870 there were about nine thousand engineers, chemists, designers, and draftsmen; in 1950 there were 741,000—more than 80 times as many. In 1910 there were about 5,000 social workers, in 1950, some 75,000. The classical learned professions (ministry, law, medicine, teaching, music and art, architecture) grew, too, but not so fast—only a sixfold increase since 1870. (163: p. 196) They cover an ever-wider range of specialties, however.

The "semi-professionals" have been growing even faster than the "professionals"; just from 1940 to 1950 they show a 50 per cent increase. (129: p. 115) Laboratory and x-ray technicians, engineering aides, electronic technicians (not only in laboratories but in production and sales)—occupations like these are multiplying. The advance in industrial and medical technology is one reason. Another reason is the allocation to less-trained persons of tasks formerly performed by doctors, dentists, teachers, engineers, and scientists, who are now in short supply—a development that should sound familiar to social work educators who are now proposing junior categories for the less-trained social worker as a means of meeting the shortage. (See Chapter X.)

CHART A. UNITED STATES CIVILIAN LABOR FORCE

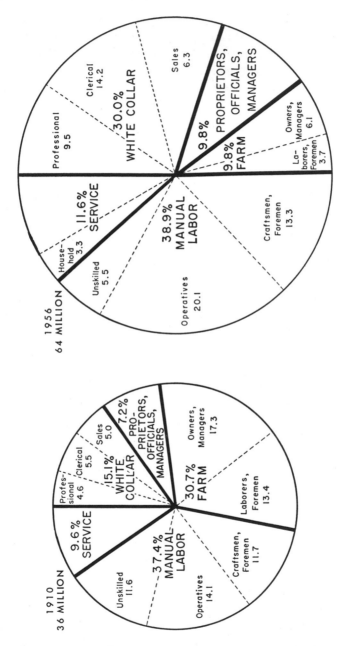

SOURCES: Data for 1910 converted for comparability by Palmer and Miller (129: p. 87). Data for April, 1956, from U.S. Bureau of the Census, *Current Population Reports*, Labor Force Series P-57, No. 166, Table 15. This analysis includes all those at work or seeking work, fourteen years of age and over, and excludes the armed forces.

A second major trend has been the growth in the proportion of "non-farm proprietors, officials, and managers" especially since 1940. This is *not* a resurgence of the small entrepreneur, for he has lost ground to the salaried corporation official. For the most part the growth in managerial ranks reflects the growth of large-scale organization in every sphere of life. Increased specialization brings an emphasis on coordination to achieve a unified product. The more specialists, the more generalists. An army of college-trained administrators, supervisors, trouble-shooters, staff advisers emerges to meet this need.

A third major shift has been within the manual worker category. The "working class" has grown only slightly since 1910 but there has been a dramatic change in its occupational composition. The percentage of nonfarm laborers dropped sharply from 12 per cent of the labor force to 6 per cent. The semi-skilled (generally machine operators) have increased from 14 per cent to 20 per cent; and "skilled craftsmen, foremen, and kindred" showed over-all modest gains, from 11.7 per cent to 13.3 per cent. There is some indication that the skilled will become an ever-larger slice of the working class. The biggest percentage gains here have been made just since 1940—especially among mechanics and repairmen; skilled construction workers and foremen (cement finishers, cranemen, hoistmen, and the like); telephone, telegraph, and power linemen and servicemen; and versatile maintenance men to service the new automatic equipment in our factories. (See "Atoms and Automation: The New Technology" on page 97).

A fourth major trend concerns the types of industries in which people work. In general, advancing industrialization first moves surplus population out of the "primary industries" which extract or produce raw materials—agriculture, mining, lumbering, fishing (which have the largest proportion of heavy, low-skilled, manual jobs) into "secondary industries" (for example, manufacturing, construction) which convert raw materials into finished products —tools, clothing, and so on. Even those left on the farm and in the mines and forests use more machinery and more specialized knowledge. At an advanced stage industrialization then moves people out of both primary and secondary into "tertiary" industries—for example, business repair services (employment relative to population up 217 per cent between 1910 and 1950); public administration (up 163 per cent); finance, real estate, and insurance (up 103 per cent); entertainment and recreation services (up 100 per cent); professional and related services (up 74 per cent); wholesale and retail trade (up 57 per cent). (61; 129: pp. 90–92) Such "tertiary" industries—industries which depend heavily on education and customer or client contact—account for almost half the entire labor force in midcentury America.

While these four trends continue—the boom in white-collar and professional and semi-professional occupations, continued growth among managers and officials, a recent move toward the more skilled manual occupations, and an over-all shift to tertiary industries—there is another development, working in the same direction, which the statistics hide. There is a general upgrading of the whole population: an ever-increasing fund of basic knowledge, occupationally relevant, goes to Everyman. "The youth of today . . . whether raised on a farm or in a city grows up in an atmosphere of machines and literacy." (163: p. 197) Before he even tries for his first job he can typically read and write, drive a car, tinker with motors, use tools. Even the "semi-skilled" job of the Census (which can be learned in a week or so) presupposes many generalized skills we take for granted. In sum: advancing industrialization brings:

1. *Over-all specialization.* This involves not only work simplification (and the dilution and obsolescence of old skills), but a vast demand for new skills, and a net shift which has raised the prestige level of the average occupational position.

2. *A net shift away from hand work and toward brain work and personal contact*—from direct participation in physical production toward services, professional and nonprofessional. Fewer people deal with the material, more deal with symbols and people.

Both developments are reflected in the fact that by 1955 approximately one-sixth of American youth of college age (18 to 24) were going to college.

Growth in the Scale of Organization

These trends in specialization are both cause and consequence of the dominance of the big organization in industry, commerce, labor, politics, the military, religion, education, recreation—in every sphere of life. Large, complex, formal organization is necessary to coordinate the efforts of large numbers of interdependent specialists; and the larger the organization the more necessity for specialization. This is true whether the specialists be clergy in a nationwide church, engineers in a corporation, scientists in a university, workers on an assembly line, or caseworkers in a family agency. Large-scale organizations with specialized personnel are characteristic of all industrial societies.

Specialization makes large-scale organization imperative; the advantages make it advisable. Modern technology costs a great deal; big organizations can pay. The amounts of goods and services this technology yields are large; big distribution channels are needed to get the products to large numbers of consumers. Markets shift; diversification of product made possible by growth and merger can often assure stability in the face of shifts. Large research, engineering, sales, accounting, personnel, advertising staffs can improve efficiency in production and sales—these and other factors converge to give the large corporation the lead in business and commerce.

Thus, in the early years of industrialization small workplaces were still dominant. In the first half of the nineteenth century the average manufacturing concern probably employed fewer than 10 persons. Even in the advanced textile industry, the typical firm employed only about 85 persons in 1849. (166: p. 759) But estimates for 1948 reported in Table 1 below suggest that 75 per cent of all employees in manufacturing (based on firms reporting under Old-Age and Survivors Insurance) were employed in firms with one hundred or more persons on the payroll; *almost half worked in firms numbering five hundred or more employees and 35 per cent in places of one thousand or more.* (422: p. 344)

Compare the figures for nonmanufacturing industries. Big workplaces in public utilities employ about the same proportion of the total employees as do the large manufacturing workplaces (for example, about one-third of the covered employees are in firms with one thousand or more workers). But services, trade, and finance remain the last strongholds of the small entrepreneur. Even here, however, the large organization seems destined to become more important, though this trend has begun so recently

TABLE 1. ESTIMATED PER CENT OF EMPLOYEES IN ESTABLISH-
MENTS COVERED BY OASI ACCORDING TO INDUSTRY
AND SIZE OF REPORTING UNIT FOR THE FIRST QUARTER
OF 1948[a]

Industry	Number of employees	Number of employees in unit			
		50 or over	100 or over	500 or over	1,000 or over
	(In millions)	Per cent in establishments covered by OASI			
Manufacturing	15.2	84	75	48	35
Public utilities	2.6	75	66	44	34
Mining	1.0	77	67	36	19
Finance	1.7	47	37	17	11
Retail trade	6.7	34	26	14	10
Contract construction	2.0	39	27	8	4
Wholesale trade	2.8	40	25	7	3
Service industries	3.5	31	20	5	2

[a] "Establishment" or "unit" or "concern" refers to a workplace or group of workplaces of the same firm (employer) engaged in the same activity and located in the same area. In 1948 OASI covered almost all private nonagricultural employers except railroads and nonprofit organizations (religious, educational, charitable).

SOURCE: Based on Woytinsky, W. S., and others, *Employment and Wages in the United States* (422: Appendix, Table 74).

and the data are so scanty that we cannot be sure. (Cf. 422: pp. 344–345.) Of course, big firm "dominance" is more than a matter of the proportion of total employees working in big places; it is also a matter of financial control, leadership in methods of operating, pricing, labor relations, and so on. Dominance may be exercised by big business even where many small firms come and go.

However acute our nostalgia for the small free enterprises and the tiny workshop, they are slowly passing from the center of the stage—surely in manufacturing, less surely in other industries. And the history of "trust busting" suggests that Bigness will withstand all onslaughts. As Theodore Roosevelt said to Congress in

1902: ". . . these big aggregations are an inevitable development of modern industrialism, and the effort to destroy them would be futile unless accomplished in ways that would work the utmost mischief to the entire body politic." (Quoted in 150: p. 226.) No President of this century has even proposed to return to the era of small enterprise, though several have let their hearts bleed in public for its passing.[1]

Large, complex organizations take on a characteristic form. They are hierarchical; they divide work and coordinate people by formal, impersonal rule, and so on. The significance of this bureaucratic form for the work of the social agency, for the very existence of a profession of social work, is spelled out in Part III, so discussion of it will be held until then.

Atoms and Automation: The New Technology

Increasing specialization and the emergence of a new middle class, the increasing importance of large, bureaucratically organized workplaces—these are trends likely to speed up with the widespread industrial application of atomic energy and "automation." It is impossible here to describe the nature of this technology; but it is possible to report what seems to be the consensus on the direction of its impact on occupational composition and size of organization.

The industrial revolution of the eighteenth and nineteenth centuries was based on new forms and applications of *power*—the substitution in a factory system of steam and then electricity for water, men, and animals. (226: pp. 318 ff.) There is little reason

---

[1] Governments and managers in the underdeveloped areas have often initiated small "familistic" enterprises in rural areas either to gain the benefits of industrialization without disruption of traditional patterns of family and village life or to recruit labor more effectively. The record of these experiences is inconclusive, but it does suggest that small-scale industry based on traditional social relations may not yield the material benefits of industrialization because the necessary organizational forms and motives do not develop. Wilbert Moore names three consequences of a reliance on light small-scale industry: (1) Some of the traditional values are preserved but this leads to inflexibility of location and skill, thus blocking further adoption of industrial technology; (2) small cottage and domestic industries tend to "sweat" their workers, which is resented by both the workers and their kin who partially subsidize them; (3) the new protective paternalism does not foster the independent capacity of workers. What is initially gained in easy recruitment may be lost in the block to further economic development, and the frustration of hopes for rising living standards. (256: pp. 31–34) This does not imply, however, that such enterprises cannot serve as an opening wedge to eventual industrialization.

to believe that a new form of (eventually cheap) power, atom electricity, will have any different effect on the organization of work from that of the continued use of electric power produced with other fuels. It intensifies the already large demand for some types and teams of engineers and scientists; and it puts a premium again on large capital outlays, thereby accentuating the need for large-scale organization. Except in rare cases it is unlikely by itself to affect plant location. (404: pp. 74–75)

"Automation" appears to be more of a departure from established ways. Heralded as the Second Industrial Revolution, it transfers the *control* function from human beings to automatic devices.[1] Three basic technological developments are covered by the word "automation." First is *integration*—the linking together of conventionally separate manufacturing operations into lines of continuous production through which the product moves untouched by human hands. This is widely used in metal-working industries; some auto engines are being made this way now. Second is the use of *feedback control* devices or servo-mechanisms which allow individual operations to be performed with no need for human control—as with the living-room thermostat or an automatic pilot. This has been used extensively in the petroleum and chemical processing industries since the 1930's. The third development is *computer technology*—the use of general- and special-purpose computing devices capable of recording, storing, and processing complex information. The new IBM machines and the famous UNIVAC are examples. Computers can be used to mechanize traditional office operations in banks, insurance companies, payroll departments—any place where routine and repetitive clerical work is done on a large scale. (169: pp. 177 ff.) All three technologies can be used in one workplace—giving us a rather close approximation to the "push-button factory" we have been hearing about.

These changes are coming—fast in some industries and companies, slow in others, but probably never in many. The long-

---

[1] For this discussion we are indebted to George B. Baldwin and George P. Schultz, "Automation: A New Dimension to Old Problems" (16); and to the very fruitful Congressional Hearings of 1955, *Automation and Technological Change* (367).

run effects are difficult to guess. But it is not hard to see the general direction of the immediate impact. Again we find intensification of previous trends. First, there is the favorable position of the large and rich concern. The equipment, at least for now, is costly to make and costly to run, and efficiency demands full-time operation. It is also so productive that it requires large marketing apparatus, advertising budgets, and the like to dispose of its vast output. The large firm obviously has the edge. Although the number of employees in some of the giants may decline somewhat, and the small workplace may still retain an advantage in flexibility, it seems likely on balance that automation will speed up the trend toward bigness. (367: pp. 25, 33–39, 95, 152, 269, 417, 615) Second, there is the upgrading of skills required. Most of the new jobs will be more challenging; most will require higher, or at least different, skills. Finally, there is the continued dilution and obsolescence of old skills and a consequent shifting around of jobs and workers. The social problems are easy enough to label, too: technological unemployment, increased leisure.

The capacities, the expense, and the complexity of this new equipment imply several things. In the factory: fewer workers handling materials or doing routine machine jobs (there will be improved working conditions, including more safety, and less heavy, dirty work); an increased proportion of engineers and very skilled maintenance men; an increased ratio of managers and supervisors to employees (jobs aimed at preserving the expensive equipment, and keeping the costly process going); a new accent on personal responsibility and conceptual skills—"ability to learn" more than ability to do. In the community: the spread of automation (especially its "integration aspects") may also accentuate the already high residential mobility of American workers. If automation gives one company in an industry a competitive advantage, it will hasten decisions of other companies to abandon old equipment and/or expand operations into new plants. These new plants are often located in outlying districts. The "suburbanization of industry," going forward anyway without automation, may thereby be speeded up, reinforcing the mobility of labor. There is a chance, too, that automation, coupled with atomic power, will make industry more mobile, resulting in a more frequent occurrence of the boomtown-ghosttown cycle. These trends hold important implications for social work in general and family-serving and community planning agencies in particular (see Chapter VIII).

The Impact on Size and Distribution of Income

There is no doubt that the changes in technical and social organization mentioned above have brought enormous increases in the efficiency of the American economy. Continued technological advance and the changes in specialization and size of organization that go with it have made possible rapid increases in living standards and, more recently, an increased equality in income distribution.

The swelling size of the American income pie is becoming legendary. While the national population tripled between 1880 and 1950, private national income grew ninefold—in 1950 prices, from $23.8 to $217.3. (89: pp. 40, 51) Total purchasing power of families and unrelated individuals almost doubled between 1935 and 1950. (243: p. 109)

Have all segments shared in these tremendous gains? The answer is "yes." Have the poorer segments been getting a larger slice of the pie than before and the rich a smaller slice? The answer is a qualified "yes." The evidence is not conclusive (adequate pre-1900 data are scarce); but the weight of it suggests that the relative distribution of income in the United States, as well as England and Germany, has tended to equalize as industrialization advanced. In fact, this may be a universal aspect of mature industrialization. (192: p. 27)

This is not to deny that the poor are always with us. Poorness is always a relative matter and some portion of the population will always be unable to provide for itself income sufficient to escape the label. Nor does it mean that the very rich are doomed to extinction. But the data do indicate that an increasing slice of the total growing national income is going to the great middle range of American families, and a decreasing proportion to the top brackets. These facts are worth examining in detail, not only because they point to the economic underpinnings of the new middle class, but also because they suggest the changing character of social welfare clientele.

Data bearing on three questions will help to portray the drift toward equality: (1) What proportion of all the families and unattached individuals, persons not living with relatives, fall in different income brackets in different years? (2) How fast does the purchasing power of different strata go up? (3) What share of the national income do the very richest families take?

First, look at the decline in the proportion of families and unattached individuals in the lower brackets between 1935 and 1955. Table 2 shows that more than three-fourths fell below $2,000 in

TABLE 2. PERCENTAGE DISTRIBUTION OF FAMILIES AND UN-
ATTACHED INDIVIDUALS ACCORDING TO FAMILY PER-
SONAL INCOME FOR THE UNITED STATES IN SELECTED
YEARS

Family personal income (not adjusted for price changes)	1935-36	1941	1944	1950	1954	1955
(In dollars)			Per cent			
Under 1,000	43.5	29.0	10.7	7.6	6.1	..
1,000 to 1,999	34.2	29.9	19.8	15.1	10.6	..
2,000 to 2,999	13.1	22.3	21.4	16.5	12.3	..
3,000 to 4,999	6.1	13.8	30.0	31.8	29.2	..
5,000 to 7,499	1.6	2.8	11.7	17.5	24.9	..
7,500 to 9,999	0.6	0.9	3.4	5.9	9.6	..
10,000 and over	0.9	1.3	3.0	5.6	7.3	..
Total	100.0	100.0	100.0	100.0	100.0	100.0
Mean family personal income (adjusted to 1950 dollars)	2,937	3,664	4,650	4,461	4,814	4,968

SOURCES: Data for 1950 and earlier are estimates developed from federal income tax returns, and sample surveys of the Federal Reserve Board and the Census Bureau. They appear in Goldsmith, Selma, and others, "Size Distribution of Income Since the Mid-Thirties," *Review of Economics and Statistics*, vol. 36, February, 1954, pp. 3–4. The 1954 and 1955 data are from Goldsmith, "Income Distribution in the United States, 1952–1955," *Survey of Current Business*, vol. 36, June, 1956, pp. 10, 12. Such data tend to underestimate actual income. Following Goldsmith's procedure, we adjusted the averages for 1954 and 1955 to 1950 dollars with the implicit price deflators for gross national product, personal consumption expenditures series, as used in the national income accounts. "Family personal income" includes monetary income from all sources, as well as certain nonmonetary items such as wages in kind, the value of food and fuel produced and consumed on farms, etc. Data for 1941 and subsequent years represent income for the calendar year; data for 1935–1936 represent an average of the estimates for calendar years 1935 and 1936.

1935 and 1936; only about one-sixth in 1954. Or consider the size of a loosely defined middle bracket: in 1935 and 1936 only about one in fifty of all families and unattached individuals had incomes between $5,000 and $9,999; in 1954 more than one in three had such incomes.

Note, however, that there are short-run variations on this theme of income equalization; and, more important, the percentages in Table 2 do not take account of changes in cost-of-living. Thus, a closer look shows that almost all the change in income distribution occurred before and during World War II. When dollar amounts are adjusted for price changes, the average family's real income did not move much in the decade after the war; in fact, from 1944 to 1950 there was actually a slight decrease in the purchasing power (in 1950 dollars) of the average family—from $4,650 to $4,461.

Whatever the short-run shifts, and despite price changes, there is no mistaking the main drift toward equality. Not only is the proportion of the population who get into middle brackets going up, but also the gap between high-paid and low-paid occupations is narrowing. Even within occupations, the trend toward equality is apparent: from 1940 to 1950 Miller found "a significant narrowing of the income gap between high-paid and low-paid workers within occupations"—and this was *not* confined to production workers or unionized sectors. (243: pp. 5, 118–119) Increases in real purchasing power have been widespread; they have affected most occupations and industries.

Changes in the relative position of rich and poor are best revealed by data on whose purchasing power has improved the most. If all families and single persons are divided into five numerically equal groups, the increase in real income for each indicates gains most favorable to the middle three fifths, and especially for the lowest of these three. The lowest of the five fifths benefited less (just held its own relative to the over-all national increase), but the top group actually lost purchasing power relative to the national trend. The swelling slice served to the third and fourth strata reflects the upsurge of lower-paid people and the decline of lower-paid jobs. Wages from 1939 to 1949 rose more rapidly in manufacturing (traditionally low paid) than in finance, transportation, and communication; meanwhile, the importance of low-paid, low-regarded domestic service has diminished. These seem to be the inevitable consequences of high levels of employment. The boom in the middle is also due to an increase in the number of earners per family. This multiple-

TABLE 3. QUINTILE DISTRIBUTION OF PER CENT INCREASE IN REAL PURCHASING POWER OF FAMILIES AND SINGLE PERSONS FOR 1935-36 TO 1948

Group	Per cent increase
Top fifth	41
Second fifth	70
Third fifth	87
Fourth fifth	101
Lowest fifth	59
National total	59

SOURCE: *Low Income Families and Economic Stability*, Appendix G, Table G-1 (adapted), p. 138. Government Printing Office, Washington, 1950.

earner pattern has taken hold more firmly among middle and lower-middle income families, thereby increasing their relative share of income. (243: pp. 121–122)

A similar picture is evident if we compare data of different years and consider the share of the total economic pie going to rich and poor. Taking 1929 and an average of 1944, 1946, 1947, and 1950, Kuznets (192: p. 4) found that the share of the lowest 40 per cent of families rose from 13½ to 18 per cent of the national income, whereas that of the top 20 per cent dropped from 55 to 44 per cent and that of the top 5 per cent from 31 to 20 per cent.

These are pretax incomes. The over-all effect of the tax structure on the trend toward income equality is a difficult question on which economists disagree. If the tax structure is on the whole *progressive* (the higher the income, the larger the percentage taken in taxes), the trend toward equalization would be even greater than that described. If on the whole the tax structure is *regressive*

(the poor taxed proportionately more than the rich), then equalization might be less. There is some evidence to support the following judgment. Taking progressive taxes like the income tax,
together with regressive taxes like federal excise and state sales
taxes, the whole structure does not become highly progressive
until incomes rise roughly beyond $7,500 (in 1948 dollars). For
people with income below that, the tax structure has no over-all
income equalization impact. (259; cf. 192.)[1]

The remarkable thing about the rich getting (relatively) poorer
and the poor getting (relatively) richer is that nobody loses.
Each decade there is so much more for all that the standard of
living of every stratum moves up. The average gain per year in
per capita real income in the eighty years before 1950 has been
1.9 per cent. If this continues for the next seven or eight decades,
our grandchildren or great-grandchildren may enjoy an average
family income (in 1953 dollars) of $25,000 per year. (342:
pp. 18–19)

Utopian prophecy based on past trends is both more shaky and
less useful than the description of the present situation to which
the social worker must orient himself. Here, the composition and
income level of the lower strata of the population are worth
special note. Even though social welfare is seen less and less as
a mere emergency activity for the destitute (see Chapter VIII),
the lower strata of the population are still the main source of need
and many services are aimed at easing their lot (see Chapter
VII).

That the percentage of poverty-stricken people has dropped in
recent decades is indisputable. Hazel Kyrk estimates that in 1901

---

[1] A second caution is in order: national income definitions exclude expense
accounts and capital gains. Both are important chunks of top-bracket incomes. The
first is not taxed at all, though it clearly becomes part of the standard of life of high-
level business, professional, and sales people. The second is taxed at a lower rate than
ordinary income—and in effect offers a real tax advantage for those who have large
sums available to invest in real estate, stocks, etc., which may yield both income
now and a lightly taxed capital gain later. The rich can even avoid a capital gains
tax—simply by retaining their investments until death, at which time their offspring
may enjoy a more advantageous tax basis. The shift of the "tycoon" from Wall
Street to Texas dramatizes still another tax advantage for the rich—the oil and gas
depletion deduction. All things considered, though, these tax facts probably do not
reverse the direction of change; they merely raise the question, "How *much* poorer
are the rich becoming (relatively)?"

at least 40 per cent of the families of wage-earners and clerical workers were trying to live on a "less than adequate" income. She judges "less than adequate" for that year to be less than $700 for a two-child family. (194: p. 210) During the depression of the 1930's, this group had perhaps contracted to the "one-third of the nation" Franklin D. Roosevelt found "ill-housed, ill-clothed, ill-fed." By 1950, taking account of price changes, Kyrk's 1901 standard could be maintained by an average-size urban, wage-earner's family of 3.4 persons for $1,700—a level below which less than 10 per cent of such families lived. (271) This ignores, of course, our vastly changed ideas of what "adequate" is, but it does show roughly that the objective conditions of the poor have improved.

Income distribution will affect the demand for, and character of, social welfare services. So will the social composition of the underprivileged groups that cannot provide for themselves the minimum level of welfare society considers essential. Some such groups have in recent decades almost disappeared (state ward orphans, for instance). The chronically unemployed are less prominent. Long-term unemployment of the magnitude experienced in the 1930's, which could reverse the trend toward income equality, is unlikely. No economist and few politicians would claim we know all there is to know about the business cycle. But we know more than we did in the 1930's. The list of anti-depression weapons available to an alert administration today is long (from variable taxes to actions of the Federal Reserve System, from unemployment compensation to deficit spending)—as long as the list of groups who create a formidable demand that depression be avoided.

The social composition of the deprived or dependent people has changed—because of the advance of industrialism and urbanism and the choking off of immigration. A half-century ago, the typical low-income family was likely to look like this: large farm family, low education, native or foreign-born, white or Negro; or large urban family, low education, white, foreign-born (southern or eastern Europe). Often one parent was dead or permanently disabled. Occupations were low in status and low in pay. For the newcomer to the city and factory, problems of poverty were complicated by language barriers and value conflicts (see Chapter III).

Today, according to a report by the congressional Subcommittee on Low-Income Families, poor families (urban consumer units with incomes below $2,000) are still characterized by low education. A large portion of the heads of these families, as before, are unemployed, permanently disabled, or retired. The occupations of the employed family heads are still at the bottom (59 per cent were laborers, service workers, and operatives in 1954). (368: pp. 11, 32)

In several respects, the poor family is now a different type of unit, however. It is likely to be a native-born, small family. Most poor families are urban or nonfarm (although about one-third are farm families, while all farm families comprise only about one-tenth of the nation's total). In 1954 about one in three of the low-income families was headed by a person over 65 years old; nationally fewer than one in seven of all families was so headed. Fifteen to 20 per cent of the poor families were headed by Negroes; nationally the figure was less than 10 per cent. (368: pp. 10, 32) Earlier data (370: pp. 5, 13) show that in 1948, about one in four of these low-income families was headed by a woman, who in many instances did not work. Although they still tend to be newcomers, the pain of transition from farms to factory and city (see Chapter III) is probably not so great; save for the stream of Puerto Rican, Mexican, and French Canadian immigrants, language and cultural barriers for our midcentury poor are less formidable.

Social Mobility and Labor Protest

In the context of America's commitment to freedom of speech and association, these shifts in specialization, scale of organization, and income size and distribution have reshaped labor protest. The labor movement today is not the amorphous, unsteady, anti-capitalist upsurge of the 1880's. As late as the 1930's, workers in Flint, Michigan, with almost revolutionary fervor, seized control of corporate property in the famous sit-down strikes. Today some of those same workers—or their sons—peacefully negotiate contracts with employers, serve on Community Welfare Council Boards, run for municipal office (and occasionally win), and live the modestly comfortable middle-class life of trade union officials. The spontaneous protest movements of yesterday have become the "business unions" of today, large stable organizations sanctioned in contracts and the law (though somewhat weakened by the Taft-Hartley Act). Labor today has limited goals: better wages, shorter hours, and improved conditions of employment. Its means are mainly economic: the establishment of collective bargaining agreements enforced in part by arbitration of grievances. Occasional legal strikes over the terms of the agreement occur, but these have become the accepted alternative to state control of labor relations. The losses are far less than those due to unemployment or illness; in the industrialized societies of the free world industrial disputes result in an average loss of about one-half man-day per year for all nonagricultural employees. (175: p. 232) Far from representing a revolutionary upsurge, American strikes probably function in part to give disaffected workers a chance to "blow off steam" in relatively harmless ways.[1]

The membership of American labor organizations is only about a third of all nonagricultural employees, compared with more than half in England, and more than two-thirds in Sweden. American labor is conservative. Compared to European labor it shows a low degree of "class consciousness." Its leaders have become integrated into the power and status structure of a private-enterprise economy and a pressure-group polity. These characteristics of American labor can be explained in large part by the impact of the trends described above on the structure of opportunity.

[1] It has been observed that the free world over, whatever the cultural setting—capitalist, socialist, or whatnot—the incidence of strikes is highest in industries which "(1) segregate large numbers of persons who (2) have relatively unpleasant jobs" (177: p. 196)—among workers who are isolated and alienated from the values of the dominant community. It is relevant, too, that in America and the Scandinavian countries the syndicalist ideology of "workers' control" gained its most solid organizational expression among the same isolated groups—seamen, longshoremen, miners, loggers, lumbermen, and miscellaneous migratory workers (who constituted in the United States the hard core of the radical IWW).

If on the whole the rich were getting richer and the poor, poorer; if occupations were becoming more manual and less skilled; if depressions were frequent and severe; if, in short, the opportunity to rise in the social and economic scale were declining while mass aspirations rose, we might expect American labor to swing in a politically class-conscious direction. The evidence, as we have seen, suggests just the opposite.

Occupational and income changes have brought a vast heterogeneity to the labor force. This heterogeneity is epitomized by the growing middle layers of American society—the new middle class of white-collar and professional people, the increasingly skilled upper crust of manual workers. Advanced specialization has made for finer distinctions of status and a multiplication of occupational worlds. Instead of two armies massed on an industrial battle field—"labor" on one side, "capital" on the other— we have immense variation in interest and attitude within the ranks of each, and a consequent decline in the solidarity of each. (257: pp. 221 ff.) On the management side, the complexity of internal cleavages follows the increased complexity of organization—with increased bargaining over power and budget, between staff advisers of specialized knowledge and power-conscious executives, between levels of authority, or on the same level of authority between rival advisers and rival supervisors. While it is still useful to distinguish between the managers and the managed, the lines are becoming a bit blurred. On the labor side, even unionized workers divide on age, sex, seniority, and skill lines, not to mention the divisions by religion, nationality, and race. Meanwhile, the upper layer of the working class, composed of men of high skill, is not only becoming more numerous, but its members are paid more than the lower white-collar workers, and there are some indications that they are adopting the same life style, and acquiring the same prestige. The lines between working class and middle class, too, become blurred.

The new heterogeneity plus the rapidity of change in occupational and income structure have made America the land of opportunity if it never was before. This does not mean that it is easy for the son of a laborer to rise to the top of a great corporation—or even that it is easier than it used to be. (The evidence on social origins of the business elite is contradictory and inconclusive; it shows mainly that it never *has* been frequent for working-class sons to become executives: 244; 340; 245; 268; 390). It *does* mean that the chances of a laborer's or farmer's or small businessman's son entering an occupation different from his father's are very great, and so are the chances that the new occupation will have higher prestige and yield better income. It also means that within his worklife the chances for change are many. These two kinds of mobility—intergenerational and worklife—show up most often in moves like these: the poor farmer (or his son) becomes a semi-skilled factory worker; the unskilled laborer (or his son) becomes a semi-skilled or skilled worker or even moves to lower white-collar work; the manual worker (or his son) sets up a small business, or becomes a salesman; the junior executive becomes the senior executive; the son of a small businessman or upper white-collar worker (bookkeeper, accountant, radio announcer) becomes a professional, administrator, or executive. Sometimes the move is down, not up.

In other words, the studies of social mobility in the U.S. suggest that: the rate of social mobility is high; the chance to get ahead, to move out of the lower strata, has improved in this century, largely because of changes in the occupational structure and the trend toward income equality; the range of movement, however, is limited; movement *across* the blue collar-white collar divide is less frequent than mobility *within* the two broad classes; there is a smaller downward movement worth noting. (305; 215; 24) Because work in modern society demands greater abilities, education is becoming the main barrier to opportunity; but it is a barrier through which more and more people pass. Since the labor struggles of the 1880's, the number of students in schools of higher education has increased about 17 times (while population increased only about two and a half times). About one in six of college age youth (18 to 24) now get to college. About 80 per cent of all youth enter high school and about 55 per cent graduate. (421: p. 170) Our hunch is that similarly high rates of mobility and a similar accent on education as a means to it may be ex-

pected as industrialization advances in Europe and in the
U.S.S.R.[1]

The existence of much opportunity to get ahead and the even
more effective *belief* in its existence, then, account in large measure for the absence of a class-conscious labor movement. The
American trade union has itself helped to keep this class structure
fluid. Unions challenge management authority in the workplace;
they share and shape decisions affecting workers; outside the
plant, in community affairs and sometimes in the national
political arena as well, they begin to offset the power of the business elite. Together with other organized groups—occupational,
religious, ethnic, veteran, farm—unions have brought about a
modest diffusion of the power which in the early decades of
industrialization was unmistakably in the hands of wealthy owners and managers of large corporations. (139; 220; 40; 392)

The Other Side: A Cautionary Conclusion

The impact of advanced industrialization on society as described above suggests that the continuing indictment of the
industrial revolution was anachronistic; in midcentury America
the old complaints were rapidly becoming irrelevant. This, we
think, is the essential truth. But it is important to put this picture
in perspective, or some live social issues will be by-passed.

Skill levels are being upgraded; the new middle class is growing. But the unskilled laborer (whose work is likely to be heavy,
dirty, and despised) and the semi-skilled machine operator
(whose work tends to be routine, repetitive, and often machine-
paced and wholly ungratifying) together make the largest category in the labor force (one in four of all those at work are semi-
skilled or unskilled manual workers). Not only do many such
workers approximate the alienated machine slave of the classic

[1] Some students even suggest that Britain, France, Germany, and Denmark
already have rates of mobility (between manual and nonmanual occupations) close
to that of America. (216; 213) It seems doubtful, however, that meaningful comparisons can be made with available data. These countries vary greatly in the scale
of organization, the ratio of managers to managed, and the degree of urbanization.
This makes for sharp contrasts in occupational structure and job classifications. The
meaning of movement from manual to white collar becomes quite ambiguous as a
characterization of social mobility in the society.

indictment (see Chapter I), but they face considerable obstacles to the upward escape. Many studies show that occupational inheritance is highest at the extremes of the prestige ladder: sons of the unskilled laborers are often stuck at the bottom; sons of professionals have more chance of staying at the top. (For example, see 305.)[1] Small wonder that investigators report sharp disaffection and class-conscious political attitudes among some factory workers—the feeling that work is oppressive and meaningless; that "success" is a matter of luck, pull, having the right connections; that a worker will be a worker for life; that management's interests and aims and power in the community are illegitimate. (57; 168; 224; 189)[2] As we have said, we think the alienated automaton is a passing figure; but in 1957 he is still with us—a minority to think about.

So, too, with the big organizations.

The economies of large size and of mechanization lead to a lush standard of living. But size creates problems of its own— problems in human relations in both factory and office. As the corner grocer falls before the chain store and the stationer before the department store, as the country doctor gives way to the big hospital or the clinic, as office work becomes standardized and simplified, an increasing number of white-collar workers, profes-

---

[1] Even in the rapidly expanding economy of Oakland, California, it was found that 68 per cent of the sons (age 31 and over) of white-collar (i.e., nonmanual) fathers had white-collar jobs in 1949 while only 47 per cent of the sons of manual workers had such jobs. The manual workers had spent 80 per cent of their careers in manual jobs. (24: p. 252; 214; p. 373) In the contracting economies of many New England textile towns, cultural blocks to mobility are far more serious; the chances of a working-class boy crossing into a white-collar or professional job are probably slimmer than the Oakland study shows.

[2] Thwarted mobility aspirations may lead to quite different adjustments, however. Chinoy (59) reports the reactions of a group of auto workers (mostly Census "semi-skilled") to the disparity between the promises of the American Creed and the realities of their own experience. He suggests that these workers have redefined "getting ahead": they scale down their ambitions to small goals obtainable in the shop; they include security and material possessions in the concept of "getting ahead"; they focus their larger out-of-shop ambitions on their children, although many of them verbally cherish the ambition of going into business for themselves someday. (Cf. 386.) Findings of the 1953 Detroit Area Study also point to the projection of ambitions onto the children. A cross-section of mothers were asked to guess their children's occupational future, with a rough choice between hand and head occupations. Seventy-seven per cent said their children would have office jobs, only 13 per cent said factory jobs—this in a population of parents in which 65 per cent of the fathers and 69 per cent of the grandfathers have blue-collar jobs. (242; 86)

sionals, and businessmen will find themselves embedded in a tall hierarchy, taking orders from others, on a factory-like production line. C. Wright Mills, who laments this tendency in *White Collar*, suggests that "management effort to create job enthusiasm reflects the unhappy unwillingness of employees to work spontaneously at their routinized tasks." He speaks of a " 'status proletarianization' of white-collar strata," and observes that men "must be serious and steady about something that does not mean anything to them. . . . The work itself . . . offers little chance for external prestige claims and internal self-esteem." (248: pp. 233, 249, 236, 243) We believe that with further automation in the office, with continued suburbanization of shopping, Mills' white-collar worlds—Macy's department store, the incompletely mechanized mail-order house, the huge typing pool, the places where piles of people shuffle paper, sort cards, wrap packages, take inventory, tap typewriters—may quickly turn out to be old-fashioned. But in the mid-fifties they are, we concede, still with us—albeit as models of the past.

Again, automation means great gains in efficiency and the demand for new skills. But not enough is known about man's adjustment to the possible strains of the new and more exacting jobs. And what about those whose old jobs are wiped out? A vast retraining program will be necessary if a large slice of the labor force is not to be abandoned. Some less-privileged workers may suffer severely unless close attention is paid to their relocation. For example, low seniority Negroes and southern whites who have just recently found a semi-skilled foothold in industry may find themselves squeezed out. Retraining and upgrading for many of them will be either difficult or costly, and their alternatives bleak—a return to subsistence farming or low-paid jobs as servants, dishwashers, night watchmen, common laborers. And even here opportunity is declining.

The familiar insistence on security has already sharpened at every level in the working class; and the old demand that the benefits be distributed in shorter hours and higher pay will become more cogent than ever. The recent prominence in labor-management agreements of wage and work guarantees, the repercussions in unemployment compensation laws—these already herald an intensified quest for security.

Incomes have risen and equalization seems to be the drift. But income distribution statistics hide some persistent inequalities nowhere justified in the American Creed. For instance, seldom can a Negro acquire land or housing on the same terms and in the same places as a white person. He may have the same money income as the white, but as anyone who has seen the ghettos of our cities knows, the Negro will have to pay more for housing and his living conditions will be far worse.

Gains have been made toward equal opportunity for all in employment, but job discrimination is still widespread. In the North and West, as well as the South, the nonwhite college graduate earns less on the average than the white who did not finish high school. (243: p. 4) College graduate or not, Negroes are generally confined to less desirable jobs.

Education, too, is more widely distributed, but in 1953 a youngster in the smartest one per cent of the population who was also in the top fifth of his high school class had about a four in ten chance of not entering college. (421: p. 316) Blocks to both motivation and opportunity played a part.

For the first time in this century more Americans own rather than rent their own homes; the middle-class package—the car, the electric stove and refrigerator, the washing machine and dryer, the deep freeze—is becoming widely distributed; leisure has come to all. But the whole structure is sustained by a heavy bet on the future—long-term mortgages for the home, the installment plan for the package. As for leisure, in millions of homes it takes two jobs and often many overtime hours (for which workers are generally eager) to put the family in the middle bracket. Under these circumstances the achievement in income equality is precarious, for even a mild recession can quickly reverse the trend (as the overtime hours and then one or two of the family jobs disappear).[1] And in a depression—well, the consequences are

---

[1] Also, for a small portion of the population—high status professionals, executives, and politicians—"leisure" so merges with "work" that there may be no more time spent in aimless play than there was a century ago.

obvious. The depression-avoidance weapons we mentioned above have not yet had a real test.

As for labor and the modest diffusion of power that has taken place since the turn of the century, a considerable concentration of power remains (for example, see 160; 228; and 246)—affecting, if nothing else, the size and character of welfare expenditures (see Chapter VIII).

For the optimist who leans toward the long view, all these qualifications may seem like minor eddies in a swift, straight stream—problems destined for quick and easy solution as industrialization flows on. For the skeptic concerned with the here and now they are the main current to watch. We believe that two things that continuing industrialization surely brings—increases in wealth and high levels of mass aspiration—will combine to create the impetus for solution of these problems. Our belief is based on two large and basic assumptions: (1) general nuclear war will be avoided; (2) major economic depressions will be avoided. Without relative peace in the atomic era, without continued high levels of employment, all bets are off.

V. Industrialism, Urbanism, and Integration: More on the Later Impact

URBANIZATION is not identical with industrialization, and cities were known long before modern industry emerged. But every highly industrialized society is also highly urbanized. The widespread dominance of the city would not be possible without the widespread use of high energy technology; city growth and industrial growth are intimately related.

An ever-larger proportion of the world's people spend at least some of their lives in the city. (About two in three Americans now live in urban areas.) And those who do not, more and more come under the influence of the city. We have purposely avoided the question of urbanism until we had described the impact of industrialization, for much that has been attributed to the crowding of many people in small spaces (cities) is due to the rise of the factory system and the changes in technology, specialization, stratification, socialization, and integration which that system symbolizes. But the city does have an independent causal effect on social relations and social problems—especially in shaping "social integration," one of the universal conditions for societal survival mentioned in the Appendix.

This chapter will discuss urbanism in the context of the question of integration—the number, kinds, strength, and stability of bonds that unite people. Special attention will be given to the impact of the city on intimate social relations, since this is so often seen as the source of an alleged breakdown in family and community life. Later, in Chapter IX, we will discuss a specific social problem, juvenile delinquency, in order to illustrate the impact of both industry and the city on one of many types of deviant behavior which concern the human relations professions.

"City," like "society," is a difficult concept to grasp. The facts to which it refers are many and complex. This is why the modern city has struck its observers in such wondrously varied ways. The city has been seen:

> As a feast—a place of novelty and excitement, of fashion and style, of ideas and artifacts, a center of sumptuous consumption, of diversity and delight.

> As a den of iniquity—a place where vice and crime abound; and political corruption rides high.

> As a fountainhead of service—a place where health and wealth, the arts and sciences, the educational and welfare services reach their highest levels.

> As a center of loneliness—a place where man is depersonalized, anonymous, alone, rootless, afraid, uniquely separated from his fellow men.

The city is all of these and more. Like industrialism, urbanism, too, has had its indictment and defense, its detractors and enthusiasts. And as in the case of industrialism, there is truth in all of these characterizations—depending upon the time and place, and upon the meaning given the terms.

The best way to proceed, for our purposes, is to begin with the classic picture of the city given by urban sociologists, stating it in its sharpest but most developed form, and then to suggest some modifications of this picture made necessary by recent changes in city life—changes reflected in recent social research exploring that life.

Urbanism as a Way of Life: A Traditional View

Urban sociologists begin with the demographic uniqueness of the city—the size, density, and heterogeneity of population. They begin with the fact that more and more people live in or orient themselves toward communities with large and dense populations having varied social characteristics (varied incomes and occupations, but also races, ethnic groups, and so on). Then they ask the question, "What do size, density, and heterogeneity of population do to social relations?" Their answers tend to follow these lines:[1]

1. *Secondary contact spreads.* Social relations tend to become impersonal, utilitarian, superficial, transitory. "Primary relations"—those which are personal, intimate, and inclusive (involve the "whole person"), which seem to the participants to be voluntary and spontaneous, and which involve a complete and mutual identity of ends (including the relationship itself as an end)—these give way to "secondary relations," which are impersonal, segmental, calculated, and embrace only a partial identity of ends.

   In the city there is constant association with strangers. Great mobility necessitates many contacts. One cannot get to know people. One must instead judge them by superficial appearances, by how they look and speak. This is not only necessary; it may even be desirable. Imagine what life would be like if you had to get to know everyone with whom you have to come in contact.

   Individuals in the city tend to meet on a rational, utilitarian basis; they view each other as means to impersonal ends. This can be attributed to the dominance of a money economy, where each thing and each person has a price. The dominance of the market is reflected in the mental life of people. Held together by a money nexus, the urban world runs by the clock—everything is calculated on a time-

[1] The following traditional picture of urbanism is based on Simmel, "The Metropolis and Mental Life" (329); Park, *The City* (279); Wirth, "Urbanism as a Way of Life" (417), and Davis' reformulation of the above in *Human Society* (78: pp. 328 ff.). Cf. Blumer, "Collective Behavior" (32). Two confusions have accompanied early discussion of urbanism. One is the jumbling of *crucial differences between cities in nonindustrial societies and cities in highly developed societies and between industrial and nonindustrial cities.* In the analysis that follows, when we speak of "urban society" or of "urbanism" we refer neither to a society which has only a few urban communities, nor to cities at a low level of economic development. Nonindustrial cities like Peiping in China, Cairo in Egypt, Poona in India, Rangoon in Burma, however large, do not make these nations "urban societies," and we would not expect the people of these cities to behave like New Yorkers. The proportion of urbanites in these societies relative to the peasant population is still small—5 to 15 per cent—because of their limited economic development. For a cogent treatment of the very different ways of life in the nonindustrial city, see Sjoberg (333). The second confusion we can only mention, without contributing to its clarification. Even in industrial cities in highly developed societies, it is *very difficult to distinguish between the effects of urbanism and those of industrialism.* This could be done by systematically comparing social relations in cities of similar demographic composition (size, density, heterogeneity) located in societies at different levels of economic growth. Since this hard task of comparison has only just begun in social science, our brief chapter must be confined to urbanism in one advanced society. Applied beyond the American scene, the analysis is at best suggestive of the situation in other urban societies with a similar standard of living.

cost basis. In short, advancing urbanism means that fewer relationships approximate that of two close friends, more approximate that of customer and clerk in a big discount house.

The shift toward secondary contact even affects friends and acquaintances. We know them as parts, not wholes. Our relations with them become segmental. Families may be affected, too. It is the city, not the country which has given us the fictional picture of the "double life"—the timid and henpecked bank clerk who is an accomplished lover on the side; or the business executive, calculating, ruthless, impersonal at work, who is known to his wife at home only as generous, kindly, and warm.

The shift toward "secondary contact" seen by these students of urbanism parallels the shift from "status" to "contract"—and from "who you are" to "what you can do" as a basis for specialization—observed by students of industrialism (see Chapter III).

2. *Social tolerance, the blasé attitude, spreads.* Given a heterogeneous population having mainly impersonal contacts, tolerance, or better, indifference is inevitable. If extreme differences are common—between banker and beggar, rich and poor, white and colored—if you see oddities often enough, they cease to be oddities. The city dweller becomes blasé—no longer surprised by anything. A recent study of American tolerance of deviation seems to confirm this notion: the least urbanized area, the South, was the least tolerant of political and religious unorthodoxy. And even within the South, the metropolitan areas were more tolerant than the small towns and farm areas. (346)

3. *Secondary control becomes dominant.* The city presents the individual with two social worlds: (1) the world of physically close but socially distant strangers (the secondary contacts described above); and (2) the world of family, friends, and acquaintances. This gives the individual a double refuge. He can free himself from the close moral control of the intimate primary group—escape into a sea of strangers. (Here is the famous anonymity of the city.) He can also escape from loneliness and isolation, from the impersonal contacts of the city, into the more comfortable primary group.

Because the escape to anonymity is possible, because primary controls can be evaded, the city resorts to secondary controls to curb the spirit of exploitation, to prevent the war of each against all (a war likely to spread where strangers in close physical contact compete for scarce goods and space). A host of control specialists arise—police, department store and hotel detectives, building inspectors, correctional officers, social agencies, civic bodies, plan commissions.

In short: legal control, based on rules which are deliberate, explicit and have a special machinery for enforcement, become more prominent; the mores and folkways, less.

4. *Private interest groups, voluntary associations multiply.* The city has many people, diverse in interest and outlook. Contact is easy—pick up the phone, get on the subway or bus, drive a car. Many different kinds of people who can easily get in touch—this is a perfect setting for the development of voluntary associations (wherever freedom of association exists). Whatever your special interest—whether it be bird-watching in the public park at 5 a.m. or the protection of your interests as a veteran of World War I—you can find others with similar interests and together form a bird lover's society or an American Legion. The multiplicity of special interest groups in the U.S. underscores this tendency in urban areas: the major fraternal orders—Masons, Elks, Eagles, and like groups—claim 20 million members; 70 or 80 thousand local trade unions claim more than 15 million members; there are 100,000 different women's organizations, 1,500 national trade associations, 4,000 chambers of commerce, and so on. (411: pp. 468–469) In the Detroit area nearly two-thirds of the adult population in 1953 had formal membership in an association other than church. Four in five had similar contacts through someone in the family who belonged. (11: p. 37) In the words of Robert Park, "What a man belongs to constitutes most of his life career and all of his obituary."

In the city there is not only the opportunity, there is also the necessity. Special interests of people are expressed and become effective only through deliberate organization. You organize or you perish. The city is the place of voluntary mass organization. (Chapter IV describes how the social organization of modern industry also puts a premium on bigness.)

5. *Social life becomes atomized, the individual stands apart, loses a sense of participation, becomes susceptible to manipulation.* If asso-

ciation is secondary and voluntary, and contacts many and superficial, if residential and social mobility is high and competition keen, then the individual is thrown back on himself. He is forced to make decisions and plan his life as a career. He is on his own, aware of himself, of differences in others. He is torn from the customs of local groups, freed from tradition. He lacks permanent ties—to particular groups or causes. His attention is on a shifting, wider universe—a complicated world with a multiplicity of competing issues, competing passions. Because he is detached from local influences, his information comes from powerful media of mass communication which easily manipulate him.

Social life is thus somewhat atomized. On the one side stands the individual—highly self-conscious and unique, calculating his future with little reference to community norms and understandings, oriented outward toward a confusing world, a world interpreted for him by the press, radio, and TV—agencies he can neither control nor check up on. On the other side stand the great mass organizations of the city—the corporation, the political party, the voluntary association—centrally controlled by officials and an active minority, as distant from the rank-and-file as the media of mass communication. And nothing stands between. A general loss in the sense of participation, and a heightened susceptibility to the demagogue is said to be the result. The "mass society," "anomie," "community disorganization" are terms used to describe a population in this state.

In this view, large, dense, heterogeneous populations come to a new way of life. Urbanism means the spread of secondary relations (impersonal, utilitarian, segmental); high mobility and superficial contact; indifference (a blasé attitude); the breakdown of primary group controls and the increased importance of formal rules and secondary controls which allow much anonymity; big mass organizations and voluntary associations, on the one hand, and individuated persons, atomized social life, on the other. Recently, many students of the city have asked, if this picture is an accurate description of urban America, how does the society maintain itself? Why does it not come apart? Americans are specialized workers living in specialized areas all dependent on the whole—but the bond of economic interdependence is not enough to maintain the solidarity of a people. (96) World order would have been achieved long ago if economic interdependence were sufficient.

A Second Look at the Traditional View

The basic problem of order in any society is maintaining consensus—some acceptance of a common set of norms and values. If groups are so diverse and interests so varied, how can the norms of different groups be consistent? And if the population as a whole is so anonymous, mobile, and their relations so atomized and unstable, how can we expect sufficient conformity to common norms? The fact is, American society is integrated in some degree —it does muster considerable consensus on a core of values (see Chapter II), and conformity is sufficient to prevent disintegration.

The precise extent and sources of integration in American society are not known. Some studies which offer clues, however, are worth mention, for they point to weaknesses in the above picture of urban life as disorganized and disintegrating.

The first set of studies deals with primary group life in the city —with the family, the urban and suburban neighborhood, and friendship cliques. It suggests, with our previous analysis, that new patterns and sources of stability may be emerging. The second group of studies deals with mass organizations in the city. It suggests that the clash of interests among such organizations and membership in them may have stabilizing as well as disruptive effects in the urban setting. The third we will merely mention: studies that suggest limits to the impact of the mass media of communication. The studies are few; we will refer to fewer. Our aim is merely to raise some questions.

Primary Group Life in the City. The foregoing picture of urban life was derived in large part from close observation of rooming-house dwellers and foreign immigrants in the little ethnic colonies surrounding the Loop in Chicago thirty years ago. The problems in these areas were those described in Chapter III—problems marking the threefold transition from farm to factory, from alien to citizen, from rural to urban. Struck with the heterogeneity and mobility of these people, the earlier students of the American city leaped to the conclusion that the breakdown of close and intimate ties and the disorganization of community life were inevitable consequences. But these people and their problems even then were not the whole story of city life; with advancing industrialization, as we have seen, they became less of the story. Continued urbanization also changes the picture.

Studies suggest first that a lively primary group life survives in the urban area, and primary group controls are effective over wide segments of the population. The alleged anonymity, depersonalization, and rootlessness of city life may be the exception rather than the rule. The typical city dweller maintains close relations with friends among either neighbors, or people in other parts of the urban area or both. One study of local intimacy in a middle-sized city reports the not-unexpected finding that close relations with neighbors are a function of residential stability and occur more frequently in high-income areas. But the lower *local* intimacy of lower-income people who moved around more did not mean a breakdown in their neighborhood friendships. They retained active friendships dispersed over the city in neighborhoods they once lived in. "Spatial mobility makes for city-wide ties; stability makes for local area ties; and most urban residents have both." (335: p. 284; cf. 309: pp. 6, 44.) The 1955 Detroit Area Study, focused on the urban family, seems to confirm this picture of intimacy in the city: only 11 per cent of this representative sample of family units have no relatives at all in the Detroit area; 54 per cent see one or more related family units (not living in the same household) once or twice a week. Fifty-seven per cent of the wives interviewed say their relatives "feel very close to each other." "Neighboring" was also widespread in this metropolis: 75 per cent of the responding families report they "get together" with neighbors aside from relatives; 55 per cent get together with "other friends" (other than neighbors or relatives) "once or twice a week" or "a few times a month." Hardly a rootless mass here, even discounting possible exaggeration (by social isolates who feel reluctant to admit their isolation).

It is true that occupational and residential mobility and heterogeneity are central to urban industrial life (see "Industrialization and Mobility," Chapter III); but they are not necessarily disruptive. In a study of migration in Chicago, 1935–1940, Ronald Freedman found that some highly "disorganized" areas (very large and diverse foreign-born populations with high insanity and delinquency rates) had *low* rates of mobility (relatively few intercity and intracity migrants come and go); while some stable, middle-class areas had high rates. He found that "the stereotype of migrants as a distressed group of low social and economic status on the fringe of the urban labor reserve . . ." was applicable only to a small part of the total stream of migrants to Chicago, mainly the rural migrants from the South. He suggests that people can become used to new experience, to changing jobs and houses, as part of the routine of modern life. (114: pp. 210, 191–193; cf. 309: pp. 62–63.) Two studies based on more recent Detroit, and Ypsilanti, Michigan, data also suggest that migrants in time fit in as participators in the formal and informal associations of the community—though, as with the nonmigrants, from one-fifth to two-fifths have no formal group membership even after about a decade of residence. (11; 324; 425)

As industrialization and urbanization proceed, the newcomers we talked about in Chapter III may no longer be "yokels" with a painful adjustment ahead; an increasing proportion appear to be people of higher status, who have lived in cities previously, and who are accustomed to urban mobility as a built-in feature of their personal and social organization. At the extremes the contrast is between the illiterate, unskilled immigrant who settled in a slummy rooming-house area on the fringe of the downtown business district and the new "corporation transient," a professional or executive who moves from city to city, town to town as part of the normal upward climb in his career, who settles in ever-better homes, takes easily to new friends of slightly higher status (if his old ones have not made the climb with him), and engages in the same types of recreation as he had found in his last residence in another suburb. (409)

This is not to suggest that great mobility of a population has *no* effect on community integration.[1] It does suggest, however, that before we conclude that the mobility characteristic of American society has a disintegrating effect, we need to consider the different kinds of people who move and the kinds of moves they make.

Whatever the mobility of the population, intimate contacts with relatives, neighbors, and friends are a universal feature of urban life at home and in the local community (as indeed they were in an earlier day among the Little Polands and Little Sicilies of the slum). Such contacts are also a universal feature of life at work. Even in the huge workplace where many thousands mass for the daily routine, the informal workgroup seems destined to go on performing its usual functions of controlling the workpace, initiating new members, deciding how far to go along with the boss, and making work a bit more like play. There is no evidence that human relations are any more atomized at work than in the local community and neighborhood, though the liveliness of informal groups may, of course, vary from place to place.

Even in the commercial markets of the big city, where urban anonymity, the impersonal secondary contact, and the spirit of exploitation should be most clear, there is room for doubt. A study of customer-clerk relations on the Northwest Side of Chicago turned up many shoppers who did not view the clerk as a means to an end, or the store as the most convenient location for an onerous economic task. There is the "ethical consumer" who feels the moral obligation to patronize special types of stores. She sacrifices lower prices or wider selection "to help the little guy out" or because "the chain store has no heart." There is also the "personalizing" shopper who shops at "my store" where "they know your name" and where clerks get to know their customers.

[1] In a study of 43 large cities, Robert C. Angell found that "moral integration" (as indexed by low rates of crime and strong local welfare effort) was least in cities whose populations were highly mobile (many migrants moving in and out of the city), ethnically and racially heterogeneous, and where a disproportionate share of the families was at the extremes of wealth and poverty. Mobility and heterogeneity together had a very high negative correlation ($-.79$) with integration. Rental spread, which probably reflects distance between rich and poor and the number of people at the bottom and the top of the income scale, was the best single "cause" of low integration ($r = -.65$). (10: pp. 17-21; cf. 309: p. 181.) Our previous analysis of stratification (Chapter IV) suggests that this source of low integration is declining.

This study suggests that the personalization of market relations among such shoppers functioned to identify them with the locality. (The personalizing consumers—though they had relatively short residence on the Northwest Side and had most of their friends outside the community—were, nevertheless, more identified with the Northwest Side than other types.)[1] (345)

All this is not to deny that a world of strangers exists, or that the proportion of a person's total relationships that are "secondary" is higher in the city than in the peasant village (where most relationships can be described in kinship terms). But the studies do suggest that the "breakdown" of primary group life and informal controls has been greatly exaggerated, and that the mobility and variety of city life can become routine instead of disruptive.

New Patterns of Family Living. Another group of recent studies point to the emergence of new, perhaps more stable patterns of family life. These patterns seem to be in part the product of continuing trends discussed earlier under the heading "The Later Impact of Industrialization on Society"—the increased income, security, and leisure afforded by the increased efficiency of large-scale organizations and specialized careers; the lessened class polarization, the decline of poverty; the changing role of women. The new patterns seem to be linked also to the rapid shift of population to the suburbs. Some students believe that continuing industrialization and the newer suburbanization that goes with it will in time bring greater stability to family life and may even lower the divorce rate.

For the first time in the history of the United States a large portion of the people who must work in big cities now have a choice: they can live in a dense urban settlement; or they can move to the less crowded metropolitan "ring"—to a satellite city, a suburban or even a rural fringe—and commute. They seem to

[1] This study must be interpreted with caution, however. The kidding and "personal" contacts between clerk and customer in a Chicago grocery store can be seen as support for the traditional picture of urbanism. Maybe it typifies the impersonal banter characterizing quickly formed casual relationships in the city. Surely it deserves contrast with the relation of clerk and customer in a general store in an isolated rural area where both parties have common friends and reciprocal knowledge of life histories and family genealogies.

prefer the fringe to the center. The population of metropolitan rings has grown almost three times as fast as central cities from 1930 to 1950. (35: p. 18) Within the ring, the unincorporated rural territory has grown faster than the rest. (37: p. 39) The central city has practically exploded and scattered itself over the countryside.

Suburbs are by no means uniform either in physical appearance or in way of life. They include small residential communities as well as thin ribbons of houses and farms along major highways. Part of suburban growth has been orderly and planned and has resulted in garden cities with adequate education and welfare facilities. Part of the growth has resulted in "suburban sprawl"— shanty towns, mud-rut streets in partially developed subdivisions, homes mixed in with factories and stores. As Bogue suggests (34), no one yet knows whether the proportion of the suburban population living under "good" conditions is larger or smaller than the proportion in our central cities—whether we define "good" in terms of services and physical living conditions, such as adequate housing, schools, libraries, churches, streets, water and sewage systems, or in terms of low indices of "disorganization" (crime, delinquency, mental disease). It is possible that if concerted effort to reshape our decayed urban centers through slum clearance, conservation, and rehabilitation were greatly accelerated it would achieve success while we let new slums develop in the metropolitan ring.

In speaking of suburbanism as a way of life, another caution is in order. On the one hand, we have a picture of the "outgoing life" in "mass-produced suburbs" like Park Forest, Illinois, or the Levittowns. Journalists William H. Whyte, Jr. (408) and Harry Henderson (145) have described young, middle-class, college-educated suburbanites "on the make," transients who expect quickly to move on and up but who meanwhile engage in almost frantic participation in neighborhood and community affairs. They participate partly because their ages, incomes, and occupations are so alike that social activity becomes the basis of prestige; and partly because the kids get organized and then organize their parents. Some recent sociological studies seem to confirm this picture. On the other hand, there are industrial cities like Flint, Michigan, whose factory-dotted suburban area contains proportionately *more* manual workers than the city. In this area, one in four home owners built his house with his own hands —a time-consuming enterprise which may be one reason why *fewer* Flint suburbanites join formal organizations, including churches, than city residents. (105) Here, life is not so "outgoing."

Variations, yes. But the evidence does seem to suggest the possibility that the suburbs are setting a pattern for a newer family form that will embrace both Flint and Levittown. The suburban family, compared to the central city family, tends to be somewhat larger. It attaches more positive value to children and becomes more important in the daily routine of its members. The parents not only try to take their child-rearing cues from medicine and psychology; many of them also try to supervise the education and recreation as well as the courtship of their children more closely than is possible in the central city. (99) The suburban family also seems to approve more than the city family of employment for mothers, especially when the children reach adolescence. (162: pp. 551, 562; 103)[1] The suburb may be the place where women are finding new identity and resolving their conflicts.

These tendencies can contribute to family solidarity. The blue-collar and white-collar workers who "live out and work in" may thus get the chance to increase their family stability at the same time that they increase their job mobility. The suburban home becomes the more-or-less permanent base; the central city *and* its ring become an economic hunting ground—with house moves tied less closely to job moves, more closely to family expansion and major shifts in income. (210; 309: p. 85)

---

[1] There is some evidence that the old pattern of "respectability" which dictated that women should work only if they had to, to make ends meet, and which kept middle-class housewives at home, is breaking down for the whole population. In 1951 "Of wives between the ages of 22 and 44 whose husbands were earning under $5,000 a year (and who had no children under eighteen), about 55 per cent were at work. At the husband's income level between $5,000 and $7,000 . . . 30 per cent of the wives went to work. In the $7,000-to-$10,000 bracket only 8.6 per cent of the wives were working. But of the $10,000-and-over group, 21.1 per cent of the wives had taken jobs." (22: p. 92) This reversal, together with other data, suggests that the newer pattern, in which a woman works because she wants to, may be emerging in the upper-income suburb faster than elsewhere. It is clearly emerging fastest among the better-educated segments of the population, whatever the income level.

Suburbanization aside, there are reasons to believe that mature industrialization will in itself bring new patterns of family life, and perhaps reverse the long-term trend toward family instability.

At work, as we saw in Chapter IV, the typical urban-industrial man, white-collar or blue-collar, suburbanite or not, finds himself increasingly in big organizations, doing a job requiring more skill or education or both than his father had. He is paid more for fewer hours, he has longer vacations. The large bureaucratic organization, which tends to be more stable and have longer lines of promotion, offers him a regularized career.[1] A vast variety of government and private welfare programs greatly increases his security. These developments on the workfront are important in analyzing the family, for there is good reason to believe that the way a man gets his living will affect the way he rears his children and spends his leisure time.

A careful study of Detroit mothers by Miller and Swanson (242) illustrates how differences in work environment can be reflected in such matters as child-rearing philosophies and practices. They found sharp contrasts between the child training of families whose heads work in large bureaucratic organizations and those whose heads were more free-enterprising or less used to urban living (self-employed, born on a farm or abroad, and so on). Parents who were nonrisk-taking wage workers or salaried employees in big hierarchical organizations put less accent on an active, independent approach to the world in their child training; they were also less concerned with "internalization," with development of strong "built in" self-control, what Riesman calls "inner direction." (300) These middle-class "bureaucratic" parents encourage an accommodating adjustive way of life. "The child's peers become colleagues whose favor he must court and whose respect he must win." He must learn to be a " 'nice guy'—affable, unthreatening, responsible, competent, adaptive." The world of work increasingly demands the human relations skills needed to

---

[1] This may be one reason why Angell found that large-scale enterprise in American cities did not appear to be a disruptive influence—it was not closely related either to their crime rate or their ability to conduct successful welfare effort. (10: p. 18)

find one's way around the big organizations; the family reflects this in its child training.

At home, despite the fact that the journey to and from work may be longer, it is a fast journey, and our typical urban-industrial man has more time for the family. His more ordered striving means less necessity for the worry and risks of a free-enterprising existence—in contrast to his father who was a farmer, a small businessman, or an independent professional.

With striking consistency the recent studies of urban life under-score the nuclear family as the basic area of involvement for all types of urban populations. We find not a madly mobile, rootless mass, disintegrating for want of intimate ties, but an almost bucolic contentment with the narrow circle of kin and close friends, with the typical urbanite spending most of his leisure with the family at home, caring for the children, watching tele-vision, maintaining the home, reading. Occasionally he makes forays into the world outside, mainly to visit relatives, sometimes to demonstrate his lightly held attachment to a formal organiza-tion or two. (335; 12; 94) When he moves, it is all part of the life plan, of the career.

As industrialization pushes us toward the four-day week, as work becomes more ordered and secure and income more regular, home and leisure are going to be even more than they are now the central interest of a man's life.

Of course, this somewhat idealized picture applies more to the growing new middle class than to the rest of the population. But this model of family life is diffusing through American culture. Two great new "melting pots" will speed the diffusion: (1) the middle-class suburb where the blue-collar worker learns to be-have more like his white-collar colleague; (2) the large bureau-cratic organization—factory, office, hospital, or store—where all come to value and practice the regularized life.

Consensus and Formal Associations and Controls. Even if family ties *are* looser and primary group controls *have* less effect (and we have seen this is easily exaggerated), American society would have an important source of stability and integration in the great second-ary associations and controls of the city. The corporation and the church, the trade union and the professional association, the political party and the veterans' organization—these are great mixers of people and points of view. They bring together diverse people in pursuit of limited goals. Since almost everyone holds membership in a work organization or a church or both, and since the active participants in voluntary associations typically hold more than one membership, these organizations have overlapping membership. Overlapping membership means that each participant is exposed to different and sometimes conflicting points of view. He also comes to an awareness of common goals that different organizations hold. Viewing it from the top side down, this imposes important restraint on the leaders of formal organizations. The American Legion Post Commander, half of whose members belong to the AFL-CIO, hesitates to attack labor unions; the union leader, half of whose members are also members of racial and ethnic minorities, feels the necessity of cooperating with minority defense organizations; the corporation official, all of whose workers are also strong union members, is cautious in his expression of his views on labor, and so on. All feel compelled to emphasize to some extent their common adherence to the American Creed of freedom and equality.

Of course, these groups often pursue conflicting interests. They adhere to conflicting norms and values. But the very clash of interests in a free society itself may have a stabilizing effect. The most obvious example is labor-management relations. As we have seen in Chapter IV, the struggles of corporations and unions with each other have led them to form new common rules as a means of accommodation, of "living together." The labor dispute has become an institutionalized form of conflict, built into our society as a legitimate channel of labor protest.

While many millions hold no meaningful membership in these great formal associations, and while the meaning of membership and participation to those who do belong is still a question worth study, it is a plausible hypothesis that such associations are powerful integrators of the society. In our view many voluntary associations, private enterprises, unions, and churches serve as a firm block against organizational and propagandistic manipulation.

(212; 225; 321; 410) These separate organizations are able to command only partial loyalties—the union on job problems, the precinct organization on politics, the bowling league in recreation, the church in religion. No one of them can embrace the entire existence of the individual. Chancellor Clark Kerr of the University of California at Berkeley has expressed the point well: "A society without strikes, without labor turnover, without business mortality is a society without independence of spirit, self-reliance, competitive urge." He sets up the ideal of a "society of accommodated conflict, rather than universal collaboration"— a pluralist society as against "the all-embracing party of the Communists and the Fascists, the all-absorbing corporation of Elton Mayo, the all-absorbing union of Frank Tannenbaum, the all-absorbing church of T. S. Eliot." (176: pp. 110–111)[1]

Consensus and Mass Communications. Just as the state of primary group life and secondary associations in the city may not herald its disintegration, so the function of the mass media of communication in urban integration or disintegration must be examined. The late Louis Wirth (416), who drew the traditional picture of urban life with great eloquence, argued that the press, TV, radio, movies may become the basis for a new consensus—a new superculture based on common exposure to common ideas. Others have argued that the mass media epitomize the disintegration of the common life, for they appeal to the baser emotions, permit easy mobilization of the rootless mass into irrational and explosive

---

[1] Perhaps one of the chief reasons for the strength of democracy in the Anglo-American world is here—in the state of *secondary associations*. A recent analysis by William Kornhauser suggests that the susceptibility of a population to mobilization by leaders of totalitarian and other "mass" movements depends in large part on: (1) a lack of independent, self-governing organizations; (2) related attitudes of alienation from work, politics, and the community. American society may provide sufficient meaningful participation in such organizations to block the anti-democratic tendencies of "mass society." Disruption of primary group life, while it may lead to personal deviance or "privatized" behavior (suicide, homocide, alcoholism) does not seem to be related to mass behavior (widespread participation in Communist and Fascist movements). It is the atrophy of those autonomous secondary groups which lie between the individual and the family, on the one hand, and the state, on the other, that creates the main political weakness of mass society—not the disintegration of family, neighborhood, and friendship clique. Kornhauser, W. A., "Anti-Democratic Tendencies of Mass Society," University of California at Berkeley, 1957. Unpublished manuscript.
For analysis of local variations in the resistance to anti-democratic tendencies (by type of community and type of issue faced) see Coleman, J. S., *Community Conflict*, Free Press, Glencoe, Ill., 1957.

social movements. (225) In our opinion, neither view is tenable, though both deserve more study. First (concerning the super-culture idea), if men are either rootless individuals or tight-knit members of special interest groups, they lack a common way of life and cannot develop common norms through these mass media. Second (concerning the manipulation idea), there is evidence that two factors limit the mass media impact: (1) while the members of the media audience may be a "mass" in terms of numbers, they select media content under pressure and guidance from local opinion leaders, and from their experience in social groups, small and large; (2) the predispositions formed in these groups make for a self-selection of exposure corresponding to previous attitude (Democrats read Democratic campaign propaganda, Republicans, Republican, and so on). (25; 199) Mass communications, as Freidson suggests (117), have been absorbed into the life of social groups. The individual adopts the patterns of exposure and response appropriate to his social class and cultural level.[1] Moreover, while the metropolitan daily may be too general to serve to *integrate* community-based activity, and too limited in impact to *disrupt* the community, Janowitz (164) found that the urban *community* press (the neighborhood "shopper," etc.) *does* contribute to community integration. The community newspaper emphasizes local news, deemphasizes conflict, plays up shared values. City people show surprising interest in it. They find it an important extension of personal communication in the local community.

Appraising the Indictment: A Concluding Note

The central theme running through our picture of urban-industrial America is this: We can perhaps view most of the targets of complaint as transitional, passing results of industriali-

[1] Of course, the media do help set the stage for public debate by structuring the issues where local experience offers no guide. Some evidence suggests that even private discussions take their cue from the media's presentation of the issues. (25: p. 460) And in turn the private discussions of key decision-makers influence what goes into the media. This is an area in which so little is known that the best we can do is to recognize that the press, TV, radio, and film are capable of reaching millions of people with stereotyped "lines" in political campaigns, at the same time that we avoid the temptation to exaggerate the easy manipulability of the mass.

zation under nineteenth century conditions. Coercive recruitment and painful transformation of peasant immigrants into
urban-industrial workers; the insecurities of the factory system,
the uncushioned impact of the dilution and obsolescence of skills;
the dehumanization of work (whether through backbreaking
labor or machine-paced, repetitive routine); class polarization;
community disintegration—these decline as economic growth
continues. A new welfare bureaucratic society emerges—more
stable than its early forms suggest, richer and more varied than
men had dreamed when they observed the harsh initial
development.

This does not mean that old problems are entirely gone or that
new ones do not face us. Perennial problems remain: problems of
fitting in newcomers (now from Puerto Rico and Mexico, from
rural areas at home, especially from the Southeast), of urban
growth, of overcrowding and slums, of unemployment and in-
juries, of mental illness and medical care, of delinquency and
crime, of the inequalities of opportunity for minorities, and more.
Other problems intensify: leisure-time use, worker retraining,
the older worker, suburban sprawl, the journey to work, preserving a creative culture despite mass education. And the uneven
development of industrialization means different problems in
different places (the median annual income of Negro male workers in the metropolitan area of Jackson, Mississippi, in 1950 was
still only $605).

Finally, economic growth brings new problems.

Worldwide, it has increased the interdependence of all peoples
at the same time that it has produced formidable ways of dividing
them—a centralization of state powers and the rise of nationalism
(in part to cope with the problems of internal stability and integration) coupled with widespread distribution of the means of
mutual annihilation.

In the United States advancing industrialism means new clientele and new settings for social work—the urban and suburban
middle classes, fresh groups of the underprivileged, brand new
communities. We turn to the welfare services and their clientele
in Part II.

PART TWO

SOCIAL PROBLEMS AND THE SUPPLY OF
WELFARE SERVICES IN THE UNITED STATES

PART TWO: SOCIAL PROBLEMS AND THE SUPPLY OF WELFARE SERVICES IN THE UNITED STATES

PART I has traced the impact of industrialization on some major features of American society. The social problems that emerged from industrialization in a capitalist setting created the *demand* for social welfare. Part II deals with one part of the *supply* side of the picture: how the problems lead to welfare services and programs.

To delimit the field, we present in Chapter VI some conceptions of social welfare current in the United States. Chapter VII briefly lays out the scope of existing welfare programs in terms of auspices and expenditures. In Chapters VIII and IX, we use family problems and juvenile delinquency as illustrative fields to show how changes in social organization discussed in Part I (mobility, the family system, social stratification) have, in the context of American values, called forth our characteristic welfare services.

VI. Conceptions of Social Welfare

WHAT IS MEANT by social welfare? Is it relief, and just for the poor? Is social insurance included? What of public recreation and parks? And if these are social welfare, why not public highways and the Tennessee Valley Authority? How about private industry's pension plans? And what of fee-charging social agencies and the "private practice" of social work?

We are not concerned here with formulating a view of what social welfare ought ideally to involve, but rather with its existing outlines and trends in the United States. Specifically, we will: (1) point out what seem to be the currently dominant concepts of welfare, and (2) state some criteria for delineating social welfare. Later chapters will discuss the implications of the dominant American conceptions of social welfare for the services and for the professional practice of social work.

Current Conceptions

Two conceptions of social welfare seem to be dominant in the United States today: the *residual* and the *institutional*. The first holds that social welfare institutions should come into play only when the normal structures of supply, the family and the market, break down. The second, in contrast, sees the welfare services as normal, "first line" functions of modern industrial society. These are the concepts around which drives for more or for less welfare service tend to focus. Not surprisingly, they derive from the ethos of the society in which they are found. They represent a compromise between the values of economic individualism and free enterprise on the one hand, and security, equality, and humanitarianism on the other. They are rather explicit among both social welfare professionals and the lay public.

The residual formulation is based on the premise that there are two "natural" channels through which an individual's needs are properly met: the family and the market economy. These are the preferred structures of supply. However, sometimes these institutions do not function adequately: family life is disrupted, depressions occur. Or sometimes the individual cannot make use of normal channels because of old age or illness. In such cases, according to this idea, a third mechanism of need fulfillment is brought into play—the social welfare structure. This is conceived as a residual agency, attending primarily to emergency functions, and is expected to withdraw when the regular social structure— the family and the economic system—is again working properly. Because of its residual, temporary, substitute characteristic, social welfare thus conceived often carries the stigma of "dole" or "charity."

The residual concept was more popular in the United States before the Great Depression of 1929 than it is now. That it is consistent with the traditional American ideology of individual responsibility and by-your-own-bootstrap progress is readily apparent. But it does not reflect the radical social changes accompanying advanced industrialization, or fully account for various aspects of contemporary social welfare activity.

The second major formulation of social welfare is given in a widely used social work textbook as "the organized system of social services and institutions, designed to aid individuals and groups to attain satisfying standards of life and health. It aims at personal and social relationships which permit individuals the fullest development of their capacities and the promotion of their well-being in harmony with the needs of the community."[1]

[1] This is a typically vague definition of the "institutional" view. Contemporary definitions of welfare are fuzzy because cultural values regarding the social responsibilities of government, business, and the individual are now in flux. The older doctrines of individualism, private property and free market, and of minimum government provided a clear-cut definition of welfare as "charity for unfortunates." The newer values of social democracy—security, equality, humanitarianism—undermine the notion of "unfortunate classes" in society. All people are regarded as having "needs" which *ipso facto* become a legitimate claim on the whole society. Business and government as channels to supply these needs have vastly broadened their responsibilities. Both the older and newer doctrines coexist today, creating conflicts and ambiguities in values which are reflected in loose definitions of social welfare.

(118: p. 4; cf. 191.) This definition of the "institutional" view implies no stigma, no emergency, no "abnormalcy." Social welfare becomes accepted as a proper, legitimate function of modern industrial society in helping individuals achieve self-fulfillment. The complexity of modern life is recognized. The inability of the individual to provide fully for himself, or to meet all his needs in family and work settings, is considered a "normal" condition; and the helping agencies achieve "regular" institutional status.

While these two views seem antithetical, in practice American social work has tried to combine them, and current trends in social welfare represent a middle course. Those who lament the passing of the old order insist that the second ideology is undermining individual character and the national social structure. Those who bewail our failure to achieve utopia today, argue that the residual conception is an obstacle which must be removed before we can produce the good life for all. In our view, neither ideology exists in a vacuum; each is a reflection of the broader cultural and societal conditions described in Part I; and with further industrialization the second is likely to prevail.

Criteria for Delineating Social Welfare

Keeping in mind this ideological dualism, we can now look at the substance of social welfare. What are the main distinguishing characteristics of activities which fall within the range of welfare practice in America today?[1]

1. **Formal Organization.** Social welfare activities are formally organized. Handouts and individual charity, though they may increase or decrease welfare, are not organized. Likewise, services and help extended within such mutual-aid relationships as family, friends and neighbors, kinship groups, and the like are not included in the definition of social welfare structure. It is recognized that there is a continuum running from the most informal

[1] All institutions, of course, undergo change over time, both in form and function. However, some continuing identity is usually clear. Thus, the historical continuity and interconnection of social welfare institutions can be traced—from hospitals first designed as a place for the poor to die, to modern community hospitals serving the health needs of all; from sandpiles for the children of working mothers, to the tennis courts and baseball tournaments of a modern recreation program; from poorhouses to Social Security.

to the most formal, and that in-between cases—the mutual-aid welfare services of a small labor union, church, or fraternal society—cannot be precisely classified. The distinction is clear in principle, however, and important.

Modern social welfare has really to be thought of as help given to the stranger, not to the person who by reason of personal bond commands it without asking. It assumes a degree of social distance between helped and helper. In this respect it is a social response to the shift from rural to urban-industrial society. Help given within the family or friendship group is but an aspect of the underlying relationship. Welfare services are a different kind of "help." We must think here of the regular, full-time, recognized agencies that carry on the welfare business.

2. **Social Sponsorship and Accountability.** Social auspice—the existence of socially sanctioned purposes and methods, and formal accountability—is the crucial element in social welfare service versus comparable service under profit-making auspices. If mobilization of resources to meet needs is not accomplished by the family or through the market economy, some third type of organization must be provided, and this is typically the society as a whole acting through government (city, state, federal), or a smaller collectivity operating through a private social agency. (Cf. 365: p. 13.)

Some mechanism for expressing the public interest and rendering the service accountable to the larger community is an essential part of social sponsorship. For public welfare services in a democratic society, the mechanism is simply the representative structure of government. For voluntary agencies accountability is typically, though less certainly, achieved through a governing board. That some of these boards are self-perpetuating, unresponsive to changing needs and isolated from constituencies, does not deny the principle of accountability, any more than oligarchy denies it in the public welfare arena. The principle is acknowledged in privately as well as publicly sponsored organizations.

3. **Absence of Profit Motive as Dominant Program Purpose.** Just as the needs-service cycle within the family is excluded from the concept of social welfare, so generally are those needs which arise and are

fulfilled within the bounds of the free enterprise system. The
services and goods produced by the market economy and pur-
chased by individuals with money derived from competitive participation in that economy are not social welfare. Profitable and
most fee-for-service activities are excluded. But there are cases
difficult to classify.

Social welfare objectives can be intimately associated with
what is basically profit-making enterprise, as when a private
business provides recreation facilities, pension plans, or nurseries
for its employees. The view may be taken, on the one hand, that
since such services attend human wants quite peripheral to the
purpose of the organization, they neither share in nor alter the
nature of the underlying profit-making activity. The latter remains nonwelfare, while the former are essentially social welfare
programs under business auspices. This view gains support from
the observation that separate structures for the administration of
welfare services often develop within the business enterprise, and
constitute a kind of "social auspice." An industrial pension plan,
for instance, usually has a trust fund separate from the financial
operations of the company; a separate office with its own physical
facilities will be set up to administer it; the policy-making group
—board or committee—will often have employee or union representation, especially if the plan is collectively bargained; and its
operation will likely come under some degree of government
regulation.

On the other hand, the view may be taken that industry-
sponsored welfare programs are simply part of the conditions of
employment, a substitute for wages. Industries provide restrooms
and run recreational programs to compete for a labor supply and
maintain employee morale and efficiency. Pensions, in this view,
are a kind of deferred wage. Programs are often administered not
through separate administrative offices, but by the business accounting or personnel office. Even when separate administrative
structures are created, this does not alter the underlying program
purpose of facilitating production.[1]

[1] It is true that men's motives vary; and businessmen are not an exception. What
we are talking about here is not individual motives but organizational purposes.

Thus, the degree to which an industrial welfare program may be considered social welfare varies inversely with extent of emphasis on a contractual relationship between two parties seeking a mutually rewarding arrangement, and directly with extent of social sponsorship and control. It is clear, nevertheless, that industrial welfare programs affect the development of social welfare institutions. The Supplemental Unemployment Benefits scheme, for instance, creates pressure for expanded unemployment insurance, and private pension plans are integrated with OASI in planning for retirement. Our discussion of social welfare expenditures (Chapter VII) will therefore include data on industrial welfare programs.

Some aspects of professional fee-for-service practice are also difficult to classify. Most Americans probably would think—and without derogatory implication—that professions as well as trades are primarily ways of making a living (often a kind of small business), and thus nonwelfare in nature. Yet it is a fact that many individual professional practitioners—physicians, lawyers, and dentists particularly—observe what appears to be a semi-social welfare practice of scaling fees according to ability to pay. Fee-scaling in private practice, however, is often a professional norm, part of a formal code of ethics. As such, its meaning and nature derive from a different context—professionalism—and it can be seen as a device by which a group with a monopoly of an indispensable service protects its fee-taking privilege. Where the professional "charges what the traffic will bear," there is no ambiguity, and his activity is clearly nonwelfare in nature.

To the extent that the private practice of social casework resembles other fee-for-service professions, it, too, is rather clearly outside the field of social welfare. Solo practice of social work is as yet so little developed, however, that it cannot be seen how close it will hew to the model of the other professions.

Many business leaders may acquire a sense of trusteeship going beyond their obligations to the shareholders. Thus, multi-plant companies have been known to avoid shutdown of an unprofitable unit because of major disruption to the local community. But one cannot say that the enterprise purpose is to save declining communities, any more than one can call dropping 50 cents in a blind man's hat Aid to the Blind.

4. **Functional Generalization: An Integrative View of Human Needs.**
Since almost any of the gamut of culturally conditioned human
needs may be unmet and since human capacities which can be
developed are many, welfare services to meet needs and enhance
capacities will be varied. Placing babies in foster homes, operating a recreation program, administering social insurance, developing medical service in a rural community—the substantive
activities here have little in common; a great variety of activities
may take on a social welfare aspect. From the standpoint of the
welfare structure as a whole, these activities are properly described as "functionally generalized"; that is, welfare services are
found attached to, or performing in place of, medical institutions,
the family, education, industry—wherever there is "unmet
need." It will be noticed that this concept is closely related to
that of residuality discussed above; what other institutions do not
do, it is the job of welfare to do. To the extent that it is the
function of social welfare to come in and "pick up the pieces" in
any area of need, it must lack attachment to any given area.

From this characteristic derives, in part at least, the comprehensive view of human needs and personality that distinguishes
social work from other professions. An international study by the
United Nations of training for social work concludes that social
work seeks to assist

> . . . individuals, families and groups in relation to the many social
> and economic forces by which they are affected, and differs in this
> respect from certain allied activities, such as health, education, re-
> ligion, etc. The latter . . . tend to exclude all save certain specific
> aspects of the socio-economic environment from their purview. . . .
> The social worker, on the other hand, cannot exclude from his con-
> sideration any aspect of the life of the person who seeks help in solving
> problems of social adjustment . . . [or any] of the community's
> social institutions that might be of use to the individual. . . .
> (365: p. 13)

Individual agencies are, of course, specialized and limited in
function; but the welfare field is inclusive. It is because social
welfare is "functionally generalized" that we exclude the school
system, which tends to be segmental in its approach to its
clientele.

5. Direct Concern with Human Consumption Needs. Finally, how are government welfare services to be distinguished from other government services, since all are socially sponsored? It is possible to place governmental activities on a continuum which ranges from services primarily concerned with the functional requisites of the society (see Appendix) and only indirectly with the fate of the individual, to those which provide direct services to meet immediate consumption needs of individuals and families. At the "indirect" end of this continuum, following the analysis of Hazel Kyrk, are government activities "inherent in the nature of the state . . . such as the national defense, the preservation of law and order, the administration of justice, the exercise of regulatory functions. . . ." Intermediate are road building, flood control, forest conservation, and other such services, "the benefits of which are so remote in time or diffused among the population that they will not be privately provided." At the direct services end are those where "specific beneficiaries can be identified, although there are also general benefits. . . . Schools and universities, recreational facilities, libraries, museums, concerts, school books and lunches, subsidized housing, medical and hospital services. In this last group of services described are those which are distinctly for consumer use and enjoyment." (195: pp. 148–149)[1]

In the last group fall the welfare services. Of course, social welfare programs serve the needs of both the larger social structure and the individual consumer. The unemployment compensation program in the United States, for example, has been designed as an anti-depression weapon as well as a means of alleviating the individual distress accompanying unemployment. But it is the latter, rather than the former, aspect of the program which from the present point of view qualifies it as a social welfare activity.

[1] An interesting parallel to the distinction Kyrk makes here has been noted with respect to Soviet state institutions where, since "everything is government," it might also be expected that everything would be social welfare. Sociologist Vucinich observes, however, that in the U.S.S.R.: "Soviet experts in jurisprudence make a sharp distinction between social institutions . . . and Soviet enterprises. Institutions (post offices, telegraphic services, scientific laboratories, schools, and the like) are, in the economic sense, nonproductive units which draw their funds from the state budgets and are not considered independent juridical persons. Enterprises, on the other hand, have their 'own' budgets . . . their 'own' basic capital (machines, tools, etc.) and working capital." (385: pp. 9–10)

A nineteenth century view of government in the United States saw its functions restricted to "activities inherent in the nature of the state." The veto of Dorothea Dix's mental hospital bill in 1854, it will be remembered, was based on President Pierce's belief that the life conditions of individuals were no proper concern of government. Today many government services are directed specifically to individuals, and it is these which tend to be identified as social welfare.

It is thus an additional distinguishing attribute of social welfare programs that they tend to be aimed directly at the individual and his consumer interests, rather than at the general society and producer interests; that they are concerned with human resources as opposed to other kinds of resources. Soil conservation, subsidy of the merchant marine, development of water power resources, much as these redound ultimately to human welfare, are not typically defined as social welfare; but feeding the hungry, finding homes for dependent children, even provision of recreational facilities are so defined. This is the point of the stipulation in the definition of welfare given by Kraus,[1] that welfare services have "direct effects on welfare and health of individuals and families," and of Cassidy's definition of the social services as "those organized activities that are primarily and directly concerned with the conservation, the protection, and the improvement of human resources." (56: p. 13)

In sum, the major traits which, taken together, distinguish social welfare structure in America (made explicit here as criteria to define the field of analysis) are:

1. Formal organization
2. Social sponsorship and accountability
3. Absence of profit motive as dominant program purpose
4. Functional generalization: integrative, rather than segmental, view of human needs
5. Direct focus on human consumption needs

The major weakness in definition occurs in the area of socially sponsored, nonprofit services which affect nearly everyone in the

[1] At a meeting of the United States Committee of the International Conference of Social Work, New York City, June 17, 1955.

society. It would seem, for instance, that public education might be classed among the social services, as it is in England (and by a few American welfare experts, for example, Ida C. Merriam). In the U.S. there is apparently a tendency to exclude from the welfare category any service, no matter how identified with welfare it may have been in origin, which becomes highly developed, widespread in its incidence among the population, and professionally staffed by persons other than social workers. Helen Witmer notes social insurance as an example of a welfare service which has tended to move out of the welfare area after it became a "usual institutional arrangement." (418: pp. 484–486) This seems to be consistent with the residual conception and its view of the welfare services as emergency, secondary, peripheral to the main show. As the residual conception becomes weaker, as we believe it will, and the institutional conception increasingly dominant, it seems likely that distinctions between welfare and other types of social institutions will become more and more blurred. Under continuing industrialization all institutions will be oriented toward and evaluated in terms of social welfare aims. The "welfare state" will become the "welfare society," and both will be more reality than epithet.

VII. Welfare Auspices and Expenditures

HAVING DEVELOPED a concept of social welfare in the United States, we can now consider the supply and organization of welfare services as a response to industrialization. What kinds of welfare services are there? How extensive are they? Who dispenses them and through what agencies? How does continuing industrialization affect them?

The analysis in this chapter will focus chiefly on auspices and expenditures: "Who takes responsibility, and who pays the bill?" In this context some idea of the range and variety of programs will also appear.

Government

Tax-supported social welfare programs in the United States are termed "public welfare."[1] They may receive legislative sanction at any of the three main levels of government—local (town, city, county), state, and federal—and are found operating separately at all levels or as joint endeavors of two or more.

Early settlers of America brought with them European notions of social welfare. As in law and language, the English cultural inheritance predominated: thus, the Poor Law was fixed here, flourishing perhaps better on the New World frontier than in the populated, commercially advanced old country. Although by 1700 governments had already accepted responsibility to aid the poor, the orphan, the widow, the aid must be minimal, deterrent, local, and it remained so with remarkably little change in the U.S. until the depression thirties. (69)

[1] Most Americans incorrectly identify the term "public welfare" with "public assistance"—relief.

148

State. During the nineteenth century state governments came to the fore as the major instruments of social welfare. "Welfare statism" was far from public consciousness. But under the stress of problems engendered by changed life conditions—cities growing, factories multiplying, heavy immigration (see Chapter III) —social services multiplied under state auspices: asylums for the mentally disturbed (Virginia, 1773), schools for the deaf (Connecticut, 1817), reformatories for juveniles (New York, 1825). There were so many, finally, that central supervisory bodies were forced into being (Massachusetts Board of State Charities, 1863). These, taking on administrative authority, evolved into the presently universal state departments of welfare, some bearing such titles as New Jersey's Department of Institutions and Agencies.

State welfare department activities are, except in a handful of states, more restricted than the title implies; usually they embrace only the public assistances, certain child welfare programs, and some supervisory functions (for example, inspecting and licensing boarding homes for children). Administratively separate from the department, and from each other, are such other major welfare programs as:

Corrections (penitentiaries, reformatories; parole supervision; youth authorities in a few states)

Mental health (hospitals for the disturbed and deficient; in a few states child and adult mental health clinics, and mental hygiene education)

Other medical services (public health; services and care of tubercular, indigent, crippled children, and so on)

Unemployment insurance and *employment service* (with federal financial aid)

Workmen's compensation (since 1948 in all states)

Vocational rehabilitation (for civilians, with federal financial aid)

Veterans' services (special aid programs varying among the states)

Public recreation (state parks and forests; financial aid and consultation for community programs)

School social services (promoting and financing local school programs for handicapped children, visiting teachers, and so on.)[1]

The immense variation among the states in number and quality of services is associated with degree of urbanization (rural states are backward), region (the southern and prairie states lag), and wealth, factors themselves intercorrelated and linked directly with industrialization. Despite such variation, and the recent great federal expansion, the state today is still a key unit in public welfare administration. Expenditure data in this connection are discussed below.

Federal. It was not traditionally conceived that the federal power, under the restricted powers granted to it in the Constitution, should extend far into the welfare field. Dorothea Dix could pressure the states into better services for the mentally ill, but her efforts to obtain federal subsidy for mental hospitals were rebuffed; the National Child Labor Committee could get state action on child labor almost everywhere, but federal laws were declared unconstitutional. The individualism of American culture (Chapter II), given potent expression by business groups, was a powerful brake on federal intervention.

Yet the interdependence wrought by industrialism (who will buy the Iowan farmer's wheat when the Detroit factories lay off?), exacerbated by the Great Depression, was an irresistible force for federal involvement. Declaring the social insurance provisions of the 1935 Social Security Act constitutional, the Supreme Court stated: "Needs that were narrow or parochial a century ago may be interwoven in our day with the well-being of the nation. . . . Only a power that is national can serve the interests of all." (379: p. 2)

Convenient constitutional loopholes—federal powers to tax, to provide for the "common defense and general welfare," and "to regulate commerce among the several States"—were forced

---

[1] There appears to be no single text dealing exclusively and in detail with state social welfare operations, broadly conceived. Fair coverage combined with some detail may be found in White (401) and Friedlander (118). The extensive discussions appear under problem or service field headings; see, for example, Bond, Floyd, and associates, *Our Needy Aged: A California Study of a National Problem*, Henry Holt and Co., New York, 1954.

wide open as the courts found ways to make the facts of government fit the facts of industrial society. Small or traditional federal programs (care of veterans and Indians, the Children's Bureau) were joined by big programs of nationwide impact—Old-Age and Survivors Insurance, Unemployment Insurance, public assistance. It is now accepted that Congress has broad authority to enter the welfare field.

Federal welfare programs are scattered among many parts of the executive establishment. A major concentration in the newly created Department of Health, Education, and Welfare (1953) includes the following:

Old-Age, Survivors, and Disability Insurance (completely federal, the country's single biggest program, radically amended since 1935 to cover nine-tenths of the working force)

Public assistance (financial aid and standard-setting for state-administered "categorical" relief programs: Old-Age Assistance, Aid to the Blind, Aid to the Permanently and Totally Disabled, Aid to Dependent Children)

Child welfare (grants-in-aid to states for Crippled Children, Maternal and Child Health, general Child Welfare programs; Children's Bureau)

Vocational rehabilitation (for civilians; financial support for state programs)

Public health (research, promotion, grants to states including mental health)

Other major federal welfare programs include:

Veterans' services (huge programs of medical care, compensation and pensions, rehabilitation, education; run by the Veterans Administration, an independent agency)

Unemployment insurance and employment service (federal legislation promoting and regulating state-administered programs; in Department of Labor)

Federal court social services and federal correctional system (in Department of Justice)

Indian welfare services (Department of Interior)

Housing programs (Housing and Home Finance Agency)

Income-security programs for railroad workers (Railroad Retirement Board)

A complete listing would fill several pages.

Two facts throw much light on the nature of the federal welfare contribution in America: in 1950–1951, when the federal share of the $15 billion for public welfare expenditure was $9 billion, or 60 per cent, only 2,074 of the nation's 74,240 social welfare workers were in federal employ. (375) In other words, the federal government is more involved in financing than in administering social services. The chief mechanism of federal financing is the "grant-in-aid"—dollar grants to the states, often with few strings attached. Another device is used in the federal unemployment insurance law. This makes it optional with the states whether they will have an unemployment program, but puts a 3 per cent payroll tax on the employers of any state which lacks one. Such devices for federal financing of state-local welfare programs represent a typical American compromise between advocates of strong central government and advocates of "states' rights," between the values of humanitarianism and security and the values of laissez faire (see Chapter II).

Local. Locally sponsored social services in America center around the ubiquitous local institutions of school, court, and general relief office. However, in most localities—practically all the rural ones—little recognizable public welfare activity is found beyond the relief program. In the schools no visiting teachers, no vocational guidance, no special education facilities for the handicapped; in the courts no psychodiagnostic clinics, little or no probation service; in the relief office no family counseling, little child welfare service—and even the financial burden of general assistance moves increasingly from the locality to the state.

Comparing types of communities, we find that the larger the community the greater the number of services. In the big cities all of the aforementioned appear and many more, in almost endless local variation, from Skid-Row rehabilitation centers to large mental hospitals and streetwork with juvenile gangs. Ogburn has shown further that rates of city growth affect services: per capita budgets for various city services are generally much larger in cities whose populations are stable or declining than in cities that are growing rapidly. (331: pp. 37–38)

Whatever the variations, however, public welfare services conceived and financed locally are comparatively scarce. It is true that cities, counties, towns, and townships are the scene on which all welfare programs reach the family; local offices of OASI, vocational rehabilitation, unemployment insurance, and the Veterans Administration dot the country. But these are not local doings. In fact, the closer one gets to the local level of government the less one finds welfare consciousness, and the lower grow welfare standards. This despite the oft-heard warning that local activity must be stepped up if domination from Washington is to be avoided.

The situation is sociologically understandable. Change always starts in the bigger centers of cultural cross-fertilization; small, isolated places lag behind. Locale is the repository of older faiths —agrarian individualism and familism, which do not regard institutionalized social welfare with favor. The problems created by interdependence among individuals, communities, states, and regions (consequent to industrially fostered specialization) can be fully felt and appreciated only from the broader perspectives of state and national capitols. The creation of cosmopolitan types of men who more easily develop that broader appreciation, and their ascent to higher headquarters is expedited by the great physical and social mobility of urban-industrial society.

Public Welfare Expenditures.[1] Another measure of public responsibility for welfare, a view of how it is divided among the various governments in the United States, and the trends that obtain, are given by expenditure data. Only recently have such authentic and comprehensive figures (Table 4) become available, and even these depart somewhat from the conception of welfare used in this analysis.

Some of the programs listed in Table 4 do not meet our criteria for social welfare. Expenditures for education (about $11 billion in 1954–1955) boost the total by more than 50 per cent. An un-

[1] For the discussion in this section we are heavily indebted to Dr. Ida C. Merriam, director of the Division of Research and Statistics of the Social Security Administration in the U.S. Department of Health, Education, and Welfare. Data on public welfare expenditures are presented and discussed annually by Dr. Merriam in the October issue of the *Social Security Bulletin*.

specified but respectable share of the nearly $3.3 billion for health and medical services goes for sanitation and environmental public health programs, which are marginal to the social work conception of social welfare. Veterans' compensation and

TABLE 4. PUBLIC CIVILIAN SOCIAL WELFARE EXPENDITURES IN THE UNITED STATES ACCORDING TO PROGRAM FOR THE FISCAL YEAR 1954–1955

Program	Total	Federal	State-local
	(In millions of dollars)		
Social insurance	9,894		
Old-age, disability and survivors		4,436	
Railroad retirement, unemployment and disability programs		789	
Public employees retirement		801	565
Unemployment insurance and employment service		354	1,760
Workmen's compensation		51	919
State temporary disability insurance			219
Public aid	3,002	1,503	1,499
Health and medical services	3,334	298	3,036
Other welfare services	1,012	325	687
Veterans' programs	4,370		62
Pensions and compensation		2,713	
Health and medical services		761	
Education		700	
Welfare and other		134	
Education (except veterans' education)	10,853	308	10,545
Total	32,465	13,173	19,292
Total excluding all education	20,912	12,165	8,747

SOURCE: Merriam, Ida C., "Social Welfare Expenditures in the United States, 1954–1955," *Social Security Bulletin*, vol. 19, October, 1956, pp. 3–10.

pensions, over $2.7 billion, have an honorific status which sets them apart from other welfare programs in the United States.

On the other hand, a number of programs which do have status as public welfare are not represented in the list. Costs of correctional systems, both state and federal (about $200 million in 1955) are omitted, as are those for court social services (probation, and the like). Welfare programs for Indians do not appear. Expenditures for school social services, such as visiting teachers, are masked by being lumped with education. Public recreation (about $0.5 billion in 1955) is not included. No exact balance can be struck between these additions to and subtractions from the

$21 billion (excluding education) for public welfare in 1954–1955 shown in the table.

As between federal and state-local outlays, the federal is larger. However, as we noted above, much federal money subsidizes state-administered health and welfare programs; of a little over $3 billion in federal grants to state and local governments in 1954–1955 nearly two billion were for welfare programs. (373: p. 19) The share of all welfare expenditure which is state-local administered is thus somewhat larger than the federal, without including education.

Moreover, as a percentage of government expenditures for all purposes, state-local allocations to welfare are much larger than the federal. Chart B includes education, but the observed rela-

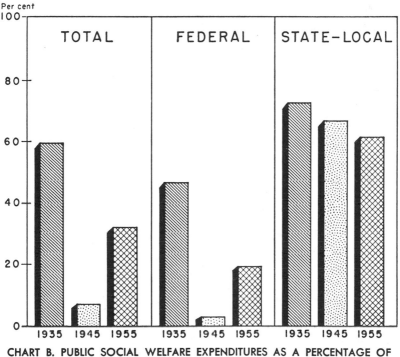

CHART B. PUBLIC SOCIAL WELFARE EXPENDITURES AS A PERCENTAGE OF GOVERNMENT EXPENDITURES FOR ALL PURPOSES, 1935, 1945, AND 1955

SOURCE: Merriam, Ida C., *Social Security Bulletin*, October, 1956, Table 5, p. 9.

tionship would be marked even without it. Over the past quarter century the state-local proportion spent for welfare has increased —about 60 per cent in 1955 compared to 40 per cent in 1929 and earlier periods; while the federal proportion spent for welfare has decreased—19 per cent in 1955 against 25 to 30 per cent in 1929. (233: p. 12) This is mainly because federal expenditures on welfare, although expanding enormously, have not increased as fast as our costly military commitments. The statistics surely do not signify either a major decline in welfare consciousness at the top or a new flowering of effort from below. Much state-local welfare activity has been coaxed into existence only by federal promotion, enticements, and legislation—money for public assistance and health programs, threatened loss of money for unemployment insurance, White House Conferences and the Children's Bureau to stir up local conscience on child welfare. Without federal aid and pressure much state-local activity would never have come into being; without it even today there would be some lapse.

To measure the "welfare effort" of the nation, expenditures must be related to our productive capacity. What share of our economic resources do we allot to welfare programs? Table 5 shows welfare expenditures as a percentage of gross national product (the total annual value of goods and services produced in the country), in averages for the later depression years (1934–1941), the war years (1941–1946), the reconversion years (1946–1950), and for individual years 1950–1951 to 1954–1955. Education is excluded.

Over the two decades shown the ratio varies from 2.9 to 6.7; excluding veterans' programs, between 2.3 and 6.1. These are large shifts—over 200 per cent—and reflect more than changing welfare values. In 1934 our productive plant was half shut down and relief needs were exceedingly high. In 1943 our energies were all at war, even ADC mothers worked, and welfare needs were put aside. In 1949 the GI's were in school or drawing "readjustment allowances." And only history will show how the Cold War and economic boom are affecting present ratios. The small but persistent increases of the early 1950's, in the total column excluding veterans' services, are due almost entirely to expansion of the Old-Age and Survivors Insurance program.

Overall it appears that today we are spending about 5 per cent of gross national product for public welfare programs, a figure that has not shifted much in the decade following World War II. Compared to other English-speaking countries our public welfare allocation appears to be low. Burns cites a Canadian study of five

TABLE 5. PUBLIC CIVILIAN WELFARE EXPENDITURES IN RELATION TO GROSS NATIONAL PRODUCT, AVERAGES OF SELECTED FISCAL YEARS

Fiscal year	Gross national product	Welfare expenditures						
		Total	Social insurance	Public aid	Health and medical services	Other welfare services	Total excluding veterans	Veterans' programs
	(In billions of dollars)			*Per cent of gross national product*				
1934–1941	87.9	6.7	0.9	4.3	0.8	0.1	6.1	0.6
1941–1946	188.4	2.9	0.8	0.9	0.5	0.1	2.3	0.6
1946–1950	247.5	5.8	1.4	0.8	0.7	0.1	3.0	2.8
1950–1951	311.8	5.1	1.5	0.8	0.8	0.2	3.3	1.8
1951–1952	336.8	4.9	1.7	0.8	0.8	0.2	3.5	1.4
1952–1953	358.4	4.8	1.8	0.8	0.8	0.2	3.6	1.2
1953–1954	360.6	5.2	2.3	0.8	0.8	0.2	4.1	1.1
1954–1955	373.1	5.8	2.7	0.8	0.9	0.2	4.6	1.2

SOURCES: Merriam, Ida C., *Social Security Bulletin*, vol. 18, October, 1955, Table 2, p. 9; and vol. 19, October, 1956, Table 2, p. 8.

such countries which estimated that the percentage of net national income accounted for by income maintenance and social security programs in 1950 was: New Zealand, 13.18; United Kingdom, 11.87; Canada, 7.99; Australia, 7.30; and the United States, 5.52. (49) Some of the apparent United States lag, however, may be accounted for by our relatively greater development of private welfare programs (though data to show this are lacking); and much of it may simply reflect the greater ability of a richer people to care for their needs through private resources.

It may be asked, finally, how have expanding population and price inflation affected our public welfare effort? With these factors taken into account, do we spend as much for welfare as we

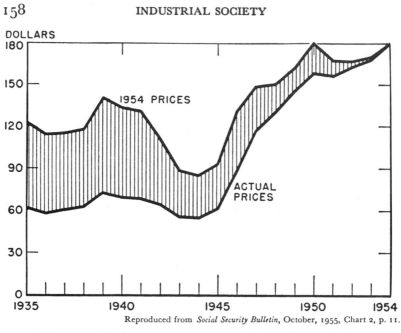

DOLLARS

1954 PRICES

ACTUAL PRICES

Reproduced from *Social Security Bulletin*, October, 1955, Chart 2, p. 11.

CHART C. PUBLIC SOCIAL WELFARE EXPENDITURES PER CAPITA,
ACTUAL AND 1954 PRICES, 1935 TO 1954

used to? Chart C shows per capita public welfare expenditures (including education) over the twenty-year period. The shaded area measures the shrinking value of the dollar; the upper line tells the story in stable 1954 dollars. Concerning this chart Dr. Merriam observes:

> The total dollar figure for 1953–54 is more than three and a half times greater than that for 1934–35; when corrected for price change the increase is 81 per cent. . . . When adjusted for population growth and price change, total social welfare expenditures show an increase of 46 per cent for this period. (233: pp. 11–12.)

This is proportionately much less than the increase in national product. But the base period used here, 1934–1935, was a time unusually high in welfare need and low in production; against a more normal economic year the percentage increase in welfare expenditure would be greater.

The Impact on Equality. The ratio of welfare expenditures to gross national product gives a direct, if rough, measure of the effort to implement the value of "*security*." There are other values these programs express and other effects worth considering. For instance, what is the effect of welfare expenditures on "*equality?*" Do social security programs tend to reduce income inequality between lower and higher income strata? Or do these programs simply spread income over time and among families *within* the lower income strata?

The answer appears to be that up to the present in the United States—and perhaps in other welfare states as well—welfare programs have had a small income-equalizing effect within the lower strata and a still smaller effect on the income distribution as a whole. The effect, moreover, varies with the type of welfare program, the condition of the economy, and the age of the population. In times of high employment and with our present proportion of old people, Old-Age and Survivors Insurance (OASI) and Unemployment Insurance (UI) may actually have increased inequality in the distribution of income. Reasons: (1) we collect more taxes out of wages and salaries than we pay out in benefits; (2) property is not so taxed; (3) since property is concentrated among higher strata, the net effect is inequality. Of course, if unemployment increases, or as spending on the aged increases, these programs could have the reverse effect. Assuming fairly high unemployment of 10 per cent, Merriam estimated that for a year in the early fifties the combined effect of OASI and UI would be to increase incomes of those receiving under $1,000 a year by about 4 per cent, and to decrease incomes of those over $3,000 a year by 1 to 2 per cent. (231: pp. 139–140) These payroll-tax supported programs tend in general to transfer income from higher- to lower-income groups *within* a broad low-income stratum "because the income of beneficiaries, whose benefits are a percentage of wages, is generally below that of employed workers, and because benefit formulas tend to favor lower-wage workers." (204: p. 306)

Programs that are financed out of general revenues (general and special public assistances, medical aid, public housing) have a clearer income-equalizing effect. Benefits here go largely to the lowest income group while revenues derive heavily from progressive income and corporation taxes. These programs, however, are small compared to the social insurances, and will become relatively smaller as OASI continues to expand.

The comparative evidence for other countries is even weaker but what there is suggests a similar picture. In the United Kingdom it has been shown that "the working class as a whole pays for its welfare benefits, and it follows that any redistribution takes place within the group." Peacock and Browning point out, however, that this observation does not take into account the benefits that go to the working class from *all* expenditures made by government—including services in kind (education, the National Health Service), subsidies such as food and housing, as well as insurance benefits (for which it is easier to see who pays the bill and who benefits). They comment: "If we offset the whole, or nearly the whole of taxes paid by the working class against various 'welfare' receipts, it follows that they receive every other government-provided service free of charge or at very small cost." (283: p. 157) They show that when all government expenditures are considered, there is a substantial income-equalizing effect felt in the United Kingdom. A similar study in the United States arrived at the same conclusion for this country. (65: p. 259)

The fact that some welfare programs do little to foster equality need not trouble their advocates. The case for OASI and UI on the grounds of family security and humanitarianism (and for UI on the grounds of stability for the economy) is strong enough without having to argue that they redistribute income. Other forces exist and other programs can be devised to secure the welfare goal of equality if it seems desirable. (See our discussion of high levels of employment, shifts in occupations, expansion of educational opportunity, the increase in multiple-earner families, pages 90–110.) The use of the tax structure to equalize property rights can go much farther than it has, and with far greater equalitarian impact than even radical expansion of welfare services could bring about.

Voluntary Welfare Efforts

Private social welfare activity in America is prominent—more so than a comparison of public and private welfare expenditures would suggest. The individualism of American culture accounts for much of this emphasis. Every Community Chest campaign is sold to corporate and individual givers partly on the gospel of preserving the private interest in welfare; if you do not give voluntarily, the warning runs, it will shortly be added to your income tax. Other factors may be nearly as important. Traditional separation of church and state has fostered a large growth of welfare structure under religious auspices. Freedom in the market economy to accumulate huge private fortunes made possible the more than $7 billion capital assets of foundations in 1954. (7: p. 15) The rapid growth of welfare programs in private industry is due to still other reasons: partial acceptance by management of the "security" demands of its employees; the effective "business unionism" of American labor; the ability of industry to support such programs, or pass on the costs in higher prices. Individualism, religious freedom, a relatively free market economy, nonideological unionism, industrial wealth—these lie back of private welfare activity in America.

The picture of private programs and auspices is complicated and shifting. A classification of private auspices, including for the moment more than what we identify as social welfare, yields the following:

Religious:
    Strictly religious purposes (nonsocial welfare)
    Church-supported schools (nonsocial welfare)
    Bona fide welfare programs

Traditional secular charities:
    The "Chest" agencies
    The national health agencies (Heart, Cancer, Polio, and the like)
    The Red Cross

Foundations:
    Welfare programs
    Research (nonsocial welfare)

Industry-union:
    Management-sponsored programs
    Union-sponsored programs
    Jointly negotiated

The first three of these types of auspices are often termed "philanthropic." (8) Of the programs under religious auspices only those with a defined welfare structure and purpose—for example, Methodist Children's Homes, Catholic Family Centers, Jewish Social Service Bureaus—are classed as social welfare. These programs often overlap the second category of auspices, since many are also community chest supported. The national health agencies, because of their research emphasis and financial autonomy, have had a status somewhat different from the local secular charities. Recent developments in federated fund-raising (the "United Fund" or "Michigan Plan" movement), however, have forced these health agencies in many communities to abandon autonomous fund-raising efforts in favor of participation in the local chest campaign.

In recent years the number of foundations has been increasing enormously. The activities they support are as varied as the interests of their donors and trustees in "religious, charitable, scientific, literary, or educational purposes." They sponsor both direct service and demonstration programs, and invest in basic science research. Although the latter activity may someday pay high dividends in human well-being, it does not qualify as social welfare service.

Industry-centered health and security plans, which bulk ever larger on the voluntary welfare scene, have so far not been thought of as "philanthropic," but they fit the criteria of social welfare used here. These programs, it should be noted, are not "industrial social work" in the European tradition of social workers offering family and other services from an outpost in the plant. The latter development, hailed for the past twenty years as a "new frontier in social work" (104: p. 134), simply has not materialized in America.[1] The actual growth of workplace-centered social welfare in America is in a quite different direction, having practically no relationship with traditional private philanthropy in financing, personnel, or philosophy; the integration is

---

[1] The only substantial discussion of industrial social work and the interesting differences between American and Continental industrial social welfare practices that has come to the authors' attention is by Miro. (251)

rather with the public income security measures, such as OASI and unemployment insurance.

Attaching dollar signs to voluntary welfare efforts is partly a matter of estimation. Thanks to the work of F. Emerson Andrews, however, estimates for philanthropic giving are now fairly sound. The figures in Table 6 reflect the bona fide church programs, secular community agencies (including special campaigns for building construction), the national health agencies, and foundation gifts channeled through the foregoing.

TABLE 6. SOCIAL WELFARE EXPENDITURES UNDER PRIVATE (PHILANTHROPIC) AUSPICES FOR 1952 AND 1954

	1952	1954
	(In millions of dollars)	
Total health	675	750
Secular services and care	375	..
Church services and care	70	..
Hospital construction	200	..
Fund-raising and central administration	30	..
Other welfare	935	1,100
Total secular services and care	645	..
Recreation, informal education, group work	170	..
Family services (mostly social adjustment)	150	..
Specialized services for children	130	..
Institutional care of adults	100	..
Services for handicapped, maternity homes, and other	95	..
Total church welfare	235	..
Fund-raising and central administration	55	..
Total health and welfare	1,610	1,850

SOURCE: U.S. Department of Health, Education, and Welfare, Social Security Administration, *Health and Welfare Expenditures of Private Philanthropic Agencies in 1954,* Table 3. (Prepared by Thomas Karter.)

Data on expenditures for industry and union health and welfare programs are less certain. The following gross estimates for 1954 have been made by Merriam (233: pp. 13–15):

	(In millions of dollars)
Retirement and pensions	500
Death benefits under group life insurance	500
Cash sickness benefits (union, industry, fraternal)	300
Sick leave benefits (including payments to government employees)	700 to 800
Estimated total	2,000

The figures tabulated above are for expenditures; contributions to the plans are larger. Already by 1950, according to the Dewhurst report, "industry spent $2.8 billion on contributions to private health, welfare and pension plans . . ." exclusive of taxes for social insurance. (89: p. 433) Most of these contributions, and those under union plans, are currently going into pension funds estimated to total as large as the OASI trust fund (about $20 billion), though benefit payments under private plans are currently less than one-fourth as large as those under public programs. (233: p. 14)

Total private welfare expenditures in 1954 were thus in the neighborhood of $4 billion (just over 1 per cent of gross national product). It is notable, however, that both community and professional social work attention is focused on the $1 billion that goes into the "traditional charities"—typically the Chest agency programs—rather than on programs represented either by the other $3 billion for private welfare or the $21 billion for public welfare. The reasons for this peculiar distribution of attention are several. Chest agencies are numerous, even though often very small, there being more than 150 in the Metropolitan Detroit area alone. As local enterprises they command much free space and time in the mass media—at annual campaign time, headlines. Also, through the perquisites of their board members, their names are welcome on the Society Page. In a well-organized community their financial needs are brought individually to the attention of every employed person in town, and to those at home by door-to-door solicitation. The Handbook of Community Welfare Resources increasingly finds its way into schools, churches, and police stations. Some programs, the Scouts and Y's particularly, serve a clientele from homes far up the social ladder, and draw a mass of volunteers from these same homes.

These Chest-type agencies command attention also because of their emphasis on services rather than financial grants, and because of their tie-in with professional social work. The $21 billion of government welfare spending in 1955, and the $2 billion of private industrial programs, went largely for public aid and social insurance benefits, which show up as checks in the mail; but the $1 billion spent by Chest-type agencies went largely for services, which show up as social workers. Professional social work concerns are predominantly focused in the traditional, voluntary agency. Professional practice was born and grew up in the Associations for Improving the Conditions of the Poor, the Child Protective Leagues, the Charity Organization Societies, and the settlement houses. Their descendants and offshoots form the core of the present Chest contingent, and this is where the professionals work today. Over the past decade about 60 per cent of the membership of professional social work associations have been

TABLE 7. CHEST APPROPRIATIONS TO LOCAL AGENCIES ACCORD-
ING TO TYPE OF SERVICE FOR 1953, AND PER CENT IN-
CREASE FOR 1935 TO 1953 IN 27 CITIES

Type of service	Per cent of total appropriations for 1953	Per cent increase in Chest appropriations for 1935–39 to 1953 in 27 cities
Care of the aged	1	210
Family service and general dependency	19	153
Care of children	18	245
Hospital care	7	148
Health other than hospital	14	191
Leisure time	40	359
Miscellaneous	1	a
Total	100	225

ᵃ Not available.

SOURCE: Dewhurst, J. Frederic, and others, *America's Needs and Resources*. (89) These figures exclude planning, financing, and common services which, according to a 1955 study of 115 community chests, absorbed 12.5 per cent of actual total chest disbursements. (64: p. 4)

employed in these settings, though by a 1950 census only 35 per cent of some 74,000 social welfare workers in the country were so employed. (314; 201; 375)

Program aims in these "social work" agencies, and some idea of trends, are suggested by Table 7 figures on Chest appropriations to local agencies by type of service.

From these figures it is evident that leisure-time programs—recreation, informal education, social group work—take a lion's share, over 40 per cent, and have had the greatest rate of growth since 1935–39 (in 1955 they were higher still). Next is family service, the most typical of private agency functions, though expenditures for it are less than half of those for leisure time, and its growth rate is among the lowest of all the services. Care of children, however, is increasingly being combined with family service, and together these cost almost as much as leisure-time services. Care of the aged is still a minor but growing function.

The program emphases revealed here—leisure-time, counseling, central planning, and specialized services—have been characteristic of the private agencies. They are also consistent with a popular theory about the proper relationship between voluntary and public welfare efforts: independence in terms of finance and administration, but coordination in the meeting of needs.[1] More specifically:

> . . . Public agencies undertake to meet, more or less adequately, basic economic, health, and educational needs. . . . To voluntary agencies remain the important tasks of filling gaps and inadequacies in these fields, of establishing standards and checking the work of public agencies, of covering many additional needs not now met by government, and of doing most of the exploratory, experimental, and research work. . . . (8: p. 112)

In practice, this division of labor is, of course, not exact; and judging from present trends it will be even less clear cut in the future. On the one hand, the privately sponsored industrial welfare programs comprise a major intrusion into the government-dominated health and income security field. On the other hand, public programs are increasing in the traditionally private fields. In 1950 public recreation expenditure—$327 million by local governments alone—already exceeded that of private agencies (89: p. 371), but if the dollar value of unpaid services by volunteers in the private agencies is considered, the balance may be the other way.[2] Although mass public recreation is not the professional social group work stressed by many of the private agencies, the New York City Youth Board is doing such group work

[1] See the excellent discussion of this interesting question of policy by George F. Davidson (74: pp. 152–159).

[2] Estimates based on Detroit area population and data of the Boy Scouts and Girl Scouts indicate that the value of volunteer troop leader services alone, rated at $2 per hour, projected to the U.S. national population, would come to approximately $300 million. A vast amount of volunteer service in addition to troop leading is given in both these programs, and, of course, there are many other voluntary programs that use large amounts of unpaid help.

with juvenile street gangs (119); "group therapy" for prison inmates is being undertaken in New Jersey and elsewhere; by 1954 more than 175 public school systems had operated camping programs as part of regular school curricula. (336: p. 61)

In the adjustmental services area, family services and the like, public services are also growing. Around courts in large cities especially are found social service staffs which are matched for size by few or no private agencies in the community.[1] In conjunction with recently increased interest in the vocational rehabilitation of public assistance clients, there are renewed efforts to provide counseling services in relief settings. (414) Even the function of exploring and experimenting grows public: streetwork with juvenile gangs, "aggressive casework," referral centers are among the important technical social work developments of the past decade, pioneered in large part by public agencies. (119) If these trends continue, the present concentration of social work professionals in the private agencies may not long continue—a point made by Commissioner of the Social Security Administration Schottland:

> By the law of averages, with the growing expansion of public welfare, with the new opportunities arising in the field—no matter what the [professional school of social work] student's initial job may be—most of them are going to wind up in public welfare. (315: p. 43)

This shift may be affected also by developments within the profession, which will be examined in Chapter XI.

[1] In the summer of 1956 the 79 probation officers in the Probation Department of Recorders Court of the City of Detroit were classified as follows: Women's Division, 11; Domestic Relations Division, 9; Men's Felony, 28; Adjustment, 8; Youth, 15; Misdemeanor, 3; Traffic, 2; Administrative, 3. (Information provided by Kenneth J. Creagh, Chief Probation Officer.) Although the officers are largely untrained, the problems dealt with in several of these divisions are of a marital or personal maladjustment nature that might well be found in a family agency.

VIII. Industrialism and Family Services

MORE WEALTH, more leisure, a changing family—the marks on American society of continuing industrialization—have implications for the giving of family service. As working people on their way to the suburbs discard old ways in favor of middle-class standards and values, new groups of clients loom in view. With new ways of life come new problems: how to choose a career, how to dispose of "discretionary" income, how to enjoy leisure, how to care for the old folk left behind. For social welfare such problems are opportunities for service. And as new social forms require behavior different from the old, culture conflict arises to pose perplexities for social administration. Is the place of an ADC mother, for instance, in the home, as we were so thoroughly persuaded just a decade ago, or is it in the work force, along with the growing millions of financially independent mothers? New client groups, new opportunities for service, new dilemmas for family service are the topics of this chapter.

The term "family service," it should be noted, is flexible. Although in modern social work parlance it is usually reserved to denote agencies which stress a counseling function for interpersonal problems, the counseling function itself is widely dispersed among agencies which emphasize other tasks. Family service merges on one side with services for deviant persons—for the mentally ill, as in psychiatric clinics for children and adults and for law offenders, as in juvenile courts and probation departments. On another side it merges with vocational and educational counseling. Historically the family agency derives from the relief agency and still has strong ties in that direction. Family service is thus given a broad connotation in the following discussion.

New Clientele

The social change most directly affecting the nature of family agency clientele is the emergence of a massive middle class (see Chapter IV). Although social work is seen less and less as an emergency service for the destitute, the viewpoint persists that most of its clientele still comes from underprivileged people. With the decline in poverty and the swelling of the middle class, the trend toward a more diversified clientele will speed up. A closer look at the groups the agencies currently serve will show the extent to which this shift in clientele has already begun.

Oft-quoted findings from a St. Paul study assert that in November, 1948, about 6 per cent (6,600) of the city's families "were absorbing well over half of the combined services of the community's dependency, health, and adjustment agencies."[1] (43: p. 9) These figures suggest that a minute contingent of "hard core" families at the very bottom of the social scale preempt the attention of the social agencies. But the meaning of such figures depends on the measure of service. If services are measured by dollar expenditures, for example, then the expensive public assistances will automatically account for the bulk of the services and of the clientele. If the whole range of public and private services is considered—not just those which reach the hard core families—a much larger proportion of a community's population is covered by social agencies; a Syracuse, New York, study "established with considerable accuracy" that 70 per cent of the city's families received services in the year 1941. (43: pp. 7–8) The actual social service picture in this regard is thus uncertain, but it seems clear that many agencies have clientele of broad social composition, especially those with a counseling emphasis, and many social workers have had experience in dealing with middle-class people. To illustrate variations, let us look at the changing clientele of different types of agencies.

[1] In correspondence with the authors, the director of the St. Paul study comments that the sentence quoted above could be more precisely stated as saying that the 6,600 families accounted for more than half of all families receiving service from the three types of agencies. The latter statement has a considerably different meaning from the published one, and has different implications from those drawn in the published report.

The social background of clients of family agencies which emphasize counseling on marital and child-parent problems varies with the class composition of the community served. The evidence suggests, however, that the agencies do not draw from a social cross-section, but from a band running downward from the middle of the community. One study of a nonsectarian agency in Detroit, a heavily industrial city, revealed a caseload composed almost entirely of upper working class and lower middle class, with the former predominating. (20) But in a residential suburb of Detroit peopled heavily by automobile company executives and subexecutives, clients of higher status predominate in the local family service caseload—only two of a sample of 96 who sought service could be classified as low as "tradespeople." (173) The very top people of this community do not use the agency— they are members of its governing board; they do, however, come in themselves to consult on problems that their maids' families may be having, and occasionally will talk unofficially with the agency executive about their own problems (no case record, please!). Clientele of sectarian family agencies seem also to reflect the social background of their respective religious communities. In Detroit the Jewish population is heavily professional and business in occupation, the Catholics are more often factory workers—a difference which naturally shows up in the agency caseloads.

Children's agencies, both public and private, that deal with adoption and with foster boarding home placement, always work with clients from the several social strata. The children, whether for adoption or boarding care, come typically from the lowest stratum—families abusive of children or broken by desertion, separation, imprisonment, or unmarried motherhood. Children are almost always placed for adoption, however, in homes ranging upward from the middle class; and foster boarding homes are nowadays found mostly among lower-middle and upper working-class families who live not in the central city but in the small towns, suburbs, and rural areas around the city. Personnel in child-placing agencies thus play all the notes on the social keyboard, and cover the rural-urban continuum as well.

Psychiatric clinics for children likewise serve a clientele of varied social background. A recent study of a large, public child guidance center in Detroit, for instance, showed that 42 per cent of the fathers of children served were business or professional in occupation; and of those fathers for whom educational data were available, nearly as many had completed two or more years of college as had received only a high school education or less. (70) Maternity homes for unmarried mothers, on the other hand, have a clientele running mostly downward from the lower middle class (girls from higher strata who "get in trouble" can usually make private arrangements). Agencies with a child protective function, congregate institutions for dependent children, and agencies working with delinquents (for example, clinics attached to a juvenile court) also have a predominantly working-class clientele.

Thus, family and children's services in some settings have already shifted quite far toward a middle-class clientele, and with further shifts in stratification, this trend may be expected to continue. Among some income-security agencies dealing with families, however, there is an opposite tendency, toward a lower-class clientele. The Aid to Dependent Children program (basically a family program) was conceived in terms of children made dependent by the death or disability of parents. "Mother's Aid," progenitor of ADC, was in most states practically restricted to respectable widows with children, and ADC took over these loads in the late 1930's. But by the end of 1952, among families on ADC rolls, the father was dead in only one case in five, and incapacitated in one case in four—a reflection of the greatly reduced number of orphans in the entire population, and the advent and expansion of Survivors Insurance to care for orphans and half-orphans. In over half the families on ADC, divorce, desertion, or unmarried motherhood was the cause of child dependency. (336: p. 400) The ADC program has not diminished in size, but the social status of its clientele has become markedly lower with no evidence in sight to suggest a reversal of the trend.

The clients of the general relief agency have similarly declined classwise. During the depression decade prior to World War II most of the general relief load was composed of the socially stable

families of unemployed workers. In the years since the war continuing industrialization, coupled with a variety of social insurance and other income-equalizing laws, has reduced poverty and
left on general relief only America's most socially and physically
handicapped people. A "typical" case in a large northern industrial city today might be a fifty-five-year-old Negro woman, without a family, with a work history of domestic service, who is
suffering from arthritis. Other types would be families whose
breadwinners are too unstable (alcoholic, neurotic) to hold a job,
and unmarried mothers judged mentally or socially incompetent
to qualify for ADC.

These most disadvantaged and demoralized families, it is true,
are not exactly a "new clientele" for social welfare. They have
absorbed a large share of the "environmental" services—relief,
medical service, child care—and are the prime objects of attention in the domestic relations (family quarrels) division of the
criminal court. But they have not been clearly seen as subjects for
positive rehabilitative "treatment" in the family agencies. They
are difficult to approach, do not come of their own volition for
help, and for the most part are lost from sight in the larger ocean
of "independent poor." Only now as large numbers of the independent poor ride the economic wave upward and outward to the
suburbs is the disorganized bottom layer left in the central city
coming fully into view, brought dramatically to the attention of
family agencies as a new clientele—the "hard to reach."

Thus, interestingly, a changing social order is bringing groups
from the opposite ends of the social pyramid into a social
welfare purview. What do these trends presage for family
service?

On the one hand, a more diversified clientele on a fee-for-
service basis will probably tend to raise the status of social agencies. On the other hand, some questions may have to be faced:
Will cultural barriers of the sort Allison Davis has found between
teacher and pupil become a factor in social worker-client relations? (76) Is there a sufficient knowledge of the new family life
patterns in suburbia to handle competently the tensions they
produce?

Regarding the question of cultural barriers, there is evidence which suggests that, among the professionally trained at least (and these dominate in the counseling type of family agency), welfare workers have been coming from progressively lower social origins over the last few decades. (200) The old question, "Can a professional teacher, social worker, minister, etc., of middle-class status and origin break through the cultural barriers of class?" may give way to the new question, "Can a professional of working-class origin, but newly won middle-class status, deal comfortably with the personal problems of clients of higher social background?" The new question would seem to be less of a challenge. Many agencies have already had extensive experience with middle-class clients without apparent embarrassment of this sort. Moreover, since social workers are highly job mobile (200), many more have worked in agencies serving middle-class clients than are so employed at any one time, so that a reservoir of sophistication exists. Nevertheless, some supervisors in social work training agencies have recently raised questions about the socially inappropriate behavior of some students in their dealings with clients.

A more serious difficulty may result from lack of knowledge about the new forms of family life developing in fringe populations (see Chapter V). Pollak has shown that social workers in a child guidance setting know too little about and pay too little attention to the structure and dynamics of the family group, an ignorance which often results in loss of important information, diagnostic errors, and ineffectual attempts at treatment. (291) He observes, for instance, that the father is often disregarded as a powerful influence in the child's life, and is rarely used as an information source. The negative effects of such blindness to the cultural and social aspects of the family will be compounded in dealing with the new middle-class suburban families, where it is increasingly the pattern for fathers to participate in all phases of family life, including child training. And there may be other changes of pattern occurring which will have repercussions on the adjustments of family members. (109) If such families are to be the clientele of the future, agency personnel will need to develop greater sensitivity to their changing ways of life.

The "new" clientele at the bottom of the social scale probably presents more difficulties to those providing adjustmental services than does the middle-class group. It is just the middle-class rational mentality which takes most readily to the notion that families and personalities can be studied and repaired like bodies or automobiles. Such an outlook is not found in the premodern mind, or to any extent in urban lower-class groups.[1] To reach the "unreached," as the New York City Youth Board terms the un-motivated and often severely disorganized lower-strata families, forms of "aggressive" casework and group work are being experimented with. (119; 278) The exploration of new methods required to help effectively such a clientele is just starting. Many difficult but interesting questions will have to be opened up in this search: how to integrate the many services bearing on a family, the applicability of current personality theory to lower-class groups, the relation of more "aggressive" treatment to self-determination of the client, the views and expectations of social service held by these clients.

Thus, a shifting class structure linked to continuing industrialization yields new clientele for the family agency, and with it new problems which represent opportunities for extending service.

New Problems—New Opportunities for Service

In the summer of 1956 a married man with two children, living on the outskirts of New York City, kidnapped a baby for ransom and abandoned him to die. His own likely fate: the electric chair. In his confession he gave as the reason for the abduction the fact that he needed money to meet payments on a new $15,000 home in the suburbs. Two lives ended, the hopes of two families shattered, for a "home in the suburbs." A bizarre episode to be sure, with overtones of psychopathology, and not one from which to generalize. But the social circumstances behind it are common enough and represent a new kind of problem: the rational use of money by those new to the ways of the middle brackets. A family

[1] Evidence for this is found in the positive correlation between social status and the willingness of a client to continue in casework treatment, that is, willingness to believe that such "treatment," without pills or monkey wrenches, is real and can help anyone. (20)

with $5,000 per year income buying a $15,000 house will, with the interest on the mortgage, put perhaps one-eighth of its lifetime income into the one purchase. Nearly as much will go into automobiles, and large additional amounts into electrical appliances, furniture, and the like. Mistakes in selection, misjudgments of ability to meet payments, ignorance of financing methods are costly, not only in money but in the social adjustment of families.

As man becomes more the consumer and less the producer, he needs help to avoid new trouble. William H. Whyte, Jr., describes 83 young couples in suburbia in the $5,000 to $7,500 bracket whose management of money would shock their counterparts of a generation past. (407) Obsessed by a desire for regularity in money transactions, they prefer the high-interest installment plan to the free charge account; they show colossal indifference to and ignorance of 12 and 18 per cent interest rates on loans at the bank, or "revolving credit plans" at the department store. Family counseling for them might well stress some simple induction into middle-class home management.

Counseling people in the buying of homes and the financing of refrigerators will seem to be functions more appropriate for the personnel of real estate offices and banks than for social workers. And what objections would arise from these free enterprise quarters if a family agency undertook skilled, hard-headed advisement of clients in the purchase of homes and expensive commodities. But here are real problems for increasing numbers of people, pressing needs met by no one; and it is the job of social welfare to meet "unmet needs."

Along with new problems in money management have come new problems in use of leisure time. As work fades into the background and leisure is pursued for its own sake, new possibilities for family strain and conflict develop. Think of a woman who increasingly feels she should be part of her blue-collar husband's leisure activities. Then think of her husband who once could "get away from it all" by retreating into an all-male world (the tavern, the ball game, the fishing trip). Today, even if his wife does not pressure him for joint participation in new and different leisure routines, he finds these last strongholds of maleness contaminated by the presence of women. Even the factory becomes decreasingly an all-male sanctuary.

Work itself, though it becomes a less prominent part of life in some ways and for some groups, changes in nature as America moves toward a middle-class mold. For ever-larger segments of the population, work is conceived in terms of a career rather than simply as a means of livelihood. A job, even a well-paying one, is not enough; it must lead somewhere, or offer "self-fulfillment." Those for whom no horizon of prestigeful vocation opens up are described by the culture as "purposeless" youth. If it be the object of social welfare to help people fulfill themselves and "achieve their highest potentials," then here in the problems of career selection and vocational counseling lie real opportunities for service.

Consider, too, the problems posed by industrial relocation. The new technology—automation and (eventually cheap) atomic power—may make industry more mobile. A plant or a whole industry now tied to a location close to coal or other relatively fixed sources of power may soon be able to locate anywhere it can get labor and raw materials. Some modern plants are so "automated" that they need not even tie themselves to a large labor supply. "Factories in the cornfields" (whether 50 miles from a downtown business district of a metropolitan area or farther out) are already part of the swing toward suburbanization of population and industry. As demands for products change, as these factories become obsolete or fail to meet the challenge of still more efficient competitors, some of them will close or move and leave their labor stranded in the cornfield. (Cf. 367: pp. 25, 35, 184, 233, 371.)

Such industrial mobility breeds a host of problems. The plight of the displaced worker, in boom or in slump, especially the older worker suddenly forced to seek a new job, is now well known (see Chapter V). We have also had experience with the booming industrial towns. Many are notorious for their deficiency in all the services and amenities necessary for a good family life. Schools, recreation facilities, and other social services, as well as streets, sewers, and the like, all lag far behind population growth. What happens to children and family life in an extreme case of this sort is documented by Carr and Stermer in their story of wartime Willow Run, Michigan. (52)

When such towns are new and booming, family-serving agencies can help to dramatize the need for adequate services and play their part in the community organization and planning efforts required. When these places decline or become ghost towns, agency personnel can provide expert testimony on the need for broadened income-maintenance programs, perhaps coupled with moving allowances. They can also experiment with new services to smooth the shift of families out of depressed areas into a new life elsewhere. More pointed methods of spreading job information, supportive treatment for uprooted families on the move, a casework approach for those obsolete workers who find the retraining programs of management, unions, and the community closed to them or too difficult for them—these are but some of the service opportunities the problem presents.

The mobility of industry described above and the mobility of urban-industrial populations described in Chapters III and IV combine to leave the central cities holding a large bag full of well-developed social problems. Racial and ethnic groups find themselves clashing as patterns of invasion and succession accompany metropolitan growth. Wildly fluctuating land values backdrop the bizarre drama in which a real estate agent on the border of a Negro ghetto panics a white homeowner into selling at a loss while the agent resells to a high-income Negro at an exorbitant price. Schools and streets, hospitals and houses become crowded and deteriorate. Family life is undermined by want of a physically secure home. Perhaps these, too, are family problems which call for family services.

New Dilemmas

Any society subject to rapid social change will experience "value conflicts," uncertainty about the "right" way to do things, indecision as to correct social policy. Family service, working as it does on the front of emerging needs and pushing always for new measures to meet needs, inevitably is faced with perplexities of this sort. For the first three decades of this century, for instance, a controversy raged in welfare circles over the extension of government action in the welfare field. The weight of expert social service opinion opposed extension in those days. Today, in line with the times, we espouse an opposite opinion, and the question is settled. But the times keep changing, and still newer ways of life bring other values into conflict, creating new dilemmas for social service. Let us look at some examples.

Most Americans hold to the belief, inherited from a nonindustrial and a frontier society, that adult children should be responsible for their aging parents. Even when such an issue arises in our own lives—do we set aside that little extra money for Johnny's college education or do we spend it now supporting grandma?—we do not perceive it as an issue in social policy. But the dilemma shows up sharply in those state old-age assistance programs (over thirty in number) which attempt to enforce "relatives responsibility" laws. No other part of relief eligibility determination (save perhaps the property lien laws, which touch on the same issue) has been found so painful, time-consuming, and unsuccessful. (38: p. 315) Even when children are financially able, the aged are apparently reluctant to make claim, the young unwilling to take responsibility. Alongside the old norm of "family responsibility" appears the new idea that the aging parent should accept an old-age pension when he has used up his savings rather than claim support from adult children. (141: p. 33) This new norm, as we have seen, fits in better with the nuclear family of industrialism. But those public officials charged with legal enforcement of children's financial responsibility for aged parents are caught in the crossfire of conflicting social directives.

Family service policy is caught in a similar crossfire when confronted with another issue of family responsibility: the obligation of parents to support their children. Many thousands of children are financially dependent upon outside help because their fathers have deserted or have for other reasons willfully refused to support them. Concern over the frequency of such behavior occasioned amendment in 1952 of the federal law governing the Aid to Dependent Children program. State agencies must now report all such cases requesting assistance to criminal prosecuting authorities before aid may be granted. Strict legal enforcement of parental duty to support young children is, of course, strongly upheld in the American value system. But at the same time social caseworkers know from several decades of sad experience that legal compulsion is rarely successful in obtaining compliance from these fathers. The dilemma for family service here is that law and public opinion require action which is technically and professionally unwise.

Another kind of perplexity for family service arises as a result of the marked trend toward outside-the-home employment of married women with children (see Chapter III). A major basis for such a financial aid program as ADC is the belief that "a mother's place is in the home" caring for her children; financial need, it has been held, is not good grounds for depriving a child of his mother's full-time attention. Americans have found this proposition easy to accept. But now increasingly we find mothers from financially independent families working outside the home. If they can, why not the ADC mother? It is notable that already some states have shifted the counseling emphasis in the program away from assuring mothers that they have a right to stay home in order to take care of their children, toward urging and helping them to obtain employment outside the home. Many family welfare workers oppose this trend, however, on the basis that suitable child-care plans are often impossible to make, or are in fact not made. The issue is difficult and unsettled.

A quite different type of dilemma derives from the efforts of family agencies to deal with problems of adjustment on a mass scale through mental hygiene education. On the one hand, agencies are urged to develop in clients through education and groupwork techniques the capacity to plan for their own development and solve their own problems—in a kind of social-psychological do-it-yourself movement. (110: p. 130) On the other hand, it is claimed that wide dissemination of scientific knowledge about personality development, appearing as "advice to parents" in the mass media and in programs of adult education, "has caused parents themselves to doubt their own effectiveness and skill in providing the proper emotional environment for their offspring." (152: p. 125) A psychiatrist, in an article entitled "The Dilemma of the Parent as Culture Bearer," comments: "The parent of today may also begin to doubt whether he is a proper person with whom to be identified and may lose his self-esteem because of the increasing shift of authority from the parent to the expert." (341: p. 303) Thus buffeted from both shores, family-life education as a function of family service seems due for a stormy passage.

The additional problems created for family service by a changing society are many. Social work has traditionally been an urban phenomenon. Suburbanization is proceeding to spread the clientele over broad metropolitan areas covering many cities, towns, and scattered country homes; how will services for a population so dispersed be distributed? How can the payroll deduction for the community chest contributed by the man in his city job be funneled back to his family needing service where they live in the suburbs? We have mentioned above the trend toward a fee-for-service status. How will this affect the agency's conception of its proper clientele? Will the poor man, and those most needing service but least able to pay, be lost from sight?

These are some of the problems and dilemmas that continuing industrialization promises to bring to the forefront in the family services field. The next chapter deals with the social welfare response to the phenomenon of juvenile delinquency. Since this problem uniquely highlights the structural and cultural changes brought about by both industrialism and urbanism, analysis of it will serve as a summary illustration of our main theme—that industrialization affects the demand for, and supply and organization of, the welfare services in crucial ways.

IX. Industrialism, Deviant Behavior, and Social Reform: The Case of Juvenile Delinquency

MENTAL ILLNESS, suicide, crime, juvenile delinquency, and other forms of deviant behavior are said to characterize an urban-industrial society. Whether or not the behavior going under these labels is more frequent than, let us say, a century ago, it seems sure that its emergence as a set of social problems demanding organized public attention is linked to urban-industrial conditions.

The social problem of juvenile delinquency in many ways provides the best illustration of the theme of this book so far: that the technological changes of industrialism lead to changes in the structure of society; these societal changes, in the context of American culture (the values described in Chapter II), produce or intensify concern about certain social problems, which creates a demand for welfare services; the supply takes the form of social agencies, public and private, manned by professional social workers and other welfare specialists. On the *demand* side, the social problem of delinquency is linked to industrialization via the changes in stratification and social mobility which industry brings about; it is linked also to distinctively urban conditions. On the *supply* side, an army of specialists has been recruited and sometimes trained to cope with the problem, and both public and private agencies converge on it; police, schools, courts, with their associated detention and probation programs, child guidance clinics, and youth boards are only the most obvious units in a complex welfare response. This chapter, then, will look at some facts and theories about the causes of juvenile delinquency, mention studies which evaluate efforts to prevent or reduce it, and suggest some implications of our analysis for the agencies which deal with the delinquent. A focus on delinquency will permit us to make explicit the uses and limits of sociological analysis, on the one hand, and of clinical and reform approaches to social welfare on the other.

Two further considerations prompt attention to juvenile delinquency. To understand the causes of delinquency is to understand the genesis of much adult crime, for the habitual delinquent has a very good chance of growing up to be a hardened criminal. And to understand the treatment of juvenile offenders is to understand the vanguard of corrections effort. As Ohlin (276: p. 13) suggests, it is in juvenile institutions that inmate self-governing techniques, group therapy, individualized case study, counseling, and program-planning have been most broadly used and developed. Programs aimed at the delinquent tend to spread to the adult prison systems and to the entire field of corrections.

Three assumptions will guide the discussion. First, as with most social phenomena, our solid knowledge is so limited that general theory, a broad understanding of the "why" of delinquency, will be more useful to the practitioner than detailed prescriptions for action or "How To Do It" recipes. The youth worker will not get the answers to his day-to-day problems here, but he may acquire a sensitivity to some major variables affecting delinquency that any action program must take into account.

Second, no social scientist can say whether a given child will become a delinquent at the age of ten—any more than the oceanographer can tell us where a cork dropped in the Atlantic will be ten days from now. But the social scientist may know the likelihood that a given neighborhood of given social composition will have a high or low rate of delinquency, just as the oceanographer may know the movements of the main currents in the Atlantic. Social science seeks to explain not the unique biography of the individual delinquent, but the differences in rates of delinquency among different strata and groups having different structure and culture.

Our third assumption is a double-barreled sociological principle: Similar motives may be expressed in different behavior patterns (for example, status-striving among lower-class boys may result in both delinquent and nondelinquent behavior; power-striving among lawyers may result in both judicious public service and political demagoguery). And the same pattern of behavior may be related to different motives (for example, Johnny's truancy may stem from neurotic inability to relate himself to schoolmates, Joe's truancy from an impulse to conform to gang standards; one doctor conforms to medical ethics because he thinks it expedient for boosting his income, another because of his altruism). Patterns of motivation and patterns of behavior both bear study, but there is no one-to-one correspondence between them.

Facts and Theories About Delinquency

Why juvenile delinquency? A veritable babel of voices is heard in reply. Ministers point to the failure of parents to teach religion; women's clubs to violence and horror in the comics, on television and film. The sociologist sees broken homes, poor housing, and disorganization in the slum; the psychologist, emotional deprivation, underlying anxieties, guilt feelings, and frustrations in the individual. A psychiatrist interprets delinquency as the product of an unresolved Oedipus complex; and an enlightened warden of a state penitentiary concludes with the inevitable, "It's always seemed to me that there are more delinquent parents than children."

Some of these partial explanations account for more of the known facts than others. Rather than setting up each explanation as a straw man to be demolished with a few well-selected statistics, we will present what seems to us a plausible interpretation suggested by our previous analysis of urban-industrial society. This theory will stress the physical and social aspects of urbanism and the stratification effects of industrialism as the master keys to delinquency. Close attention will be given to the gaps in the evidence.

Urbanism, Culture Conflict, and Social Disorganization. Delinquency is probably more characteristic of urban than rural areas. Cities crowd heterogeneous populations into small spaces. Even the physical aspects of city life—decreased space for harmless physi-

cal activity, the existence of private property in forms easier to
destroy or steal, the anonymity of the crowd—offer a superior
chance for law-breaking.

Another less obvious argument holds that social disorganization and cultural conflict produce a high delinquency rate among
the heterogeneous, poverty-stricken, highly mobile people of the
slum. On the culture side, the city mixes people of diverse cultural backgrounds, offering youngsters their choice of diverse
standards of behavior, including "normal" patterns of crime; on
the organization side, the slum lacks the community spirit, the
social cohesion of a stable community, necessary to induce conventional behavior and control deviants (see, for example, 326).
The parent of the youthful offender is often heard to exclaim,
"He never learned that from me!" But in the city, especially in
the slum, there are many other channels for learning: the street,
the gang, the movies.

Much data can be mustered in support of the "social disorganization" and "culture conflict" argument. But, as with the general
theory of urbanism of which it is a part (see Chapter V, pages
116–121), some notable evidence suggests its limits:

1. *The slum is seldom a lawless "jungle"; it is highly organized.* One
can hardly read the classic description of an Italian slum in
Boston, Whyte's *Street Corner Society*, without being impressed
with the large amount of "integration" described therein.
The organization and the ambitions of the population may
be centered around racket structure, crime syndicate, and
political machine; the concern with reputation may be
local; the integration may be internal, not within the larger
community; and the sense of community may take the form
of hostility to respectable institutions. It is true, too, that
the integration of the slum sometimes tends to minimize
mutual helpfulness and responsibility and maximize ego-
centric considerations. ("We all want to bet, so we protect
the bookies from the cops.") But organization there is, and
the image of an anonymous mass of struggling humanity,
a vacuum into which the delinquent moves, is misleading.

There is also a logical error: the indices of "social disorganization" to which these studies point often include
crime, delinquency, broken homes, prostitution, and the

like. The loosely defined whole is then used to explain one of its parts, delinquency. (196: pp. 9–10)

2. *Areas of high mobility sometimes show high delinquency rates, sometimes low.* As we have seen in Chapter V, mobility does not necessarily disrupt a stable social life. A careful study in Baltimore shows no significant relation between the delinquency rate of an area and its population change. (196: pp. 29–30) Confirming other research on urbanism, a study of Omaha (350) suggests that areas where families change houses often but better their conditions while they are at it, have low rates of habitual delinquency. The idea that highly mobile families are necessarily rootless, too loosely attached to the community to control their youngsters, does not stand up. It is when high rates of *residential* mobility are not accompanied by *social* mobility that we find instability— as reflected in high rates of crime, dependency, and the like.

3. *Poverty or substandard housing as such does not cause delinquency* any more than high rates of tuberculosis and child mortality found in delinquency areas cause delinquency. The Baltimore study (196: pp. 79–80) shows no real relationship between delinquency rates and the physical aspects of housing. Several neighborhoods with very low rents and atrocious overcrowding could not even qualify in the upper 25 per cent of the ranking delinquency areas. Again, as with mobility, it is only where poverty and slum housing are associated with delinquency-inducing ways of life—social disorganization, culture conflict, and the presence of a delinquent subculture—that they are related to delinquency rates. Thus, while Lander found that in Baltimore the delinquency rate is not specifically related to socioeconomic conditions in an area, it *is* related to "anomie"—that is, social instability indexed by many disadvantaged Negro migrants and few owner-occupied homes.

4. *Young people in delinquency areas are only to a limited degree confronted with a moral vacuum or moral confusion due to culture conflict.* The cultural diversity one finds in the slum, the standards of conduct at odds with the larger community, the hostility to police and courts—these may hide a very sizable agreement that habitual truancy, vandalism, and stealing are indeed "wrong." Even the delinquents themselves, let alone predominantly law-abiding adults, will provide ready rationalizations for their crimes which reveal

some awareness of community standards (for example, stealing or destroying property is fair only if "the guy was insured," "the house was vacant," or "it's a big business—they can afford it"). Finally, the mere existence of two or more minority groups with conflicting standards—Negro and white, Jewish and Irish—does not appear to ensure a high delinquency rate. Indeed, "culture conflict" as a factor in delinquency areas seems to be important only where the smaller of two clashing groups in a neighborhood is large enough to threaten the dominance of the larger. (196: p. 65; cf. 358: pp. 120–121; and 320: pp. 91–93.)

With all these reservations, it is true that distinctly urban conditions play their part in the genesis of high delinquency rates. Targets for vandalism and stealing are readily available; the anonymous escape into the sea of strangers is more possible. While primary-group controls are not absent, the slum family in the city is less cohesive (see Chapter III). Moreover, legal control is a larger part of the total machinery of control throughout the city—and impersonal laws are not only more numerous and varied but they are easier to flout or evade than the rural mores. While delinquency rates are often low in areas where one minority group is dominant, areas of maximum heterogeneity (for instance, half Negro, half white) do offer opportunity for culture conflict and gang warfare. The presence of many clashing values seems to weaken the hold of any of them.

In general, the "poverty and social disorganization in the slum" theory stands up with this qualification: the delinquency rate in an area will be low despite bad housing, bad location, and poverty *if* the area is socially stable.[1] Social instability under the physical conditions of slum life provides the opportunity for the development of delinquency.

The opportunities are there; the motives are more elusive. In fact, it is the chief deficiency of the theory of "social disorganization and culture conflict" that it explains delinquency wholly in terms of the absence of restraints and the absence or weakness of

[1] For instance, Lander found that "in completely stabilized Negro areas, i.e., areas of 90 to 100% Negro population, the Negro delinquency rate is the *same* as the corresponding white rate when the influence of other factors [home ownership, income, and the like] is eliminated." (196: p. 60)

shared goals and values. Granting that city slums offer opportunities for deviant behavior, why do youngsters develop the particular patterns of behavior they do? How do we explain the impulse to delinquency rather than to some other form of behavior?
Here we must turn from urbanism to a consideration of, first, the
delinquent subculture and, second, of the impact of industrialism
on the class structure.

The Content and Distribution of Delinquency as a Culture Pattern. The
best sociological treatment of patterns of motivation accounting
for the development of habitual delinquency is Albert K. Cohen's
Delinquent Boys: The Culture of the Gang (62), a book that has
received considerable social work attention. It is a synthesis of a
vast literature that describes, explains, and predicts delinquent
behavior. This section will present a modified version of Cohen's
argument, which we will reformulate in the subsequent section,
"Gaps in the Evidence."[1]

In all discussion of delinquency causation we first need to know
what types of youngsters commit what unlawful acts how often, for this is
what we are trying to explain. Here, because of well-known
limitations of both official and unofficial records, we are on shaky
ground and can only offer our best judgment.

Children learn to become delinquent by becoming members of
groups in which delinquent behavior is the thing to do. There is a
delinquent "subculture"—ways of acting, thinking, and feeling
learned by association with delinquent models. This subculture
may be learned by any kind of personality if the opportunities
afforded by the physical and social facts of city life described
above are many and the opportunities and resources for learning
*non*delinquent behavior are few, although there must also be
reason to learn it. The boy who becomes a delinquent, then, has
gone through the same process as a boy who becomes a Boy Scout
or a Future Farmer. The difference is in the cultural pattern to
which he is exposed, the skills necessary to learn the appropriate
behavior, and the motives that prompt his learning.

---

[1] We refer to other work on delinquency only where it elaborates, confirms, or
denies Cohen's thesis, or is cited as incidental in Cohen. For citation of other references, and details on the subculture of the delinquent gang, see Cohen (62).

What is this delinquent cultural pattern? What behavior is typical and expected?

1. *Solidarity with the gang, hostility, or indifference to the world outside.* Delinquent behavior is typically gang behavior. Continual demonstrations of one's loyalty to the in-group and contempt for out-groups are a feature of many groups organized for conflict—nations, unions, political parties, and smaller friendship cliques. But the delinquent gang develops in-group solidarity to a high principle, intensely felt. They must keep the gang independent, autonomous, free from adult control. They must maintain their "rep" at all costs.

2. *Acts which do not bring financial or at first glance any other gain.* "Juvenile crime" in many ways is unlike "adult crime." Acts which epitomize the spirit of the delinquent subculture are nonutilitarian, apparently *purposeless*. The gang steals "for the hell of it." They steal clothes they cannot wear, toys they do not use, food they throw away. While stealing they commit vandalism, trespass, truancy. Like adult criminals, they may exert much effort and court much danger while they are about it; but the end product is not so much the possession of a coveted object otherwise unattainable as it is the adventure itself.

3. *Acts committed with an eye to immediate pleasure.* Consistent with this is the element of *short-run hedonism:* except for mapping the strategy of intergang warfare, the gang seldom plans, or shows interest in long-term gains or costs. They hang around the street corner, rough-housing, chewing the fat, waiting for something to turn up. Most of their fun is quite ordinary; they swim, play ball, cards, and so on—only a small fraction of the daily round is specifically delinquent. Note, for instance, this boy's description of gang life (quoted in 119: p. 13): "Now, for example, you take an average day. What happens? We come down to the restaurant and we sit in the restaurant, and sit and sit. All right, say, er . . . after a couple of hours in the restaurant, maybe we'll go to a poolroom, shoot a little pool, that's if somebody's got the money. O.K., a little pool, come back. By this time the restaurant is closed. We go in the candy store, sit around the candy store for a while, and that's it, that's all we do, man."

4. *Malice and negativism; the flouting of rules.* Of course, this routine is interspersed with the occasional bursts of delinquency that excite the community and make headlines. Such bursts are characterized not only by purposeless, short-run hedonism, but also by the feature which gives them their drama— their malicious tone. The gang enthusiastically enjoys the defiance of taboos and the discomfiture of others. Aside from gang wars, "there is keen delight in terrorizing 'good' children, in driving them from playgrounds and gyms for which the gang itself may have little use, and in general in making themselves obnoxious to the virtuous." Gang members do not just *break* the rules of school and community; they *flout* them. Cohen points to "an element of active spite and malice, contempt and ridicule, challenge and defiance, exquisitely symbolized in an incident described to the writer by Mr. Henry D. McKay, of defecating on the teacher's desk." (62: p. 28)

The behavior typical of the delinquent subculture, then, is characterized by gang solidarity; an apparently nonutilitarian, short-run hedonism; and malice toward respectable out-groups. Now among what parts of our population do we find this subculture? The answer seems to be: among boys much more than among girls; among lower socioeconomic strata much more than among middle and upper strata. The statistics on which these generalizations rest are by no means conclusive and cannot be discussed in detail here. But the best evidence points to their accuracy. (See, for instance, the assessments by Cohen, Lander, and Kvaraceus, in 62; 196; and 193, pp. 82–110.)

Practically all official sources agree that male delinquency is at least four times as frequent as female. Moreover, what female delinquency there is does not fit the delinquent subculture as well as male delinquency. One problem immediately comes to mind: some types of offenses committed by girls (for example, a girl gang breaks a window or rolls a drunk) are less likely to find their way into the record than when committed by boys. (What man would admit to being beaten by girls?) On the other hand, boys are less likely to be referred to the police and courts for sex offenses than girls. It is probable that incomplete reporting for boys' sex offenses would at least balance incomplete reporting for girls' nonsex offenses, so, when boy-girl comparisons are at issue, official statistics remain a good index of the actual frequency of delinquent acts.

The same logic applies to the class distribution of the delinquent subculture. Almost all statistical analyses agree that delinquency, especially gang delinquency, is mainly a working-class phenomenon; the less prosperous, less respected, less powerful neighborhoods and families produce the high delinquency rates.[1] But what about off-the-record delinquency? The record could reflect the usual bias of courts and police—the fact that the lower-class boy is an easy mark for complaint, arrest, and prosecution. Some delightfully skeptical studies describing unofficial delinquency, white-collar crime, and adult transgressions generally, have taught us that many crimes are committed by middle-class persons, both young and not-so-young. The child who never breaks the law is as rare as the adult who never breaks a speed limit.[2] The catch is that working-class youngsters *also* commit undetected and unrecorded delinquencies—probably both more serious and more frequent. Careful studies of off-the-record delinquency—in Passaic, the District of Columbia, and Cambridge-Somerville—all show a very large amount of unofficial delinquency among lower-class youth. One study of 114 underprivileged boys (40 of whom were official court delinquents) conservatively estimates that they had committed a minimum of 6,416 infractions of law in five years—only 95 of which became a matter of official complaint. (Cited in 62: pp. 40-41.)

[1] This seems to hold even for rural areas. For instance, Merrill compared 300 cases referred to a rural county court in California with a control group matched for locale, age, and sex. Delinquents were more than 4 to 1 male; they were disproportionately from dependent or low-income and manual-worker families. Among the delinquents, boys were more likely than girls to be recidivists. (235: pp. 15-16, 77-79, 345)

[2] Porterfield (292: pp. 38 ff.) asked 437 students, not official delinquents, how many times they had ever committed any of 55 offenses (driving noisily by schools or churches; prowling; using abusive language; loafing in a pool hall, as well as more serious offenses). Precollege men averaged 17.6 offenses, college men averaged 11.2, precollege women averaged 4.7; all had committed one or more offenses. Wallerstein and Wyle (388) listed 49 offenses under the penal code of New York and got 1,020 men and 678 women to confess to undetected violations. The sample was probably biased toward the upper-income brackets. Ninety-nine per cent confessed to one or more crimes (e.g., opening someone else's mail, misrepresenting a product old, gambling, assault, stealing hotel towels).

Of course, no one has taken a representative sample of the juvenile population, followed them around twenty-four hours a day, and *then* compared delinquents and nondelinquents as to sex, class, and frequency of different types of acts. Until we obtain such data, however, the best evidence seems to indicate that all youngsters engage in delinquency, but the ones who make it a habit, a way of life, are overwhelmingly working-class boys. Here lies the bulk of juvenile crime. When you want to think of an act epitomizing modern urban delinquency, think of vandalism on the property of a respectable community institution (for example, a school) committed by a male gang whose families have low status and live in working-class neighborhoods.

The Status Anxiety of Lower-Class Boys. Why is the delinquent subculture concentrated among lower-class boys? The delinquency pattern, like all culture, consists of solutions to shared problems; to explain it, we must look at the typical problems of the lower-class boy, problems he and his family share with others in like circumstances.

If industrialization does nothing else, it creates a working class whose status, power, and security of income are relatively low. At the same time, it raises the level of mass aspiration—it makes those of low status *care* about being at the bottom.

That lower-class youth (mainly the sons of dependent families or of low-income laborers and service workers) are disadvantaged in the struggle for "success" is certain. Two decades of solid research have reminded us that schools and churches, courts and social agencies, uphold middle-class values and virtues, and peg the working-class child at the bottom. His opportunities to acquire the vocabulary, health, personal characteristics, social skills, and manners approved in these places are few. At home, the occupational models he encounters among his older brothers, friends, relatives, father and father's friends are generally of low status; the sustained pressure for school performance is lacking. At school, he experiences consequent discomfort. The testing and grading system puts a premium on information and abilities developed in middle- and upper-class homes. Discipline will be unequally administered by middle-class teachers—to his disadvantage. The conduct thought proper and rewarded by the school—stay on the job, learn your lessons, budget your time, obey authority, develop the ambition, initiative, self-control, good character, and sociability needed to get ahead—this ideal conduct supports the home and neighborhood training of the middle-class child, contradicts that of the slum child. (Cf. 391; 97; 151.)

That lower-class children nevertheless acquire and retain American success goals is less certain, though crucial to this explanation of delinquency. The notion is that the lower-class boy, though relegated to the bottom of the status pyramid, does internalize the free-mobility ideology—or at least he values the opinions of those who have. Just as the Negro comes to accept the dominant white caste's view of dark skin as inferior, so the working-class boy in some degree comes to share the values of a dominant middle class: manual workers are inferior to non-manual workers; those with ability and ambition will get ahead; all have the duty to try; those who fail, lack virtue and should feel shame. If he does not pick up these beliefs and values in school, he gets them from the mass media, which still celebrate the rich, the powerful, the well-born as models of success, and emphasize the inferiority of working-class people and practices.

Cohen recognizes that different working-class boys absorb different values in varying degrees; that many of these values may be absorbed side by side with working-class values (having ambition and self-reliance, on the one hand, having fun here and now, and standing by one's friends, on the other); and that not all life situations compel a choice between them. (Cf. 62: pp. 104 ff., 123–127, 168.) He argues, however, that "most children in American society, of whatever class, assimilate to some degree, the middle class value system. Some assimilate it in almost 'pure' form, others in various attenuated versions and . . . uneasy combinations . . . sometimes submerged by the working-class system but rarely altogether stifled." (62: p. 104) What few data we have suggest this may be true.[1]

---

[1] For example, Chinoy's study of *Automobile Workers and the American Dream* shows that few workers, upon finding the road to success blocked in the factory, abandon or reject middle-class success goals outright. Instead they scale their ambitions down a bit, emphasizing security and material possessions rather than occupational

In short, the lower-class boy, disadvantaged in the struggle for status measured by middle-class values, anxious about the fact that he and his family seem to have lost that struggle, has a problem of adjustment. He is in the market for a solution.

The delinquent solution is the most satisfactory of the alternatives. Conceivably, he could try to play the middle-class game by middle-class rules. But he is already handicapped by family and neighborhood experiences which give him inferior resources and limited opportunities for conformity to such standards. He solves the problem by sharing it with other boys; together they create and maintain the delinquent subculture. They reject the school, the church, the settlement house—the entire apparatus manned by middle-class people, sustaining middle-class values. They play truant because "good" boys do not. They flout the rules which stigmatize them as inferior. They single out middle-class targets for acts of vandalism—with special pleasure in the aimless, violent destruction of property, visible symbol of the rewards for middle-class virtue.[1]

The delinquent gang in this view is a form of protest against a status system which places lower-class youth low. It is also a way of creating an alternative system with criteria of success they can meet. The delinquent gang permits the lower-class boy to turn middle-class morality upside down: to define merit in terms that contradict the norms accounting for his anxieties; and to approve aggression against the persons and institutions who uphold these norms.

The foregoing theory accounts not only for the "aimless" and malicious character of delinquency, but also for its distribution in

---

prestige; they project their ambitions onto their children; they verbally cherish small-business aspiration for themselves. (59) Directly to the point, Merrill's comparison of the aspirations and expectations of 100 fifteen-year-old, low-status delinquents and 100 higher-status nondelinquents of the same age shows that the delinquent boys had much lower *expectations* of getting ahead occupationally, but when it came to what they would *like* to achieve, their ambitions were about the same as middle-class nondelinquents. (235: p. 148) See pp. 198–199, 202–203 for the further research needed on this point.

[1] So strong is the hold of this subculture, once developed, that it is only a slight exaggeration to say, with Denney and Riesman, that a lower-class boy who is *not* delinquent in a delinquency area is fairly sure to be either "headed up the class ladder or . . . psychologically deviant or both, being unwilling or unable to join in the group activities sanctioned by his peers." (85: p. 471)

the population. Boys are more exposed than girls to the demand for job achievement; lower-class youth are more disadvantaged than other youth in the scramble for the "success" they all want. It is thus in the male, working-class sector that there is a common core of status anxiety and discontent, for which the delinquent subculture seems an appropriate solution.

To recapitulate: Some deviant behavior exists in all societies. What industrialization seems to do is to create conditions under which transmission of a consistent, communitywide set of values becomes more difficult, the paths to nonconformity become easier, and the problems of social mobility more poignant. For both motive and opportunity, then, look to the status anxiety of lower-class boys in the physical and social setting of the urban slum and you will have an explanation that fits most of the facts of delinquent life.

Anxiety About Male Identity as a Possible Cause. What about that boy from a "good" family in a "respectable" neighborhood who gets into trouble? Reporters and editorial writers, confronted with the middle-class delinquent, rise to heights of moral fervor. They display an anguished resentment at what they allege to be a vast increase in vicious crime among "overprivileged" youth.

The first thing to note is that the picture we get from the popular press about "middle-class delinquents" is often misleading. A typical article mentioned boys from "middle-class" families with "incomes of $3,000 to $6,000," living in "two-family homes on a clean street." But such income brackets include many two- or three-earner homes (for instance, mother a laundress, father an unskilled laborer), where the status dilemma of the children is as distressing as it is in the slum. Moreover, social classes, defined in terms of income and occupation, are not completely homogeneous as to culture: a home with middle-class income and even occupation may provide its children a set of working-class experiences, with little encouragement and training that will pay off in "success" in school and community—although this is unlikely in most high-status families. Finally, middle-class delinquency in terms of frequency is only a small fraction of lower-class delinquency.

A more debatable and possibly more important question is this: Is middle-class delinquency of the same *quality* as lower-class delinquency? If the behavior and the genesis of one are sharply different from the behavior and genesis of the other, each must be understood and handled differently.

Cohen, drawing upon the work of Parsons, offers the following hypothesis: While the development of a delinquent subculture among lower-class boys is a solution to the typical *status* anxiety they experience and share, the delinquent solution among middle-class boys is their way of coping with a basic anxiety about the achievement of a *male identity*. We do not agree with this argument, but it is important to consider it and in fact offer further supporting elaboration in order later to reformulate it. Briefly, here is the argument.

Three features of the social world of the middle class make the boy's masculinity a problem: the central importance of the mother as disciplinarian and socializing agent; the "feminizing" of work; the "feminizing" of leisure.

The smaller nuclear family, with the home often far from both relatives and work, and sometimes far from the central city, makes the mother the dominant value disseminator for both girls and boys (see Chapter III). On less solid ground, the argument goes a step farther to assume that the middle-class father is more often absent from home than the lower-class father, and that the former's absence makes the mother not only the transmitter of values, but also the dominant object of identification, which for boys becomes a source of sex-role anxiety.

That work, especially in the growing middle class, has become less visibly and distinctively masculine is clear from our previous discussion: more and more jobs are white collar, professional and administrative; more and more are open to women. Although sex is still one basis of job assignment, ability to perform is increasingly the key. And women, as well as men, can sit at desks, neatly dressed, read and write, shuffle paper, deal smoothly with customers and clients, and perform the light manual operations required in the mechanized office or store. The boy is expected to become "manly" like his father, but where in the middle-class family is the unambiguous model of manliness he can follow?

Leisure in the middle class, like work, has also become less distinctively masculine. Try to classify the leisure activities our culture fifty years ago defined as "manly" (fighting, drinking, gambling, stoking a furnace, carpentry, active sports), "neuter" (reading, traveling, eating, going to church) or "feminine" (caring for children, cooking, washing dishes, decorating the home). Then list the percentage of leisure hours your *grandfather* gave to each type and compare it with the percentage *you* (or your brother or father) give today. The balance has surely shifted in the feminine direction. Even the activities restricted to men, let alone the hours allotted to them, are fewer. (Think of once-masculine gambling and then look at midcentury Las Vegas.)

In short, the middle-class boy, in contrast to both his sister and his working-class peers, finds, in his family routine, in the available models of identification, no "assurance that he is indubitably, in his own eyes and those of the world around him, a representative and recognizable specimen of his sex." In Cohen's words:

> He knows it is shameful for a boy to be like a woman and he feels constrained to rebel against all those impulses which he feels might be suggestive of femininity and to exaggerate all those traits which set him apart from the other sex. . . . Since mother has been the principal agent of indoctrination of "good," respectable behavior, "goodness" comes to symbolize femininity, and . . . "bad" behavior acquires the functionof denying his femininity. (62: pp. 163–164)

During that long preparation for an adult job (which itself may not provide an assured membership card in the fraternity of males), he resorts to juvenile crime to prove to himself and everyone else that he is really a man. Here, Cohen argues, lies the common core of motivation among middle-class delinquents: anxiety about sex role.

This hypothesis, to do it justice, is not expected to hold unless the conditions leading to such anxiety are well developed and unless the boy's opportunities to share and express it with others in the same boat are many. The low delinquency rate of the middle class suggests that few boys reach the height of anxiety which prompts a delinquent solution to the problem of achieving a male identity and that alternative solutions are typical. We would add that research may show another explanation of sex-role anxiety, consistent with delinquency statistics and suggested below, to be more accurate.

Gaps in the Evidence: Some Needed Research

With the exception of the treatment of sex-role anxiety, the theory presented above, a modified version of Cohen, seems to be the best explanation of the accumulated data on the nature and distribution of delinquent conduct. As we have already indicated, the data are not always reliable; and the gaps in the evidence are many. But the theory has the merit of being testable—we know from it what facts we must look for to prove us right or wrong. A brief reminder of some unanswered questions will help to clarify the uses and limits of this explanation of delinquency causation and will serve to introduce a discussion of delinquency prevention.

Some of the main problems for research are: (1) the frequency of delinquency in certain social categories; (2) the types of acts by social categories; (3) sex-role anxiety in delinquency causation; (4) the group setting of delinquency; (5) why so many lower-class boys escape delinquency; (6) the psychology of delinquency in the individual case.

    1. *The frequency of delinquency: rates by categories* The discussion above of the problem of unrecorded and undetected crime concluded that the class and sex variations in official delinquency probably hold for unofficial delinquency, too, though more work is needed to clinch the case. There are some hints that the boy-girl differences may be diminishing. One study (223) reports a drop in the sex ratio from 60:1 to 8:1 among cases brought before the Children's Court and classified as delinquents in New York City from 1902 to 1932. Nationally, and in the years 1938 to 1947 the ratio continued to drop for police arrests, though for juvenile court cases it fluctuated closely around one girl to five boys. (318: p. 13) If this reflects shifts in actual rates and the trend continues, then the status-anxiety, male-identity explanation may need modification. Are girls becoming ex-

posed to increased demand for achievement in ways uncon-
nected with sex? Or is sex delinquency among girls on the
increase, and, if so, why?

Too little is known about urban-rural differences, as well.
It is conceivable that the higher official delinquency rate in
the city may not be due to culture conflict, social disorganization, and other distinctively urban conditions; it may
merely reflect the greater willingness of urban populations
to call in outside authority to settle disputes. Rural people
do not readily resort to the police, courts, detention facilities, and social agencies to handle cases of truancy, stealing,
family conflict, property damage, trespass, and the like—
though these may occur as often as in the city. (Cf. 240:
p. 13.) Of course, this may be another way of saying that
the hold of the folkways and mores in the urban area is less
important and legal control more important than in the
rural area—which does not contradict the theory that delinquency should be more of a visible social problem in the
city than in the country.

2. *The content of the delinquent subculture: types of acts by categories.*
More serious are the gaps in the evidence about the character of delinquent acts committed by working-class and
middle-class boys and girls. How "purposeless," "short-
run," and "malicious" *are* the patterns of delinquent
behavior?

Court records show that *theft* is the most common type of
offense for male delinquents; even records of unofficial delinquency place stealing second only to truancy as the leading juvenile crime. (17: pp. 50–51) Is this purposeless; is it
"negativistic"? One can argue, as Cohen does, that stealing,
like destruction of property, is "an attack on the middle class
where their egos are most sensitive"—expressing contempt
for a way of life which judges lower-class boys to be inferior.
(62: p. 134) But the evidence is lacking. How is status among
middle- and lower-class boys related to their aggressiveness
toward the rules which determine status? How are hostile
sentiments toward middle-class values related to stealing
and other acts of delinquency? What do these boys do with
the stolen goods? Are "passive" crimes (for instance,
truancy) to be taken as products of status anxiety as much
as "active" crimes (stealing, vandalism)? These are some of
the missing facts needed to give the theory a good test. Even
if the earliest adventures in stealing prove to be at once

playful and malicious, "just for the hell of it," with practice it may become more like adult crime, more calculated, more purposeful.

One fact which may or may not prove to be uncomfortable for the theory is the finding of Wattenberg and Balistrieri (394) that "in contrast to other boys charged by Detroit police with misconduct, juveniles involved in automobile theft come relatively in higher proportion from good neighborhoods and favored ethnic groups." Again, is auto-theft "nonpurposive, malicious" crime? Do any boy gangs engaged in car theft have, or develop, connections with adult criminals who dispose of cars for profit? Or is almost all of it, as Jerome Hall suggests (131: pp. 249 ff.), "just for fun"—a one-night joy-ride? Are these boys showing they are men, are they experiencing more status anxiety than other middle-class boys, or neither?

3. *Male identity as a source of anxiety.* One way to test the "masculine identity" idea of delinquency causation would be to contrast four groups—middle-class delinquents and non-delinquents, lower-class delinquents and nondelinquents—as to: (1) the role models to which they have been significantly exposed; (2) the pressure they have felt for achievement; (3) the mobility patterns of their fathers. Those middle-class boys whose fathers have lost status while the boys were children but who have internalized middle-class success goals might experience as much status anxiety as lower-class boys (and behave in as delinquent a way) without having any unusual anxiety in the achievement of "manliness." There are many possibilities for research of this sort.

Mobility of fathers aside, it can be argued that the middle-class boy, because of long-delayed entry into careers, is more worried about becoming an adult than a man, while masculinity is more a problem for the working-class boy. Anything resembling femininity brings the latter more ridicule from his less-equalitarian family. The very clarity of his parents' demand for unequivocal manliness, coupled with their harsher sex discipline,[1] suggests that the lower-

---

[1] A careful comparison of native-born working-class and suburban middle-class mothers (372 cases with five- or six-year-old children) showed that sex training is clearly more severe in the lower stratum. Lower-class mothers applied more pressure against masturbation and group sex play; they were also less permissive regarding nudity and began modesty training earlier. All but one of the other major studies of class differences in child-rearing picture a punitive tendency in the lower strata. (217) Kinsey's data on sex behavior of different educational strata are also consistent. (183: pp. 365 ff.)

class boy may experience more intense anxiety about sex role. This is not to say that middle-class boys have no male identity problem of the kind we have described above. Cross-cultural comparison shows that some aspects of sex role—for example, a man should be active vs. passive, dominant vs. subordinate—are universal and are perhaps based on innate differences, cross-cutting social classes, as well as societies. But the middle-class boy can play off societywide (or worldwide) definitions of maleness against the more tolerant ambiguities of middle-class life; while for the lower-class boy "there's no hiding place down there."

Finally, it has not been proved that middle-class fathers spend less time with their children than do lower-class fathers. And it seems doubtful that middle-class boys identify with their mothers more strongly than lower-class boys. Even if the middle-class father *were* more often absent from home, this would not block a strong identification with him. Such identification is more than a matter of proximity and more than a matter of love; it may depend mainly on the respect and deference the mother demonstrates toward the father (the boy wants to be like the parent who gets the larger number of rewards in the family). If in the lower-class family the mother shows contempt toward the father for not "bringing home the bacon" and resentment when he goes off to the bar with the gang, the male children will have no strong desire to be like Dad, and hence will be more amenable to feminine identification. The reverse may be more typical of the middle-class family, where father may seem to get more rewards (be treated with more respect and affection)—and serve as the desired model for his boys.

If research supports these ideas, the theory could be reformulated as follows: (1) status anxiety is greater in the lower class and the delinquent solution is both appropriate and more available; (2) anxiety about male identity is also greater in the lower class, but for this the delinquent solution is one among many appropriate solutions (for example, alcoholism, dope addiction, neurosis); (3) for those middle-class boys who have much status anxiety and who are able to share it with others, but unable to solve it by reorienting their ambitions, the delinquent solution though less readily available is appropriate (and the male identity problem is negligible). This theory is consistent with the statistics of delinquency—a high rate for lower-class but a low rate for middle-class boys; it would predict even sharper contrasts than the official statistics show.

4. *Big gangs, small gangs, and lone wolves.* That much if not most habitual delinquency is gang delinquency is plain. That the gang is one road and often the only road to prestige and power denied these boys in school, church, social clubs, and the economic system, is also suggested by many observers of gang life.[1] Moreover, if one contrasts gang delinquents with nongang delinquents one finds it is the lone wolf who shows evidence of disturbed, "tense or depriving" family relations; the gang boys, in contrast, typically "do not fit a picture of weak supervision or poor home relations"—they are all too normal. (395: pp. 749, 752) This is familiar enough and nicely fits our discussion of the delinquent subculture. But it also points to the fact that the theory does not cover that portion of delinquent behavior which is primarily psychogenic—a point which will be clear when we deal with the "unadjusted delinquent" below.

A second consideration that may be obscured or left out by the theory is this: there are gangs and gangs. A casually formed play group of four or five boys who spend their spare time together and occasionally "raise hell" with fists, sticks, bottles, and rocks is one thing. A large-scale organization with a hierarchy (topped by a Leader, a War Counselor, and two Main Guys), recruitment policies, judicial procedures (the death penalty is sometimes imposed), a rank-and-file of a hundred boys equipped with knives and home-made "zip guns," intergang relations replete with claims to sovereignty over a "turf," mediators and arbitrators from the Youth Board, outpost commands in enemy territory, pacts negotiated with allies—this is another. Some gangs are so bureaucratically organized that it is hard to assess what we read about either their members' motives or the workings of their organizational machinery. With the large number of "street workers," reporters, clergymen, and caseworkers approaching them for off-the-record, confidential stories, the leaders, like officers of other large organizations, must have developed by now considerable sophistication, in the form of a pat public relations line.

---

[1] Speculative, clinical, and sometimes systematic, these studies are carefully reviewed in W. W. Wattenberg's and J. J. Balistrieri's "Gang Membership and Juvenile Misconduct." (395)

Is the big bureaucratic gang different from the small informal gang in the nature and consequences of its crimes?[1] Is the big gang different in the functions it fulfills for its members? Or is it merely an extreme form of the same protest against middle-class values, stemming from the same status anxiety? Answers to these questions will form part of the large body of data on who commits what kinds of acts how often in what settings—data we need in order to arrive at useful classifications of delinquents and of patterns of causation.

5. *Why so many lower-class families escape delinquency.* The answers concern: (1) middle-class values among lower-class delinquents; and (2) ethnic variations in delinquency rates, reflecting variations in family integration and in skills for urban living.

The first is implied by the theory and was discussed above: middle-class values and criteria of status are not internalized by all with the same intensity (thus, low status would not produce the same anxiety in all); skills and resources such as intelligence and language ability vary among lower-class families, with some better equipped to overcome the obstacles to the upward climb than others (so that the children's opportunities to achieve success by middle-class standards are greater).

Only comparison proves, and the theory cannot be shown to be wrong unless we design studies with adequate controls. For instance, we need to compare lower-class delinquents and nondelinquents as to: (1) which of the success goals they have internalized with what intensity; (2) the resources and skills available for status achievement; (3) who experiences how much status discontent; (4) their relative opportunities for learning delinquent behavior. Do lower-class nondelinquents, compared with lower-class delinquents of the same age, neighborhood, ethnicity, and race, have greater resources which can pay off in status

---

[1] A survey of 1,477 American cities by the Federal Bureau of Investigation shows that at least two in five of those arrested in 1955 for major crimes (murder, negligent manslaughter, rape, robbery, aggravated assault, burglary, larceny, and auto theft) were under 18 years of age. Youngsters under 18 accounted for two in three of the arrests for auto theft, about half the arrests for burglary and larceny, and more than one in four for buying or receiving stolen property. (374: pp. 112–115) This suggests that a large number of teenage crimes (1) are purposive and planned, the kind of thing a well-organized gang might accomplish; (2) closely resemble adult crimes, and may even have an organizational connection. Cohen's description of gang life does not fit some large, dope-addicted gangs of New York City who mingle with pushers, become involved in the traffic, or commit crimes for the money to get the dope. (Cf. 190.)

achievement? Do they have fewer chances to contact delinquent gangs? Or take nondelinquents who have equal opportunity to learn delinquency and who also lack resources for middle-class achievement. Have they absorbed less of the American Dream than anxiety-filled delinquents? And among delinquents, does the character of delinquent acts vary with variations in the degree of status discontent?

The second answer—ethnic variations—may offer further support for the theory. It is often noted that some ethnic groups—mainly the Jews, Chinese, and Japanese—produce remarkably few delinquents. (17: p. 56; 358: pp. 109, 125; 222) More significant, even when they live in delinquency areas—in the same slums at the same social and economic level as delinquent-prone ethnics—they seem resistant to the delinquent subculture.[1] (219; 320: p. 89)

Why are there delinquency-resistant minorities? The theory suggests that we look at the degree of exposure to the delinquent subculture, and the opportunities for arriving at nondelinquent solutions to the problem of status anxiety. These ethnic groups tend to be more self-contained, more isolated from the mainstream of slum life, than other ethnic groups. Their families, even in the second generation, seem to remain more integrated. In effect, these youngsters are less exposed to the delinquent subculture.[2]

[1] From the *New York Times* of August 19, 1956: "Youth Board executives could recall only one Chinese delinquent in all their years of experience and only one family of Moslem children, all psychopathic. Few Jewish children are adjudged to be delinquent, but comparatively many are emotionally disturbed, these social workers said. . . . Only 2.2 per cent of all children brought into Children's Court for misbehavior in 1952 were Jewish, while about 31.5 per cent of the total city population was Jewish." Delinquency rates are in general low among children who are Jewish, or foreign born, or second-generation Orientals. (17; 358) Like urban-rural differentials, these ethnic contrasts may be due in part to the success of the more cohesive groups in keeping violators from the eyes of outside authorities. (Cf. 320: pp. 73-74.) For the reasons mentioned below, however, it seems likely that the frequency of unofficial delinquency (covered up by the group) is also low.

[2] A study of five ethnic groups (321 cases) in a Boston suburb found that lower-class Jews made more use of reward in disciplining their five-year-old children than did lower-class Italian, Irish, Old-American, or British parents. On the assumption that use of reward leads to closer bonds in the family, this suggests that family integration among Jews is a block to absorption into a delinquent subculture. (364) A study in May, 1955, of assimilation and parent-child relationships based on reports from 2,138 high school students in the Boston area whose parents were first and second generation is similarly suggestive. It points to large differences in family integration among working-class ethnics. French-Canadian parents, and to a slightly lesser degree, Italian and Portuguese, put strong pressure on their children to maintain language and religious differences, and in general to conform to ethnic customs and stick with friends of their own kind—in contrast to the rapidly assimilating Irish. (363; cf. 320.) If family integration is a factor in delinquency-resistance, then we would predict high delinquency rates among the Irish, compared to the others

On the skills and resources side, too, the lowest-delin-
quency ethnic groups are favorably situated: Jewish immigrants come more often from urban areas, and already
possess some of the skills required for competitive survival
in the city. Even if slum-located, they or their relatives often
have entrepreneurial talents developed in the retail trades;
their children consequently encounter a wider range of occupational role models to follow, and they acquire more
economically relevant information. Add the special place
of scholarship in the Jewish tradition, the survival of Old
Country language and customs among Oriental-Americans,
and we see that the sources of delinquency-resistance are
many and powerful. Contrast the Polish or Mexican immigrant or the Negro migrant from the South—rural, unskilled, lacking the resources which would help him get
along in the urban-industrial setting, his family less isolated
from external influences, less integrated internally, more
vulnerable to the delinquent solution.

Systematic comparisons of ethnic groups of similar social-
economic status but with varied delinquency rates could
provide a strategic test of the theory.

6. *Causes in the case; confirmation from psychological studies.* Finally,
what about the individual delinquent? Every youth worker
has encountered cases that do not fit the theory—cases that
cry for explanation on a different level, boys whose mental
or physical deficiencies, neurotic anxieties, or family relationships seem paramount in their delinquency. To this
criticism, Cohen gives a good answer: First, this theory aims
not to catalogue the great range of causes in the individual
case, but to seek the common core of motivation and opportunity which explains the bulk of delinquent behavior.
Second, the theory *does*, nevertheless, help us understand
the individual case.

Here are three points to consider in understanding the individual delinquent from this point of view: (1) Too often
"the explanation of delinquency stops short with the demonstration that the child has problems. . . . One can only
say, 'Who doesn't have problems?' " To discover that a
case has guilt feelings, insecurities, mental conflicts, and the
like, is not to show that the solution (delinquency) is appropriate to or even connected with the problem. We must ask,
"Why does this boy with his particular problem of adjust-

ment choose a delinquent solution (the 'symptoms' of vandalism, truancy, and so on) instead of some other solution?" The unique details of his life history may contribute to the answer, but it would seem more economical to find out first whether he has been searching for a solution in association with others who have the same adjustment problem. (2) Status anxiety and anxiety about sex role are components of motivation that are often ignored, yet they are pervasive in the groups that produce and sustain delinquency as a culture pattern. (3) Established theories, as Cohen suggests, "have tended to ignore that world outside the family—the school, the street, the playground, the settlement house. This world too is a crucible of personality and proving ground as well, with its own exacting judges of failure and success." (62: pp. 154-155)

To this we can add, moreover, that psychological studies are not inconsistent with the theory, though they do suggest its limits. For instance, several students of deviant behavior have observed psychological types of delinquency which match the social types (lower-class status-anxious, middle-class *and* lower-class masculinity-anxious) we discussed above. Fritz Redl (295: pp. 368-369) points to the "genuine delinquent," whose strong identification with delinquent subgroups takes place "on a class basis" (lashing out at the middle class), "on a development basis" with age peers, or "on a neighborhood gang basis." Alexander and Staub, in a psychoanalytic interpretation of crime, describe a type they call the "normal, non-neurotic criminal whose Super-Ego is criminal." (3: p. 148) Hewitt and Jenkins studied records on 500 cases in the files of the Michigan Child Guidance Institute and Hewitt isolated three syndromes—one of which is "Socialized Delinquency Behavior." The socialized delinquent, as Jenkins describes him, has a normal shell of inhibition toward members of the gang but not toward out-groups. He is a product of "parental negligence and exposure to delinquency patterns." They note that types of delinquency vary with their psychological types—habitual truancy and stealing are highly correlated with the "socialized delinquent" syndrome but not with the others. (147: pp. 10, 22-32, 45, 68, 81-89, 94)

It is clear that these "normal" types, while varied in precise specifications and sharply different in their theoretical roots, parallel the gang boy on whom we have concentrated. By the same token, it is likely that our theory does not cover Redl's "neurotic" type (whose "delinquent behavior . . . is part of a neurosis, or . . . is developed in order to disguise one"), or Hewitt's "Unsocialized Aggressive Behavior" syndrome (rooted in parental rejection) and "Overinhibited Behavior" syndrome (closely associated with physical deficiency). In general, we have argued that these latter types are not frequent among habitual male gang delinquents (in comparison to nondelinquents), though they may appear more often among lone-wolf delinquents, and, less surely, among middle-class boys. We have also argued that while there are individual differences in delinquency-conducive personality tendencies, the chance for given types of personality to become delinquent varies with the social and cultural situations we have described under the labels "lower class," "middle class," and "ethnic group."

It would seem, finally, to be consistent with our theory that the "normal," "socialized" delinquent has proved to be almost impervious to psychological treatment. Redl notes that his "genuine" delinquent is the type that poses the toughest problem for the psychoanalyst. (295: p. 368) Programs aimed toward resolving personality disorders in order to prevent delinquency apparently have not been successful with the kinds of boys who become chronic delinquents. (Cf. 419: pp. 30, 40.)

These, then, are a few of the main gaps in the evidence we need in order to test and reformulate the sociological explanation of delinquency. It is by no means a complete list of the research possibilities. Besides better answers to the question of who commits what kinds of acts with what meaning how often—including comparisons of delinquent and nondelinquent children of both sexes at each class level and in varied ethnic groups, of youngsters engaged in different types of delinquences, of big gangs, small gangs and lone wolves—we need comparisons of delinquents and nondelinquents within one family, of one-shot delinquents versus recidivists, and more. Here is a challenging area for research in which social workers and sociologists as well as other social scientists can collaborate with profit.

The rest of this chapter considers the implications of our analysis for delinquency-prevention efforts.

Evaluating Programs of Delinquency-Prevention

Although much time and money have been devoted to stopping or reducing delinquency, reliable studies evaluating programs of delinquency-prevention can be counted on one's fingers. This is not surprising, for most of the studies asking "Did it work?" fail to define and analyze either "it" (the preventive measures under study) or "work" (how well the measures have been applied to what youngsters with what degree of success). It is safe to say that most programs are never evaluated, and most evaluation studies do not permit judgment of the programs which *are* evaluated.

The most cautious and careful review of the best studies was done by Helen L. Witmer and Edith Tufts of the U.S. Children's Bureau in 1954. (419) Their sober assessment of evidence on the effectiveness of prevention programs confirms our view of the prime causes of most delinquency, at the same time that it emphasizes variations on the main theme. They define delinquency as unlawful behavior whether or not it brings the child to the attention of the police and courts. By "prevention" they mean "both the forestalling of delinquent behavior and . . . the reduction in its frequency and seriousness." (419: p. 5) They classify delinquency-prevention programs in terms of their underlying ideas in two broad categories: (1) programs that aim to improve the environment (housing, school and recreational facilities, neighborhood solidarity); (2) programs that try to prevent delinquency through educational or therapeutic measures applied in individual cases. They exclude the service aspects of police courts and training schools as well as many social agency programs which, though possibly relevant, do not have delinquency prevention as a main aim. Because the environmental approach has been least tried and least evaluated, and is most indirect in its effects, the Witmer-Tufts review of results gives little attention to it. (It may be that drastic changes in family income would reduce delinquency, but the test of this idea is yet to come.)

This section will draw heavily on the Witmer-Tufts report, but the reader is advised to consult the original for a full and sympathetic understanding of both the difficulties of evaluation research and the limits of even the best studies to date.

Education and Therapy for the Case: The Clinical Approach. Some programs aimed at reforming the individual delinquent involve parents; others, children; some, delinquents; others, predelinquents or "problem" children. Their methods range from training courses in "How to be a better parent" to psychotherapy in a child guidance clinic, from friendly counseling by volunteer adults (compare the Big Brother Movement) to long-term casework designed to bring the entire range of community health, education, and welfare services to a child.

An especially ambitious program based on friendly counseling plus community resources, the Cambridge-Somerville Youth Study, illustrates typical results. Eleven trained professionals worked for about seven years with 234 "problem" boys. The boys and their families were sought out and given friendly counsel, psychological and medical services, tutoring; they engaged in recreation (for example, trips) and other activities with the counselors. After service was terminated, the police and court record of the treatment group was compared with the record of a matched control group. Relatively good matching and complete evaluation data forced the conclusion that the program did *not* reduce delinquent acts or keep habitual delinquency from developing.[1] "The services," Witmer and Tufts (419: p. 30) note, "were especially ineffectual . . . with the kinds of boys who became chronic delinquents: slum boys with indifferent, neglectful parents; seriously neurotic boys, from various kinds of neighborhoods, who had even more emotionally unfavorable homes; and feebleminded or neurologically handicapped boys whose homes, too, were poor."

Similar, if less dismal, results appear for child guidance clinics. Here, casework with willingly cooperative parents is coupled with

---

[1] The most optimistic thing that can be said about the results of this study is that there are some hints that given more time, greater differences in *seriousness* of official offenses between treatment and control groups might have appeared.

psychiatric treatment of the child, and, in the best clinics, supplemented by other tailor-made services (medical and dental care, supervision of foster homes, visits to schools, tutoring). A series of careful studies of one such program, the Judge Baker Guidance Center ("characteristic of the best of child guidance"), suggests that: (1) study, diagnosis, and social recommendations to the court did not reduce recidivism (boys not exposed to the clinic had about the same rate); (2) direct treatment (including provision of medical care, economic aid, recreation, employment, foster care, and psychiatric treatment) was somewhat more effective—especially when intake policy eliminated cases of gross social pathology, though such treatment was ineffective with cases of markedly abnormal personality. Heroic efforts over long periods seemed to pay off for most of those delinquents accepted for treatment, including many who were seriously neurotic. But who is accepted for treatment in the typical clinic? Even the Judge Baker studies do not tell us the basis of selection. Witmer and Tufts suggest the likely situation:

> . . . Child guidance aims at the resolution of personality and behavior disorders that are attributable largely to difficulties in parent-child relationships. Consequently, clinics try to restrict their clientele to cases of this sort. Moreover, since clinics usually maintain that parent-child relationship difficulties can be resolved only if parents can recognize their existence and are capable and desirous of doing something to improve the situation, they are inclined to further restrict their intake to cases in which parents give evidence of these abilities and desires. . . . The result is that the delinquents whom child guidance clinics serve are not representative of the total delinquent population. They are more likely to be children of middle class than of lower class status and to be reacting to adverse parental attitudes alone rather than to such attitudes combined with adverse social conditions. (419: p. 40)

No good evidence is available to show the effectiveness of alternative casework approaches. The Passaic (New Jersey) Children's Bureau combines school and police services with joint social agency effort to provide psychiatric and social services for all misconduct cases in the area. The St. Paul Experiment in Child Welfare, set up by the U.S. Children's Bureau, used a

Social Service Exchange to locate cases and went after them, adopting various approaches to overcome parent resistance to clinic services (for example, offering help with educational or health problems rather than with the problem that occasioned the referral). The New York City Youth Board tries to identify and treat children as early in the development of their problem behavior as possible. Its referral unit workers and its caseworkers have developed significant ways of getting in touch with the very cases missed by child guidance clinics. Through "aggressive casework"—friendly persistence despite doors being slammed in its face, parents refusing referral to treatment agencies, and other rebuffs—the Youth Board has made real breakthroughs with lower-class families. And through its unusual work with delinquent gangs it has reached the very core of the delinquent subculture. Unfortunately, none of these programs has yet been evaluated adequately.

It is fair to say that where programs based on the clinical approach have been evaluated, they have not been shown to reduce or prevent delinquency among the delinquent-prone portions of the population. This is not to say that therapy and other clinical services are not justified on other grounds. Counseling or psychiatric aid, plus efficient use of community facilities to supplement the care of well-intentioned but ill-equipped parents, may not reduce delinquency, but it may improve the child's health, reduce emotional disturbance, or have other beneficial effects. Psychotherapy for the individual delinquent, however, must not be mistaken for delinquency-prevention, any more than humanitarian reform of prisons should be mistaken for rehabilitation.

Work with gangs and work with neighborhoods, though they involve casework or groupwork techniques, have the effect of restructuring the child's social environment. These programs, which show more promise in reaching the unreached typical delinquent, are discussed below.

Area Projects and Group Work for Neighborhood and Gang: The Environmental Approach. Witmer and Tufts found no evaluations of delinquency-prevention programs aimed at improvement of home or school environment.[1] The delinquency-reduction effect of changes in income distribution, job and housing opportunities for minority groups, and other ways of increasing security and equality in the delinquency areas were beyond the scope of their report and have not been evaluated anyway. That leaves only two types of programs representing an environmental approach that have been even tentatively assessed: recreational reform and neighborhood reform. The first says: "Give children a good place to play and good supervised recreation and there will be less delinquency." The second, broader program tackles the entire neighborhood and seeks to reduce delinquency by increasing neighborhood cohesion through encouragement of local self-help projects, and sometimes by rechanneling gang activity.

The recreational approach assumes, with Denney and Riesman, that delinquency is largely a form of recreation—"activities in which gregarious theft and gang warfare by the boys and gregarious sex by the girls appear to be channels for the playful, sociable and conformist impulses of the lower-class youth." (85: p. 471) Could not delinquency be reduced if these playful impulses were acted out in well-chaperoned playgrounds and community centers? The three most complete studies that assess groupwork programs with a recreational emphasis make this idea doubtful. Thrasher (360) in 1927–1931 compared offense records of members of the Boys' Club of New York University before and during club membership. Reed (296) in 1942 studied the use of groupwork-agency services by delinquent boys and girls in Cincinnati, compared members of groupwork agencies with non-member delinquents, and traced the official delinquency rates of agency members over time. Shanas and Dunning (323) compared delinquents and nondelinquents in their use of recreational facilities, and official and unofficial delinquency rates of users and non-

[1] R. J. Havighurst and others (142), however, report a ten-year experimental youth development program which aims to discover and help both problem children and talented children. It was begun in a small city—Quincy, Illinois—in 1951. It involves an elaborate screening of fourth graders, who will be studied for a decade, coupled with coordination and improvement of community youth services, both school and nonschool. Evaluation, including comparison with a control group, is built into this research-action project, but results are as yet unreported. However, a fifth-year progress report describes the problems of screening, establishing contact, developing community resources, and using expert advice. (39)

users in four slum areas and one middle-class area in Chicago, 1938–1939. At minimum these studies add up to the following:

1. Delinquents *do* participate in recreation and groupwork programs. While in some areas they participate less than nondelinquents, in others they participate more. Delinquents seem to take to game rooms and competitive sports as enthusiastically as they take to crime.

2. But the participants allocate only a very small slice of their daily routine to supervised recreation (for example, Shanas and Dunning note that boys, delinquent or nondelinquent, spent about twice as much time at the movies).

3. Delinquency may decrease slightly or increase, sometimes sharply, while participation goes on. Factors other than recreation activity probably explain whatever shifts in delinquency rates take place among participants—for example, increased age increases chances of becoming a delinquent, especially in slum areas. Participation in recreation programs and avoiding delinquency were slightly associated in one study but this may be due to self-selection of clientele (the less seriously delinquent boys may be the ones who use the facilities). Reed showed that groupwork activities, though not excluding delinquents, tended to attract a delinquent-resistant population. The participants, compared with nonparticipating court delinquents, included more whites, girls, and youngsters under fifteen.

These findings are entirely consistent with the proposition that if boys are moved to delinquency, and a delinquent subculture is available, they go on learning to become delinquents while using whatever recreational facilities they find. In fact, delinquent gangs have been known to convert clubs, playgrounds, or community centers into bases of operation, if not targets for vandalism.

As we have suggested, most delinquency is more than mere recreation and has its roots in the status anxiety and perhaps sex-role anxiety of lower-class boys. The provision of adequate recreation facilities is commendable in its own right, but it does not hold much promise for the reduction of delinquency.

Programs which aim to reorganize life in delinquent gangs or high-delinquency neighborhoods, or both, are based more squarely on the view of causation presented above. They recognize the concentration of delinquency in gangs formed by "normal" boys in underprivileged areas. Explicitly or implicitly they also recognize the delinquent subculture as an ambivalent protest against middle-class standards among boys who subscribe both to conventional values and to criminal values. The fact that these boys and/or their parents display not only a protest against a status system which pegs them low but a latent desire for achievement of status within that very system, becomes the lever for social action.

Since the early thirties when Clifford Shaw and his associates set up the Chicago Area Project, several neighborhood committees have been organized in delinquency areas in Chicago and elsewhere. (Cf. 419: pp. 11–17; 45; 4; and 328.) Their programs vary, but the general idea is to involve the "natural leaders"— slum residents who already have high prestige and power, "big shots," however disreputable they may seem by middle-class standards—in committee work aimed at making the neighborhood a better place for children. Trained outsiders are kept to a minimum; money is raised and staff recruited as much as possible from the community itself. A local community council becomes the sponsoring agency. It may establish a neighborhood center. It operates clubs, sends children to summer camps, carries on informal education and recreation activities. It supervises the area's probationers and parolees. Programs are designed to draw adults and children together and to increase the sense of community in the area. Self-help, local autonomy, local responsibility are the watchwords in these area projects.

Witmer and Tufts summarize the results: "(1) Residents of low income areas can and have organized themselves into effective working units for promoting and conducting welfare programs. (2) These community organizations have been stable and enduring. They raise funds, administer them well, and adapt the programs to local needs. (3) Local talent, otherwise untapped, has been discovered and utilized. Local leadership has been mobilized in the interest of children's welfare." (4) The work of the committees probably reaches most delinquency-prone youngsters.

Did these shifts in the social environment reduce delinquency? The claims of project organizers are modest, but their programs come out rather well, in the judgment of Witmer and Tufts. From 1930 to 1942 official delinquency rates in three out of four project communities fell; and the work with parolees has been very successful (for example, one community committee supervised 41 persons, including many habitual offenders, over a decade; only one was recommitted). This is suggestive, but hardly conclusive in the absence of adequate data, including unofficial delinquency rates, for comparable areas in which projects are not operating. More evidence, especially on the effect of long-term work with chronic delinquents, is said to be forthcoming.

Work with delinquent gangs, or what has been called the "boring-from-within" approach, is another program that has at least made contact with the typical hard-core delinquent, whatever its effect on delinquency prevention.[1] Here, trained group-workers or "streetworkers" or "detached" workers locate gangs in their usual hangouts, and try to gain their confidence. This is a slow and difficult process. The worker learns the boys' lingo and their current lines of interest, shoots pool with them, keeps up his end in buying sodas and cigarettes and in playing juke boxes and, in time, acts as a kind of counsel when they get into trouble (for instance, argues their cases in judges' chambers). He visits the boys in jail, helps them get jobs when they are released. He seldom, if ever, reports their illegal acts. When and if acceptance is won, the worker then tries carefully to redirect gang activities along more conventional lines. He offers to mediate gang wars. He arranges fair fights. ("No guns, bottles, rocks or sticks. No bats. Just knucks. No kicking, no gouging.") He helps them organize athletic teams, dances, parties, and the like. In general, he tries to reshape their social environment, as well as move them toward a better understanding of themselves.

While "boring from within" has been tried before on a small scale in Chicago, Cleveland, Detroit, and Los Angeles, the New

---

[1] Two very interesting short reports describe this work in New York City: one by Crawford, Malamud, and Dumpson (67); and the other by Furman (119). For a colorful, but honest journalistic account see Kramer and Karr (190).

York City Youth Board has adopted only recently the most ambitious program. The Board has claimed that this approach has prevented some gang wars, and made gangs more democratic. Gang members, through trips, discussions, and other constructive activities, have learned new skills and have been brought closer to conventional society. Less success is reported "in changing the gang members' attitudes toward family, church, police, school, and work" and no success with boys who have "serious personality problems." (419: p. 34)[1] No systematic comparisons of behavior of infiltrated gangs and gangs not reached, or of the subsequent careers of their members, have been reported through 1954.

It is instructive to note that gang members exposed to the "boring within" approach are typically mystified. Streetworkers behave like no other adults they have seen. Gangs often take them for "cops," FBI agents, dope peddlers, or social reformers. The boys have no other categories for adults who accept their behavior. A member of a gang in a slum with a traditional delinquency-pattern does not readily give it up upon the approach of this outsider. Frequently, if the streetworker is not rejected outright or tolerated as a "sucker," the best he gets is the opportunity to substitute less serious delinquencies for major crimes or to supplement the latter with conventional activity.

Nevertheless, work with gangs and work with neighborhoods seem to hold some promise for delinquency control if undertaken on a large scale. The stubborn resistance such work encounters, however, at the same time dramatizes the hold of the delinquent subculture on delinquency-prone boys. And the slim evidence of delinquency-reduction effects reminds us to be cautious.

Deviant Behavior and Social Reform

Given our analysis of the causes of delinquency, and the limited effect of delinquency-prevention efforts based on alternative

---

[1] Evaluation studies consistently conclude that nothing thus far tried prevents delinquency among the very severely disturbed. Treatment of psychotic or neurologically disabled children, whether the approach be "clinical" or "environmental," seldom proves to be delinquency-preventive. (Cf. 419: pp. 30, 34, 38, 49.)

views of causation, where do we turn for the solution to this problem?

At times the sociologist seems to be saying: "Look, the experience of western countries is consistent: all this devoted effort, all these varied techniques, and yet delinquency, if it does not increase, still persists. There is nothing much the social welfare agency can do about it." Indeed, there is a respectable tradition in American sociology which conveys this very message. It was the guiding assumption of Robert E. Park and his students, who told us so much about the uprooted, the deviant, the deprived people of the urban slum, that the communitywide and even nationwide links between social problems are so numerous that piecemeal solutions will not work. In a Chicago slum the problem may look like juvenile delinquency, but the neighborhood is what it is because of those basic inequalities of income and opportunity which sustain the slum. The city as a whole creates the demand for a labor supply to do its less desirable, lower-paid work; the city as a whole creates the demand for the gambling joint, the prostitute, the bookie, and the dope peddler—and their protection by the police. The slum and its people feed these demands. Who is responsible?

Who is responsible for those courts and penal institutions which earn the label "schools for crime"? Who is responsible for a shortage of schoolrooms and schoolteachers, for a curriculum and a routine that bores, and a value system that humiliates the child of the slum? Who is responsible for corruption of the police and the politician? Not the family, not the neighborhood. The city as a whole.

And what appear at first glance to be citywide problems turn out to be intercity and nationwide. Take a sleepy textile town in the South which finds itself awakened by violent race conflict and industrial strife. Look closely and you will see a Supreme Court in Washington reaffirming the American Creed, a New England mill-owner planning lay-offs in Massachusetts with an eye to expansion in the South, a union headquarters in New York determined to protect wage standards by extending its organization, a minority defense agency in Chicago determined to move faster toward equality. Or, to cite an example of an intercity social problem: When the heat is on to clean up Skid Row in Chicago, we find an increase in panhandling and petty crime in Milwaukee, the next convenient big-city freightstop. Turn the Chicago heat off and the situation returns to "normal."

In short, what Park and his students say to us is: All problems are connected; few problems are local. If we want real change, if we want the problems to yield, we must place the lever where the greatest leverage is—under the whole social structure; and, to face the hard truth, the whole social structure, short of revolution, can be moved only slowly, only slightly.

A no less dismal message seems to come from Freud and his followers, at the other extreme. Here it is not the entire society we must restructure; it is the entire personality. This is not only slow and difficult—whatever theory of personality guides the effort—but it is also largely irrelevant to delinquency-prevention on any grand scale. What evidence we have on the psychotherapeutic aspects of clinical programs suggests that they do not reduce or prevent delinquency in the areas where it flourishes most, or among the youngsters who are most vulnerable.

Our analysis of delinquency is consistent with Park's observations about the interdependence of social problems and their roots in the social structure. Delinquency rates may not be lowered much in the long run save by basic changes in our society: either less accent on achievement, to reduce the status anxiety of those who do not achieve; or more equal opportunity for achievement, to reduce the discontent of able youngsters among the underprivileged; or both. Since values change only very slowly, the point of maximum leverage is, indeed, the social structure. Tax laws which favor low-income brackets by wiping out regressive features of our tax structure; measures to stabilize employment where it remains unstable; expanded insurance against the risks of unemployment, illness, and accidents; measures to reduce discrimination against minorities in education, housing and employment and politics—these would comprise a most efficient program of delinquency-prevention. In our view, every middle-class child who *lacks* ability but is given a college education and high occupational position, every lower-class child who *has* ability but does not receive such privileges, every family exposed to American "success" goals which lacks the income and opportunity to realize them for its children, constitutes a prop for the maintenance of delinquency. Either we must value equality and equal opportunity less or live them more—or we must suffer the cost of the delinquent subculture.

Gloomy inferences need not be drawn from this proposition, for three reasons. First, the societal trends described in Part I suggest that our social structure is moving in the required direction. Major accompaniments of industrialization—shifts in the distribution of power and income, the stabilizing effects of changes in occupations, the necessary drift toward more rational job assignment—these should reduce the pressures toward delinquency felt by the less privileged. The reorganization of urban life described in Chapter V should also reduce socially costly deviant behavior. In so far as "culture conflict" is a factor in delinquency, any integrating force that reduces differences among subcultures (based on race, nationality, and other advantage or disadvantage) should reduce delinquency rates. The suburbs where more and more people live and the big organizations where they work, plus the even more pervasive merging of the working class with an expanding middle class, should accelerate the process of assimilation, and bring about a blurring of subcultures.

The second reason why we need not despair concerns a point that students of social reform have often missed. As citizens or as welfare professionals we can no more deal successfully with the "total society" than we can deal with the abstract "total individual," torn from his societal setting. What we *can* tackle with modest hope are the groups in between—gangs, schools, neighborhood organizations, and other secondary associations in the community, as well as families—the groups that mediate the relations of individual to society. (Cf. 110: pp. 13 ff.) Whether social action directed toward these groups and social reform through these groups is a proper or possible function for social work will be discussed in Chapter XI.

Finally, as evaluation studies suggest, traditional social case-work has achieved many successes—especially with those cases where moderate personality disturbances are involved—and there is no reason to suppose that these successes will cease.

Implications for Agencies Dealing with Delinquents

Whatever the long-run solutions, whatever forces beyond the welfare agency are working to reshape the social structure in delinquency-preventive ways, there is still the day-to-day job of administering programs aimed at the juvenile offender, the "predelinquent," and children generally. There is the uneasy task of protecting the community against serious crime. There is the question of what to do with the chronic delinquent now, in the short-run, with the resources available.

Agencies in astonishing number and variety converge on children in trouble—some public, some private, some staffed by social workers, some not. In New York City alone, there are about 379 *voluntary* agencies with programs in some way related to prevention and treatment of juvenile delinquency. In 1953 they spent a total of more than $36 million. (400: pp. 25–26) Add to this private effort the entire apparatus of police and courts (with their detention, parole, and probation facilities) and schools (with their attendance bureaus, recreation centers, visiting teachers, and guidance and remedial teaching services), and the size of the effort becomes truly impressive.

What specialists converge on the deviant child and how they handle him is described in the vast literature on corrections and delinquency.[1] Here we will merely list some of the most troublesome of the recurrent dilemmas the specialists encounter. For the beginning student or mature youth worker, these are good topics for sober thought:

1. *The label "delinquent."* Juvenile delinquency is what the law says it is. And the law is typically broad and often vague in its definition. Every legal definition of delinquency in-

[1] Two good summaries of this literature, containing overviews of the entire field are those by Tappan (355: Parts 3–4), who is very critical of the concept of school and court as social agencies; and H. A. Bloch and F. T. Flynn (30), who are a bit more sympathetic to this concept.

cludes not only violations of laws and ordinances by children, but also other items, an average of eight or nine, beyond these—behavior which would not mark an adult as an offender. Items in the Juvenile Court Acts of some states include: smoking, drinking; sexual misconduct; late hours; refusal to obey parent or guardian; "incorrigible"; acts of "carelessness" or "mischief"; habitually wandering about railroad yards or tracks. In general, it may be said that any behavior which is unconventional by communitywide standards tends to be labeled "delinquent." (Cf. 310.)

To the extent that our juvenile courts are inadequately staffed and unimaginatively run, to the extent that the label "delinquent" popularly or even officially connotes an evil only slightly less extreme than "criminal," to the extent that "treatment" (detention in a jail or reform school) perpetuates and even reinforces the behavior labeled "delinquent," such definitions are recklessly broad.

Does the typical exposure to the juvenile court tend to move the child to more conventional conduct, or does it create and strengthen an image of himself as antisocial and maltreated? (To play the role of delinquent effectively one must first convince oneself that one *is* a delinquent.) A few juvenile court acts avoid the delinquency tag; instead they describe situations and classify children over which the court has jurisdiction. Does the change in label (for example, "neglected" vs. "delinquent") make a difference, or does the mere appearance in a juvenile court, however well staffed, however enlightened, mark the child in his own eyes and the eyes of important others?

While many juvenile courts are well aware of this point and treat early offenders with great solicitude, accepting their behavior as temporary, others are less sensitive. It seems likely that if the community (through police, courts, and other agencies) views a ten-year-old child's casual acting out of criminal roles as the behavior typical of him and treats him accordingly, it will help him acquire a self-image that fits. We do not know to what extent our police and courts help in the flowering of criminal careers.

2. *Custody, punishment and revenge vs. treatment; protection of the community vs. protection of the child.* We have come a long way from jailing, flogging, branding, and mutilating children of seven, which was the age of legal responsibility in nineteenth century America. (358: pp. 69–71; 355: pp. 170,

391–393) Today, there is the juvenile court, and wide use of suspended sentence, probation, and individual treatment techniques. The age of criminal liability has generally been moved up; the notion that the child is responsible for his behavior has been challenged. In general, the basic idea of the juvenile court movement, "protect the child—help him adjust," is in ascendance over the basic idea of the traditional criminal court, "protect the community—punishment will deter."

What is dominant philosophy, however, is not dominant practice. A large proportion of youthful offenders find themselves in the hands of criminal courts with punitive ideology. The quality of juvenile courts is often no better than the criminal courts. (Cf. 354.) An estimated 50,000 to 100,000 children are confined each year in jails—often illegally. (218) Temporary detention facilities are sometimes used by juvenile judges as punishment—they become long-term jails. (171: p. 269)

The agencies that deal with juvenile offenders reflect community values in all their contradictions and ambiguities. One judge, confronted with a teenage vandal, is morally outraged at the wanton destruction of private property, lectures him, and sends him to a tough training school; another looks not at the vandalism but at the boy and the circumstances that shaped him, and refers him to a probation officer or caseworker in a family agency for sympathetic supervision and family visits. One policeman who witnesses sex play between young boys in a railroad yard ignores it; another, incensed by what he considers to be abnormal, beats them up and brings them to court for "moral depravity," "sexual misconduct," "bad associates," or wandering about railroad tracks.

So long as important segments of the community are primarily concerned with protection of life and property, and at the same time hold to the belief that punishment deters crime in direct proportion to its severity, so long as police and courts and detention facilities recruit personnel indoctrinated with neither a "humanitarian" nor a "scientific" approach to deviant behavior, then so long can we expect our practice to belie our profession.

a. *Paternalism vs. justice; the court as social agency vs. the court as dispenser of justice.* More complicated, perhaps, are the dilemmas represented even by the well-run, well-staffed court for children. An enlightened juvenile court judge in Pittsburgh sums up the distinctive philosophy of the juvenile court in a way that highlights the problem. He points to the difference between the question, "Did you or did you not?" and the quite different question of the juvenile court, "Why, under what circumstances, and what can be done to help?" (316: p. 107) The conflict in functions is not hard to see, though it is extremely difficult to resolve. Should the court assume that the delinquent act is a symptom of underlying psychological or family maladjustment, take jurisdiction over an increasing variety of cases, and seek to operate as a sympathetic substitute parent, with adjustment of any youngster who comes before it as the aim? Should it, in short, be a generalized social agency? Or should it instead be primarily a dispenser of justice, giving careful attention to standards of justice—guarantee opportunity for defense, legal counsel, and appeal, never presume delinquency without proof and a definite charge—with the hope that this will decrease court exposure where the child's behavior does not warrant apprehension? Are not the facts of delinquent behavior often in dispute? How much attention should the court pay to the nature of the delinquent act? By virtue of its authority and the training of its functionaries, is not the court on firmer ground when it sticks to the legal questions (what is the legal status of the child, who shall have custody, does the community have the right to intervene in his life, and so on), leaving social services to agencies specially equipped to diagnose and plan treatment?

Is the court to be *both* a paternalistic social agency and a dispenser of justice? Are such practices as arrest, revocation of probation and parole, police access to court records, and the other authoritarian sanctions it is required to use, compatible with the casework principles which inspire judges and trained probation officers in the most progressive jurisdictions? Can justice, which must be impersonal (a fixed type of response to a specific type of act), be reconciled with personalized treatment and clinical rehabilitation? Should the job of adjudication be sharply separate from the job of disposition? Or should we assume that wise decisions about the need to intervene (adjudication) require some notion of the impact of different kinds of intervention as well as knowledge of the services available?[1]

[1] An excellent discussion of the possible and desirable functions of the juvenile court, with analysis of the problems encountered under each alternative, can be found in Kahn's *A Court for Children* (171, especially chapters 10 and 11), a study of the operation of the New York City Children's Court. Cf. Tappan's *Juvenile Delinquency* (355). On the question of the compatibility or incompatibility of casework treatment and authoritative disposition, see Elliot Studt's "Treatment of Persons in Conflict with Authority." (349)

b. *Streetworkers vs. the police.* The punishment vs. treatment and justice vs. casework dilemmas are reflected in the clash between "detached" groupworkers who infiltrate gangs and aggressive policemen who believe in being tough with gangs. The boring-from-within approach (coupled with neighborhood organization) seems to offer the best chance for reaching the habitual delinquent in his natural habitat. But we should not let this promise stop us from looking at the hard questions the police and others raise.

Does the presence of the youth board's streetworker, who refrains from reporting illegal activities in the interest of building a long-term relationship with the boys, serve unwittingly to give quasi-official sanction to a delinquent way of life? Is this respectable representative of the community, whatever his personal behavior, however intense his effort to redirect gang conduct into more conventional channels, seen by the deviant boy as a sign of middle-class weakness, an admission that his aggressive (and therefore manly) acts are justified? If this has not yet been the case, what would happen if a major expansion of such programs took place—a groupworker on every street, in every gang?

Can the streetworker ever be successful if he does not appear to condone crime at some point in his confidence-building? If he is too successful in identifying with the boys, does he lose his identity as a community representative, a symbol of alternative values and ways of life? If he identifies with them too little, can he ever exert enough influence to change gang behavior? Streetworker is a delicate role to play, a sensitive balancing act where slipping either way can mean curtains for the play— a sort of death-by-absorption, on the one hand, death-by-rejection, on the other.

There are answers to these questions. One obvious one is the apparent failure of the alternatives tried. This is not answer enough. And firmness of faith is no substitute for the evidence now lacking. For instance, no one has yet tried to: (1) double the police force in one delinquency area with instructions to crack down and keep the lid on for two or three years; (2) put an equal number of streetworkers into another, comparable delinquency area; (3) compare the effect of the two approaches on the severity and frequency of delinquency.

Other questions concern the relevance of traditional casework training and practice for work with the unwilling clients of the court and the street; further, whether the supply of dedicated workers skilled enough to do this sort of job can be expanded enough to exert a major impact.

c. *Schools, child labor laws, and delinquency.* One of the most persistent of the doubts that plague a modern democracy concerns the wisdom of insisting that all children stay in school until they are sixteen or so, and that no youngster be allowed to earn a living. If all schools could meet the increasingly varied demands put upon them, if each teacher could give the problem child her undivided attention, if all curricula were tailor-made to fit the tremendously varied needs of youngsters differently situated, if our schools were not a microcosm of the larger community (with the same ethnic and racial tensions, the same conflicting values, the same barriers to equal treatment of the smart and the dull, the poor and the rich), then compulsory school laws and laws prohibiting child labor would make clear sense. As it is, the delinquent-prone child—the boy from the slum, with neither the motivation nor the resources to get along in school—is bored or threatened by what we offer him. His school experience, if it does not encourage delinquency, at least fails to block it. Would it be undemocratic to set up special screening programs to find children who cannot profit from the standard routine, to set up special training programs to permit earlier entry to jobs? Is it democratic to require compulsory school attendance and at the same time to put youngsters into reformatories if they find school unchallenging, frustrating, or irrelevant to their needs? Is it any more democratic to put them into special classes and schools for "problem" children run harshly and punitively, some worse than prisons?

Two approaches for dealing with such youngsters have been discussed in recent years. One is to reorient all or part of the school program toward more "practical" ends. Some work-study projects now under way with high school children in New York City and elsewhere represent this sort of realism. It seems likely, however, that any formal training program will miss some chronic but salvageable delinquents, as well as many potential delinquents. For these, a second, more drastic approach has been proposed—something like a revival of the Civilian Conservation Corps of Depression fame, or a similar channel for the removal of city youth who hate school to the country for a work-health-study program.

Both of these approaches argue that it is more economical to pay problem children rather high apprentice wages in work-study projects, Youth Camps, or other activities, than to suffer the cost of criminal careers. Difficult problems—beyond the possible threat to universal citizenship education—spring immediately to view: Would such untried programs work? (At the logical and ludicrous extreme, would a second-hand Cadillac Eldorado for every sixteen-year-old delinquent deter delinquency?) Would not such special treatment, with the necessary screening and selection process, and segregated facilities, "tag" the potential delinquent, creating or affirming an undesirable self-concept, itself conducive to deviant behavior?

3. *The problems of specialization, coordination, and overlapping jurisdiction.* We have argued that delinquency has its roots deep in the structure and culture of American society. The organized efforts of whole communities and ultimately the whole society are required to cope with it. Immediately questions about the coordination of specialized services are raised. And immediately the standard observations are made regarding the need for an effective social service exchange, interagency case conferences, strategic location of services, coordinated attacks on delinquency-inducing environments (problems of schools, slums, and the like), improved liaison between welfare services and courts or schools, and so on.

Who should intervene in the child's life, on what occasions? When the court and when the school adjustment service? When the parent, the policeman, the minister, the agency representative? When the private agency, when the public? When the sectarian, when the nonsectarian? Should "neglect" cases come to court? When? Who should play what role in arrest, detention, adjudication, probation, parole? Should the basis of specialization be *type of client* defined legally ("truant," "neglected," "delinquent," "defective"); type of client defined in some other way (for example, "psychoneurotic"); *auspices* (Catholic, Jewish, Protestant); *purpose of service* (punishment, rehabilitation, shelter, detention); *type of process* (psychiatry, family casework, psychological testing and diagnosis); *geographical location,* or what?

These problems of specialization and coordination are not unique to children's services, or to the welfare services as a whole. They appear wherever men organize to pursue a goal. Who shall give what service under whose control; by what criteria shall work be divided? Discussion of these questions will be reserved for a general treatment of the structure of welfare services and the social agency in Chapter X. There we shall see that neater areas of jurisdiction and greater coordination of specialized effort entail both costs and gains, and in any case are never simple to achieve.

4. *The gap between knowledge and action.* Treatment and rehabilitation, even simple classification, of deviant youngsters assumes considerable knowledge of what made them deviate. The phrase "predelinquent" currently in use epitomizes this assumption. Our analysis of causation (which is seldom

the view held implicitly or explicitly by the judge, the probation officer, or the policeman) suggests how tenuous some
of this knowledge is. And our picture of delinquency-
prevention and delinquency-treatment programs and problems suggests that even this limited knowledge seldom gets
put to work.

A final set of important questions, then, concerns the
ways research can be tied to practice, and practice can
better be evaluated.

Whatever the problems and dilemmas facing agencies which
converge on the delinquent, it is a sad fact that most of them get
there too late. The ineffectiveness of institutionalization of the
serious (and sometimes not-so-serious) offender is too well known
to discuss here. With a few distinguished exceptions (see 17:
pp. 297 ff.), the training schools and detention homes reinforce
rather than reform delinquent behavior. The recidivism rate of
boys and girls who have been detained in such places attests to
their lack of promise for both child and community.[1]

The alternatives to institutionalization most in use seem to be
parole, probation, deferred prosecution, and foster-home placement. Here again, though the costs are less than those for detention and the chances for treatment and rehabilitation are greater,
such alternatives as typically carried out have not achieved much
success. Take, for instance, probation. A study by Kahn of one
of the best juvenile courts in the country, based on 89 representative probation "treatment" records, reports "uniformly inadequate service. . . . In general, the records show that the officer's
conception of his major duty is to 'check up' on children and
parents. . . . Beyond that, contacts usually consist of random

---

[1] It is helpful in thinking about the functions of various programs aimed at the
juvenile delinquent to ask, "What would happen with some degree of certainty if we
wiped out all (jails, training schools, detention homes, and the like)?" If, for instance,
we release all the children we now detain in jails and reform schools, would there be
an increase in juvenile delinquency? Rubin cites a suggestive example from California: "A judge closed a juvenile institution because he was disgusted with the absence of sound treatment. The children had been neglected and abused in the institution. Most were simply sent home by the judge, some were placed in foster homes.
The police predicted a crime wave; it never came. Six months later, out of 140 children taken out of the institution, only ten were in trouble again." (310: p. 5) And
institutionalization has been estimated to cost ten times as much as satisfactory
probation. (171: p. 222)

advice-giving and warning about the consequences of further infractions of the law." (171: p. 189) Typically, the child "reports," the officer "checks up" and throws in a "pep talk." It is likely, moreover, that most habitual gang delinquents by the time the court has dealt with them are so firmly a part of the delinquent subculture that even if the services were better the obstacles to rehabilitation would be too great.

All this is not to disparage the many services which have been developed as alternatives to detention. A child is placed in a carefully arranged and selected foster home where he finds a new life and is able to blot out a long history of crime in the street and despair at home (where a near-psychotic father had terrorized him). Another is released from reform school to find for the first time a real friend and wise counselor in a well-trained parole officer. Still another is put under the supervision of a private social agency known for its unusual psychiatric facilities, and after three years of intensive therapy for himself and his parents, he carves out a brilliant career in college.

No one who has seen the great and obvious good that can come from these services at their best will underestimate their importance and the necessity of expanding their quality. But the probation or parole officer is so often undertrained and overworked, his tenure on the job so short and his salary so low, his caseload unserved; the foster home or boarding home so often an exercise in repetitive failure to adjust; the psychotherapy so superficial (if not irrelevant for the type of delinquent subjected to it), that we would be hard put to say they block more than they contribute to delinquency.

Nor is all this to ignore the possibility that effective policing could do something to suppress delinquency and even help to reduce it. The police might well benefit from some training and supervision by people who are social-work trained or social-work oriented—with the possibility that the gains in controlling or suppressing crime in an area could eventually be translated into more positive community attitudes toward the police.

Even at their best, however, all these are clean-up tasks designed to tidy up the societal mess. Delinquency prevention seems to be the most rational answer. Traditional casework techniques seem to have their best chance in the case of the moderately disturbed personality. But the greatest leverage seems to reside in changes in the social structure aimed at increasing equality (both in the relative rewards going to the lowest stratum and in the opportunities they have for moving up), coupled with expansion of those delinquency-prevention programs which, like work with gangs and neighborhoods, take account of the content and distribution of the delinquent subculture, and attend to the stubborn fact of the "adjusted" as well as the "unadjusted" delinquent.

PART THREE

THE ORGANIZATION OF WELFARE
SERVICES IN THE UNITED STATES

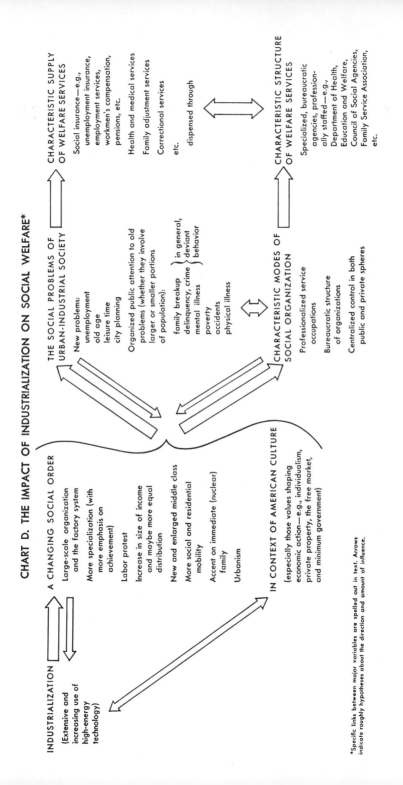

CHART D. THE IMPACT OF INDUSTRIALIZATION ON SOCIAL WELFARE*

INDUSTRIALIZATION
(Extensive and increasing use of high-energy technology)

A CHANGING SOCIAL ORDER

Large-scale organization and the factory system

More specialization (with more emphasis on achievement)

Labor protest

Increase in size of income and maybe more equal distribution

New and enlarged middle class

More social and residential mobility

Accent on immediate (nuclear) family

Urbanism

IN CONTEXT OF AMERICAN CULTURE
(especially those values shaping economic action—e.g., individualism, private property, the free market, and minimum government)

THE SOCIAL PROBLEMS OF URBAN-INDUSTRIAL SOCIETY

New problems:
unemployment
old age
leisure time
city planning

Organized public attention to old problems (whether they involve larger or smaller portions of population):

family breakup
delinquency, crime } in general, deviant behavior
mental illness
poverty
accidents
physical illness

CHARACTERISTIC MODES OF SOCIAL ORGANIZATION

Professionalized service occupations

Bureaucratic structure of organizations

Centralized control in both public and private spheres

CHARACTERISTIC SUPPLY OF WELFARE SERVICES

Social insurance—e.g., unemployment insurance, employment services, workmen's compensation, pensions, etc.

Health and medical services

Family adjustment services

Correctional services

etc.

dispensed through

CHARACTERISTIC STRUCTURE OF WELFARE SERVICES

Specialized, bureaucratic agencies, professionally staffed—e.g., Department of Health, Education and Welfare, Council of Social Agencies, Family Service Association, etc.

*Specific links between major variables are spelled out in text. Arrows indicate roughly hypotheses about the direction and amount of influence.

PART THREE: THE ORGANIZATION OF
WELFARE SERVICES IN THE UNITED STATES

IN PRECEDING CHAPTERS we have described various social welfare services as responses to the social problems created by urban-industrial conditions in the context of American culture and history. We have dealt, in a word, with the impact of industrialization on the demand for and supply of social services. Chart D diagrams the main line of our analysis. The services have thus far been treated in relation to the problems which call them into being.

But industrialization affects the services quite apart from the problems they deal with, in ways subtle but nonetheless important. In this final part of the book we ask: How does industrialization affect the organization of welfare services and the formulation of welfare policy? The theme appears on Chart D: industrialization ⟶ changes in social structure ⟶ a characteristic organization of social services which acts on ⟶ the supply and definition of appropriate services.

How are the social services organized? What characteristic organizational forms do the dispensers of social service develop? What are the main features of these forms? What uses and disuses do they have for service? What groups and individuals have power to make welfare policy decisions, and what are the forces that play upon them?

The major organizational forms involved in the supply of services are the social agency and the social work profession. Virtually all welfare service is dispensed through social agencies, public and private, and virtually all social workers operate through such agencies. The agency will be discussed in Chapter X, the profession in the final chapter. This division is merely a matter of convenience. Agency and profession at many points are in fact one in their influence on welfare work—a result of their common origin in the specialization of modern life. Agencies are created to integrate specialties based on technical knowledge; professions are organized to claim and realize jurisdictions based on technical knowledge. The "supervision complex" in social work, for instance, is a feature of both agency and profession. Thus, discussion of social work as a profession, though reserved mainly for Chapter XI, cannot be entirely excluded from the analysis of agency structure and social welfare policy.

X. Agency Structure and Social Welfare Policy

SUPPOSE AN INDIVIDUAL wants help on a personal problem from a family counseling agency. Except in case of emergency, he cannot apply for and expect immediate service. He must first talk with a receptionist, who will give him an appointment with a caseworker for a more or less distant date.[1] Already, in a minor way, service has been controlled: by a receptionist, working under agency rules, and by the use of a waiting period, possibly "therapeutic."[2]

When the appointed time comes the client will meet with the caseworker not in his home but in an agency office, furnished with a desk behind which the worker sits. The "intake" interview will last, typically, about an hour. If his case is acceptable he will "continue in treatment" on some regular weekly basis, not because life's problems turn in a weekly cycle, but because the agency as a complex social structure finds it necessary to regularize activities if it is to function at all. Thus far, agency rules and professional codes of conduct have shaped the client's experience in obvious ways.

Beyond the worker are a supervisor and perhaps a case consultant with whom the worker will share case information and responsibility for diagnostic and treatment decisions. They help to decide what will be done with the client. Above them still is

---

[1] Even getting this far may be difficult and discouraging. A receptionist who acts like a clerk can be disturbing to someone seeking help on a delicate, personal problem. A description of how the steps prior to counseling may feel to an applicant is given in "The Better Mouse Trap" by Morton Sontheimer. (339: pp. 354–355)

[2] Some agencies have maintained, with professional backing, that a waiting period may have therapeutic value in motivating a client to accept help when it is finally given. Research at one counseling agency, however, indicates that a two-month waiting period resulted in more resistance, greater lack of emotional control, and more likelihood of dropping out of treatment. (304: pp. 92, 94, 190)

the agency director. All of them, from receptionist to director, make decisions about the casework service—either general policies and rules or specific case decisions. Codes, agency and professional, written and unwritten, formal and informal, govern *their* interaction, too, and thereby what is done for the client.

The caseworker, however, will not help him in just any way he needs and she (the worker) is able. Rather, the agency has certain "functions." If the client's needs lie outside the declared limits of these, he will be "referred" to another agency. He may be passed on through several before he receives service. He may find none to fit his need, or give up the search. Or he may receive service simultaneously from several agencies, each dealing with an aspect of his problem. He is faced, probably unwittingly, with the fact that agencies are themselves specialized, dividing the total welfare function in a web of interdependence whose complexity has fateful consequences for service.

Decisions affecting daily practice in and among agencies, matters of "small policy," will be made by all their personnel. Where "big policy" is concerned, however—large expenditures, major shifts in service—authority resides at a higher level. For the voluntary agency there is almost always a "lay board," legally responsible and the final arbiter of which clients will receive what services. But if the agency is "Chest"-supported even the board's authority is circumscribed, for there remains a "budget committee," typically including "hardheaded businessmen," to decide the amount of money the agency may have. In the public agency such decisions will be made, within the confines of existing legislation, by local or state "welfare commissions," and by public officials running up to federal Cabinet level. And most of these board members, commissioners, and officials come by these positions so crucial for welfare as a result of their power and status in the larger society. Their interests, and the stereotypes and opinions they hold about social welfare and social work, powerfully affect the nature of services available to the client.

This brief picture of social agency operation reveals an organization marked by specialization of function among workers, who are arranged in a hierarchy. Their relations are, to a degree, formalized, their activities routinized. The agency is, in short, a *bureaucracy*, a form of organization typical of the complex industrial society. The agency is, further, one of a host specialized by program purpose, skill emphasis, clientele, location, and auspices. It exists in a state of *interdependence* with other agencies, creating needs for communication and cooperation which are met through a superstructure of coordinating mechanisms, such as councils and chests, which themselves take on bureaucratic form. Whenever important decisions on welfare matters are to be made, the *power structure* of American society will come into play. All these organizational characteristics of the agency and its environment reflect the changes wrought by industrialism in the larger society discussed in Chapters III, IV, and V: complex specialization and stratification, with a major shift toward service occupations; increasing scale of organization; the increased productivity and income to underwrite the whole.

Patterns of organization and control of social welfare activity have had little study. We can here suggest only their grosser, typical outlines. The label we give to these patterns, "bureaucracy," is a model to which actual agency practice conforms in varying degree. Where possible, we will indicate the conditions under which actual behavior will "fit" the bureaucratic model least and most.

Bureaucracy: Intra-Agency Specialization and Coordination

Bureaucracy (or, simply, formal organization) exists in degree —the degree to which certain distinguishing characteristics are present and emphasized. Many people would list these characteristics as red tape, buck passing, inaction, inflexibility. These, however, are but the "pathologies" of bureaucracy—they derive from a number of more basic features of organization. The purpose of this section is to discuss essential characteristics of bureaucracy, the implications of these characteristics for social service, and the conditions which promote their development in the social agency.

Distinguishing Characteristics. To say bureaucracy is to say *specialization;* and to say specialization is to say *hierarchy.*[1] Most

---

[1] The list of main characteristics used here is taken from the various writings of Max Weber. They are conveniently summarized by Blau (28: pp. 28-30). Cf. Dahl and Lindblom (71: pp. 235-236).

social agencies have, broadly speaking, two main levels of authority and status (representing also the major functional division)—
the clerical-technical staff, typists to accountants, and the professional staff, each subdivided in standard ways. Within the professional staff the major ranks of worker, supervisor, and executive
are found. From one to six or seven caseworkers (or groupworkers) may be directed by one supervisor who, if his supervisory
load is light, may also carry a caseload. In a large agency there
may be a case supervisor, supervisor of supervisors. We see here
the standard pyramid of the "line" organization. (331: pp. 130–
216) The essence is authority; the right to command by virtue of
position passes successively from many hands to fewer to an
integrating peak.[1] Any organization of appreciable size and complexity, comprising people of different but interrelated skills,
inescapably is driven to such a system in order to achieve a
framework within which goals can be set and efforts can be mustered and coordinated with maximal efficiency. Internal agency
hierarchy is most fully worked out when the agency is public, or,
if private, participates in joint fund-raising. Then central authorities create finely graded classifications or civil service schemes,
running from the lowest filing clerk to the topmost brass.

The hierarchy is also a congealed model of the career pattern.
It provides a set of steps through which the individual may advance, a promotional horizon for the motivation of those lower
down. The caseworker aims to become supervisor, the supervisor
to become an executive. Social agency structure thus accords with
the need in industrial society for a highly motivated work-force
(see Chapter V). Not all achieve their goals, of course, but there
is some evidence that the hierarchical organization of social work
allows a comparatively large opportunity for advancement above
the basic caseworker and groupworker jobs. Among all welfare
workers in 1950, 37 per cent were above client-contact jobs;
among members of professional social work associations some 60
per cent hold the higher positions (though not all of these are

---

[1] The advisory, or "staff," function in social agencies, existing outside the line
organization, is performed by consultants, usually psychiatrists, but sometimes home
economists and other nonsocial work professionals.

supervisors and directors—some are teachers, public relations specialists, and the like). (375: p. 38; 201) An ironic commentary on the extraordinary speed with which social groupworkers become supervisors came from an experienced social worker observing operations in a modern settlement house: "Heaven forbid that a groupworker should lead a group!"

Although the supervision pattern may be required by bureaucratic organization in the agency, the ways in which authority is exercised, the styles of leadership, are quite as much an outgrowth of unique elements in social work professional culture. In an extensive literature devoted to developing effective supervisory technique, and in courses in supervision in schools of social work, leadership is more often conceived in terms of education than of command, as a channel for obtaining collaboration among workers on difficult problems than as a method of case review by higher authority.[1] Supervision is also a key element in the training of caseworkers, who spend about half their two years of graduate training in an agency under a selected teacher-supervisor. Since sensitivity to the motivational and emotional states of the client—perhaps the prime objective of social work training—must be preceded by self-awareness, the student is himself subjected to a near-psychotherapeutic experience. He is persistently called to account for his own behavior, not in cognitive but in emotional terms—not "Why do you think this way?" but "Why do you feel this way?"

This supervisor-trainee relationship has tended to carry over into general practice, leading to a recent upsurge of doubt about the social work supervisory pattern. Does the work of an experienced worker need to be subjected to persistent, routine review? Does this not foster excessive dependency in the worker? Is it logical and efficient to place responsibility for education in a person whose fundamental role in the hierarchy is command and review? (344) The increasing use in psychiatric settings of a professional-team approach raises further questions; the psychi-

[1] This emphasis is found to a lesser extent in supervisory training programs in industry, too—reflecting an attempt to humanize the mass organization and a growing concern with the morale of employees.

atrist and psychologist members of the team operate as independent practitioners, but the social worker still reports to a
supervisor outside the team structure. The result is confusion in
lines of authority and responsibility, and in concepts of professional role. (332) In some places the supervision structure is
being tacitly abandoned. Back of these doubts probably lies the
drive for professionalization of social work (see Chapter XI).
Public opinion, it is observed, accords higher status to professionals who practice independently—outside administrative hierarchies. Stress on supervision is thus seen as an impediment to
full acceptance of social work as a profession. If this belief is
widespread among social work leaders, further erosion of the
present supervisory pattern may be expected.

First, then, we have specialists, and to coordinate and motivate
their efforts we have hierarchy. A second feature of bureaucracy
—and agency—is an emphasis on rules, on doing things "by the
book." This appears as *routinization of activity* on the one hand, and
on the other as *formalization of relationships* between functionaries
and clients, and to a lesser extent among functionaries themselves.
Compare the handout at the door of the monastery in fourteenth
century Europe, or at the relief agency in nineteenth century
America, or at a Salvation Army slum mission today, with the
two-inch thick "Manual of Regulations" guiding the administration of contemporary public assistance. Or contrast the informal
mixing and exchange of "culture" between University "settlers"
and slum dwellers envisaged by the founders of the Settlement
House movement with the elaborately planned program of activities offered by settlement houses today, even though they are
among the least formal of our modern leisure-time agencies.

Formalization of colleague-relations within the agency should
be distinguished from that of practitioner-client relations. The
former derives more from the requirements of bureaucratic structure, the latter more from professional culture. Thus, in a small
agency where the impress of bureaucracy is less, colleague relations will be more informal; but the worker-client relationship
will be much the same whatever the agency size, so long as it is
staffed by professionally trained people. There seems to be a

tendency in social work, however, to extend the ideal of objective, impartial, socially distant relations with clients (see Chapter XI) to colleague relations, as well.[1]

Within any good-sized agency rules and some formality will be found. They function to smooth communication and command between the hierarchical ranks, to regulate relations between occupational specialists working side-by-side, and to realize the objectives of a planned program. Without stable, comfortable, certified ways of talking and writing to one another, people of different rank or different function do not easily maintain harmony. Without prescribed goals and rules that fit the goals, specialized efforts tend to be random and to cancel one another.

Because a bureaucracy coordinates interdependent specialists, each person must be proficient in his task, and must not presume to intrude upon anyone else's. Thus, further features of the social agency are *assignment of roles on the basis of technical qualifications,* and clear and official *areas of jurisdiction* for the several roles. In the nonbureaucratic organization—an early-day social agency or a contemporary agency not yet caught up in the swing toward professionalism and formal organization—little attention is paid to technical qualifications for role performance. In rural areas teachers without formal certificates of training are still hired, judges without law degrees are elected, and juvenile court probation officers and Children's Aid Society workers need only "be of good character." To qualify for employment in a modern, high-standard agency, in contrast, the worker must possess a MSW degree at least, and often also a "specialization" in psychiatric, family, or child welfare work. The supervisor not only must have such training, but in addition must give evidence of years of experience, and of interest in "professional improvement" by attendance at postgraduate institutes and the like.

[1] A well-known lecturer on mental hygiene in a school of social work used to insist that workers should not draw their friends from among their coworkers. Although rationalized on professional and mental hygiene grounds, such a rule of conduct seems but a glorification of one of the pathologies of bureaucracy. If it were followed, it very likely would tend to disrupt informal, task-relevant communication (e.g., exchange of professional news, of information about client needs, agency problems) and thereby reduce agency efficiency.

In the nonbureaucratic organization, areas of jurisdiction will be hazy—anyone may do anything, within limits, even if he is unskilled at it. In the family, father may cook dinner and diaper the baby, mother may drive the car and mow the lawn. In the early-day social agency, anyone might pitch in to help investigate a rush of relief applicants. But in the modern agency, the case-worker will not take over a dictaphone in the stenographic pool, even if she is able; the stenographer would not dream of conducting a treatment interview; and, although alternation of roles occurs, the worker who is not "on intake" will not casually wander in and do an intake interview.

Effects on Service. Bureaucracy, especially as it becomes joined with professional culture, plainly has many implications for agency operation and social service. The essential characteristics of formal organization—specialization and hierarchy, emphasis on rules, technical qualifications for functionaries operating in clearcut areas of jurisdiction—are not designed to interfere with the giving and getting of service. Quite the opposite. From the viewpoints of both client and worker, however, they often appear as obstacles and impediments.

The rules and red tape that swathe the agency within, for instance, also reach out to mold the client. He has a role to play, too; he must behave like a "case" if he is to use the service. He must fall into certain categories by need or other attribute—a dependent child, over 65, a marital problem, "motivated for treatment." There are applications to complete or sign, appointments to be kept. He must be willing to cooperate, to bare his life's secrets in relevant areas, to bring spouse or children to the office, to file charges in court, to be "cleared" through a Social Service Exchange.

Within the agency, specialists in a hierarchy find effective communication an increasingly severe problem. There is much truth in the observation that ours is the "paper age" (soon, perhaps, to become the "magnetic tape age"), that we are a nation of paper-shufflers and file-keepers. Small, informal groups can maintain identity, continuity, and tradition through word of mouth. Families need few records, and those, such as income tax returns, are required by the outside bureaucratic society. But anyone who has worked in either small or large agencies or in business firms knows that paper-work is central to all operations; in the largest organizations, whole divisions simply maintain records. Several necessities of organizational life prompt the piles of paper. First, these organizations have a long time-perspective. They undertake long-range tasks, and therefore need to perceive long-range changes and to make continuing evaluations of organizational efforts and results, unclouded by personal or memory bias. Second, in so far as they assign positions on the basis of technical ability, they must keep records for periodic review of individual performance. Third, agencies are accountable to some board or legislative body or other authority; so they keep records to justify themselves should they come under attack or scrutiny. Most important, continuity of function dictates that records be kept, for people die, retire, quit, fail, are promoted. The next occupant of the position, the next worker on the case must get oriented. Some of this is done informally. But contacts and information are of such complexity and scope that even the memory of an "old office Joe" with a reputation for knowing everything cannot be trusted. To the extent that their time perspective is long, that accountability to officials is required, and continuity of specialized roles must be maintained, even small organizations will devote much effort to the record department.

The well-run social casework agency is a champion record-keeper. The Hill and Ormsby cost study in the Family Service of Philadelphia (primarily a casework agency) arrived at the following distribution of a $100 expenditure for casework services (148: p. 168):

Interviewing costs	$42.49
Case recording	32.15
Supervisory conferences	13.17
Case consultations	5.77
Miscellaneous	6.42
Total	$100.00

Thirty-two per cent of all expenditures related to providing casework services were for recording. Moreover, if we focus not simply on recording but on the total process of *maintaining communication* within a bureaucratic structure, then supervisory conferences and case consultations may be added to case recording, resulting in a total of 51 per cent of all expenditures for this purpose. These bulk so large along with other necessary costs that only 42 per cent is spent for direct contact with clients. The expense of maintaining communication appears to be very great. But where there is a long-range program with outside accountability, a complex division of labor, and frequent changes of staff, communication within an organization becomes necessarily a matter of prime importance—we do not know, really, whether or not a cost distribution such as the above is optimal for a family agency.[1]

Because of the time that must be spent in maintaining communication, and the general intricacy of its inner workings, bureaucracy affects the speed with which service is given. The writers know of an instance in a small city where a midday radioed public appeal for bedding for a burned-out family brought fifty mattresses, flung upon their doorstep, by evening. Agencies oppose public appeals of this sort, but that is the way informal welfare operates. The formal agency, in contrast, has its own built-in tempo and reaction time. Although not typical, the time schedule of one large high-standard family agency in early 1955 was substantially as follows. When a prospective client first made contact with the agency, unless a well-defined emergency existed, he was asked to call back some two or three weeks later to arrange an appointment. When he called back, he was given an appointment three or four weeks later for an intake interview. At the completion of this, if he needed further consultation, he was scheduled for a second appointment some three to six months later. From then on he was seen every week or fortnight on

---

[1] As a result of the publication of the Hill and Ormsby study, several agencies have experimented with methods for reducing time spent on conferences and recording. Detailed recording of interviews is being abandoned for most purposes, and some agencies report considerable savings in recording time without hindrance to results. It is unfortunate that there is so little knowledge of the relative effectiveness of different organizational structures. There appear to be no studies which compare any measure of performance for agencies which are similar in size, function, and clientele, but differ as to supervisor-worker ratio, number of levels of authority, caseload, and so on. Studies which relate such variables are hard to design and harder to carry out, but they are sorely needed to supplement administrative wisdom.

regular schedule. This situation is perhaps extreme and may have been due largely to lack of personnel to meet the demand.[1] But the impress of bureaucracy is plain; no informal organization can ever operate with such deliberation in the face of a request for help.

Bureaucracy tends to minimize urgency, which may be counted a disadvantage. But the gains associated with it are clear: reliability, continuity, fairness. Although he may wait as long as six months for service, the client will receive dependable attention. The agency will not forget him, as the public will forget its mattress-buried family after a few days. Those same files whose maintenance eats up 32 cents of the agency dollar assure him definite attention at the appointed time. Other agency procedures also assure continuity of service—not just this burned-out family but others to come will get predictable help. Finally, while bureaucratic procedures may seem impersonal to the client—he cannot have his favorite worker, or perhaps even the one to whom he unburdened at intake—by the same token he is assured of equality of treatment. Class background, the worker's feelings, "pull," personal charm or lack of it, make little difference to the agency; in informal welfare they are often the very basis on which aid is given.

The model for the foregoing discussion has been the "ideal type" bureaucracy. (399) Along with its gains—efficiency, reliability, precision, fairness—come what many students have called its pathologies: timidity, delay, officiousness, red tape, exaggeration of routine, limited adaptability. (237: pp. 396 ff.) The agency as a means, a mechanism—the *agency*—for carrying out welfare policy becomes an end in itself. Between the altruist with his desire to help and the client with his need lies the machine, with its own "needs." These needs can result in an emphasis on technique and method, on organizational routines and records, rather than on people and service.[2]

---

[1] By the fall of 1956 this agency had managed to shorten the time span between initial request and regular service to an average of about four months.

[2] There is some reason to believe that in a large social agency, preoccupation with the rules, a strong "procedural orientation," will be found most often among middle ranks (long-service staff and supervisors). On the one hand, the top administrators

Footnote continued on page 244.

Factors Affecting Degree of Bureaucracy. Much of what goes on in social agencies fits this model of bureaucracy. And much does not. Several factors affect the degree to which bureaucratic gains and pathologies will be present in an organization. Among the most important are size, proportion of personnel which is professionally oriented, and degree of public control.

First, consider size: the bigger, the more bureaucratic. Even in large organizations, however, a network of informal, personal relations among workers infiltrates the bureaucratic skeleton, infusing it with qualities quite unbureaucratic. In the social agency lines of communication may by-pass the supervisor, a client will be seen out of turn or transferred to a worker he knows, hours set for "dictation" will be disregarded—all with the knowledge and tacit approval of everyone in the agency. This so-called "informal organization," which arises in part as a reaction against the pathologies of bureaucracy, is often essential to the survival of the agency and the accomplishment of its goals. It sometimes has a powerful effect in reshaping the goals of an organization. (303; 29)

In the small agency informal colleague relations and a deemphasis of hierarchy and rules are still more common, and the model of bureaucracy a still poorer fit. But even in the small agency many fundamental elements of bureaucracy—assignment of roles on the basis of technical qualification, division of responsibility, record-keeping—must still exist, with effects heightened by the professional culture of social work. It seems clear, also, that the day of the small agency is nearly past. Many such agencies exist, but mergers—both by geography to cover metropolitan areas and by program purposes to cover related functions

---

Continued from page 243.

not only have an overview of the whole agency, but they must also relate it and justify it to the larger community in terms of program purposes—so they are likely to be goal-centered ("drop what you're doing and see this man"). On the other hand, the lower ranks are too close to the task and what it takes to get it done, to become enamoured of procedure. The middle ranks, most insulated from both the day-to-day task and the overview of agency and community, are most vulnerable to "technicism." (Cf. 112: pp. 162 ff.) Also vulnerable are the less competent, less successful, and therefore most insecure functionaries: insecurity breeds rigidity and over-conformity; the insecure fear change and seek security in fixed rules. (Cf. 29.)

—are now frequent. Finally, there are a limited number of ways to organize work—and if the schools and churches we attend, the stores we patronize, the voluntary associations and political parties we belong to, the government agencies we encounter, and the defense establishment we support all accustom us to elements of bureaucracy, we become predisposed to adopt this organizational form in new areas for different problems, appropriate or not. The atmosphere and pattern of bureaucracy tend to be copied in small agencies even when size and degree of specialization do not require them.

A second major factor affecting degree of bureaucracy in the agency is *the proportion of personnel that is strongly committed to a profession.* A professional orientation among functionaries works both ways—toward accentuating and toward reducing bureaucratic tendencies—but on balance the reduction effect may be stronger. Considering that both professionalism and bureaucracy are responses to complex specialization in modern society, it is not surprising that they play into each other at many points. The impersonality of relations governed by rules that the formal organization requires finds its counterpart in the professional emphasis on formality of client-worker relations. Insistence that recruitment and promotion of workers be on the basis of technical qualifications is common to both; and both strive toward clarity in the definition and jurisdiction of roles. We have also suggested that some unique stresses in social work culture may further accentuate bureaucratic tendencies, for example, the emphasis on supervision and records, and a possible tendency to carry rules for worker-client relations over to colleague relations.

On the other hand, to be professional is to behave in many ways counter to the bureaucratic pattern. The service code of the professional (see Chapter XI) requires him to give foremost attention to the needs of the client, with several unbureaucratic results: he may disregard or short-circuit formal rules and regulations in order to meet client needs; he will be concerned about red-tape impediments to efficient operation, and will be ready to make adjustments; he will strive to maintain or improve existing standards of work (330); he will often seek to evaluate service on the basis of results achieved rather than by techniques used. Professionalism gives one not only the incentive but also the strength to avoid excesses of bureaucratic proceduralism—for membership in a cohesive group with its own standards, and with roots outside any given agency, frees the functionary from the fears and insecurity which would lead him to take refuge in fixed rules. "A professional orientation neutralizes feelings of dependency. . . ." (29: p. 188) Where professionalism is strong, Blau finds, the feeling of freedom is also strong, and the proliferation of rules less necessary.

A third factor affecting bureaucracy is *auspices*. Among the various types of auspices, the public versus private alternative is most crucial on the American scene. The public agency is larger on average than the private agency, and less often professionally staffed. Thus, the factors discussed above, size and method of staffing, enter again. Not only has the public agency a bigger local operating office, it is also more often tied in with extensive state and federal hierarchies of control. People in the ADC program, for instance, or in unemployment insurance, work in local, state, regional, and federal offices; a mass of regulations issues at all levels; and there may be a dozen supervisory layers stacked above the local-bureau visitor and employment-office interviewer. Such towering organizational pyramids require an emphasis on the basic characteristics of bureaucracy and invite the exaggerations which we have called "pathologies" of bureaucracy.

Two other conditions of public agency life tend further to accentuate bureaucracy: public welfare programs are framed in law, and the agency operates in a "goldfish bowl." The basic law setting up a program is usually brief; administration of the program requires an endless flow of regulations which comprise the ever-changing "Manual." Operation in the glare of publicity may create an atmosphere of insecurity which, as Blau shows, tends to foster rigidity and proceduralism. It is no accident that Weber found his model of the bureaucrat in the public official.

Much of what social workers accept today as normal agency practice is but the universal face of bureaucracy. The personal, piecemeal, immediate, unstructured, informal, and haphazard welfare practices of yesteryear find less and less place in the welfare world of today. Given awareness of the possible pathologies of bureaucracy, and some ingenuity, the inherent disadvantages can be minimized. Certainly, ways can be found to reduce a six-month waiting period for service. When the organization becomes top-heavy, needlessly hierarchical, preoccupied with procedure, deaf to the needs of individuals, then alternative lines of communication and change can be found—by pressure from without (consider how veterans' groups reach into and manipulate the massive bureaucracy of the Veterans Administration), or by pressure from within (witness the many solutions to organizational and service problems instituted spontaneously by staff subordinates without administrative direction). And it is not impossible for agency administrators studiously to minimize bureaucratic pathologies.[1]

Bureaucracy: Interagency Specialization and Coordination

Not only does specialization within the agency give rise to bureaucracy, but specialization among agencies in a community also creates an interdependence which requires coordinating mechanisms. The basic problem, whether *within* the agency or *among* agencies, is the same—how to attain effective integration of specialisms. Among agencies, however, the bases for specialization are more varied, and an authoritative structure for exercising over-all control is lacking. Further, the need for coordination among agencies is often obscured. It is less easy to see the community as a functional whole, with interdependence among all its

[1] Detailed observation by Blau of people at work in a state employment agency and a federal law-enforcement agency led him to list five main factors that minimize bureaucratic pathologies, i.e., factors that increase the agency's ability to change itself and initiate adjustments that further organizational goals: (1) job security for employees and staff (which can be achieved by sensible financing and personnel policy); (2) a professional orientation toward the work (which can be encouraged by high standards of recruitment and performance); (3) established workgroups that command the loyalty of the workers (to lessen the need for individuals to seek security in fixed rules and familiar routines); (4) the absence of basic conflict between workgroup and management (so that workgroups do not sabotage organizational goals); and (5) organizational problems experienced as disturbing (a challenge for change such as a case overload). (29: pp. 208 ff.) In addition, agency administrators and supervisors can use all the skills of the democratic leader that fit so well the training and ideology of social workers.

parts, than it is to see the essential unity of a single agency. Nevertheless, the division of labor which binds us all together in a web of mutual dependence, though sometimes obscure, is a basic fact of community life. (Cf. 143.) In welfare, as in all areas of endeavor, no one can do the whole job; there must be an extensive division of welfare work. But on what bases is the work divided? What problems arise? What methods are used to meet the problems?

Bases of Specialization in Social Welfare. Work can be divided in a great many ways. But a close look at any array of specialties in an organization or any array of organizations in a field shows a limited number of criteria by which they justify or define their special work. The major bases of specialization among social agencies are listed and exemplified in Chart E.

CHART E.   BASES OF SPECIALIZATION IN SOCIAL WELFARE

Basis of specialization	Exemplified by such specializations as:
Purpose (or program)	Public assistance, corrections, recreation, vocational rehabilitation
Skill (or process)	Social casework, group work, vocational counseling, psychiatry, community organization
Clientele	Children, adults, aged, veterans, nonveterans, religious background, financial ability
Auspices (or sponsorship)	Government (federal, state, local, state-local), voluntary (sectarian, nonsectarian, joint-financed)
Geography (or location)	Geographic jurisdictions and boundaries of service

Specialization on any of these bases can, of course, occur within, as well as among, agencies. A very large agency may be regarded as a complex of specialized subagencies. The Veterans Administration, for example, offers vocational rehabilitation, social service, pensions, and so on (specialization by purpose or program), employs psychiatrists, social caseworkers, and the like (specialization by skill), and has district, regional, and local offices (specialization by geography).[1] Our focus here, however, is not on the internal structure of a single administrative unit but on the aggregate of separate agencies typical of the welfare scene in most American communities.

The Reasons for Specialization. The general advantage gained by specialization, of whatever mode and on whatever base, is efficiency—economy, speed, accuracy in performance of a task. (331: p. 137) But efficiency is only one of the factors leading to specialization. Consider some cases of specialization by clientele. Separation of adults from children in outpatient psychiatric service is probably motivated almost entirely by a desire to enhance the degree of skill that can be brought to bear—which should increase efficiency. Separate family agencies for Catholics, Jews, and Protestants, however, stem from religious sentiments, and probably decrease over-all efficiency. The dual school system of the South, based on specialization by race, certainly decreases efficiency, though it may realize other values of some citizens in that area. The "special" public assistances, ADC, OAA, and the like, arise for political reasons—popular support can more easily be generated for old folk and orphaned children than for the generality of poor.

Similar reasons explain some of the specialization that occurs on other bases. Geographical dispersion of agencies makes services physically available and allows for regional variation in standards and needs, for example, lower relief grants in Mississippi than in New York. But it also serves, especially among government agencies, to forestall or silence outcries against "centralization in Washington." Some of our present specialization by skill—marital counseling, rehabilitation counseling, educational counseling, parent-child counseling, vocational counseling, and family casework, for instance—probably owes as much to con-

---

[1] The V.A., of course, has but one clientele, veterans (though they may be subdivided into pensioners, compensation claimants, etc.), and one auspices, the federal government. A single auspices is the usual pattern for welfare agencies in the U.S.; in England it is quite common for an agency to be sponsored jointly by government and private groups. (167: p. 5) An example of multiple sponsorship in the U.S. is the Michigan system of community child guidance clinics, which is instituted by the State Department of Mental Health only on condition of local (government or voluntary or both) sharing in financing.

siderations of professional jurisdiction and prerogative as it does
to actual gains in efficiency. And so on.

The fact that specialization often occurs for reasons irrelevant
to efficiency does not mean that it is "wrong" or even that it
lowers efficiency. The specialization among relief programs mentioned above, though it may have some undesirable consequences,
may be the best balance of social welfare losses and gains that can
be achieved under the existing social and political circumstances.
If separate family casework facilities for religious groups are
favored despite their possibly greater economic cost, then religious values and not economic efficiency are the weightier
criteria. The desirability of a given mode of specialization in a
particular situation can be judged only in terms of the priority of
values pertinent to the situation.

Disadvantages of Interagency Specialization. Whatever the motivations behind them, the fact of specialization and the particular
basis on which it is undertaken do affect both the efficiency and
the goals of service. Some of the problems they present for social
welfare can be grouped under four headings: gaps in service,
dividing the client, segregating the client, and duplication.

(1) *Gaps in service* are currently recognized as a most serious
problem in the provision of welfare services. A case cited by
Virtue in a study of children's services in Michigan illustrates how
specialization on several bases works to create gaps:

> Two boys, 10 and 11, are bedridden and paralyzed with muscular
> dystrophy. Prognosis is death within five years. Previous aid through
> the Crippled Children Commission has been terminated upon diag-
> nosis, owing to the poor prognosis and the unavailability of hospital
> care for purely custodial cases. After full investigation by welfare,
> educational, judicial, and private agency personnel, no aid was given.
> At last contact, the mother was caring for these boys together with
> her other children, in a house with no plumbing, and with no help
> other than that supplied by an occasional visit from an orthopedic
> therapist and a volunteer neighbor who read to the boys one after-
> noon a week. The judge of the juvenile court reported that the mar-
> riage of the parents appeared to be in jeopardy, as a result of long
> physical and mental strain. Reasons given by various agencies for
> not extending aid were:

1. Juvenile court: no neglect or other basis for jurisdiction.

2. Health department: no local health department.

3. Welfare and relief authorities (state and county): father is employed and thus ineligible for financial assistance; suggest foster care through special educational services.

4. Crippled Children Commission: statute interpreted not to authorize home care.

5. Local school: insufficient personnel to furnish home tutoring.

6. State department of public instruction, special services division: locality not eligible for state-furnished special services.

7. Michigan Society for Crippled Children and Adults, Inc.: public agencies could help if they saw fit; private agency should not invade public agency field. (384: pp. 9–10)

In this case, the juvenile court, relief authorities, and the Crippled Children's Commission could not act because of real or imagined restrictions imposed by specialization on *program-purpose* lines. Services of a health department and of the special services division of the state department of public instruction were not available because of gaps in *geographic* coverage. The local school board had insufficient personnel to provide home tutoring, presumably from lack of funds; this results from a specialization by *auspices*— many localities are too poor to provide special educational services and need help from the state or federal government. Notions about proper auspices also apparently account for the private agency's refusal to act.

Gaps in service also result from specialization by *skill* (or process) and *clientele*. In a paper on "The Limits of Social Service" psychologist Gordon Allport suggests that narrowing of "agency function" has progressed to the point where

> . . . The problem is growing acute in social work. Increasing emphasis on defining agency function can lead to a rat-race of referrals, sometimes demoralizing to the client and hence unethical. Even if referrals themselves do not damage the client, he may find at the end of his trek that for his distress there is no rubric and therefore no agency to help him. An unmarried girl in a certain town could find no help; she was seven months pregnant and the only appropriate agency had a rule that no applicant more than six

months pregnant could be accepted. Good casework, the agency said, could not be done at this late stage of pregnancy. . . . (5: p. 204)

Here the agency, though it deals with unmarried expectant mothers, specializes in a clientele less than six months pregnant. The more controlling specialization in this case, however, is by skill— "good casework" dictates the restriction on clients. Presumably agencies which do not specialize in good casework should exist to care for girls pregnant longer than six months. In both the Allport and the Virtue cases, it is clear, specialization has so far distorted the presumed goals of service that no service is in fact given.

(2) *Dividing the client*, in social welfare as in medicine, is regarded as a serious problem. It occurs when the client—individual, family, or community—has a problem whose solution requires two or more skills, or has several problems involving a variety of programs. The extent to which multiple problems in a single case is the rule rather than the exception is suggested by Buell's finding in St. Paul that the majority of health, dependency, and adjustment services were absorbed by multiple-problem families. (43: p. 9) It is common occurrence in any good-sized American city for a public assistance worker, a probation officer from the juvenile court, and a family caseworker all to be visiting the home of a single family—and it can happen that a visiting teacher, truant officer, and public health nurse will meet them there. In social welfare, dividing the client takes place mostly on the basis of specialization by program; division by skill is better illustrated from medicine where a general practitioner, an internist, a urologist, a gynecologist, and a proctologist may simultaneously serve a female client who has an infection of the pelvic area.

The existence and availability to the client of such varied specialties is not the problem—they may all be necessary. The problem is that services are not integrated, a situation increasingly hard to avoid as services grow ever more specialized, numerous, and technically arcane. Consider a fairly common big-city social syndrome: family on ADC because father is disabled with a heart condition, one or more children delinquent.

The relief investigator, in pursuance of agency policy, urges the father to seek work; the visiting nurse counsels rest on doctor's orders. The assistance agency hunts a part-time job for mother; the probation officer bids her stay home to keep Johnny out of mischief. The truant officer warns Johnny against any more absences from school; the probation officer admonishes him not to miss his school-hours appointment at the court. This picture, though hypothetical, is not much exaggerated. Only the clients know the full story of conflicting counsel, and they do not write the case records. From the point of view of service both by agency and profession, inconsistent, partial, and contradictory treatment plans result—inefficiency. From the client's viewpoint, puzzlement and resentment ("inability to respond to treatment") result—and the goal of service is lost. Many of the "hard to reach" families now receiving so much attention are the product of such treatment; their disaffection is understandable.

(3) That *segregation and stigmatizing of the client* may result from specialization is little recognized in social welfare literature, though they constitute a serious disadvantage of some types of specialization. Of course, some segregation—children from adults in psychiatric service, for example—carries no stigma. Even segregation that would be disapproved by preponderant public opinion—separation of clients on religious or racial grounds—if done with "malice aforethought," with knowledge of and willingness to pay the consequences, is at least overt and can be opposed openly in terms of the pertinent values. But segregation and stigmatization are too often the unanticipated, and often overlooked, effects of specialization.

Americans, for instance, have not yet ceased to think of the mental hospital as a "nut house," rather than as a medical facility, though it is surely not the aim of special facilities for the mentally ill to stigmatize their patients. Because such attitudes toward mental hospitals and the mentally ill interfere with patient recovery, there is now a movement to incorporate psychiatric facilities into the general hospital. This amounts to knocking out geographic and, to some degree, program bases of specialization in order to avoid the stigma attached to segregation. Specialization by skill would remain; that is, psychiatrists would now work in the general hospital, alongside other medical specialists, under the mantle of a general health program.

The juvenile court offers another example of how specialization by program and clientele can lead unwittingly to stigmatization, and hence to poor service. Although the juvenile court was in part created just to avoid a criminal court record for children, it has developed according to some observers (cf. 355) its own stigma, and the vast growth of social services under its aegis serves to suck in an ever-larger population of children to take the brand. Appreciation of this is a main motive in the recently growing movement to trim back the court to more strictly legal functions. (Cf. 30.) Pressure to expand court social services, it should be noted, has come not from within the court itself (until recently at least), but from the outside community. The court, as part of the police power of the society, has in effect been forced to accept responsibility for handling such problems as other agencies, public and private, have been unable or unwilling to accept.

Because populations are socially, racially, or otherwise segregated by residence, geographic specialization of a service often begets unanticipated stigmatizing effects. The agency becomes identified with the neighborhood. In late 1956 there was established in the Jeffries public housing project in Detroit an experimental nursery school, sponsored by the Housing Commission and a university college of education. Expertly staffed, and with excellent physical facilities, the nursery was planned, in part, as a demonstration of the feasibility and desirability of "integrated" education—across lines of race and economic class. To obtain so mixed a group of children it was necessary to draw on white and better-off Negro families who lived outside the housing project. But no outside mother, even though she lived just 40 feet across the street, would at the start send her child into the "project nursery."

It is unavoidable that specialization, especially on the basis of location of clientele, will often have segregative effects. In many instances, this will make little difference, either in efficiency or for the goals of service. When disadvantages do appear, however, these must be weighed against the advantages gained by the given mode of specialization. Is it better to have a (voluntarily) segregated nursery than none at all? It may be more difficult and costly, again, to design life-cycle (all ages) communities than it is to build mass housing for the aged to live in apart. But if the latter does not in fact realize our goals of health and happiness for the old, the economy of specialization should perhaps be forgone.

(4) Eliminating *duplication of services* was a foremost objective of the first large-scale attempt to "organize charity," eighty to ninety years ago; and duplication is still a favorite *bête noire* of critics of social welfare organization. A close look, however, might suggest that what is called duplication is often in fact justified by the advantages of specialization by clientele, auspices, and so on. The most commonly cited example of flagrant duplication is the array of veterans' services, paralleling at many points those available to "ordinary citizens." But are these duplicate services, or are they a realization of a value the American people hold (or are presumed by legislators to hold) about how veterans should be treated? Looked at closely, the veterans' services are not "just the same" as those available to the general community. The veterans' pension is administered quite differently from relief; getting a nonservice connected disability taken care of in a V.A. hospital is quite unlike applying for hospitalization under the "afflicted adult" provisions of the poor law; veterans' vocational rehabilitation is structured and staffed differently from the civilian rehabilitation program. If there were no V.A., veterans would not be getting the services they now have. Whether they *should* get them is, of course, a different question, not to be confused with the charge of duplication.

Experienced public assistance administrators have recently proposed establishing employment services within, and under the administrative direction of, the assistance agency. This would seem to be duplicating the services offered everywhere by state employment service offices. To some extent this may be true. But the more important truth is this: despite conferences and agreements, the general employment service is not geared to give the kind of patient, painstaking, individualized, and long-term attention to any one case that is often required to get a relief recipient back in the work force. Yet this is exactly the kind of service the public assistance agency wants and is prepared to set up. When the relief recipient is referred to the general employment service, nothing happens; when the relief agency does its own employment job, it is often successful. By most criteria of efficiency or goal-achievement, two such employment services do not duplicate each other.[1]

Much criticism of "duplication," and much of the reorganization undertaken to eliminate it, may be traced to "political" motives (331: pp. 162–164)—a desire to get rid of or take over existing agencies and units which threaten the hegemony of other units, a desire to weaken, strengthen, or change the goals of programs by placing them under departments with hostile or friendly views. Something of this may be seen on the community welfare scene in the current movement to close the many, small, Chest-supported community centers found scattered about large American cities, and replace them with a centralized agency employing roving neighborhood workers who utilize existing school and church buildings to put on a program. The shift is defended on the grounds that it eliminates the expense of "duplicate" physical facilities—the community house. Other things equal, such a saving would evidently accrue. But the further consequences are that control of the program moves out of the hands of the local center board, and the nature of the program itself changes. It seems likely that those who engineer such reorganization are aware of these consequences, and count on them. Whether the consequences are desirable in themselves is not, again, the question here.

In the multi-problem family case used above to illustrate "dividing the client," the relief worker, the probation officer, the family caseworker all take identical "face sheet information" from the client, and may tread each other's footsteps in extensive

---

[1] The relief agency-administered employment service may be less efficient in so far as it lacks the technical knowledge of occupational categories, job descriptions, employer preferences, and labor market conditions possessed by the general employment office.

explorations of the client's life history. This sort of duplication is wasteful and probably harmful to the client, as is also the overlap in service programs offered, and skills used, by the workers.

It should be emphasized again, however, that duplication, dividing the client, gaps in service, and all the other problems that come with specialization, are not to be regarded as total evils to be destroyed root and branch. Rather, they are costs to be balanced against gains that result from specialization on one base or another; they are factors to be weighed in our efforts to obtain an optimal division of labor in the social welfare job, once we have decided what welfare job we want done.

Specialization as a Technical Problem. It is clear that the choice among types of specialization (by program purpose, skill, clientele, auspices, location, or some combination of these) is fateful for both the shaping of welfare goals and their efficient accomplishment. It is clear, too, that once we have decided what values we want to pursue or emphasize (for example, strengthening child-supervision by keeping an ADC mother at home versus raising family income by getting her a job), the problem of specialization is mainly a technical one, a matter of know-how. What special programs will be appropriate, what skills should be applied, with which of the possible auspices should responsibility rest?

Let us return to the examples given in Chapter IX of the treatment of children labeled "delinquent." We saw there that agency practice reflects community values in all their contradictions and ambiguities. But even if we should deliberately clarify and rank our values as, first, "protection of the child," second, "justice," and, third, "deterrence of serious crime," we would still have knotty problems of organization. Kahn, in his intensive study of court services for children in New York City, notes that, though there is an abundance of programs available to help the child in trouble with the law, *these programs are structured and specialized in ways largely irrelevant to the problems children have.* Present program specialization for juvenile court cases is in terms of methods of case-finding and community stereotypes of clients ("neglected," "delinquent," "defective") or in terms of symptom-labeling ("truant," "conduct disorder," "stealing"). Such labels "do not differentiate between children in terms of how they can be understood, what their needs may be, or how they should be served." (171: p. 6) The truant may prove to be either a bright child who needs a more stimulating school program, or a schizophrenic who needs hospitalization. The child who steals may simply be obeying the codes of his gang (see Chapter IX), or a kleptomaniac expressing emotional conflicts. It will be noted that Kahn is concerned here not with duplication of service, or segregation of the client, or dividing the client, but with program divisions that are inappropriate to the problem. The present array of programs would be comparable, using a medical analogy, to hospital clinics specialized in "fevers," "aches," and "rashes."

Inappropriate program specialization creates havoc in the development and deployment of skill specialties. The purpose of specialization by skill is to create, through intensive practice and training, exceptional efficiency of performance in a restricted area. With the present organization of programs, however, any worker in any agency is likely to have in his caseload so wide a variety of problems requiring different skills that no effective skill specialization is possible. Or, if one skill carries high status, then everyone strives to claim or attain that skill, and other necessary skills are neglected. Every caseload, for instance, is likely to contain some children needing psychotherapy, resulting, Kahn notes, in the "attempt to transform each staff member into a psychotherapist. . . ." (171: p. 7)

The problem of adapting means (specialization) to ends (service) is further illustrated in Burns' discussion of auspices for public social security programs. (48: pp. 212–223)[1] At what level of government should responsibility for unemployment insurance reside? Why is OASI federally, but the unemployment program state, administered? What level of government is best suited to finance and administer public assistance? It is evident that political forces play a large part in what actually happens—witness the shifting of unemployment service back and forth between

[1] Burns, in Chapters 11 to 13 of the book cited, gives the best analysis in print of social security programs in relation to basis of specialization.

state and federal auspices. But political considerations aside, the answers to such questions depend on knowledge about such technical factors as: the relative taxing powers and tax bases of the different auspices, effect on mobility of labor and industry, effect on productivity, regional and industrial differences in unemployment rates, regional variation in living standards.

Thus, both Kahn's question (what is the best way to divide programs for children in the court?) and Burns' question (what is the optimal allocation of income maintenance programs among public auspices?) are not only value questions whose answers depend upon one's ranking of the goals of these programs, but also technical questions whose solution requires scientific knowledge. For children's services, we need to know more about administration—the effects on the child of different types of courts and schools, different encounters with specialists variously organized and controlled; and we need to know more about the factors of personality and social structure that produce various types of delinquents. For social security programs we need to know more, for example, about the health of children in ADC families (federally subsidized) as compared to children in families on local relief.

The present structure of children's services is justly criticized, but, both because of the confusion of goals being pursued and the lack of relevant knowledge, a more appropriate structure is hard to determine. We may wonder at the present haphazard arrangement of social security programs but until we know whether the economic rehabilitation of public assistance clients is better achieved by use of a relief agency-administered employment service than by use of the general employment service, or whether unemployment benefits are more adequate under federal rather than state sponsorship, a better arrangement cannot be determined. Questions of this sort have only recently come into focus as pressing problems for research in social welfare.

Coordination. Once we have decided how to divide work—on the basis of both goals and organizational know-how—we still have the problem of coordinating the special agencies we set up. Some of this is handled in the routine process of agency operation. But much of it is done more deliberately by welfare planners operating in the field known as "community organization." Improved coordination through planning cannot solve all the problems created by specialization. It is, however, of major help in tackling the problems of dividing the client, gaps in service, and duplication.

One of the oldest coordinative devices is the *social service exchange*, developed in the early charity-organization period to control duplication of relief-giving by the many private relief agencies of the time. Today duplication in relief is no longer a problem, and the exchange is used mainly as a means of letting one agency know which other agencies have been active on a case. Theoretically, the exchange could help to solve the problem of dividing the client, by allowing agencies to collaborate and integrate their services on a case. In practice, it is doubtful that much of this happens.[1] Other agency listings on the clearance slip carry only identification data; for useful case information one must read the agency record, or consult the worker on the case, which are both time-consuming processes. The number of other agency listings is often too large for a caseworker to track down and there is no way to establish priority among them for follow-up. Even when other agency records are read, integration of treatment does not automatically result. In recent years, moreover, agencies have increasingly adopted the practice of "selective registration" of cases, so that there is now no assurance of obtaining a complete picture of agency involvement in a case. Because of doubts about the usefulness of the exchange function, and concern about the breach of confidence involved in registration (is it sound professional ethics to register a client without his knowledge or permission?), some communities have dropped the exchange.

Another time-honored device for obtaining integration of services among agencies is the *case conference*. Informally, a vast amount of telephoning goes on among social workers in a community, ascertaining activities and policies of other agencies,

---

[1] Although the extent to which agencies clear cases through the exchange can be readily ascertained, there appears to be no evidence on the extent to which actual integration in service results from such registration.

checking who does what in a given case. Much of this conferring is useful; some of it probably represents attempts to untangle snarls resulting from earlier lack of integration of service. There is apparently no research information on the amount, nature, and effects of telephonic communication among social workers in a community. In its more formal guise, the case conference involves a planned meeting of supervisory as well as worker personnel from two or more agencies, in which, besides discussion of the exigencies of the immediate problem, agency policy with respect to similar cases is threshed out. Such conferences, because they are time-consuming, are convened only for exceptional cases; they are called to deal with emergencies, rather than to facilitate the daily integration of services.

A fresh approach to the problem is being explored by the Family-Centered Project in St. Paul, where, by agreement among the agencies serving a family, one worker is usually assigned to the case and administers all the services. (149) This device has been used before but has not had the benefit of extended and systematic application; results so far in St. Paul are promising. Of course, there are serious obstacles to this approach. For example, when a public assistance agency and a court probation service are active in the same family, how can the court's powers be given legally to the relief worker; or how can the probation officer assume legal responsibility for determination of relief need? Further, and perhaps more serious, how can the benefits of specialization be realized if specialists are not allowed to deal with the case? Some evidence suggests these obstacles can be surmounted by *selective use of specialists, after relationship with a family has been cemented by one worker*.

A different set of coordinative devices is addressed to the problem of gaps in service. When needed services simply do not exist, specialization, of course, is not the cause, nor is coordination the cure. But the equivalent of service gaps occurs when the client is not steered to the proper existing service—which can happen simply from a worker's inability to know all of the several hundred possible resources in a large community, or from his failure to go through the right channels to get an agency's attention.

There is no measure of, nor any research that has attempted to measure, the amount of nonuse and misuse of existing social services in a community. Such studies as Virtue's of public services to children in Michigan, however, suggest that the amount is large and the consequences wasteful and sometimes disastrous. (384: pp. 6–18)

One method of dealing with the problem is the *welfare resources handbook*, now issued, usually by the community welfare council, in nearly all large communities. Handbooks receive wide distribution and much use by such welfare "threshold" institutions as the police, schools, and churches, but they can help the unsophisticated clergyman or police sergeant only a little way toward the goal of precise agency selection and referral. For the family problem appropriate for a family agency, there will be found scores of agencies listed under the "Family Services" heading in the handbook; and brief bits of information about agency function, intake policies, and the like may mean little to those not already informed. On this basis bad referrals are often made. A better practice involves further telephoning until an agency that accepts responsibility is found. Even then, the case may have to be referred further; and, if accepted, may only get onto a long waiting list, as we noted earlier. The sophisticated social worker also uses the handbook, but in a different way. He already knows the community welfare structure and how to refer cases. For him the handbook is a convenient-sized telephone directory, to check addresses and phone numbers, or sometimes the geographic jurisdiction of an agency. Handbooks have their value but, as with dictionaries, one must first know the language in order to use them.

The *community information service* is a tool designed for much the same purposes as the handbook, and is in many ways superior. All a worker needs to know is a telephone number—the resources specialist on the other end of the wire, given a few pertinent details, selects the best agency for the case in hand, and gives directions for getting there. On first glance, this is more expensive. The resources handbook is sold at a price that pays for its cost; the cost of an information service cannot be so recaptured. But the savings from reducing fruitless agency contact, wasted time for workers, and the runaround for clients must be weighed against that cost.

Virtue suggests that "where many agencies, spanning several specialized professional techniques" offer various services, "adequate choice-making or 'threshold' personnel must be developed to ensure that the resources are known, integrated, and appropriately used." (384: p. 18) She mentions children's consultants of a state department of welfare, visiting teachers, and staff members of child guidance clinics as examples of "threshold" personnel. But such workers are hardly more specialized in the liaison function than any of a score of other kinds of workers—family caseworkers, probation officers, and the like—and what seems called for is not specialized personnel for referral work, but solid knowledge of resources and skill in referral as part of the standard equipment of welfare workers in all agencies. Professional social work training, more than training in the other occupations involved in welfare work (medicine, education, law), aims specifically at imparting such knowledge and skill. It is interesting to note that this important task of liaison, which only social work makes a definite effort to discharge, is often overlooked in descriptions of the social work function.[1]

The specific devices mentioned above operate within a framework for coordination provided in most large communities by the *council of social agencies* (variously called community welfare councils, health and welfare federations, and so on). The council, of course, is a general, social welfare planning organization, with coordination only one of its functions; and councils are only one of the many types of bodies devoted in whole or part to welfare planning.[2] The council, however, is the key coordinative unit at

---

[1] Janowitz' study of "Public Perspectives on Social Security" shows that few people know their rights and benefits under even such a well-known program as OASI. (165) It is clear that welfare professionals in an increasingly complex society must take major responsibility for knowing welfare resources and how to steer people to them.

[2] The central offices of public welfare departments, at the state and federal levels especially, emphasize such a function. In the voluntary field, the 1954 *Social Work Year Book* devotes 83 pages to a listing of agencies at the national level alone, most of them concerned with planning and coordinative activities. There is even a body—the National Social Welfare Assembly—whose task it is to coordinate the work of the national coordinating agencies.

the community level; at its best it represents a high point in democratic participation in American communities.

Out of the council's coordinative machinery, however, new problems arise. It is possible, and not uncommon in large communities, for councils to become a block to agency planning and working together. Once the coordinating function is centralized in a single center, there is a natural tendency among agencies to leave the planning function to the central body, awaiting its call to action. Other channels of communication tend to dry up; there is felt a responsibility to move only through the formally constituted planning center. (111) This is a loss to cross-agency communication; and since the center itself becomes a bureaucracy, distorting incoming messages as it passes them on to suit its own needs, a further limitation is placed on cooperative action. However, if there is leadership in the planning center, the gains far outweigh this sort of loss.

More difficulty occurs when the central planning body does not provide a staff adequate to the coordination task. In the Detroit metropolitan area, for instance, the welfare council in 1957 employed about 25 professionals (exclusive of top administration) distributed as follows: work with suburban division, 4–5; publicity and community information service, 4; volunteer services, 4; research department, 3; budgeting, 3; special projects, 2; coordination of agencies grouped by program field, 3; coordination of agencies on a neighborhood basis, 1. The four persons working in program fields and neighborhood councils carry most of the load of coordinating the work of the city's some 200 officially chartered public and private agencies, plus a possibly greater number of unofficial groups active in social welfare. There is, of course, no standard formula for allocation of personnel to the various subdivisions of a central planning body. Certainly, wide variation would be found among councils across the country. One wonders, however, why the number of professionals now serving the program fields is the same as twenty years ago—three —though population, number of agencies, and specialization in welfare services have all increased greatly in this period. One wonders, too, why the number working in neighborhood coordination of agencies has dropped from six or seven in 1950 to only one or two today. Whatever the reasons, from the agencies' point of view it is a fact that machinery for interagency cooperation is less adequate now than it was a decade or two ago.

The situation can be worsened, moreover, when the planning agency is under undue control, direct or indirect, of the fund-raising arm, the Chest. This can come about through organizational structure, for instance, when both council and Chest are under the same board of directors and top administration; or informally through financial dependence of the council on the Chest. It is here that the influence on social welfare of the power structure in American communities becomes most clear.

Power Structure and the Social Agency

Power is the *ability of one social unit* (group or person) *to influence the behavior of another social unit and thereby condition its access to social values* (objects that groups of men want as shown by their behavior toward them). Men in some positions exercise considerable power over men in other positions. To speak of a power structure is to locate these positions and their connections. A full understanding of the operations and policies of the social agency requires some knowledge of the power structure of both American society and the local community—for the agency takes account of men of power in ways worth study. The aim of this section is to speculate about these ways.

The Location of Power in the United States. In different societies and times, different classes and groups have been powerful. In tenth century France it was the nobility and clergy; in thirteenth century Venice, the great merchants. In early New England there was a type of theocracy. In the U.S.S.R. power has resided in the Communist party, perhaps sharing with industrial managers, military leaders, and key scientific groups.

Solutions to problems in one sphere (or role system) in a society tend to limit and control solutions in other less dominant spheres. Thus, if a society gives top priority to war and expansion beyond its boundaries, such priority will limit the way in which the problems of internal order and domestic economy will be handled (for example, the amount of freedom and the standard of living allowed); it will also increase the power of military leaders. If a society gives top priority to the production and distribution of material goods, this will limit the possible power of religious leaders; it will also increase the power of the industrial elite. (Cf. 252: p. 180.)

Power in America, as we suggested in Chapters IV and V, has been considerably diffused with the advance of industrialism. Comparing the 1880's with the 1950's, we can say that power has become amorphous, hard to locate, shifting. The heterogeneity of occupation and income, the upsurge of organized farmers and laborers, the multiplicity of voluntary associations pursuing special interests—these make the notion of a "ruling class" untenable. As David Riesman suggests (300: pp. 242–255), any one of the many power blocs converging on Washington can usually veto a measure which strikes at the core of its interests, so complex are the mutual stalemate and mutual backscratching arrangements.

But while power is more diffuse than it was in the Gilded Age, some groups still have more than others, and in a general way they can be located. Men of great power are mainly but not exclusively found in the economic, military, and political spheres. The men and problems of these spheres tend to take precedence over the men and problems of other spheres.

Men at the top in the economic sphere—investment bankers and corporation lawyers as well as business executives—make fateful decisions not only about the kinds and quality of goods available for consumption, about jobs and credit and who will get them, but also about the level and kinds of welfare expenditures and who will control them, a point we will discuss in detail below. To protect and expand their interests, the economic elite make liaison with other spheres; their power is felt in politics, religion, social welfare, as well as in industry and business. Their personnel is increasingly interchangeable with that of government; there is a heavy traffic between them.

A second major locus of power is the military. Mainly because of what we view as a permanent military threat and a consequent shift of elite attention from domestic to foreign affairs, plus the increased cost of up-to-date military technology, the generals, admirals, and administrators of the defense establishment have vastly increased their power, a fact demonstrated in their enlarged budgets and their control over men and material.[1] The effect on social welfare is obviously crucial, if indirect; the more spent for military purposes, the less available for social insurance, public aid, health and medical care and other welfare services.

In order to understand the control of welfare policy at the national level, developments within the political sphere (the third major locus of power) are especially important. It is a commonplace that the classical view of democracy—in which the people presumably discuss issues, arrive at definite and rational opinions, and elect representatives to carry out their will—does not even come close to the realities of modern government. That the "general public," by which we mean those who are not organized into active and politically relevant pressure groups, have little effect on government operations, in the welfare field as in others, is the widely accepted truth. The place of Congress, of the President and his Cabinet, of the higher civil service, and the pressures to which each is sensitive are discussed in a vast literature, in which few systematic empirical studies of welfare policy appear.[2] Who does make policy and who reshapes it, once made, however,

[1] Since 1941, the percentage of the entire government budget spent by and for the military has never gone below about 30 per cent. Since the Korean War, about two of every three federal budget dollars have gone for defense. "Even more significantly, national security expenditures in [the peacetime year of] 1954 amounted to nearly one sixth of total national income." (53: pp. 292, 894) When the President sent to Congress in January, 1957, his proposed budget for the fiscal year 1958, he called for military expenditures of more than $45 billion, or 63 per cent of the budget. Contrast the proposed total bill for domestic welfare measures including veterans' benefits, public assistance, health, education and housing; it came to less than $17 billion, or 24 per cent. (U.S. News and World Report, January 25, 1957, p. 149; New York Times, January 17, 1957, p. 13.) Excluding veterans' benefits, welfare expenditures would be less than 17 per cent of the entire federal budget. (Cf. 53: pp. 801–802, 892.)

[2] See, however, these case studies: Macmahon and others, The Administration of Federal Work Relief (221); Kesselman, The Social Politics of FEPC (179); and Meyerson and Banfield, Politics, Planning, and the Public Interest (239), a study of the Chicago Housing Authority in action. For excellent case studies of the legislative and administrative process on issues or in areas further removed from social welfare, see Selznick, TVA and the Grass Roots (322); Schattschneider, Politics, Pressures and the Tariff (313); and Bailey, Congress Makes a Law (13). Among the general treatments of these problems, see Key (180), and Gross (128).

are large questions with no easy answers. We can note here only two developments in both state and federal government that seem fairly clear. First, the number, variety, and influence of pressure groups—religious bodies, labor unions, manufacturers' associations, the organized professions—have grown, and there is hardly a welfare program enacted or a welfare agency administered without these special interests making themselves felt. Second, the influence of the higher civil servants, the administrator and the staff expert, has grown. Those public welfare executives and technicians who are program-minded, in collaboration with relevant pressure groups, clearly affect much welfare policy. They have the technical knowledge and experience which their political superiors (for example, cabinet officers) and legislative committees lack; they can use both executive and legislative channels to shape welfare programs. Such experts, grouped in formidable bureaucracies, also bridge the wide gulf between legislative "policy" and "execution"; they do not "make" policy, but they "crystallize" the policy when the policy is loose, sharpen the definition of the problem when its specificity is low, fill the vacuum when the boss is busy or time is short, use official policy pronouncements as a lever to strengthen and broaden welfare programs. (Cf. 410: pp. 194–195.) All this has long gone on in the field of health, where physicians, by virtue of strong internal organization, financial affluence, and technical indispensability, have shaped the course of government policy. Even the least powerful professions such as social work now have their "representatives" in Washington, and together with professionally trained and committed technicians and administrators, they can have a say. It is mainly within the political sphere that social work leaders must operate, if welfare policy is to show their mark.

It can plausibly be argued, with C. Wright Mills (246), that the political elite has lost ground in the fifty-year rise of the new coalition of business executives, political leaders, and military men. But to what extent the three spheres coordinate their efforts is still an open question. The three often represent an uneasy coalition, loose even in informal organization, vague or contradictory in policy, each internally divided, and sometimes breaking down. There is no doubt, however, that relative to the leaders of religion, or labor, or social welfare, the economic, the military, and the political elite is each overriding in power. There is also no doubt that all three have their ultimate effect on the size and character of welfare expenditures, and on the control and operation of the social agency. The impact of the military and political elites is obvious and is best seen on a national level in the enactment, financing, and administration of welfare programs. The effect of the business elite is less obvious and is best seen on a community level, and especially in the voluntary agencies.

The Social Agency Board in the Local Community. With the exception of some agencies under sectarian auspices, private agencies in the United States typically have a lay board in control. Such boards have evolved from the early years when a group of wealthy persons would constitute themselves the patrons of a charity. Their major function then, since welfare work was mainly confined to relief giving, was often little more than supplying funds out of their own pockets and those of their friends. With the growth of federated financing, the direct involvement of service-agency boards in fund-raising has declined; but indirectly, through their influence on the allocation of jointly raised funds, their importance in this area remains. In other areas the functions of the board have expanded. The board assumes legal responsibility and becomes the entity of incorporation. It represents the agency in community and interagency relationships and, most important from the viewpoint of everyday welfare practice, it has the power to set policy in all phases of agency operation, from rules governing client eligibility to pay scales for professional staff.

Decisions made by these boards vitally affect the lives of large segments of the community. Who then sits on them? Although democratic representation from all sectors of the community might be ideal for an agency board, it usually serves the financial and other needs of the agency better to obtain what is known in social work circles as a "power board," i.e., to take the American power structure into account. The results are seen in a recent study of the governing boards of 17 voluntary health associations in the Detroit metropolitan area, where labor is relatively articu-

late regarding democratic representation.[1] The boards averaged
22 members in size. Membership was distributed occupationally
as shown in Table 8.

TABLE 8. REPRESENTATION OF POWERFUL PEOPLE ON VOLUNTARY AGENCY BOARDS

	Per cent
Businessmen	21.0
Physicians	15.1
Industrialists	8.8
Wives of businessmen	8.6
Wives of industrialists	5.7
Attorneys	5.2
Educators	4.1
Labor representatives	3.9
Financiers	3.6
Employees of welfare agencies	3.4
Government officials	2.3
Clergy	1.8
Editors and journalists	1.8
Registered nurses	0.8
Others (mostly housewives)	13.8
Total	100.0

SOURCE: Engel, Robert L., *Representativeness of Governing Boards* (100).

The business interests and their wives, plus physicians and at-
torneys, total 68 per cent. The businessmen and industrialists
were noted as being "presidents, vice-presidents, treasurers, and
chairmen of the boards of the largest industries in Detroit." (100:
p. 19) The high percentage of physicians is accounted for by the
special health function of these agencies. Some 38 per cent of all
board members lived in a group of small, upper-class suburbs
which represent but a minute portion of the area's total population. About 70 per cent were in the top 20 per cent of income

[1] It is worthwhile listing, as an example of the growth and specialization of volun-
tary welfare work in America, and of the need for coordination, the fields of these
agencies working in the one area of health in Detroit: Cancer, Crippled Children,
Arthritis and Rheumatism, Cerebral Palsy, Infantile Paralysis, Tuberculosis, Heart,
Mental Health, Mentally Retarded Children, Muscular Dystrophy, Blindness,
Multiple Sclerosis, Planned Parenthood, Visiting Nurse, Epilepsy, Rehabilitation
Institute, League for the Handicapped. And this is not an exhaustive list of Detroit's
health agencies.

receivers. Nine of the 17 boards are self-perpetuating, new members being selected by action of the board itself.

This Detroit picture is probably typical of urban areas. A study of a sample of agencies in Springfield, Massachusetts, in 1951–1952 showed 85 per cent of board members to be managerial or professional in occupation, as compared to 20 per cent of the area's population fourteen years of age or older. (383: p. 7) A nationwide study of board membership conducted by Community Chests and Councils in the mid-1950's, using a sample of more than 2,000 agencies, counted 36 per cent employers and executives, and 31 per cent professionals other than social workers. (63: p. 6)[1]

Agencies, of course, vary in their ability to attract prominent members of the community. The smaller, younger, and otherwise less important agencies have correspondingly less powerful people on their boards. On the other hand, there is usually an even greater concentration of the business elite or their representatives on the boards of central fund-raising agencies; the nationwide study mentioned above found Chest, Fund, and Council boards to be composed 40 per cent of employers and business executives.

It is clear that top community power figures—from business, industry, finance, and the high-status professions of medicine and law—get channeled into commanding positions on social agency boards.[2] To note where power lies, however, does not say how

[1] In this same study similar information was gathered on a sample of 184 public-agency boards in charge of tuberculosis hospitals, public assistance, and public recreation programs, and the like. Occupational distribution of their members is not markedly different from that of the voluntary agencies: 24 per cent employers and executives as compared to 36 per cent, and 38 per cent professionals as compared to 31 per cent. The public boards thus have fewer members from the business community, more from the professions. The public boards also have a higher proportion of wage-earners (not labor representatives)—7 per cent as against 3 per cent.

[2] C. Wright Mills (246: p. 280) reminds us to "be careful of any simple and direct inference from origin and career to political career and policy. . . ." For: "(1) Men from high places may be ideological representatives of the poor and humble. (2) Men of humble origin, brightly self-made, may energetically serve the most vested and inherited interests. Moreover (3), not all men who effectively represent the interests of a stratum need in any way belong to it or personally benefit by policies that further its interests. Among the politicians, in short, there are sympathetic *agents* of given groups, conscious and unconscious, paid and unpaid. Finally (4), among the top decision-makers we find men who have been chosen for their positions because of their 'expert knowledge' " instead of family background and present connections.

often, or to what purpose, it will be used. We turn now to that question.

The Consequences of Power Structure for Welfare Policy: The Case of Business. For the sake of simplicity we will concentrate again on the implications of business power for the voluntary agencies, where most professionally trained social workers work. A guiding generalization can be stated at the outset: The business elite is by and large concerned with "big policy," not "lesser policy." By big policy we mean issues involving major welfare programs; that is, those programs which affect many people, or cost a great deal, or both. Big policy is best exemplified in the determination by central fund-raising bodies of the general level of welfare expenditures and their distribution. By lesser policy we mean decisions involving minor costs, affecting small populations, or both, as well as supervision of the technical conduct of social welfare affairs. In these matters, business leaders avoid involvement.[1]

Seventy-five years ago board members often took a direct and personal interest in agency operations and clientele.[2] In the early form of the Charity Organization Society members of the board would constitute the case-review committee, investigating what resources a family might have and deciding what relief might be obtained for it. Frequently they themselves undertook "friendly visiting" in the homes of the poor. As social work has grown more professional and agencies more specialized, and business interests have become more regional or national than local in scope, board members have largely withdrawn from participation in agency operations and do not exercise their policy-making powers in day-to-day operations.

Professional social workers, aware of the board's ultimate responsibility, often feel uneasy at this apparent abdication of

---

[1] We are talking here, it should be noted, not about the motivations of individual businessmen, but about the interests of the business community. Individual businessmen have been known to favor the closed shop; but Chambers of Commerce and the NAM back "right to work" laws.

[2] And in small cities and towns sometimes board members still do, to the distress of professional workers. Even in small places, it is only in older agencies with traditions reaching back into the 1800's that board members will insist on personal information or direct contacts with clients.

power by the board. Thus, the executive of a family service agency wrote in 1956:[1]

> I've been concerned and at the same time both amused and somewhat guilty about the fact that the Board of Directors makes policy decisions, both by authority of the by-laws and in the actual voting they do; yet actually in the present day family casework agency the staff has to "educate" the Board constantly and persistently and it certainly does choose the elements of education which lead toward the conclusions of which the staff approves. In other words, we tell them how to vote and they vote and we call that process "the Board sets the policies of the agency." . . .
>
> I can frankly cite very few instances when Board opinion has influenced my judgment about policy and practices during the [many] years I have been Executive of this agency, although the Board has made every important policy decision and has been "informed" ad nauseum before every decision. . . .
>
> Of course, the really valuable thing here is that if they are in disagreement with me, they have a right to say so and no doubt there come times in every agency's history where this happens. So in spite of all the above ridicule of our present system, I think the best thing to do is to continue the process.

This inside view of the agency is not caricatured. It is a typical picture of board behavior where small policy matters are at stake. Even in decisions of the middle range (medium cost affecting medium-sized populations)—for example, decisions to establish a children's clinic or well-baby center, movements to knock out traditional building-centered settlement houses in favor of roving neighborhood workers—welfare professionals are skilled in interpreting need, and powerful community leaders are used to making a routine financial contribution, taking care not to become too much involved.

But on "big policy" the economic interest of men of power may be controlling, whatever their humanitarian spirit, their sense of community responsibility, or reluctance to get caught on time-consuming welfare committees. Such problems as slum clearance, or unemployment compensation, or the total level of welfare expenditures are "big policy" and men of wealth and power are

[1] In a personal letter to the authors.

well aware that either through taxes or large voluntary contributions they will foot a big chunk of the bill. Here agency administrators no longer "tell them how to vote"; and professional welfare workers are less likely to determine policy.

Floyd Hunter, in one of the few systematic studies of power and community welfare in an urban area, illustrates the point about "big policy" and "lesser policy" with the case of Joe Cratchet. Cratchet was a professional social worker in a large southern city who ran a locally sponsored neighborhood club for underprivileged boys. He was an outspoken man and slum clearance was among his interests. Top leaders of the community, men of great power and wealth, were divided on the issue of housing reform, for which there was considerable public demand. They compromised one year by deciding to aid "a women's group which had as its platform 'paint up and clean up the undesirable neighborhoods.' " Cratchet "publicly attacked the 'clean-up-paint-up' campaign as being sponsored by the power interests to shunt off any vital approach to the housing problem." A furor followed, during which the Community Chest Board instructed the director to devise some way of getting rid of Cratchet. Cratchet stood his ground, and it was not until his agency budget was up before the Chest that the matter came to a head. After much debate and maneuver, during which Cratchet's personal life was investigated (without result) and his agency program won approval, he was dismissed. "Big policy" was involved and he had been too outspoken on the issue. (160: pp. 189–193)

A second case, Denny North, was executive secretary of a civic planning association in Regional City. Hunter observes:

> His job is dependent, to some extent, upon his convincing the top structure, through intermediaries, that he is "all right," because many of the projects in his office are concerned with civic improvement, and the top leaders are watchful that no reformer or agitator be long in the job. . . . Many of the conditions which need remedy are expensive propositions and are long held in abeyance by the men who could really make decisions to move toward solutions of the various problems. . . . If he organizes too well, and sells his program too effectively, he is in danger of becoming what is known as a

controversial figure in the community and of meeting the same fate as his predecessors who were considered reformers. (160: pp. 53–54)

The kind of welfare situation in which the business community feels impelled to take a controlling hand is well illustrated in these cases. They suggest, further, that there is built into social agency structure a considerable social and psychological distance between the makers and executors of fundamental welfare policy. The board member lives on The Hill, the welfare professional somewhere down the slope. The social circles of their lives rarely intersect—a gap in society lies between. Client needs and difficulties, around which the professional builds his life, are but leisure-time interests to his board of control; and the professional's plea for some new service for the "underdog" may lose its urgency when strained through a "bird-dog" philosophy.

In such a situation—with the pressures for conformity to "big policy" of "big men," the gap between policy and client needs, the social distance between board member and professional—the social worker may develop feelings of impotence. Again quoting Hunter:

> The professionals in Regional City, in their social gatherings, are rather likely to discuss their frustrations and dissatisfactions in terms of hopeless or resigned despair. Much of their discussion centers around disparaging remarks concerning the powers that be and the feeling that they have little opportunity to help in matters of community policy and decision, in which they feel they have definite contributions to make. (160: p. 56)

Probably most social workers, being less concerned with broad social reform and community planning, and less acutely aware of "the powers that be," would not speak so darkly. Social workers do not typically despair; few board members are entirely insensitive to welfare problems. Moreover, Regional City is in the Deep South, where Organized Labor and other welfare-minded groups are not yet strong enough to become an effective curb on business power. In the rest of the country one might expect to find business power used with more restraint. It is even possible that more skill in techniques of communication, in the tactics of social action, more use of the machinery of patient "reporting" and "clearance" might have lessened Cratchet's troubles with the Regional City elite.[1] Yet, like any extreme but true case, Regional City highlights what goes on less visibly, less dramatically, in everyday life and in all urban areas, and points to some consequences of the power structure for welfare policy—unstudied and unmet needs, underdeveloped welfare services, and frustrated welfare workers.

Another illustration of the issues which excite business attention, and hence board member concern, is federated fund-raising for voluntary social welfare. Because federated financing simplifies and rationalizes what is otherwise a chaotic struggle by a myriad of individual agencies competing for donations both from the businessman and from his employees (who must be solicited in his place of business), because by its very size it is "big policy," community business leaders usually give it active support and look sharp to its proper control. Central financing provides a channel for the expression of business interests in the spending of welfare funds. Nonearmarked funds raised for a group of agencies must afterward be divided among them; thus, allocation also becomes a function of the central body. And who gets what—which services will be expanded, which contracted, whether a new agency will be opened or an old one foreclosed—is decided by a budget committee on which businessmen sit.

Now, on many decisions the lay powers will follow the lead of welfare professionals, as in the case of agency boards described earlier. But where boards lead instead of follow—that is, generally on "big policy"—the fact that they are attuned more to matters of finance and business, and the fact of their social-class identifications, have subtle and far-reaching effects. Thus, one study suggests that centralization of fund-raising in the context of American power structure may introduce irrelevant standards for allocation, interfering with the rational and equitable deployment of welfare resources—rational, that is, by any criterion of

[1] In a community organization course in a school of social work, Cratchet's troubles would be used as a case study in "how not to do it." It would not be claimed, however, given the Regional City situation, that much could be done quickly even by skilled practitioners of welfare planning.

public interest. In a situation of limited resources, the social-economic level of an agency constituency (board and clientele) rather than the substantive content of its program becomes the standard for allocation. (205) For example, assuming equal need, a long-established and nationally known recreation agency with a "power board" and middle-class clientele using its swimming pool and handball courts stands a better chance of getting a budget increase than a little, local community center whose board president is the corner groceryman. Back of this, in part, lies the fact that the weak constituency cannot threaten, with the same force as a strong one, to do its own fund-raising. But whether fund-raising is done jointly or not, the business community tends to control it and, hence, fund allocation. This is achieved, often without intention, by the size of donations by leading business-men, plus their ability to get or discourage contributions from their friends, and their ability to devote their own or their staff time to the campaign.[1] (308)

With only rare exceptions (and then with irrational or inequi-table results), top business leaders concern themselves with big policy, not lesser policy. Two trends may be in the making, how-ever, which will change this picture. On the one hand, the busi-ness elite, in and beyond the community, in so far as they represent national, multi-plant corporations, tend to withdraw entirely from direct control of local voluntary welfare efforts, giving way to lesser local figures. This should work to reduce business interest in big policy at the community level, especially in the industrial suburbs and satellite cities. On the other hand, the business elite tend more and more to use voluntary welfare as a testing ground for rising business executives and as an avenue for public relations. This should work to maintain business con-trol over big policy and perhaps increase concern with small policy as well, especially in large central cities.

[1] The technique of federated fund-raising also depends to a considerable extent on the presence on the Chest board of the voice and will of the givers. As campaigns are commonly run in America, a goal is publicly announced and solicitation from the general public starts. Prior to this, however, a good portion of the goal, perhaps more than half, has already been pledged in "big gifts," and information on these is divulged piecemeal during the campaign to maintain public interest and morale.

The first point finds support in two studies: one by Schulze of changing power structure in "Cibola," a small satellite city of Detroit, and one by Mills and Ulmer of the relationship between "civic welfare" and the extent of big-business domination in small and medium-sized cities.

Schulze found that over the past 100 years there has occurred "*a marked withdrawal of the economic dominants from manifest participation in the socio-political life of Cibola.*" (317: p. 359) The "economic dominants," those who occupied the top occupational positions in the local economic system, had given way to "public leaders" —local merchants, educators, salesmen, public officials, clergymen, realtors—in the control of community life, including welfare policy. This withdrawal by the economic dominants extended to "big policy" matters such as change to a manager form of city government, and a fight over expansion of the city by annexation. Schulze argues that nonintervention by economic heavyweights is a general concomitant of urbanization, resulting from increasing dependence of economic units upon populations and organizations beyond the local area, and a consequent withdrawal of interest from local problems. This would hold, though in lesser degree, for men on the interlocking directorates of local banks and industry, to the extent their interests (for example, bank deposits and loans, business contracts) extend beyond the local community, as well as for those in control of the nationwide firms. (317: p. 357)

Mills and Ulmer also found that executives of large, absentee-owned corporations tend to avoid active, positive involvement in the welfare problems of the local community where the plant is located. This study compared three pairs of small cities, one city in each pair being "big-business," the other "small-business," as measured by number of employees per employing organization. Each pair of cities was matched as to geographic location, population size, and race and nativity of population. Mills and Ulmer attribute the following differences between the big-business and small-business cities to the size-of-business factor. In the *small-business city:* there is a larger middle class, composed of independent proprietors rather than corporation officials; specialization in production is less and there is less domination of the community payroll by one or a few industries; range and quality of retail services are greater; business leaders take a more active role in local civic affairs; middle-class women are more active in civic affairs; labor and business groups cooperate better. In general, participation in local civic affairs, and consequently "civic welfare," are higher in the small-business cities. The authors argue that this is because corporation officials who set the social tone of the big-business community are not themselves much interested in local civic enterprises but may, nevertheless, exercise a negative, "veto power" over civic action which threatens corporate interests, thus preventing anyone else from taking leadership. (250)

Three distinctions must be made, however, which suggest modifications of Schulze's and Mills and Ulmer's conclusions as applied to the general urban welfare scene. They are: (1) resident managers of local firms *versus* managers of absentee firms who work in plants in the local community and either live there temporarily or not at all; (2) satellite cities or industrial suburbs whose plants are controlled from afar *versus* central cities containing both the main plants and the central headquarters of gigantic corporations; and (3) fast-growing *versus* stable or declining communities.

Some of the economic dominants in satellite Cibola, for instance, are resident managers of multi-plant companies whose central offices are in Detroit. Some of these live outside and commute to Cibola. Commuters *or* residents, many expect to move on to other jobs in other communities. All are oriented toward Detroit headquarters, where their fate is determined. Meanwhile, the growing public-relations consciousness of large corporation executives militate against their "meddling" in the affairs of the local community, though friendly gestures of a noncontroversial kind are, of course, still approved. From the viewpoint of the absentee firm, the managers who live in or commute to Cibola cannot afford to get too involved with the local politics and social welfare of a small satellite city. From the managers' personal viewpoint, the same holds true, for they are temporary residents whose main commitments are in the company and its way of life, not the community and its way of life. But contrast the economic dominants who run local firms. Schulze found that while these men were less active in local affairs than the "public leaders," they were more active than the absentee-firm dominants. Moreover, there is little evidence that the top executives of the automobile companies in Detroit with plants in satellite Cibola are becoming less active in the financing and control of welfare activity in the central city. The withdrawal of local economic dominants from welfare policy in the satellite city, and of central-city dominants from central-city policy seems to be going on in lesser degree if it is going on at all.

Finally, concerning the effect of big-business participation or withdrawal on the development of "civic spirit," some of the differences between big-business and small-business cities may be due not to the factor of business size but to *rate of population growth*, a factor Mills and Ulmer did not control in their analysis. Two of the three big-business cities had explosive rates of population growth from 1890 to 1940 compared to the small-business cities with which they were paired (1500 and 1200 per cent growth as compared to 150 and 300 per cent). In the third pair of cities, where growth rate was low in each case, there was also the least difference in "civic welfare." What Mills and Ulmer attribute to big-business domination may be simply the lag in per capita welfare expenditures generally associated with swift population growth. (Cf. 272; 331: pp. 37–38.)[1] This objection, however, applies more to observations about how much welfare effort there is than it does to conclusions about who controls welfare policy and agency operation.

---

[1] Goldschmidt's study of three industrialized farming communities in Kern County, California (124), found civic participation to be inversely related to *size of landholding*, and accounts for the relationship on much the same grounds as do Mills and Ulmer. But note, again, it is the big-farm community which has had the greatest rate of recent population growth. Note, too, Angell's finding that his Integration Index for American cities (based on crime rates and welfare efforts) was correlated *positively* with the Mills-Ulmer index for degree of big-business domination. Angell comments: "This surprising result is probably a consequence of the greater frequency of small businesses in mobile and heterogeneous communities rather than of any direct causal influence of large business on integration. At any rate, it is clear that the scale of enterprise is not closely related to moral integration, as the congressional committee supposed." (10: p. 18)

We have previously noted the withdrawal of agency board members from active participation in the daily conduct of social agency affairs. We have in the Schulze and Mills-Ulmer studies, perhaps, evidence of a further stage in the same process. If so, welfare professionals may expect shifts in the composition of agency boards, especially of the powerful fund-raising agencies in the suburban or satellite city, in the direction of "wider community representation," a fundamental goal of social work philosophy. Whether this would simplify the job of working with board members is not clear.

The second trend—increasing use of welfare activity as training for future executives—would seem to slow down the withdrawal noted above. The overrepresentation on agency boards of businessmen is not due exclusively to their desire to control welfare functions. The agency's striving for powerful patrons and the sense of community responsibility of such persons are also factors in their board service. Equal willingness and ability to serve are probably less frequent in lower social ranks. However, a study by Ross of organized philanthropy in "Wellsville," a large city in eastern Canada where voluntary welfare organization is quite in the U.S. pattern, points to two motives for business participation which may be overriding. Although she finds that "philanthropy, most particularly the organization of financial campaigns, is a substantial activity of successful businessmen" (308: p. 274), she also finds that such activity is not a matter of *noblesse oblige* or spirit of community responsibility. It is instead a matter of: (1) facilitating business careers, and (2) maintaining good corporation public relations. In a story that casts a strange light on "voluntary" welfare organization, we are told by 70 businessmen respondents that businessmen have "philanthropic careers" as well as business careers. For each rung on the business ladder there is a rung on the philanthropic ladder, and a man has to show his mettle on the latter to qualify for advancement on the former. Before the development of organized fund-raising in Wellsville, church membership, activity in church work, and family background were the important adjuncts to business careers. Now it is more important to identify with philanthropy, both for individual advancement and for company publicity purposes. (308: p. 280) Such activity, moreover, is not seen as a matter of choice for the man who wants to get ahead or for the corporation fighting to stay in the public eye. It is part of the sober game of business, and one result is that the attitude of those who play it soon changes from enthusiasm to "one of apathy and weariness." (307: p. 485)

It seems likely that "the gradual monopolization of money-raising campaigns by the business world" over the past fifty years noted by Ross in Wellsville (308: p. 280) is a general development in urban-industrial America as well—though the withdrawal of big corporations from direct involvement in the affairs of satellite communities may be a variation on the theme. It is likely, further, that the changes this pattern of control has brought to Wellsville have occurred elsewhere, too: from giving by the pious and wealthy only, to giving by all sections of the community; from giving as a means of securing reward in heaven, to securing good public relations on earth; from church control of fund-raising to less-direct but still effective business control; from stress on people in need to stress on the efficiency of agencies; from leadership by amateurs to trained personnel working in professional organizations coupled with careerists from business; from reliance on a sense of individual responsibility to reliance on group pressure. (307: pp. 485–486) Like so many main tendencies of urban-industrial society, the shift in control of welfare agency and welfare policy has brought mixed blessings. Without more knowledge of this area, only the bold and hasty would tell us where the good and where the bad lie.

XI. The Emergence of a Social Work Profession

ANY CONSIDERATION of how the welfare services are organized must deal with the people who man the agencies. The professionalization of social work is therefore one of the more important developments in American social welfare. This is a reflection of the growth of the professions that accompanies industrialization everywhere, but in America the process has perhaps gone farther than in other countries and with greater repercussions.

Professionalization of any occupation involves several characteristic processes and effects. It means that efforts will be made by the professional group to control the type and standards of work done in its area of competence; that practitioner-client relationships will assume new forms; that decisions about the proper methods of supplying services and directions of future development of practice will tend to be delegated by the larger society to the organized professional associations and to the professional schools; that the profession will assume a certain status in the hierarchy of professions, influenced by and influencing popular stereotypes of the profession and economic returns to the practitioners; that certain ethical obligations will be self-imposed by the practitioner group; that jurisdictional disputes over areas of competence with related professions will arise.

Many of these characteristics of professionalization are evident in American social work. Since they have not been intensively studied, the picture presented here must be regarded as partial and suggestive only.[1]

---

[1] The following analysis of professionalism is indebted to the work of Professors E. C. Hughes of the University of Chicago and R. K. Merton and W. J. Goode of Columbia University. Cf. Caplow, *The Sociology of Work* (50).

What Is a Profession?

What is the difference between an autoworker and a physician, or an electrician and a lawyer, that makes us speak of one as a professional and deny the label to the other? Both in the minds of the lay public and professional groups themselves the criteria of distinction seem to be two: (1) The job of the professional is *technical*. (2) The professional man adheres to a set of *professional norms*. The degree to which an occupation fits these criteria is the degree of its professionalization.

A profession claims *exclusive* possession of competence in a specified area. This competence is "technical" because it comes from a systematic body of skill and knowledge acquired only through long, prescribed training. The profession represents a monopoly of skill, which is linked to standards of training and which justifies a monopoly of activity in an area. It is felt that not just anyone can do the job, so the job territory is marked "off limits" to the amateur, often by law.

The basis of the claim to technical competence varies—with each profession emphasizing the distinctive features of its own background. Medicine, since its "reform" in the United States some fifty years ago, has emphasized its roots in a scientific body of knowledge along with high, rigorously defined and enforced standards of training designed to impart that body of knowledge. Contrast the ministry. It, too, stresses rigorous standards of training. But clearly it does not claim possession of a science-based body of knowledge (though its doctrines are well-codified and systematized). It is medicine and not the ministry that has become the preferred model for social work, and a close relationship has developed between them. One result of this has been the recent increase in social work efforts to undertake the research needed to establish a unified scientific base—exemplified in programs of research developing at several schools of social work. Just as there is no mistaking the sphere of competence of a physician, no confusion about how one becomes an M.D. or who has a right to the title, social work has hoped through science-based effort to achieve similar status, to enable it to render service and achieve rewards befitting its spirit and its professions.

The criterion of "technical" is not enough, however. The barber goes to a trade school, has an apprenticeship, and forms an occupational association to uphold standards, regulate entry to the trade, and get legal sanction for his practice. But the success of the claim to professional status is governed also by the degree to which the practitioners adhere to a set of moral norms that characterize the established professions. These norms dictate not only that the practitioner render *technically competent*, high quality service; but that he be *impersonal, objective* (the professional avoids emotional involvement), *impartial* (he does not discriminate, he gives equal service regardless of personal sentiment), and be motivated by a *service ideal* (devotion to the client's interests more than profit should guide decisions when the two are in conflict). These norms function to govern conduct among members of a profession and between them and their clients. Professional codes of ethics help to maintain such norms.

The degree of professionalization, then, is measured not just by the degree of success in the claim to exclusive technical competence, but also by the degree of adherence to professional norms of conduct. We will consider these norms further when we discuss client-professional relations.

Why Does Professionalism Increase?

The "demand" for a profession of social work, as for other professions, has arisen in the context of, and as a result of, several trends discussed in Part I. Specialization itself, a prerequisite to professionalism, is the result of the underlying industrialization process. Rising productivity and income not only permit but *force* the eventual withdrawal of population from farming and manufacturing. These people are channeled into the tertiary service "industries"—service professions and occupations of all kinds, from physicians and social workers to beauticians and television repair service men. Specialization in the service industries, of which social work is one, is bound to increase with industrialization's advance.

The growth in scale and complexity of social organizations—business corporations, labor unions, professional groups, social agencies, units of government—is likewise a factor, because it creates a demand for liaison and contact men of all kinds. We need guides, so to speak, through a new kind of civilized jungle. Social work is an example par excellence of the liaison function, a large part of its total activity being devoted to putting people in touch with the community resources they need but can hardly name, let alone locate.

Also involved in the shift toward professionalization is the prestige of science. Every practice modeling itself on medical lines wishes to shine with the light of science, real or simulated. Quite early the devotees of the human adjustment arts began to yearn toward a goal of "social engineering." The empirical, critical, rational spirit of science has found its way into nearly every type of activity in America. And it has become particularly important to social work because the neighboring, established professions, especially medicine, to which social work looks for its model of professionalism, stress scientific knowledge as the basis for professional practice.

Finally, in any complex society with strong traditions of freedom, there is a general tendency to preserve the autonomy and privacy of the different spheres of life—familial, religious, professional, political, cultural, military, and the like—and for each to respect as well as influence the others, while running itself by its own standards. This is essential to the maintenance of the freedom and efficiency of each. (Cf. 327.) Professionalism, involving as it does the use of esoteric skills and knowledge, is conducive to such autonomy. This autonomy, combined with professional prestige, makes it easier for the occupational group to resist the interference of lay opinions and pressures. Professionalism thus extends, in a measure, the power of an occupational group, both over its own members and the client public.

Aside from these organizational pressures toward professionalism, there is a big push from the workers themselves. What is happening to real estate dealers (realtors), junk dealers (salvage consultants), and laboratory technicians (medical technologists) is not professionalization in any exact sense. But it is true that hundreds of occupations aspire to a prestigeful label and use the established professions as their model—both for their label and ultimately for the organization of their work.

At least three rewards of professional life provide impetus for this trend. First, the professions have high status. Research consistently reveals that Americans place the professions at the top of the occupational prestige scale. Second, the professions have high income. Although starting incomes for many professions are low, and average annual incomes for some remain below many craft and business occupations, lifetime earnings and lifetime security for the professions are very high indeed. (312: p. 99) Third, job simplification and standardization for one portion of the labor force (see Chapters III and IV) reduce intrinsic job satisfaction; the job becomes a necessary evil. The drive toward professionalization, through stress on the moral and ethical aspects of work, through celebration of the service ideal and creation of a sense of internal community, may be seen as a way to give new meaning to the job.

Social Work: The Area of Competence

In the long run, the social workers' move toward professionalism—the establishment of formal training programs, the learning and celebration of professional norms—will not be fully successful without the delimitation of a clear area in which social work, and no other occupation, has technical competence.[1] Social work has made strenuous efforts in this direction, but has been faced with difficulties deriving from its traditions and its field of activity.

Historically social work consisted of a tradition of concern for the welfare of people, especially the disadvantaged. But no group can claim monopoly of humanitarian philosophy, or create a profession out of it. To the extent that people believe that every citizen has the duty to improve the common life, social work (as

[1] Nor will licensing, currently pursued by social workers, "make" the profession. Egg-graders have been licensed for some time in Indiana, well-diggers in Maryland, horseshoers in Illinois, plumbers in many places, and so on.

social reform) looks like everybody's business. As psychologist Charles Dollard puts it, "social work has had to fight a constant rearguard action against the pervasive notion that any man with love in his heart can do the job." (92: p. 233)

The crucial move toward delimiting an occupational area appeared when the Charity Organization movement provided a system wherein a Visitor came frequently and systematically in contact with "cases"—the heads of poverty-stricken families primarily—with special attention given to what were seen as the individual or family causes of difficulty and as individual resources to meet the problem. Thus, a setting and vehicle were provided for the observation of human behavior and for the practice of skills in helping people out of trouble. Casework, as Helen Witmer observes, was "born in the dilemma of poor relief," that is, as a method to break the long series of failures in dealing with poverty. (418: p. 127)

Casework, of course, is only one of the specialties in social work; but it is so dominant that it is doubtful that there would be any such identifiable entity as professional social work without it. Emphasis on casework evolution can index the evolution of the whole profession.

In its early days casework carried a strong "sociological" emphasis: an interest in the social-economic environment—conditions of factory labor, housing, income maintenance. Quite early, however, casework became centered on the individual, on his personal strengths and weaknesses, on individual psychological mechanisms, and on broad social forces only as these were interpretable in individual behavior terms. Mary Richmond is reputed to have said, "I have spent twenty-five years of my life in an attempt to get social casework accepted as a valid process in social work. Now I shall spend the rest of my life trying to demonstrate to social caseworkers that there is more to social work than social casework." (41: pp. 186–187)

Reinforcement of this trend came from the rapid adoption by casework, particularly after 1920, of large parts of psychoanalytic theory, which was introduced into America in the second decade of the century. Casework was already so individually focused that it seems likely it would have developed in this direction anyway. Psychoanalysis, however, with its relatively coherent theory of personality, provided a rationale for "diagnosis and treatment" that had hitherto been lacking.

Thus, an area of competence began slowly to be carved out. Social work knowledge at first consisted largely of sophistication in the use of community resources and the insight of "wisdom" into human motivation and behavior. Social work skills even today consist in large part of an extension and refinement of information on how to interview, how to obtain facts about the client's background, how to identify and distinguish surface from underlying problems, what community resources exist, and how to refer. Such practice is pragmatic, based on rule-of-thumb experience rather than on theory.

In recent decades, however, a theoretical base for practice has been built up, largely by borrowing from psychoanalytic theory, but also by creative conversion of such theory to social work usages, and by borrowing from other dynamic psychologies and, to a lesser extent, from academic social psychology, sociology, and cultural anthropology. Curricula in graduate schools of social work today commonly have as a central requirement courses in "human growth and development" designed to present an integrated theory of human personality.[1] Many of the major concepts (defense mechanism, transference, counter-transference, ego strengths, sublimation, libidinal attachment, psychosexuality, instinctual drives, the Oedipus complex, and so on) are Freudian, but, as noted, usages from other areas are increasing.

Against this knowledge background, then, casework takes form as a type of counseling process which emphasizes helping an individual to identify, clarify, and understand his own difficulties to the point where he can free himself from them, or accept help. The resemblance to psychotherapy is close. Casework operates on the premise that any individual facing social stresses which he

---

[1] This designation and emphasis derives in part from the publication in 1952 by the American Association of Schools of Social Work of a curriculum policy statement which marked out "Human Growth and Behavior" as one of the three major areas of social work education. The other two are "The Social Services" and "Social Work Practice."

cannot deal with has strengths and inner resources which, if freed from the shackles of fear, inhibition, and other types of psychological blockage, will enable him to become effectively self-responsible (excepting, of course, psychotics, babies, and the like). A man out of work, for example, will not usually be supplied with a job, but will be helped to understand why he will not seek, or cannot hold, one—or why one is not available to him on his terms. Casework's motto is "help people to help themselves." To this end training stresses knowledge and insight into psychological processes, both of the client and worker. Exhortation and coercion are avoided.

Caseworkers hold that social welfare programs cannot be built except on a sound comprehension of these aspects of human behavior. Although the importance of economic and other environmental factors in creating and conditioning individual problems is recognized, and "environmental manipulation" (for example, referring a jobless man to an employment service using community resources) is considered a proper part of treatment technique, this aspect is not stressed.

We have been speaking here of casework. But it is worth noting that in recent decades even group work has absorbed into its knowledge base a good deal of the same dynamic psychology with which casework is imbued.[1] Social group work, as compared to other types of group leadership, is personality-focused rather than activity-focused. Its object is to use group processes and structure —leadership opportunities, social pressure, and the like—to improve or develop the individual's personality and help him learn to live successfully with others. Acquisition of skills, activities for their own sake, competition are usually subordinated and controlled to the ends mentioned above.

In some quarters even community organization for social work (social welfare planning), which would seem to have its natural basis in sociological rather than psychological perspectives, is construed in interpersonality terms. An alternate concept of

[1] See, for instance, the article on "Social Group Work" in the 1954 *Social Work Year Book* (336) or Gertrude Wilson's and Gladys Ryland's *Social Group Work Practice* (413). Quite recently, and not to any extent in print, this emphasis has been challenged in favor of a "group dynamics" theoretical background. (Cf. 412.)

community organization currently in vogue focuses on the *process* of working with groups in the community rather than on the substantive problem of identifying areas of social need and organizing to deal with them. This approach uses the term "intergroup work" rather than community organization but here, too, psychological perspectives are dominant.

Social Welfare Occupations: The Extent of Professionalization

We have been speaking informally of "social work professionalization." The fact is, there are a number of social welfare occupations, diverse not only in skill and job content, but also in degree of identification with and preparation for social work as professionally conceived. Some groups are actively engaged in pressing for professional status; some are passive toward the idea of inclusion in the profession; while still others may be consciously opposed. Before discussing some of the implications of professionalization for practice, it will be useful to present the existing pattern, using formal social work education as the best available measure of professionalism.

Extensive data on the social welfare occupations and on the social characteristics and working conditions of welfare workers are contained in *Social Workers in 1950*, a report prepared by the Bureau of Labor Statistics of the U.S. Department of Labor and published by the American Association of Social Workers.

Table 9 shows the estimated distribution of welfare workers by "program" or field of service, and the degree of professionalization of each as measured by the percentage of workers in the program who have completed two or more years of training in a graduate school of social work. Of the estimated total of 74,240 persons in the United States in social work positions, as defined for purposes of this study in 1950, only 16 per cent had completed the full two-year graduate curriculum. An additional 11 per cent had one to two years, 13 per cent something less than a year; 60 per cent had no study at all in a graduate social work school. Comprehensive data of this sort have not been gathered since 1950. However, there is reason to believe that the picture presented here has not changed appreciably (see section on "Recruitment," page 309).

Public assistance workers, by far the largest group (41 per cent of the total), are in the main without professional school training. However, public assistance is considered by people both inside

TABLE 9. DISTRIBUTION OF U.S. SOCIAL WORKERS ACCORDING TO PROGRAM AND PROFESSIONAL EDUCATION FOR 1950

Program	Number of workers	Per cent	Per cent in each program with 2 or more years in graduate social work school
Public assistance	30,110	41	4
Work with physically handicapped	1,756	2	8
Work with adult offenders	2,298	3	8
Work with aged in institutions	652	1	6
Group work (including recreation and informal education)	8,764	12	11
Other services to individuals	3,999	5	19
Community organization	2,675	4	22
Child welfare work:			
Noninstitutional (except court)	6,645	9	29
Institutional	2,599	4	23
Court services	1,943	3	11
School social work	1,210	2	17
Other family services	4,749	6	42
Psychiatric social work:			
In clinics	1,071	1	83
In hospitals	1,182	2	48
Medical social work	2,804	4	49
Teaching social work	518	1	74
Not reported	1,265	2	..
Total for all programs	74,240	100	16

SOURCE: U.S. Department of Labor, Bureau of Labor Statistics, *Social Workers in 1950* (375: Table D-3, p. 39, and Table D-14, p. 48). Percentages do not add to 100 because of rounding.

and outside the field, and by the public at large, a social work operation. Public aid agencies, in cooperation with state and federal authorities, have constantly tried to raise the standards of social work training among their employees, and have supported fairly extensive stipend and work-training programs toward this end. Also, where trained supervision is available, professional schools of social work frequently use public assistance agencies for student field work placement.

Obstacles to further professionalization of this program exist, however. First, public aid is largely locally administered, and changes are therefore difficult to effect, however strong the desire of many state and federal administrators for higher standards. The local welfare worker's job is still viewed as one of eligibility determination by "relief investigators." Second, public welfare personnel are among the lowest paid professional and semi-professional public employees. A recent study in the state of Florida, comparing salaries of Department of Welfare personnel with those of other departments in the state government shows

TABLE 10. DISTRIBUTION OF PUBLIC WELFARE EMPLOYEES AND OTHER PUBLIC EMPLOYEES IN FLORIDA ACCORDING TO SALARY FOR 1954

Monthly salary	Department of Public Welfare	34 other state departments
(In dollars)	*Per cent*	
Under 300	*87.6*	*46.7*
300 to 450	*11.6*	*39.8*
450 to 600	*0.7*	*8.7*
600 to 700	*0.1*	*2.3*
700 and over	*0.0*	*2.5*
Total	*100.0*	*100.0*

SOURCE: Florida Department of Public Welfare, *1955–1957 Legislative Program* (106: p. 11)

this clearly. Figures in Table 10 show percentage of personnel in each salary class, as of September, 1954. Since the bulk of those who earn less than $300 per month in the Welfare Department are "visitors," who must in most cases possess a college education and provide themselves with a car, more than training or ability is reflected in these figures.

Thus, both incentive and resources for expensive professional training are lacking. Finally, the size of the group needed in this program has rendered substantial professionalization unlikely, since in 1950 there were only about 20,000 employed social workers in the whole country with one or more years of professional education in an accredited school of social work. (375: based on Table 2, p. 6, and Table 5, p. 9) In this field, therefore, professionalization as measured by present social work standards can occur only slowly.

The nature of the clientele of public assistance programs, especially Aid to Dependent Children, has changed in recent years. In many cases the ADC families need not only financial aid—a matter of bookkeeping and eligibility checking—but skilled, rehabilitative casework service. This challenge to provide more skilled service has received increasing attention. The Bureau of Public Assistance in the Department of Health, Education, and Welfare has sponsored several regional conferences, aimed at awakening the states to the need for casework service in the ADC program. In 1956, for the first time, federal grants were authorized for the training of public assistance workers, and for research in the rehabilitation of public assistance recipients (though a bill to appropriate funds under the authorization was later defeated). Several states (for example, Michigan) have begun to place training supervisors in local public aid bureaus and have approached professional social work schools with plans for the casework training of public assistance workers.

There is evident in all this a recognition of the complex tasks comprising the public assistance function and an attempt to identify and segregate those aspects which justify professional skills. Studies are presently under way to see which of the tasks in public assistance are sufficiently routine to be allocated to semiprofessional positions—much in the way that scarce physicians have yielded small slices of their job to new technical and semiprofessional personnel (x-ray and laboratory technicians, and the like). Three outcomes of job evaluation are possible: provision of expanded professional service to supplement a streamlined eligibility determination operation; maintenance of only the limited amount of casework (including skilled referral) that has been present in the combined job in the past—as ever larger portions of the total operation are taken over by personnel with little professional consciousness; or complete elimination of the casework aspect of public assistance.

Work with the physically handicapped is an uncertain area with regard to social work identification (only 8 per cent of its workers have full training). Although many private agencies (for instance, League for the Handicapped) are clearly in the social work tradition and strive to raise their professional standards, the major rehabilitation program in this country, run by the states with federal financial participation, is typically administered by state departments of public instruction or similar bodies having an educational orientation. In consequence, the training emphasis in many states has underplayed social work. In some states there is even a definite antagonism to social work in this program. Whether in the future more social workers will be employed in it depends on general developments in rehabilitation work (the 1954 federal legislation expanding the program promises a heavier social work investment), and on the availability of trained personnel, especially medical social workers. Part of the responsibility for the situation may rest with schools of social work themselves, for social work education, except with regard to medical social work, has not given much attention to training for this field. That the rehabilitation counselor's job is not a casework specialty seems to have been accepted. Whether it is essentially therapy, or education, or something else, is not clear.

Work with adult offenders, mainly in probation and parole programs, has not been social work oriented. Until very recently, professional schools of social work have evinced only minor interest in the field, and there is considerable question whether the caseworker as presently equipped could operate effectively in an atmosphere of high authoritativeness and "toughness." Moreover, most adult offenders are male, while most caseworkers are female, which might make a poor fit for this type of work. The federal probation system employs some trained social workers, and recently a few local and state probation and parole offices have been seeking trained casework supervision for their workers, and investigating opportunities for training the staff itself. One has the impression that this is a field that will move toward social work identification, but, as the 8 per cent figure on social work education shows (Table 9), it is likely to be a slow process. The chance for speed depends on the ability of social work education to be flexible in meeting the peculiar needs of this field, and on the salary and other incentives offered.

Child welfare work presents a varied picture of professionalization. Court services comprise mainly probation officers in juvenile courts (some of whom will be working with dependent rather than delinquent children). In many places court social workers are still political appointees; even where under civil service, they may be required to have only a college degree and "good character." Recently there has been an increasing degree of awareness among public hiring authorities that casework skills are needed for this sort of work, and some tentative exploration of methods for providing the training has occurred. Professional consciousness in this area remains on the whole low—with consequences we will discuss below in the Role Conflict section.

School social work, more commonly known as Visiting Teaching, straddles two disciplines. In some jurisdictions social work training is required for employment, in others the stress is on training in the field of education combined with some lesser preparation in casework. The professional organization of these workers, the School Social Work Section of the National Association of Social Workers, is fully identified with social work. However, the high educational requirements of the NASW which went into effect in October, 1955, will henceforth prevent all but those who complete graduate social work training from joining the professional association.

Community organization workers (22 per cent professionally trained) are employed mainly in Chests and Councils of Social Agencies, with some additions from state and national planning, coordination, and social action agencies. Such agencies are on the whole closely tied to social work, and have played a key part in promoting professionalization. Social work training for community organization work, however, is not widely offered, and the literature in the field is scanty, compared to the flood of books in casework. Because of the limited number of community organization positions relative to other jobs in social work, the flow of students has been too small to support a community organization major except in the larger schools. The need for skills not characteristic of social work—public relations, research, accounting— also helps to account for a rather low degree of social work training in this group, which by other standards is professionally conscious.

Group work, including recreation and informal education, is again a divided field with respect to social work allegiance. Many of the employing agencies in this type of work (YMCA and YWCA, Girl Scouts and Boy Scouts, settlement and community houses) are large and venerable and in the absence of a crystallized, established occupational specialization for the kind of work they do they have tended to cultivate their own specialties. The YMCA has for years looked to George Williams College and Springfield College as its major sources of trained personnel, and "YMCA work" is widely recognized as a separate occupational category if not profession. The Boy Scouts, though perhaps not so training-conscious, similarly maintains a training center for careers in "Scouting." The YWCA and the Girl Scouts, on the other hand, have tended to look to the accredited schools of social work for their paid staff members, although the limited supply of personnel from this source has made it necessary to recruit staff from a variety of sources. Jewish community center work has also been social work identified, and the settlements have been moving in that direction, though more slowly. Rural programs (4-H, Future Farmers of America) have little social work orientation.

Some programs that classify themselves as "character-building" are somewhat antagonistic to social work. Part of the difficulty here has been the inability of practitioners in the recreation and leisure-time activities field to understand the objectives of group work, and to grasp the ways in which it differs from what they customarily do. Finally, recreation workers are often trained in Schools of Education, adding an element of divided allegiance to an already complex situation.

Family services other than public assistance show a high degree of professionalization. These services include employees of the high-standard member agencies of the Family Service Association of America. There are some family agencies under religious auspices, as well as those under court auspices, which have lower standards, at least as far as social work is concerned. On the whole, however, family service is highly identified with social work and is well on its way to complete professionalization.

Medical social work is a solidly social work occupation, with high professional standards. Inability to obtain adequately trained people, rather than lack of desire, is the main obstacle to more complete professionalization.

A high degree of professionalization is evident in the psychiatric field, especially among social workers in mental health clinics (83 per cent have had two or more years of graduate social work). Many of the large state hospitals, particularly in more rural areas, still employ "psychiatric social workers" with little or no training. Clinics, however—both child and adult— exist mainly in urban centers and have from the first maintained high standards for all professional employees. Moreover, because of their high prestige and relatively favorable pay scales, they have consistently been able to attract trained people when other agencies, aiming at equally high standards, have gone begging for help in an undermanned field. Although psychiatric social workers are very highly identified with social work, it is among members of this group that we find most strongly the "psychotherapy" conception of casework, and a tendency to extend the social work role in the direction of medical, and more particularly psychiatric, practice, in order to achieve the rewards of professional status that psychiatrists have. There is a difference of opinion among social workers as to whether persons entering "private practice" are still in the field. To some it seems that the few who go it alone adopt a professional stance at the cost of abandoning social work.

The above analysis, though it gives only a rough picture of the peaks and valleys of social work professionalism, provides the background for discussion of some universal aspects of professionalization and its consequences for welfare services.

The Development of a "Professional Self": Client-Worker-Colleague Relations

Schools of social work, like all professional schools, try to transmit more than technical skills and knowledge. A prime concern in training for professional work is the creation of a "professional self." While there is variation between professions in the nature of such a self, it tends to be oriented toward a similar set of norms—standards and guides to proper or expected conduct in the professional role. Four ideas about the ideal professional-client relationship are especially well developed in the healing and helping occupations. They center around the words impersonal, objective, impartial, and selfless. They stem from the basic fact that the job is both technical and humanitarian. As sociologist Talcott Parsons suggests, these four norms are especially strong in the medical profession, the current model for many less established professions, including social work. (282: pp. 433–439, 454 ff.; 280: chap. 8)

The Impersonal Relationship: Functionally Specific. As we saw in Part I, work relations in modern society tend to be "functionally specific"—the rights and obligations covered by the relationship are clearly defined and delimited. The human relations professions emphasize this sharply.

Many of the problems both the physician and the social worker must face require extensive exploration of the client's personal life. The physician must have access to all parts of the body of the patient; the caseworker to many aspects of the emotional and financial condition of the client. How can a stranger be permitted such intimacy and such knowledge? Given the intimacy, how can the professional restrain himself from involvement with the client in areas where he has no competence and how can the client be prevented from making demands in such areas?

The profession deals with such problems by accenting the technical aspects of the situation, and limiting the relationship to the task at hand. If personal information is sought, it is information relevant to the performance of the technical task; if rapport must be established, it is rapport for a purpose. The situation is defined in diagnostic and treatment terms, not in terms of personal interest in the client. Think of the physician's rectal or vaginal examination. The intimate contact is defined as nonintimate.

Social work practice illustrates this in many ways. Inquiry into the client's life is defined as legitimate, not as snooping. The worker typically does not "make friends" with the client. He does not reveal his personal life, entertain the client socially in his home, or visit with the client on a social basis. As far as possible, the social worker insists that service be given in the office rather than in the home, because the latter threatens a more extensive personal involvement than is good for professional relationship. The client is kept to a strict appointment schedule, symbolizing formality of relationship and measuring restriction of contact.

Emotional Neutrality. Related to the injunction to keep the relationship within bounds is the norm which says, "Be *objective*—be aware of and control emotional involvement with the client." The person who brings his problems to a social worker or other professional is in trouble. His emotions will be aroused by this, and intensified by internal resentment at having to expose his weakness to an outsider. This situation confronts the professional "helper" with something of a dilemma. If he becomes emotionally involved himself he loses objectivity, his ability to see facts in clear perspective, and his power to help; but at the same time a sufficiently close relationship must be established to convince the client of the worker's identification with his problem and of willingness to understand and help. There must be involvement and no involvement at the same time.

All human relations blend social nearness and distance; and the dilemma of involvement and detachment is not new to our time.[1] But never before has it been built into a society so formally and explicitly for so many roles—roles segregated and labeled "job." For social work (as well as for psychotherapy) the term "objectivity" (or emotional neutrality) takes its place beside "rapport" as a characterization of the client-professional relationship. Together they comprise in Mannheim's words a "strange combination of intimacy and objectivity, nearness and distance, attraction and repulsion, friendship and estrangement"

[1] The problem is dealt with in many different ways. In Roman Catholicism, for instance, the priest maintains social distance from the confessor by interposition of a physical barrier. The Zuni have created the role of "ceremonial father," sponsor and guide to the male child in initiation rites—a relationship marked by intimacy in limited, prescribed areas only, distance in others. The ceremonial father is not a blood relative but is supposed to act like one upon occasion.

(225: pp. 324–325), a combination which the professional in training (especially one who works in an intimate field like social work) finds difficult to comprehend and incorporate into his habit patterns. When it is grasped and "learned in the muscles," then the novitiate has developed the essence of the "professional self."

Impartiality and the Ideal of Service. Formality and objectivity serve to protect the professional and keep otherwise intimate relations within bounds (thus indirectly making possible technical service to meet the client's need). But two further norms which directly protect the client arise out of them and strengthen them: "Don't discriminate among clients on a personal basis," the norm of impartiality; and "Keep personal and commercial interests subordinated to the client's needs," the norm of altruistic service.

To the client the professional helper is a stranger and vice versa. In the eyes of the other, each may have undesirable personal or social characteristics. If the practitioner were free to give or withhold his services, to serve poorly or well, on the basis of personal characteristics, then there could be no confidence and no ground for establishing professional helping relationships. Moreover, if likes and dislikes were to be made the basis for service, then the client would tend to develop attitudes and behavior to win the practitioner's favor. Often this would involve the attempt (not necessarily conscious) to develop personal relationships, and client-practitioner contact would be made on grounds irrelevant to service. Thus, all professions come to observe the norm of impartiality—the best possible service regardless of race, religion, politics, or personal traits of the client. Social work not only incorporates this norm into its professional practice, but makes it an important part of its whole philosophy. It becomes part of the professional self.

The fourth major norm governing client-professional relationship is *service*. All professional associations and all groups aspiring to professional status espouse the ideal of service. This is more than lip service. It *has* to be a working ideal because the client is peculiarly vulnerable: he is in trouble and ignorant of how to help himself out of it. (282: p. 445) If the client believed that the practitioner was interested simply in making money, ready to use his confidences and to exploit him for personal gain, then he would not be willing to enter a professional-client relationship. He would demand a guarantee of specific results in a specific time. This is the way to get houses built and milk delivered. Problems dealt with by professionals cannot be handled this way. No physician or lawyer or social worker can guarantee results, even though he must be paid. In exchange for this latitude the professional submits himself to the service norm which guarantees to the client not results, but devotion to his interests and his cause.

Because of the client's belief in the professional's service ideal he does not typically attempt to bind him to a contract; he has confidence in and gives his confidences to the worker. Such trust is especially necessary in the helping professions where intimate matters are involved. Among some of the established professions, like law, medicine, and the ministry, this confidence even becomes legally sanctioned in the form of privileged communication. In social work, client-worker confidences do not as yet have this legal status, a fact which has occasioned difficulty for both client and worker in some types of social work practice.

All of these norms help to guide the professional in his relationship with the client. They define the situation for both client and practitioner; they protect both. Social work as a fledgling profession, along with all the other occupations in process of professionalization, absorbs them from the existing culture of professionalism or discovers them afresh out of the necessities of its own practice.

The emergence of the professional-client relationship in the "intimate" fields reflects in interpersonal relations what has been happening in the larger society. The demand that the large and impersonal bureaucracies of industry and government, education and justice be "humanized" is part of a general tendency of advanced industrialization in a free society. What we have here is an attempt to combine the intimacy of the social relations of the small, nonindustrial community with the impersonal, segmental, contractual relationships necessary to a large area of urban-industrial life. The human relations professions function to smooth the workings of the bureaucratic welfare state with a formalized personal touch.

Norms Governing Colleague Relations. Professions and professionals derive their self-images not only from relations with clients but from relations among fellow-workers. Day-by-day, hour-by-hour, the professional self developed in Graduate School is affirmed and sustained or changed by colleagues at work—in the labels they apply to one another, the technical information they pool, the experiences they share that the practicing professional and no one else has. (Cf. 21.) It is the colleague group, ideally a society of equals, that celebrates and enforces the norms governing client-professional relations. The colleague group also develops a second set of norms that cue the newcomer to the "right" ways to relate to other professionals.

Colleague relations form around two poles: competition within the group; unity toward out-groups. Group members compete among themselves for jobs and status; but they also unite against outsiders who threaten the privileges and rewards of the group. The major norms that shape colleague relations are centered in these two areas. They concern recognition of formal qualifications and maintenance of professional standards of work; the airing of problems and complaints; the utilization of specialties within the profession; and the interpretation of colleague behavior in professional terms. It may be that the unique history, tasks, and functions of each profession lead to distinctive norms for each, but our emphasis here will be on the norms that seem general to all service professions located in bureaucratic structures. Needless to say, the research to establish the existence of these norms, the proportion of practitioners who adhere to each and the intensity of their adherence has yet to be done.

The first norm governing colleague relations may be stated in this form: *Do what you can to maintain professional authority and professional standards of work.* All professionals honor the technical competence of the formally qualified. An MD, RN, or MSW after a name creates the presumption that the individual is competent in the designated occupation and should be recognized as such by all others who have the same credentials. Four corollaries of this guiding rule are: reluctance to criticize or rank qualified colleagues; criticism of less trained practitioners; self-regulation of workload to maintain standards; and, perhaps unique to social work, an accent on close personal professional supervision of the individual practitioner.

The reluctance to criticize or rank the abilities of a colleague before the client public, or expose him to criticism by others, is illustrated in the teaching and medical professions. Organized schoolteachers carry on a perennial fight against proposals of administrators and parents that promotion and salary increases be based on merit, rather than seniority. One reason why physicians oppose public medical service is that, in the absence of a market mechanism for determining who should acquire most income and authority, they would have to grade each other, or suffer nonmedical administrators to do so. (48: p. 141) A local medical society asked to recommend a physician will simply present a register composed of all physicians in the desired specialty and require the client to make the individual choice. All professions tend to foster the myth that all practitioners are equally able.

All professions are also anti-amateur. Competing practitioners who are not regarded as professionally qualified are condemned. An attitude of disgusted outrage accompanies the refusal of MD's to recognize the claims of osteopaths and chiropractors. The latter groups are not in a position to reciprocate such feelings, and develop defensive attitudes. (389)

In social work the situation is more ambiguous. Most welfare jobs are filled by persons without a Master's degree in social work or equivalent. The widely used epithet "untrained" has therefore been applied to these persons with increasing uneasiness, since they are the main reservoir for badly needed recruitment to the profession, and it is important that they not be estranged. "Trained" and "untrained" often work side by side on the same jobs in the same agency. Sometimes the untrained—especially the older and more experienced—supervise the trained. Generally, on the job, not much is made of the distinction; everyday social and work relations are overriding. Sometimes the fledgling School graduate will adopt the scoffing attitude of the untrained toward professional tenets—much as the young "progressive education" trained teacher will often abandon College of Education mental hygiene precepts in the handling of child discipline problems under the coaching of the old-timers in the school.[1]

Yet the distinction between "trained" and "untrained" has important consequences. Promotion may be open to the one, not to the other. Personal relations have to be handled delicately to avoid offense. The young trained worker can join the professional association, the older experienced one cannot. As the whole field gets further professionalized, the distinctions will get sharper—as they are now in professionally advanced settings like child guidance and family service.

Another corollary to the norm, "Maintain professional authority and standards," is seen in the tendency, universal among both professional and nonprofessional occupations, to regulate the workload. In the professions this takes the form of the rule, "Don't do too much or too little work if it lowers standards." Where there is a system of record-keeping for the compilation of administrative statistics, this can be translated, "If you report too much work (client contacts, collateral visits, case conferences), you're doing a sloppy job; if you report too little, you're shirking professional responsibility." This problem of regulating the workpace is seen in complaints among physicians that their colleagues either take on too large a practice, or refuse service to borderline cases at inconvenient times (for example, three o'clock on a rainy morning). The idea that there is an optimum workload or workpace seems widespread in the professions; it is generally rooted in the collective desire to protect work standards, lest the profession lose its authority.

Concern with bona fide service is seen, finally, in the emphasis on proper professional supervision of the novitiate. This is more

---

[1] One vehicle for the effort of the trained social worker to create a *modus vivendi* with his untrained colleagues is the "Social Work Club," found in many communities, to which anyone interested in social welfare may belong. Trained professionals help to sponsor such clubs, but do not monopolize leading roles and, more importantly, do not pressure fellow professionals into joining, as they do with respect to the National Association of Social Workers.

than the surgeon's supervision of the intern's closing of the wound, or the Chief of Surgery's review of the Staff Surgeon's operative performance. In social work, supervision is both more detailed and lasts longer. What begins as field work training under very close watch of agency personnel continues for a lifetime in the "supervision complex" (see Chapter X). The supervisor-worker relation has in it some of the elements of a training analysis. The idea that the professional social worker should not do anything without close (if permissive) supervision is perhaps more pervasive among social workers than in any other profession.

A second norm governing colleague relations is this: *Do not air professional problems, complaints, and mistakes publicly*—do nothing and admit to nothing which will discredit the profession in the eyes of outsiders. Within their own circle, professionals will often ridicule the pretentions and limitations of their own vocation; they will also discuss the problems of malpractice. Physicians will joke about patients they call the "psychos" whom they treat with placebos or send "on vacation" via Blue Cross. Surgeons will admit privately that mistakes are made, that some of their hasty colleagues perform unnecessary operations, and that some slips of the knife do occur. Similarly social workers will laugh with one another at what they consider the absurdity of some personality theory learned at school; they will also wonder on occasion whether they have helped or hurt a client, admit to having sloughed off an importunate case, and so on.

Errors of judgment and deficiencies of skill are inevitable in any occupation requiring much judgment and high skill. All professions develop ways of spreading the risk of inevitable mistakes. (Cf. 158.) One way is to keep them quiet, view them as matters for strictly professional concern. The tendency to close ranks against any outside complaint of malpractice, commercialism, or incompetence seems plain. Thus, it is difficult to get one doctor to testify against another in lawsuits for malpractice, whatever the merits of the complaint. Fee splitting, apparently endemic in medical circles, and in many states illegal, is often called to the attention of medical societies, and the typical answer is a convention resolution that the profession should police itself.

Although the norm that soiled professional linen should be washed in private is relatively weak in social work, there are occasions when it is clearly expressed and affects colleague behavior. For instance, if a client is psychotic and commits suicide before the need for referral to a psychiatrist is recognized, the talk will tend to stay in the fraternity, with silence or statements of justification greeting the complaining public. Or, for a less dramatic occasion: social workers tend to avoid public criticism of the administration of welfare programs. The profession is thought to be under fire enough ("Relief scandals!" the newspapers cry); to give information to the public that can be used out of context is to add fuel to the fire.

In general, however, internal problems of social work seem to be aired in public with uncommon frequency and frankness. Several reasons may account for this. Since social work is composed of a number of occupations, some of which are not professionally conscious, the centrifugal pulls on it are many and strong. Legal aids to control of members—licensing, certification—are not yet well developed. Moreover, the profession has a philosophical commitment to democratic discussion of all issues. It is possible also that the unique connection between social work and sociology affects the situation. Sociologists in social work, due to their own professional predilections, are prone to turn their research attention not only to substantive questions of social work practice, but also to the social organization of social work itself. Their studies typically emphasize the problems, paradoxes, and dilemmas of the profession (a tendency to which the present volume is not immune) and this may add to the self-critical strain indigenous to social work.

The third norm governing colleague relations is this: *Be aware of the limited competence of your own specialty within the profession; honor the claims of other specialties; and be ready to refer clients to a more competent colleague.* This is expressed in obvious ways in the referral systems of the more established professions; the internist does not claim the work of the ophthalmologist, the latter does not claim the work of the brain surgeon; each supports the prestige of all by making appropriate referrals. In the less well-established professions this norm sometimes creates dilemmas: when, for instance, should the nonmedical psychotherapist terminate treatment and refer a patient to a psychiatrist? In social work, because of the commitment to a generic curriculum and recently growing official opposition to internal specialization, this norm is not strongly developed. But it does exist. For instance, a psychiatric caseworker who takes a job leading a group of convalescent psychotics in a recreation setting accepts as valid the disapproval of group workers, and feels that a group worker should be hired for the job. Or a family caseworker on a difficult child case will consult a child welfare specialist, or refer the client to a clinic for psychiatric casework service.

Finally, there is a norm which may be unique to social work: *Interpret colleague as well as client behavior in professional (for example, casework) terms.* The colleague group expects the social worker to be alert to the unconscious motivation of overt acts, to display his knowledge of the "deeper" causes of behavior, and to do this in a way that will remind everyone he is part of the fraternity. As one caseworker put it, "You're not one of the crowd if you let a Freudian slip go by unnoticed." If there is any norm unique to the colleague groups in social work it is this one—a reflection, perhaps, of the self-consciousness of a fledgling profession, as well as the uncertain state of the social and psychological knowledge on which social work rests.

The four norms we have described—maintain professional authority and standards of work; do not air problems, complaints, and mistakes publicly; recognize the bounds of special competence and be ready to refer; interpret both colleague and client behavior in professional terms—all function together to regulate internal competition, build the solidarity of the group in its relations with outsiders, and enhance the success of the jurisdictional claim which any profession must stake out. For the individual social worker, these norms function to affirm the professional self he began to develop in training.[1]

[1] In all professions there is some discrepancy between the norms inculcated in professional training and the requirements of practice. In social work this would be so if for no other reason because of the varied jobs available after graduation and the relatively standard curriculum used before graduation. "Reality shock"—a label

Some Consequences of Social Work Professionalism

The development of professionalism sketched above has had several effects on the practice of social work. Four will be commented upon here: problems of recruitment, interprofessional relations, role conflict among social workers, and definition of the field for future growth.

Recruitment and Public Images of the Profession. Recruitment of new practitioners is a particularly critical problem in the drive toward social work professionalization. Figures on the number of professionally trained workers greatly underestimate the true growth of professional consciousness, and public recognition of the profession in recent years. The evidence is that many more people identify themselves as social workers than graduate from schools of social work, and many more positions calling for trained social workers exist than there are trained people to fill them. A situation has arisen in which the public demand built up for social workers cannot be met because too few students are presenting themselves for training. Although this makes for "good pickings" for present workers, and is tending to push salaries up, it also tends to frustrate public expectation, and invites preemption of the jobs by other occupations. Table 11 shows the number of graduates from the two-year social work curriculum in recent years, and gives a ratio of social work graduates to the total number of college graduates two years earlier. It is clear that these numbers, whatever their trend, are not enough to staff a profession of 75- to 100-thousand members.

The reasons for these recruitment difficulties are partly social, partly economic. The social aspect relates in part to the public image of the profession—always an important element in career choices. Too little is known about the current content of popular stereotypes of the social worker. The obvious negative phrases

---

suggested by Everett C. Hughes for the experience of the new graduate on his first job—is minimized by field work training in the social work curriculum. However, it seems possible that agency practice typically contrasts sharply with professional ideology. In less well-established professions such as social work or psychology, the norms dealing with client-professional relations as well as those governing colleague relations may be less a working code than a set of ideals advocated by the leaders of the profession (and partly summarized in a code of ethics).

"do-gooder" or "cold snooper" may reflect more the social workers' anxieties about a hostile public than the actual feelings of that public. Research on this matter is needed.

There are, however, three suggestive studies of the relative prestige or social status of social work. A national cross-section of the population was asked in the spring of 1947 to rank prestige-wise a list of 90 occupations. (263: pp. 412–413) Social work was not among the occupations listed but "welfare worker for a city

TABLE 11. TRENDS IN GRADUATE SOCIAL WORK EDUCA-
TION

Year	Number of graduates from two-year social work curriculum	Per cent of all college graduates of two years prior
1949–1950	1,804	.67
1950–1951	1,923	.52
1951–1952	1,946	.45
1952–1953	1,844	.48
1953–1954	1,651	.50
1954–1955	1,590	.52

SOURCE: French, David G., "An Estimate of the Number of Persons Who Will Be Graduated from Schools of Social Work in the United States, 1955 to 1965." (116: Table 1)

government" ranked forty-sixth in the list of 90—around "electrician," "trained machinist," "undertaker," and "reporter on a daily newspaper." The only other welfare-type occupation was "playground director," which ranked fifty-fourth, around "tenant farmer" and "traveling salesman for a wholesale concern," "policeman," and "railroad conductor." The "welfare worker" noted above had a score of 73, compared to the following for some other occupations:

Professional and semi-professional workers as a whole	80.6
Physician	93
College professor	89
Lawyer	86
Public schoolteacher	78

The only other studies that have come to the writers' attention show similar results. One used as raters 700 high school seniors in two Cleveland suburbs; the other used 72 Wayne University students (288). One suggests that social workers rank higher among lower-class students, lower among middle-class students (402: p. 162). All three studies show striking consistency: it is fairly clear that the public does not rank social work as one of the high prestige professions. It is a plausible hypothesis, however, that the image held by the middle-class public will become more favorable as the clientele of social work shifts upward (more middle-income families have firsthand exposure), and as the education level of the average social worker rises. But at the moment, in so far as the status of a profession is a factor in occupational choice, we have in the middling prestige of social work one reason for recruitment difficulties.

The different amounts of prestige attached to specialties within the profession also affect recruitment. Psychiatric social work has been, and still largely is, the specialization with the most prestige, a fact which has a definite effect on work opportunities and conditions. A psychiatric caseworker is welcome in a family agency, but a family caseworker does not usually qualify for a child guidance clinic job. Often there is a salary premium attached to the psychiatric job classification. It is no accident that students choose the psychiatric sequence in preference to family or child casework, or to social group work.[1]

Low pay is a second block to easy recruitment. Dean Fedele F. Fauri of the University of Michigan has discussed the unfavorable position of social workers as compared to other professions requiring a similar amount of training. (102: pp. 47 ff.) The public schoolteacher, for instance, earns the basic professional education degree in four years of college, and goes into jobs with a pay range like that in social work. The Master's degree in education requires but one year of study, and that can be done during summer vacation periods. The basic professional social work degree, in contrast, requires two years of graduate work beyond the A.B. level—a pattern laid down in the 1920's and 1930's and now

---

[1] But in 1956 a study commission of the Council on Social Work Education (the accrediting body for schools of social work) made the drastic recommendation that "there should be no accrediting of any specializations by any definition." (174: p. 45) If this aim is achieved, the psychiatric tag is likely to lose its value.

standard in the 60-odd Schools of Social Work in the U.S. and
Canada. Only rarely can the two years be shortened by summer
school classes, because in the vast majority of schools the "integrated curriculum" requires that classroom "methods" courses be
taken simultaneously with the "field work" assignment, and field
work is tied to the nine months of the normal academic year.
Many a career-seeking college junior avoids the path to social
work when he learns that social workers train longer to earn
about what teachers get.

Proposals to shorten the two years of graduate training, or to
permit admission to professional school at the end of the college
junior year, have so far met with disfavor by professional associations and accrediting bodies.[1] It is felt that any relaxation in
training requirements would undermine professional standards
and thwart the achievement of solid professional status. The
major device used to overcome the economic handicap to recruitment, aside from publicity, is substantial subsidization of students
through work-study plans (salary while in training), agency and
Community Chest "stipends," training grants offered by units of
the Department of Health, Education, and Welfare. A handful
of Schools have for a long time offered plans which spread the
training period over more than two years, so that a student may
hold down a nearly full-time job while earning his Master's
degree. Such programs, now spreading rapidly to other Schools,
do not cut the training period, but do sacrifice the "integrated
curriculum" concept.

Recruitment, in the sense of winning the allegiance of already-
employed groups, has also been affected by the way in which
social work competence is defined, and the standards set for
membership in professional associations. A pattern has crystallized which tends to disaffect persons in social work positions who
do not meet the membership standard set by the newly merged
professional association, the National Association of Social Workers. This standard calls for two years of graduate education in an

---

[1] The National Association of Social Workers has recently declared it "strongly
opposes vocationally oriented undergraduate programs" of social work education.
(262)

accredited school of social work. In the past many persons have entered social work programs who had obtained their training in other fields, and indeed some of the outstanding leaders in the field of social work are in this group. Several of the larger schools of social work have had as deans social workers who did not hold a social work degree, and the first two nominees for president of the National Association of Social Workers, which proclaimed the two-year degree standard, both lacked social work degrees.

It may be predicted that the new membership standard in the professional association, if sustained, will have the effect of strengthening the place of casework in professional social work at the expense of other types of practice. The schools of social work under the new standard become the sole channel through which persons may enter the professional association. And the schools have for years invested their major resources in developing competence for the field of casework. The best available index of student specialization in schools of social work is the type of field work students take in their second year. The 1956 figures reveal the following:

TABLE 12. TYPE OF FIELD-WORK PLACEMENT OF SECOND-YEAR STUDENTS IN SCHOOLS OF SOCIAL WORK AS OF NOVEMBER 1, 1956

Type of field work	Percentage of students
Casework	*86*
Group work	*10*
Community organization	*2.5*
Administration	*.8*
Research	*.3*
Total	*100*

SOURCE: *Statistics on Social Work Education,* 1956. Council on Social Work Education, 1956.

The new doctoral programs being offered in schools of social work seek to give emphasis to broad social welfare programs as well as to casework, but it is safe to assert that the professional image which the schools both reflect and reinforce puts casework, and as a poor second, group work, at the core of professional social work. Administration, community organization, development of social policy, social insurance, research—these are in danger of becoming even more peripheral to the professional image of social work than they were under the more loosely defined professional associations which existed prior to the establishment of the National Association of Social Workers.

Interprofessional Relations. The drive toward professionalization in social work—reflected in raised training standards, crystallization of the area of competence, and restriction of entry to the professional association—leads social work into hard competition with neighboring occupations.

Social work may be classified roughly in the "human relations" area of occupational specialization. As such, it is among the service occupations, based on wealth and division of labor made possible by advanced industrialization.

All occupations in the human relations field have only tenuous claims to exclusive competence. This results not only from their newness, uncertain standards, and the embryonic state of the social and psychological sciences on which they draw, but also from the fact that the types of problems dealt with are part of everyday living. The lay public cannot recognize the need for special competence in an area where everyone is "expert."

The problem is especially evident in "interpreting" social work to the public. Inability to implant in the public mind and the minds of other professions a clear image of social work is a matter of constant concern to the profession. However, this is a problem shared with sister occupations in the human relations field, resulting predictably from the nature of the task and the as yet modest degree of professionalization.

Social workers concerned about the negative stereotypes of social work held by other groups should note a recent study of interprofessional relations. Zander and others (424) interviewed 156 psychiatrists, 165 clinical psychologists, and 159 psychiatric social workers—all working in teams in large metropolitan areas. They found that "psychiatrists stereotype their own professional group less favorably than do social workers." And, although social workers describe themselves with many pleasant labels, "they also view themselves as more 'mercenary,' 'condescending,' and 'striving' than do the psychiatrists." Clinical psychologists, it was found, are more critical of their own profession ("dogmatic," "mercenary," "condescending," and "striving") than are either social workers or psychiatrists. Social workers in general display a penchant for public self-criticism and a strong concern about acceptance by other groups—though this is less true of those whose status and professional commitment are unusually high. (424: pp. 54–58, 191–196) From this study (especially pp. 72–75) one might hypothesize that the more prestige a profession achieves, and the stronger its inner fraternity, the less it will be concerned about negative public images and the opinions of other professionals.

Social work knowledge and skill are such as to create ambiguity in contacts with related professions. Social work's orientation to psychoanalytic theory was stressed above; from it, serious problems of professional jurisdiction have arisen, because several other professions or would-be professions (analytic psychiatry, the counseling branch of clinical psychology, the several brands of "guidance") have evolved which base their practice on much the same body of theory.

Social work claims distinction from the others on grounds of greater attention to the social environment. The stress on the *social* is counterposed to preoccupation with intrapsychic phenomena, though as we have suggested, this is played down in practice. Social work claims further distinction by incorporating humanitarian sentiments into its body of technical "principles" ("the right of an individual to fullest expression of his capacities," and so on)—in other words, by a general attempt to wed science to ethics.

In practice, however, the types of problems and clients treated by the several groups are often overlapping, theoretical formulations of diagnosis and treatment may be similar or identical, and certain treatment techniques are used in common. The matter has come to a head in recent years in discussions of such questions as: What is psychotherapy? Who has a right to practice psychotherapy? Is casework a form of it?

The growth of professional social work has taken it into a relationship increasingly typical of modern professional practice—the professional "team." The focus of each discipline on its own technical interests has tended to slice up the client and parcel him out. As the worried medical specialists say, "Who sees the patient as a whole?" By gathering complementary specialists into a team, the stereoscopic view destroyed by specialization can be regained. The hospital team of physician, nurse, and medical social worker is one example; the mental hygiene clinic team of psychiatrist, clinical psychologist, and psychiatric social worker is another. The mutual understanding which such arrangements provide may be needed in other areas, too. Lawyers in child welfare work, for example, have complained of difficulty in working with social workers because of ignorance of the law among the latter. Social workers in turn may feel lawyers are blind to child needs.

The problem of jurisdictional conflict in and out of teams is highlighted by the Zander study of interprofessional relations mentioned above. Analysis shows that these three kinds of specialists agree pretty well about one another's proper functions, but "of the social workers 30% see [interviewing] as a unique ability that they possess, while only 12% of the psychiatrists attribute this skill to them" (p. 59). Social workers seem to feel more secure regarding their jurisdiction over case-history writing and community contact work than when doing diagnosis and therapy, but they are strongly attracted to the latter functions and "many wish they were psychiatrists rather than social workers" (pp. 14, 57, 62). In general, however, though they want more responsibility, the social workers accept their subordinate status. One reason for this is the fact that in this case interprofessional relations are also cross-sex relations with the dominant profession also being dominantly male. (Cf. pp. 117–119.) The major cleavage in this trio seems to be between dominant male psychiatrists teamed with female social workers, on the one hand, and subordinate male psychologists, on the other. For instance, skills in psychometrics are seen both by social workers and psychiatrists as "almost the *only* contribution of the clinical psychologists," while fewer than half of the psychologists claim this as a major skill—aspiring instead to therapy, diagnosis, and other tasks (p. 139).[1]

If in what may be the clearest and most stable working relationship in the mental health field we find unsolved vital issues concerning who should do what, how best to collaborate and maintain professional status, then it is easy to see how in other interprofessional contacts among the human relations professions the cleavages might be deep. Ultimate division of function among occupations in areas such as psychotherapy will be determined, of course, not only by the criterion of technical competence, but also by ability to mobilize public and political support, as illustrated by the already considerable success of the medical profession in achieving legal preemption of the "mental healing arts."

Profession, Agency, Social Movement, and Sex: Role Conflict Among Social Workers. The nature of the area of competence, professional norms governing relations with clients and colleagues, and interprofessional rivalry and collaboration are not the only factors shaping the social worker's behavior on the job. For the social worker is more than a professional: he is, among other things, an agency staff member, a humanitarian, and a representative of his sex, male or female. The interplay between these identities presents the social worker with some dilemmas fateful for the development of both the practice and philosophy of social work.

In this section we will first consider two types of "role conflict" evident in all of social life, and then apply this concept to the situation of the social worker. The aim is to bring together our analysis of agency structure and operation, and social work professionalism.

---

[1] This looks very much like one of the classical games of social life—a very big and powerful unit (psychiatrist) and a very small unit (psychiatric social worker) ganging up on a third, medium-sized unit (clinical psychologist) which the established power sees as an aggressor. One can find this phenomenon in jurisdictional conflicts among siblings, unions, nations, and other social units. (Cf. 51.)

If Johnny, aged ten, comes upon his father while the latter is telling an off-color joke to adult friends, the father will falter in his tale, display mixed emotions, perhaps fall silent. If a male social worker receives an order from a female supervisor of similar age, he may experience vague discomfort. In the first instance, the behavior appropriate for a father is inconsistent with the behavior appropriate to an adult friend in a peer group; in the second, behavior expected of a subordinate is inconsistent with the behavior typically expected of a man.

Or take examples of a different kind: a family physician who has become Mr. Jones' friendly confidant feels uneasy collecting fees from that same Mr. Jones when the latter is short of cash. A casework-trained probation officer finds himself torn between behavior expected of a permissive counselor aiming at rehabilitation and the authoritative behavior expected of an officer of the court to keep the "con" in line.

"Role conflict" is the label sociologists use to describe this pervasive phenomenon. It refers to cases in which a person playing a role is obligated to behave (that is, act, think, feel) in incompatible ways simultaneously, all of which ways are defined as proper to the role or roles he is playing. Two types of role conflict are illustrated above: conflict involving (1) two roles in two groups which expect, prefer, or allow contradictory behavior —father versus adult friend, social worker versus male; and (2) one role containing conflicting expectations of behavior—the doctor who must be at once friendly confidant and businesslike fee collector, the probation officer who must be at once permissive and authoritative.

The opportunities for role conflict are many in a complex and changing society. Most behavior is structured in roles—we take the parts of parent, worker, supervisor, theater-goer, guest, stranger, and so on, acting out their rights and obligations. Often behavior called for in one role does not "fit" another. Since we play many roles in continual succession and sometimes simultaneously, and since roles are continually being redefined (note Chapter IV on the search for new identity among women), role conflict pervades our experience.

The person caught in the cross-fire of competing claims typically makes some kind of adjustment: he tries to reshape the role or roles to make the demands compatible; he quits the role; he adapts to the role by playing up one set of obligations, playing down another, and so on. Whatever strategy of adjustment he uses, it is easy to see that these resolutions of role conflict exert a strain toward change in both the person and the groups in which he participates. Here lies the significance of role conflict: if we understand the structured strains in the role of social worker we can better understand the transformations that occur in the worker as he moves through his career and experiences these recurrent dilemmas, as well as the pressures the worker in turn exerts for changes in the welfare organizations in which he works.

The main sources of role conflict among social workers are these sometimes conflicting identities: (1) profession versus agency; (2) social movements and reform groups sustaining humanitarian sentiments versus agency and profession; (3) sex versus agency or profession.

Social work, like every skilled occupation, *develops work standards and other norms which may deviate from those enforced by agencies* in which workers are employed. In school and in the professional association the worker is indoctrinated with these standards, which will include notions about the proper sizes of caseload and grouoload, the right to professional supervision, access to consultants (for example, a psychiatrist in a family service agency), the amount of time to be spent on an interview, the number of interviews per day or week, the necessity of private offices for interviewing, confidentiality of case material, the rights of clients (for example, permission must be obtained before speaking to relatives), exclusion from the staff of the professionally untrained, and so on. In varying degrees agencies incorporate professional work standards and norms into their own operating standards. Thus, Simon and others (331: p. 123) note that the practice of consultation is highly developed and approved by administration in agencies staffed by social workers. Often, however, agencies have operational requirements, set by law, tradition, policy, or public pressures, which depart from professional standards. This is particularly true of public agencies operating within a legal framework, a situation which sets the stage for role conflict.[1]

The administration of public assistance, for instance, presents many points of profession-agency disagreement. The crisis in public assistance after World War II—with legislators, newspapers, and public welfare commissions crying "fraud" and "mollycoddling," while social workers responded, "undermining of professional standards"—hinged on such conflicts. Professional social workers who had hung on in line and administrative positions from the depression thirties considered it good professional casework: (1) to disregard for budgeting purposes some kinds of financial resources (paper-route earnings of a boy in the family, the occasional contributions of an estranged father); and (2) to refuse to impose moral standards as a condition of financial eligibility (overlook expenditure of relief grant for cigarettes or liquor, the presence of a "boy friend"). The public assistance agency manual, however, is explicit: all family income must be deducted from the grant, relief funds may not be spent on beverage alcohol, the birth of a second illegitimate child to an unmarried mother on ADC calls for a review of her moral "suitability" to receive a relief check. The worker is caught between conflicting directives of agency and profession.

In the field of corrections the professional social worker is subjected to even sharper contradictions. Social workers, as Ohlin observes, "have approached correctional problems with a well integrated philosophy and clearly defined casework principles and procedures" which are at variance with traditional

---

[1] The discrepancy between professional and agency norms stems from a basic conflict in principles of organization which appears in all bureaucratic systems—in factories (with engineers, accountants, personnel managers), in universities (with faculty, nonacademic administrators, and the like), in hospitals (with doctors, technicians, nurses). In all of these organizations, different professional groups are arranged in a hierarchy. Thus, the *colleague principle* (a group whose members have *similar* technical training and occupational position, common professional norms developed by training and initiation, and who are formally equal) is in conflict with the *hierarchical principle* of the bureaucracy (a group whose members have *dissimilar* training and position, are formally *un*equal, and who in on-the-job training and indoctrination develop common *organizational* norms.) Macmahon and others in a chapter entitled "Rival Claims of Hierarchy and Specialty" in their study of the WPA, give a detailed account of how professional specialists in education, art, and construction engineering fought with the line command of the hierarchy for control of the work relief programs for unemployed professionals. (221)

correctional practices. (276: p. 17) The social worker as parole or probation officer expects to have neutral, nonjudgmental relations with a client who has selected the agency and comes motivated for treatment, access to skilled casework supervision, the right to treat the client in accordance with the latter's individual needs, agency protection from the pressures of public opinion in the exercise of professional skills. (277) But, in fact, the typical probationer or parolee has not "selected the agency," is not motivated for treatment, does not recognize that he has problems with which the practitioner can help, and usually refuses proffered assistance. The man who has been promoted to supervisor is not the skilled professional caseworker, but a political appointee or a fellow skilled in public relations or high in seniority, who is very often indifferent or hostile to social work precepts. Far from being able to individualize the client, the worker is bound by "rules of client supervision" which arose historically as a defense for the agency against public criticism of coddling the offender. The parolee must observe a curfew, abstain from drink, avoid old pals, get permission to change jobs or living quarters—and the worker is expected to enforce these rules no matter how they clash with his professional views on proper treatment plans for the client. (277) At almost every point the worker is torn between agency and professional norms.

A second source of role conflict is the *clash between humanitarian values and agency and professional norms*. Many, if not most, social workers are "graduates" of liberal, social-reform movements, and carry with them into school, profession, and agency, identification with such movements, expressed in humanitarian sentiments about how people should be treated. In some agencies and programs, however, humanitarianism is not the controlling philosophy. General relief offices up and down the country are still largely wedded to pauper law principles of harshness and deterrence. The practice of correctional institutions likewise reflects their traditional purposes of punishment and deterrence. In such circumstances the worker will often break agency rules in order to treat the client humanely—the probation officer will knowingly permit infractions of curfew, the relief worker will advise recipients to keep beer bottles (and boy friends) out of sight. But any worker who tries to be a good humanitarian and a good agency representative at the same time is in for torment of conscience.

Humanitarian sentiments clash also with professional norms. This shows up most clearly in the student beginning his professional school training. He comes to school, as cursory examination of applications for admission will show, imbued with a desire "to help people"; and from the school he wants training in the techniques of help. To his distress, however, he soon finds out that clinical therapeusis is expressed in ways quite alien from those suggested by the naive impulse to help. The humanitarian in him would bind the client's wound directly; the professional clinician, he is taught, explores the wound with seeming indifference to the client's pain. The humanitarian would meet the need as expressed; the clinician teaches that expressed needs are rarely the real ones. The humanitarian takes people at face value; the clinician is sure that faces are but masks for deeper drives that must be probed. The humanitarian, feeling that all men are brothers, offers friendship to those he succors; the clinician knows he must maintain social distance from those he would help. Some students are simply unable to reconcile the contradictions, and drop out of school. And the ambivalence of the professional social worker toward participating in social action on the local scene suggests that those who do go on into practice seldom resolve the profession vs. humanitarian conflict completely.

A third area of conflict derives from discrepancies between sex role and agency and professional roles. It is mainly the rank-and-file male social worker and the female supervisor who experience this clash—which helps to explain why men do not long remain in direct service positions, and women are not often assigned to top administrative posts.

Social work jobs for women can be seen as extensions of sex roles derived from norms governing the behavior of wife and mother. As woman she is traditionally expected to provide care to children, the aged, the sick; to be nurturant, gentle, kind, receptive; in short, feminine. As caseworker, though professionalism and agency procedures hold this in check somewhat, she functions in a similar way—as does the nurse or the elementary schoolteacher. So far, there is some, but not much discrepancy between occupational and sex roles. It is when she becomes a supervisor with male subordinates that her troubles may begin. There is a norm still prevalent in American culture which says, "Women should not be in authority over men of roughly the same social class and age." Further, the next step up is likely to be blocked for the female supervisor, because of the notion that women are not good risks for top administration. The rationale goes like this: if they marry, they may quit; if they do not quit, they may have difficulty getting along with their husbands, since it is still thought that women should not exceed their husbands in status and authority. In addition, the active, aggressive entrepreneurial behavior needed to develop professional and community contacts and to gain access to men of power—both essential for agency survival—is often deprecated for women.

For the young male social worker, these same definitions of sex role present an even more poignant problem, at the same time that they spur his upward climb. With the present sex ratio in social work, his supervisors will most often be female; and despite the partial shift toward equality of sexes, most men still feel demeaned and threatened, their self-image wounded, by subordination to women at work. The male social worker is surrounded by many other reminders of the conflict between his sex role and occupational role. Popular stereotypes of the social worker—whether as motherly healer, cold snooper, or Lady Bountiful—are almost exclusively female. In popular literature, the model of the social worker is a flat-heeled female; even in the daily press, personal items about social workers will likely appear on the Woman's Page. The major historical figures that leap to mind—Jane Addams, Mary Richmond—are women; the men are more likely to be remembered as reformers—Charles Loring Brace, Harry Hopkins. There is a noticeable trend in current professional social work literature to use "she" rather than the standard English "he" to refer to a worker of indeterminate sex. In hospital settings—medical and psychiatric—a host of female ancillaries (nurses, nurses' aides, social workers, medical technicians, receptionists) swarm in comfortable, acknowledged subservience around the dominant doctor. The male social worker in such settings is classed with the female helpers rather than with the male doctors, and he may thereby feel his masculinity threatened.

These illustrations are sufficient to indicate the implications of role conflict among social workers. The problems of recruitment to the profession, and staffing of agencies with trained workers, are particularly affected. Conflicts among professional, agency, and humanitarian identities drive social workers to avoid or abandon some important social welfare fields, to loosen connections with the profession, to give less than full allegiance to the agency. Students are baffled or repulsed by the inner contradictions of the roles they are asked to learn. Much-needed recruitment of males to the profession is blocked by the difficulties they face in maintaining a self-respecting sex identity, though at the same time this difficulty may act as a pressure to achieve higher administrative position once they get into social work—which could be one explanation of the skyrocketing careers observers note among young men in this field.

Analysis of the sources and kinds of role conflict, the points in the career pattern where the dilemmas are felt most urgently, and the typical strategies of adjustment by which they are resolved could increase our understanding of the behavior of social workers on the job. More important, such analysis could tell us something about the circumstances under which role conflict adds a bit of needed flexibility, change, and novelty to the profession and when it hinders its proper functions and threatens its future. Thus, the Ohlin group, although they also emphasize the need for further research, on the basis of their study of role conflict among social workers in the correctional field, are able to recommend specific revisions in preparation for the field: (1) recognition of the real divergence of interest between agency and social worker that often exists in the corrections field, and training in how to deal with it; (2) the discovery and teaching of treatment skills which are effective in situations where alternatives are circumscribed (as opposed to the exhortation that "the worker must accept the limitations of the agency"); (3) training in how to deal with the client who has limited capacity for change, or is "not motivated for treatment." (277: pp. 224–225) Recent contributions to the social work literature on training for correctional work, notably those of Elliot Studt, underscore the importance of Ohlin's observations. (347; 348; 349).

Study of role conflict in settings other than corrections and subsequent planning to reduce the elements of strain in the social worker's role would be worth the effort. It is by no means certain, however, that we would want to eliminate all the conflicts described above even if we could. If the humanitarian sentiments sustained by sex role and reform groups were all eliminated wherever they interfered with rigid adherence to professional and agency standards, and no one ever experienced a second thought about them, the welfare world might be a bleak one indeed.

The Future of Social Work

In September of 1955 a teacher of social work from New Zealand visiting the United States made this comment: "I notice some of you people in America are objecting to your emphasis on individualized services and are trying to reorient the field toward broad welfare programing, social welfare policy, and social welfare administration—away from psychology and toward social science. In New Zealand our social work school is called a School of Social Science. Our curriculum stresses social administration, and social and political science as opposed to psychology. Most of our graduates go to work in government welfare programs. *But they don't have any professional identification as social workers.* We'd like to know how you manage to develop that spirit."

From Environment and Reform to the Case and the Profession. In this century American social work has made a major shift in its intellectual orientations: From viewing the case as a product of impersonal forces in the social and economic environment, social work came to the image of the case as a product of unconscious impulse, needing restoration to an unchanged environment by self-mastery.[1] This shift in theory is intimately related to a major shift in practice: from preoccupation with reform to preoccupation with technical professionalism.

Social work leaders in the period of environmental reform (1900–1914) were describing the "Spirit of Social Work" in these words:

> . . . The dominant idea . . . is . . . to seek out and to strike effectively at those organized forces of evil, at those particular causes of dependence and intolerable living conditions which are beyond the control of the individuals whom they injure and whom they too often destroy.
>
> Other tasks for other ages. This be the glory of ours, that the social causes of dependence shall be destroyed. Other work for other agencies. This be the chosen field of philanthropy, that relief shall come at last to those who in the very nature of the case—the child, the sick, the weak—cannot help themselves. (87: p. 194)

Preceding and paralleling this brief upsurge of reform interest was a tendency that quickly became dominant. While Edward T. Devine was rejoicing in the glorious reform task of his "age," Mary Richmond was viewing the reform movement as a diversion from the basic task of mastering the difficult details of investigating individual cases. She later recalled, "During all that period, I know, it was uphill work to interest either the public or the social reformers in any reform that dealt with people one by one instead of in great masses." (299: p. 587)

"One by one" is the theme of the last forty years of social work. Interest in reform declined.[2] Social workers took the position that professional leadership should be assumed only in areas where social workers are technically expert. (203) The tendency has been to construe even these areas narrowly in terms of casework and groupwork process. By bringing public agencies to take over the burden of financial assistance, the Great Depression, though

[1] It is not much of an exaggeration to say that social science in our universities was making a comparable shift: from the problems posed by Marx to the problems posed by Freud, though now the attempt to wed the two accounts for some of the most stimulating work in the social sciences.

[2] As individuals, social workers may be "liberals" in spirit and voting habits— there is evidence that most of them are. (125) But in the arena of society and agency the forces creating professionalism override individual orientations toward reform.

it prompted a resurgence of interest in social reform, also had the effect of freeing large numbers of the professional-minded in voluntary agencies from the responsibility of dispensing relief and gave them the opportunity to develop still further their technical interest in the psychology of the individual.

The flight from reform accelerated after the 1930's, but not without uneasy words of warning from social work leaders and considerable restiveness among the rank-and-file. "Social work, in principle and in tenet," wrote Donald Howard in 1954, "is not separable from social reform . . . reform activities . . . must be reintroduced into professional thinking, organization and training." (155: p. 159) Similar comment came from Benjamin Youngdahl, when he retired in 1953 as president of the American Association of Social Workers. He concluded his address with the rhetorical query "Is our function as social workers limited to the treatment of pathologies; or do we also have a positive or preventive function to perform?" (423: p. 111) Hollis and Taylor in a much-discussed study prepared for the National Council on Social Work Education in 1951 observe that for the last quarter of a century "The profession has accepted too little of a unified responsibility for appraising and improving social welfare institutions." (152: p. 142) A report to the American Association of Group Workers in 1949 reminds them of "the need for group workers to be more actively involved in maintaining general social welfare services. . . ." and of their responsibility to take a stand on major social issues of the time. (336: p. 451) The 1956 Alumni Day address at the New York School of Social Work by Agnes E. Meyer is a forthright example of militant advice from the outside. Exhorting social workers as "the conscience of our American society" to the task of "community reorganization," she observed that the older professions, law, medicine, and education, "have become encrusted in bureaucracy, respectability and economic rewards." Social work in contrast "is still free—to some extent—from this lock-step towards success which most Americans worship." (238: p. 9) The volumes of the National Conference of Social Work have been peppered with such observations for years. To go professional is to corrupt the reform tradition; to neglect the social causes of maladjustment and broader programs of prevention is to abdicate professional responsibility—these are recurrent themes in contemporary debate in the social work community.

Usually, discussion of these themes revolves around two questions: (1) Is professionalism entirely incompatible with a social work commitment to reform, and, if so, in what specific ways? Or (2) Accepting professionalism as necessary to the proper organization and growth of social work, what is the proper relation of the social worker to the welfare policy-maker? To flog the social worker for his alleged desertion or corruption will not answer these questions. For the answers we must look to the forces, inside and outside the profession, which account for the flight from reform.

One set of pressures has been in the realm of ideas. Social science in the United States during this period was becoming separated from social philosophy and social reform; from the new social science social work borrowed the idea that the technical expert should check his values at the door—leave questions of policy to others. Meanwhile, theories of dynamic psychology turned the social worker's attention toward the inner person—toward a search for change in the case rather than in his social opportunities, in the personality rather than in the social structure. Psychological perspectives were in turn linked to a general tendency in the mental health movement to define "adjustment," "normality" as conformity to the dominant values of private initiative, personal responsibility, and individual achievement. (See "The Culture of Capitalism," Chapter II; cf. 80.) Social work became firmly tied to psychological science and the two reflected neatly the central tendencies of American culture.

A second, possibly more important, pressure away from reform was the slowly growing recognition that this activity was becoming shaky as a basis for professional specialization if, indeed, it was ever strong. The massive shifts in specialization and stratification discussed in Chapter IV—the upgrading of skills, the slow equalization of income, the diffusion of power—these were bringing changes on the social action and social reform front. Social reform activity became widespread, the common property of so many organizations that it became difficult for any one group to stake out a claim to prior leadership rights, or even to see itself in such a light. Organized labor can now fight for its broad welfare programs more vigorously and effectively than social work ever could. The minority defense organizations and the farm bloc give important influence to other once-voiceless groups. Private social action associations abound on every side. It can almost be said that a social reform outlook has pervaded our political structure—witness the willingness of both major parties to carry on with welfare legislation, albeit with different enthusiasm and emphasis. Thus, social work as reform has not seemed to have much professional future. The people of poverty have become fewer. (See "Distribution of Income," Chapter IV.) Increasingly, they can speak for themselves—and it could be argued that they do not need social workers to speak for them.[1]

Finally, although this is seldom stated, it has seemed doubtful to many that community organization and welfare planning (the main carriers of the reform tradition) have thus far developed a really scientific base for professional status. Where is the body of knowledge and skill that the social welfare planner exclusively claims as his own? The reform-minded can answer that professional social workers are close to the grass roots—they know the troubles people have, the state of community resources, and can therefore advise politicians and administrators on what is needed and what is feasible. But, just as there are many others besides caseworkers who can carry on a therapeutic interview (from the psychiatrist to the up-to-date minister), so there are many others who are in just as good a position to keep in touch with the community's grass roots and who may work at it harder (from the precinct captain or policeman to the parish priest). On a higher level of operation, once removed from the grass roots, social workers as now trained are less equipped as reformers by school curricula than lawyers, labor leaders, politicians, public adminis-

---

[1] Although it should be added that the society continuously casts up new groups who are not organized to speak for themselves—the mentally ill, young and old delinquents, the physically handicapped, and the like.

trators, and others who know the political-social map and how to find their way around it.

Once the process of professionalization is begun, there are forces from within the occupation which, if they are not incompatible with a reform spirit, at least exert subtle pressure against its full-blown development. The notion that professionalism is corrupting because it brings economic rewards and social recognition, making its adherents fat, comfortable, and lazy, is much too simple. Missionary spirit and public service dedication, as evidenced in hard work for the social welfare, appear too often among well-paid executives, politicians, ministers, and labor leaders for us to believe that achievement of a secure and profitable career through prescribed training or long tenure necessarily transforms a man's basic values. More impressive is the argument that a professional absorbed in the technical side of his work, aiming mainly at full use of his skills and training, preoccupied with that competent, efficient performance of which his professional colleagues would approve—this person does not have the time, energy, or inclination necessary for social reform, for dedicated attention to the broader public purpose. Nor will those who conform to the professional injunction, "Be impartial, be objective," let their humanitarian sentiments affect their work very much. If the "do-gooder" is not eliminated in the first place (by being screened out in the process of self-selection into and recruitment by Schools of Social Work), he is reoriented by his professional training.

Even here, however, there is a compromise the professional can work out. In many a corner of the bureaucratic machinery of modern society, one finds the "program professional"—the specialist in depth (for example, experts in social insurance, recreation, rehabilitation, public assistance, housing) whose professional competence and commitment are beyond question, but whose commitment to particular programs and policies (for example, health insurance) is just as strong. By virtue of his technical prowess, he makes himself indispensable as a policy adviser. In his job moves—between government and private agencies, civic organizations, foundations—he follows the programs to which both his skills and his social philosophy are bound. (Cf. 410: pp. 129–143.) In his work he strives to make creative the tasks of planning, administering, and evaluating. Social work occupations provide many chances for such persons to enhance income and prestige at the same time they fulfill their commitment to social welfare. As the caseworker or groupworker becomes a supervisor or administrator, his ties to the larger community of civic organizations, pressure groups, and politicians become wider and stronger. Social action in the role of representative of social work becomes more feasible.

Whatever his initial subject-matter specialty, the social worker can acquire at least as good knowledge of the power structure (and how to work with it and through it) as the lawyer and the public administrator. If a council of social agencies lacks representation from a group whose participation is crucial in implementing a welfare program, the program professional we speak of is the fellow who will recognize the fact and find ways to get the group involved. This sort of know-how may not represent an exclusive competence, but it may be a vital one for the jobs that need to be done.

Keeping an eye on the development of the program professional role, curriculum planners in social work can accept the inevitability of increasing specialization within a growing profession and begin to spell out career paths that go beyond traditional casework and group work. Specifically, this means among other things the encouragement of a theoretical base for the field of community organization comparable to dynamic psychology, the base that has been used for casework. It implies a sustained commitment of manpower and resources both in schools of social work and in the social science disciplines—to develop people who can spot promising leads in sociology, anthropology, and social psychology, test their relevance for social work, and translate them into terms that fit the tasks and outlook of the social worker.

Of course, not everyone can become a social work leader and move on a stage which is communitywide or nationwide—bargaining, pleading, advising, pressuring in the cause of social welfare. But thousands can become members of a professional association. Many social workers have felt that organized professional associations themselves can become efficient carriers of the reform tradition. These associations can encourage a unified voice for the profession—a voice never silent on the size and direction of welfare programs, always clear on the continuing existence and possible prevention of social problems to which the lay public is indifferent. And not just in Washington, but in the community, close to home.

Policy vs. Technique. Both those inclined toward social reform or social administration and those absorbed in professional technique have had to make their adjustment to the enthusiastic shift toward professionalism. Whether they play the game as policy-oriented professionals or as apolitical technicians, social workers in midcentury America face some sharp dilemmas.

The dominant tendency toward psychological individualization coupled as it is with the flight from reform raises the question of the proper relation of the professional social worker to the policy-makers and administrators. Arthur Altmeyer suggests one outcome of the trend so far: "The persons most active in shaping and administering these large-scale welfare programs will be trained in other professions, or will acquire such training as they possess in a purely pragmatic manner." (6: p. 87) To abandon a lively reform interest has seemed to some not only to abdicate professional responsibility but also to abandon major fields of employment.

Opposed to this is the view that without technical social work training (casework, group work), one can neither be a good social agency administrator, nor participate intelligently in shaping policy. This means above all an understanding of personality. Writes Gordon Hamilton:

> . . . One cannot successfully solve problems of inter-relationships without a sound economic and political structure, but it is also true that one cannot solve—and this is less easily granted—economic problems without profound understanding of human behavior. . . . There are those who urge social workers to become community organizers and administrators, but do not yet realize that an adequate concept of personality and behavior is as essential to sound

legislation, to programs, to institutions and to administration, as it is in treatment. (134: pp. 317–321)

In essence, the caseworkers complain that the policy-minded lose sight of the psychological understandings necessary to help the case, while the policy-minded complain that the caseworkers lose sight of the community structure that creates the case in the first place and fail to use their case-history information to shape the size and character of welfare service. The argument between the apolitical technician and the policy-minded "program professional" is an old one and is carried on wherever staff experts who have knowledge work in large organizations under other people who have power. (410) It seems to us that whatever way social work decides to play the game, it is faced with the fundamental problem of its knowledge-skill base. Whether the social worker wants to abandon his social conscience and concentrate on the case, or rise above the case to shape the course of welfare events, he must look sharp to his scientific support. If he wants to be a technician he must get technical. If he wants to become a planner, he has to demonstrate a superior competence here.

In our opinion, this requires a long-range effort to build more solid bridges to the social sciences—with plenty of traffic across. But a flow of traffic need not involve the risk and confusion of a traffic jam. There is danger in a quick professionalization of social work (and the accompanying preoccupation with the goal of an exclusive, science-based competence). The danger is *not* that it takes the steam out of reform; *not* that it promotes a trained incapacity to see how the social structure affects the problems of the welfare practitioner and client; and surely *not* that its rewards paralyze the will to press for change. The danger lies instead in the underdeveloped state of the social and psychological sciences and the tendency to oversell their immediate practical implications. Public relations experts, family relations experts, personnel psychologists, advertising men—all risk a premature packaging of limited intellectual perspectives in the hasty drive for professional status, a job territory, and expanded business. Social work, too, is exposed to the temptation to crystallize its organization around unnecessarily restricted and still-loose bodies of thought.

Social work can do much, we think, to avoid the enthusiastic pushing of a tenuous package. It can cultivate closer ties with the social sciences, while seeking to understand their uses and limits; set before the student not only the model of the technician who is a skilled caseworker or groupworker, but also the model of the policy-sensitive program professional who is a skilled community organizer and planner; keep under continuing scrutiny the implications of a psychological orientation for technical practice and social policy; expand and define its area of competence so that social administration and policy are embraced as fields of social work training and practice, and so that those "untrained" welfare workers who are now denied status may more readily find their way into the profession; and maintain a general tolerance of the aims and claims of other groups, lay and professional, working for social welfare.

APPENDIX

INDUSTRIALISM, SOCIETY, AND SOCIAL CHANGE: A THEORETICAL POSTSCRIPT

APPENDIX: Industrialism, Society, and Social Change: A Theoretical Postscript

Our discussion of the impact of industrialization on American society and the welfare services has been guided by some implicit assumptions, about which the reader should be informed. These assumptions concern: (1) the features of societies that are "basic"; (2) the role of technology in social change; and (3) the relevance of our analysis to an understanding of industrialization and social welfare in other countries, especially those with less-developed economies.

Basic Features of Societies: Some Conditions for Societal Survival

To characterize a whole society is a large and risky task. To describe the relationships among a husband, wife, and two children one has known intimately for years is difficult enough; to describe the entire web of social relations making up American society is much more difficult. Though social scientists and historians have studied many parts of this society intensively, and have speculated often and imaginatively about its future, our knowledge of it is not firm. Almost all we have said about it, then, should be taken as informed guess, hypothesis, best judgment— given the state of social-science evidence as we see it.

In answering such a simple question as, "What is the Jones family like?" we would probably begin with how many persons make up the family, their ages, their sex (size and characteristics of population). We would concentrate on its major features. We would mention what Mr. Jones does for a living (as a guide to the family's place in the economic system and its position in the community). We might tell who is boss in the family—and in what areas of family living (the allocation of authority). We might say how close-knit and integrated it is (the strength of its solidarity), possibly adding that Mrs. Jones married Mr. Jones for money but Mr. Jones is blinded by his love for his wife (the nature of the bonds—affectional or economic—that hold the group together). Perhaps we would also describe the daily routine of the Jones family—what the children do and are expected to do, what tasks fall to the husband and to the wife (the degree and kind of specialization). We would be interested, too, in how the Joneses are training their children—what they want to make of their children, how "permissive" they are toward them, how many of their prejudices and preferences they pass on to them, and so on (perpetuation of the group via socialization). With a few major characteristics like these we would have a pretty fair picture of the Jones family.

All social life arises from men's attempts to solve problems they share. Our picture of the Jones family is fairly well-rounded because the features described reflect universal problems of group life. These problems—indeed, these necessary conditions for societal survival—include: (1) population; (2) specialization and stratification (including the division of labor, the allocation of authority, and assignment of persons to child-rearing); (3) solidarity or "integration"; (4) perpetuation of the social system (which involves the socialization of new members, a system of communication, and so on). (Cf. 78; 1; 242.)

Our selection of aspects of American society for discussion in this book, especially in Chapters III to V, was guided by these important and universal problems. Here is a brief explanation of why they may be called necessary conditions for societal survival.

First, a society has to have *population*. It must provide its members food, protect them against injury, and assure the reproduction of new organisms. This means some patterning of sex relationships to ensure motivation and opportunity for a sufficient rate of reproduction. Without people, there is no society.

Second, a society must have some system of *role differentiation and role assignment*. It has to get essential work done, so it assigns different activities to different individuals. For instance: all societies face the universal problems of: (1) *scarcity* (our wants exceed the available supply of goods and services; everything does not grow on trees to be picked off at will); (2) *order* (the war of all against all must be held in check); and (3) *child care* (the infant everywhere is born helpless).

To cope with scarcity all societies develop an *economic* role system—some accepted division of labor and some allocation of property rights to assure the production and distribution of things that have value. Different tasks are specified and assigned to individuals trained and motivated to carry them out.

To cope with the problem of keeping order, every society develops a *political* role system—an organized allocation of control over the use of violence within and from outside the society (a police force and an army, for example). Different individuals are given different amounts of authority. (198)

Similarly, every society must make some reliable provision for child-rearing and assigns these essential tasks to specific persons or groups. It may be the biological mother or father, or neither. But it has to be someone. Differences in *age* and *sex*, which are a basis for dividing up work in all societies, are drawn upon here, too.

In short: everyone cannot do everything. Neither can everyone do nothing. No specialization, no activity—no society.

The necessity of specialization—economic, political, age, and sex—leads to another universal feature of societies: *social stratification*. People classify one another in categories and place these categories above or below one another on a scale of superiority and inferiority. The criteria of ranking vary; anything valued and unequally distributed may suffice: wealth, power, magic, women, and so on. This type of role differentiation is called stratification.

Despite the recurrent dream of absolute equality—for example, the "classless society"—every society past or present has had some system of stratification. Distinctions are made. Some positions are honored, others not. Some are accorded more authority than others. Who is and who is not honored—the priest, the workman, the scholar, or the warrior; the distance between top and bottom positions—the difference between rich and poor, leader and rank-and-file; these and other features of stratification systems vary from place to place, time to time. But power and prestige differences do appear everywhere.[1]

"Solidarity," "cohesion," or "social integration"—these are some of the words used to describe a third major condition for survival. The degree to which the parts of a society hold together —the number, kinds, strength, and stability of bonds uniting its members—is called its *integration*. To say that a society must have integration to survive is to say that its members must be motivated to: (1) tolerate one another, lest they destroy one another; and (2) resist outsiders, lest they invite extinction (note the Tasmanians) or absorption (note the Inca of Peru); (3) plan their conduct to fit in at least roughly with what others expect. The sources of integration are many: economic interdependence; a shared set of values or goals (not unanimity, but some broad consensus as for instance there is consensus in America that the nation-state is a proper object of allegiance); some rules governing the means for achieving the goals (for example, prohibition of murder as a means of eliminating occupational competitors); some common definitions of what is real in situations all share (for example, a mile is so long, the President is elected by voters going to the ballot box every four years).

Finally, societies have to have some way to continue their systems of social relations beyond the life span of one individual or one generation. To survive they must *perpetuate the social system*, pass on their ways of life to new members. This involves: (1) some system of communication and socialization as well as (2)

[1] Among the reasons are these: (1) Any society has to distribute people among its different positions and induce them to perform essential duties. (2) Every society has a hierarchy of values based on the fact of scarcity. (3) Differences in the distribution of these values (e.g., income, power, etc.) move people to go after positions and perform once they are in them. (4) So long as the family has anything to do with bringing up children and so long as some of the behavior and possessions unequally valued and unequally distributed are learned or acquired in the family, then some inequality will be perpetuated. (5) The different criteria of stratification are interrelated—e.g., power differences among men are universal, those with power can use it to obtain for themselves and their kin those things which are valued (a man of power can use connections to get his son a good job, a man of wealth can buy his son a good education). (Cf. 83.)

effective control of disruptive behavior—techniques for handling the inadequately socialized, the deviants (this does not exclude the deliberate toleration of deviants). In the absence of shared linguistic symbols, a society cannot maintain the common norms or the sanctions (rewards and penalties) that sustain cooperation and accommodation. Moreover, without language few skills could be transmitted to the next generation. Everywhere the infant must learn the language, as well as the attitudes appropriate to the goals and means and definition of reality of the larger society; and the adult must learn the behavior appropriate to his age, sex, occupational, and other specialized roles.

Urban-industrial America, like all other societies, faces the universal problems of specialization, stratification, integration, and socialization. In analyzing the impact of technology (or anything else) on a society it is useful to focus on each of these main problems and ask, "How does technology affect the way the society meets that problem?"

Technology and Social Change

The invention of the printing press, it is said, is the basic cause of modern democracy. "The printing press has made popular education possible. . . . General education . . . has made plausible the contention that all adults should have a vote. . . ." (302: p. 165)

The invention of contraceptives, the steam engine, and steel, it is said, are the basic causes of the downward trend in the age of marriage in the United States since 1890. Contraceptives made possible early marriage without the burden of children; the steam engine and steel made railroads and factories possible, which brought about the growth of cities and a rise in income, which in turn made marriage easier, diffused knowledge, reduced the hold of religious rules of conduct and thereby increased the willingness to use contraceptives. (274: pp. 89 94)

The steam engine is invoked to explain in the same way the weakening of kinship ties, the declining authority of the man in the family, the transfer of functions away from the family, the increased divorce rate, the rise of commercial recreation, and more. (274: pp. 89–92)[1]

And so the argument goes, until technology (or the machine as a symbol of modern technology) would seem to be the master of man's destiny—all-embracing, self-inventing, self-accepting, self-perpetuating, self-changing, *the* cause of social change (or in more moderate formulations the most important cause).

The technological determinist argument is sometimes stated like this. Culture has two parts: (1) material culture (machines, tools, artifacts) and (2) nonmaterial or adaptive culture (ideas, knowledge, values, institutions). "Social maladjustments" stem from the fact that changes in material culture precede changes in nonmaterial culture—material culture changes at an exponential (ever-accelerating) rate while nonmaterial culture lags behind. The mores and folkways and institutions fail to adapt to the ever-increasing pile of new inventions. (272: Part IV) Cultural lag, the argument holds, is due to many factors, but it is especially due to vested interests—the interests of those who stand to lose their preferred position by use of the new inventions. (273: pp. 525 ff.)

There is a better way to put the matter. Culture is a useful abstraction, not a pile of physical objects. It is a system of beliefs ("the world is round"), values ("equality of opportunity is morally right"), and expressive symbols (art forms) which governs man's relations to his fellow man and to his environment. It is passed on to new generations via communication. It consists of

---

[1] Or if you prefer examples of the impact of technology on primitive societies: A change in technique of rice cultivation was introduced among the Tanala, a stable primitive tribe with a subsistence economy and communal ownership of land. Exhaustion of jungle compelled them to give up the dry-rice for the wet-rice method. There followed a mad scramble for the few fertile valleys. According to Kardiner, this shift in method of cultivation caused dramatic social changes: (1) the extended family system was broken up (irrigated rice fields could be tended by one family, so why share the product?); (2) property became important as a measure of prestige and land could now be inherited; (3) tribal democracy was replaced by a king with absolute power and a feudal hierarchy with permanent land tenure; (4) slaves—of no economic importance in the old setup—became assets both as workers and as sources of revenue by ransom; (5) the new fears of poverty and oppression stimulated the hoarding of wealth, an increase of crime and homosexuality, and the introduction of concepts denoting "evil spirits." (172: pp. 418 ff.)

ideas shared by a group concerning the ways to act, think, and feel.[1]

"Technology" is that segment of culture which represents the application of knowledge of nature to empirical ends, to ends which can be attained in this world—for example, getting work done, lifting a weight, and the like. Technology is "instrumental" —it can be shown to be a means directly connected to an empirical goal. The power-shovel moves dirt, the atomic bomb destroys life around it, the metronome trains the sense of rhythm, the mastery of press, radio, and TV helps to win an election, the pacifier permits the mother to offer oral gratification to the infant, the prayer wheel enables Buddhist monks to increase the number of prayers—these are examples of the use of technology in the economic, military, artistic, political, kinship, and religious spheres (or role systems).

In analyzing the entire history of human societies a good procedure is first to assume that changes in technology are more basic, more causal, than other social changes, and then to look for exceptions and specify conditions. Changes in men's ways of getting work done do often require or make possible changes in other segments of their culture. For example, in American society it turned out that the transportation system changed more rapidly, via the invention of the automobile, than did our sex mores. And there is little doubt that this quick adoption of the automobile in time helped to take courtship out of the front parlor and put it on the road. Here industrial technology determined an aspect of the social order. (See also our discussion in Part I of the impact of industrialism on specialization, stratification, and mobility.) The reverse is also true, however: the customs of people in one sphere of life often limit and shape the technology

[1] Culture consists of ideas governing social interaction as well as interaction with the physical environment. "Social structure" or "social system" or "social order," as we have used these terms, designates a segment of culture: those ideas which define the rights and obligations comprising the positions people occupy in groups—i.e., those norms and values which define role systems. Thus, "a mother should be nurturant toward her children" is an idea which specifies certain obligations for the position of mother in the kinship system—which, in turn, implies the right of the child to physical and emotional support. When we have spelled out all such rights and duties for the interrelated positions in all of the spheres of group life, we have described a "society."

they use. For instance, it seems likely that the increased importance of the nuclear family is a "cause" for the adoption of the
six-passenger car rather than some other kind of car. The question for analysis is, "Under what conditions will technological
change be a cause of other social changes and under what conditions will it be an effect?" No precise answer is available from
present knowledge. A line of approach, however, is suggested by
many students of social change. (See especially the works of
Kingsley Davis, Gerth and Mills, and W. F. Cottrell cited in the
bibliography.)

First, for technological change to be the basic cause of changes
in the social order, there must be a strong commitment to the
value of economic progress, and to the belief that the adoption of
technological change is the best way to get it. In a society which
places highest priority on technical efficiency—the maximum
contribution of rational, acquisitive individuals to production—
technological changes will often be basic, because such innovations will be adopted quickly and, should other features of the
culture prove incompatible (for example, an extended family
system), it is they and not the technology that will be adapted
and made to fit. American society, at least in the past, has placed
high priority on such values and beliefs (see Chapter II). It has
shown a willingness to adapt its social life to the demands of high-
energy technology.

Second, even where high priority is given to efficiency and
economic progress, both the adoption and the direction of development of technology is often determined by other beliefs and
values. This is especially true in the short run and may be illustrated by America's emphasis on military technology since 1941.
In large measure, this emphasis is due to the high priority which
we place upon the value of national security (which involves the
sentiment that the nation-state is a proper object of final allegiance), and our belief that the development of nuclear weapons
is the main way to secure it. Here, technology is less cause than
effect. To implement our values and beliefs we appropriate many
billions for defense. We allocate these billions to certain industries, research establishments, and military installations. These

decisions have great impact on: (1) the internal organization of science (for example, which specialties will receive greatest rewards, which universities and research organizations will flourish, which research problems will attract the best talent, and so on); (2) the kinds of technology developed; (3) the timing of its adoption.[1]

Suppose that saving the aged from degenerative diseases and improving their living conditions had taken clear-cut priority over national defense in the last two decades. The possible effects on technology are many: the prestige, power, and income of the biological and social sciences relative to the physical sciences would have increased; the applications of their findings in the field of medicine might change the age distribution of the population, which in turn would affect income distribution, patterns of recreation and family life, the demand for housing, and so on. Applications to city planning could have repercussions in the styles and location of residential building; consequent changes in the technology of the building industry might be revolutionary (assuming billions in resources went to implement these values regarding the care of the aged).

Deciding how much change in the social structure can be explained by technology and how much by values is a matter of how specific one's predictions must be, and how long the time span.

At lower levels of technology, and for the very long run, some general predictions may be made on the premise that changes in technology determine changes in the social order more than the reverse. For instance, it is likely that among a set of societies competing for scarce resources, one will be moved to adopt a more efficient technology (with its repercussions in social organization and culture), and the others will tend either to follow, or become absorbed or destroyed. The history of primitive societies as reported by anthropologists Kroeber, C. D. Forde, and others, offers impressive confirmation. Food gatherers in competition with more efficient food raisers have typically lost their inde-

---

[1] The production of underwater vessels, large jet planes, and atomic energy plants was surely hastened by our values and beliefs regarding national security.

pendence—or have been forced to an even more precarious existence in areas where food raising is impossible. That this makes a difference in social organization and culture can be seen from these examples. In order to survive, food gatherers must move often to new sources of supply. Given primitive transportation methods, their tools and housing must be light and simple. Size of population is severely limited by limited energy resources. Everyone spends much time gathering food; division of labor is therefore simple. Not much energy is left for the support of priests, government functionaries, or internal or external warfare —so religious, political, and military organization is simple. And so on. Technology as a crucial limiting factor is plain.

With higher levels of surplus energy, however, the limits of existing technology are less fateful, cultural variation greater, and predictions of the consequences of technological change less specific. We can say, for instance, that advancing industrialism imposes an increased emphasis on the immediate family (see Chapter III). But technological determinism will not explain differences in child-training among German and American fathers; the accent on private vs. public welfare services in the United States; the greater equalitarian tendencies of American culture as compared with that of Britain, or Britain's stronger tradition of civil liberties; the appearance at similar levels of economic development of revolutionary syndicalism among Italian laborers, parliamentary socialism in Britain, and "business" unions in America. In short, many of the most important variations we see before us, for 50 to 100 years of the recent past, demand that we take account of values and beliefs as well as technology.

It is easy to overlook the interdependence of values and technology in dealing with short-run (let us say three-generation) social change in modern society. Social change, while it is sometimes fast and sometimes slow, tends to be cumulative—that is, change on one front brings change on another. This is because: (1) social change consists of changes in role systems (military, economic, political, kinship, religious); (2) these systems are interdependent. Now in modern societies, the main innovators of technology—those who develop and adopt new technology quickly and on a large scale—are men at the top in the military and economic spheres. These men happen also to occupy very powerful positions in society—which means that their technological innovations will, in so far as power can be effective, and so long as their values do not change greatly from what they are, be given priority over the demands of other segments of the culture. (See Chapter X. Cf. 121: pp. 388 ff.) If, for instance, it can be demonstrated that military tests of atomic weapons in Nevada represent a threat to the health of a few thousand unborn babies, and scientists and church leaders clamor for cessation of tests, the more powerful military and industrial leaders who are charged with developing weapons for national defense will override objections to the tests—in the name of the overriding value of national security. Since these men of power are also in a position to articulate and reaffirm the value of national defense and the belief in nuclear deterrence, it is unlikely that the assertion by less powerful men of alternative beliefs and values will shift the technological effort. Thus do the beliefs and values of powerful military and economic elites committed to technological progress overcome those of less powerful groups—thereby making it appear that technology is the driving force in history.

The example of nuclear technology is instructive—offering caution to both the "technological determinist" and the "ideological determinist" views of social change. It suggests that:

(1) *The kind of technology developed and the speed of its adoption are affected by variations in the beliefs and values of groups having unequal power and unequal access to the means of communication.* Note the importance for the atomic program of the ideas of military and industrial leaders about economic progress and national security.

(2) *Men's beliefs and values are in the long run affected by their knowledge of the physical possibilities before them.* Nationalism as a value would be unlikely in the absence of the centralized military force made possible by high-energy technology. Note, too, that the invention of atomic weapons makes it probable that any elite that engaged in general war would find itself weaker at the end than it was before. Without anyone intending it, the development of this technology may either induce regression toward a pre-modern society (which might well follow a general atomic war), or create

the conditions for regional, if not worldwide, values and forms of organization (which might flow from widespread knowledge of the consequences of atomic war). (Cf. 66.)

In short, the relation between technology and the social order is reciprocal. On the one hand, man's values and beliefs determine the technology he develops and uses; on the other hand, technology sets limits to what man *can* do and influences what he *will* do in all spheres of life.[1] These limits are especially important in determining which societies survive in the very long run.

Limited Application to Other Societies

There is a tendency for *modern* industry and its major social effects to come wrapped in an all-or-nothing package. (254; 206; 154) Part I of this book has spelled out this thesis. But there are many things men do to slice up the package and take it piece by piece. And there is nothing to prevent them from rejecting the whole thing on the grounds that it costs too much. Thus, even though we have stressed the importance of the technological and economic contents of the package and have assumed the interrelations of its parts, it is with the understanding that there are many variations in the way the package is opened and consumed.

Industrialism first took firm root in late eighteenth and early nineteenth century England. America followed in the last half of the nineteenth century. Since England and America are the targets of much of the social criticism mentioned in Chapter I, it makes sense to ask whether their experience was typical of later industrialization in other countries or of present industrialization in the underdeveloped areas.

[1] Fred Cottrell makes this point in contrasting industrial and nonindustrial societies: ". . . it will be precisely in those societies where increasing amounts of energy are being used that groups favoring values which require more energy for their achievement [e.g., economic growth, military strength, possession of material goods] will be able to promote those values. For example, [industrial societies] can utilize advertising, propaganda, and education to promote the use of . . . newspapers, magazines, railways, airplanes, television, and radio. The use of these will in turn sustain increased demand for them and for goods whose use can be promoted by them." By the same token, in nonindustrial societies values which do not depend upon industrialization are more likely to survive because they do not have to compete with mass campaigns to promote material possessions as evidence of worth. (66: p. 299)

Even if the nature of past British and American experience with industrialization were *not* in dispute, in many respects it could not serve as a guide to other peoples today. Industrialization in both countries depended on conditions which did not recur in places later following the British lead.

First, as we just indicated in our discussion of technology, men's values shape their approach to the problems posed by industrialism. Human societies have displayed great variation in their priority lists—some emphasizing commerce, others military expansion, or religion or something else. Economic development is not always at the top of these lists. As Wilbert Moore suggests, "For the world to beat a path to the door of the inventor of a superior mousetrap, it must first be interested in catching mice." (256: p. 182) Few countries have attached as much importance to rational economic activity and the accumulation of practical knowledge as did England and America in the nineteenth century.

Aside from variations in value systems, there are many variations in the economic, demographic, and technological factors which promote or impede the pace of industrialization and shape its social impact.

For instance, the latecomers to industrialization are in a good position to avoid some of the early British experience. They are less dependent upon local innovations; they can and do import some technical skills and borrow from a great range of modern technology that portion that fits their needs.[1] They can and do

---

[1] It is not necessary to import a bulldozer into a local economy affording no alternative employment to the farmers it will displace, who cannot afford its upkeep in the first place; nor is it necessary to demonstrate agricultural machinery to farmers too poor to purchase it for farms too small for its effective use. Maybe an improved hoe or plough will suffice at first. (230: p. 242. Cf. 66: pp. 135, 142 ff.) These are lessons that all parties to technical assistance programs are learning to the advantage of all. That men need not be slaves to any particular technology is underscored by the choices a developing country faces between its present technological level and more efficient ones. There are many roads to increased production: "In Indian agriculture, for example, current average farm size and labor intensity in agriculture can be continued, and different fertilizers used. Or, several individual farms may be consolidated and operated with more complex machinery on a cooperative basis. Or, the land may be transformed into large estates, each operated with the most modern machinery, again collectively or as a state enterprise." (58: p. 22) Each road requires different changes in social relations, property institutions and the like. The choice is always there.

usher in economic change, largely under the control of central
governments with comprehensive development plans which seek
to anticipate social problems created by industry; for example,
housing may be built by an expanding industry as part of the
plan. They can and do nurture infant industries to suit their purposes and the possibilities of world trade. They can and do locate
plants to minimize local community disruption (230: pp. 236 ff.).
And the availability of cheap power, a prerequisite to industrialization, gives these latecomers quite an advantage over
nineteenth century British industrialists. (42: p. 125)

Conversely, some of the barriers to rapid industrialization may
be greater than those Britain and America faced. On the economic side, the underdeveloped areas today cannot obtain large
sums of foreign capital with the ease the United States did in the
nineteenth century. Nor can they so easily get food by conquest
while they industrialize—in the manner of the colonial powers of
yesteryear. On the social side, in southern and eastern Europe
and in most of China, the rule of equal inheritance of farm
property by all heirs appears to have lessened the willingness of
peasants to seek other avenues of employment. Contrast Britain
in the past (or French Canada today): there, the "push" out of
agriculture into urban-industrial employment was hastened by
customs of inheritance providing for succession by a single heir;
the other heirs *had* to move out. (256: p. 51) Or, on the demographic side: When England's death rate plunged downward and
the birth rate remained high, widespread starvation was not the
result; but as industrialization brings lower infant mortality and
somewhat longer life to the dense populations of Asia, the gain in
wealth is continuously diverted to the support of a mushrooming
population at the same low living standards. The latecomers to
industrialization cannot get rid of surplus population by emigra-
tion as England once did.

A final caution: industrialization sets in motion a process of
social and cultural change that goes on (1) continually and (2)
unevenly—worldwide as well as within the United States. One
cannot help being struck by the very unequal rates of change between northwestern and southeastern Europe, between the Far

East and North America, between regions within the United States (where much of the Southeast is still an underdeveloped area). We do not know why industrialization began earlier and progressed faster in Japan, with its limited resources, than in China, with its superior resources. And, though our knowledge of western societies is more extensive, we cannot say with certainty why France and Italy, despite an earlier start, are so little industrialized compared to England and Germany. For some of the best attempts to explain these variations without, however, abandoning the search for the general process, see the work of W. E. Moore (256); M. J. Levy (206); W. Arthur Lewis (209); D. S. Landes (197); and W. F. Cottrell (66).

Bibliography

1. ABERLE, D. F., A. K. COHEN, A. K. DAVIS, M. J. LEVY, JR., and F. X. SUTTON, "The Functional Prerequisites of a Society," *Ethics: An International Journal of Social, Political, and Legal Philosophy*, vol. 60, January, 1950, pp. 100–111.

2. ADDAMS, JANE, *Twenty Years at Hull-House*. Macmillan Co., New York, 1910.

3. ALEXANDER, FRANZ, and HUGO STAUB, *The Criminal, the Judge, and the Public:* A Psychological Analysis, translated by Gregory Zilboorg. Macmillan Co., New York, 1931.

4. ALINSKY, SAUL D., *Reveille for Radicals*. University of Chicago Press, Chicago, 1946.

5. ALLPORT, GORDON W., "The Limits of Social Service" in *National Policies for Education, Health and Social Services*, edited by James E. Russell. Doubleday and Co., New York, 1955, pp. 194–214.

6. ALTMEYER, ARTHUR J., "Training for International Responsibilities" in *America's Role in International Social Welfare*, by Alva Myrdal, Arthur J. Altmeyer, and Dean Rusk. Columbia University Press, New York, 1955, pp. 57–91.

7. ANDREWS, F. EMERSON, *Philanthropic Foundations*. Russell Sage Foundation, New York, 1956.

8. ANDREWS, F. EMERSON, *Philanthropic Giving*. Russell Sage Foundation, New York, 1950.

9. ANGELL, ROBERT C., *The Family Encounters the Depression*. Charles Scribner's Sons, New York, 1936.

10. ANGELL, ROBERT C., "The Moral Integration of American Cities," *American Journal of Sociology*, vol. 57, July, 1951, part 2, pp. 1–140.

11. AXELROD, MORRIS, *A Study of Formal and Informal Group Participation in a Large Urban Community*. Ph.D. thesis, University of Michigan, Ann Arbor, 1953.

353

12. Axelrod, Morris, "Urban Structure and Social Participation," *American Sociological Review*, vol. 21, February, 1956, pp. 13–18.

13. Bailey, Stephen K., *Congress Makes a Law:* The Story Behind the Employment Act of 1946. Columbia University Press, New York, 1950.

14. Bailyn, Bernard, *The New England Merchants in the Seventeenth Century.* Harvard University Press, Cambridge, 1955. See also review of this book by Seymour M. Lipset in *American Sociological Review*, vol. 21, October, 1956, pp. 660–661.

15. Bakke, Edward W., *The Unemployed Man.* E. P. Dutton and Co., New York, 1934.

16. Baldwin, George B., and George P. Schultz, "Automation: A New Dimension to Old Problems," *Industrial Relations Research Association Proceedings*, 1954. University of Wisconsin Press, Madison, 1955, pp. 114–128.

17. Barron, Milton L., *The Juvenile in Delinquent Society.* Alfred A. Knopf, New York, 1954.

18. Bauer, Raymond A., Alex Inkeles, and Clyde Kluckhohn, *How the Soviet System Works.* Harvard University Press, Cambridge, 1956.

19. Beard, Charles A., and Mary R. Beard, *The Rise of American Civilization.* New ed. rev. and enl., 2 vols. in one. Macmillan Co., New York, 1933.

20. Becker, Charlotte, *Styles of Life of Clients of a Family Service.* Master's thesis, Wayne State University, Detroit, 1955.

21. Becker, Howard S., and James Carper, "The Elements of Identification with an Occupation," *American Sociological Review*, vol. 21, June, 1956, pp. 341–348.

22. Bell, Daniel, "The Great Back-to-Work Movement," *Fortune*, vol. 54, July, 1956, pp. 90–93, 168–172.

23. Bendix, Reinhard, *Work and Authority in Industry:* Ideologies of Management in the Course of Industrialization. John Wiley and Sons, New York, 1956.

24. Bendix, Reinhard, Seymour M. Lipset, and F. Theodore Malm, *Social Origins and Occupational Career Patterns.* Institute of Industrial Relations, University of California, Berkeley, 1954. Reprint 53. See also *Industrial and Labor Relations Review*, vol. 7, January, 1954, pp. 246–261.

25. BERELSON, BERNARD R., and MORRIS JANOWITZ, editors, *Reader in Public Opinion and Communication*. 2d ed. Free Press, Glencoe, Ill., 1953.

26. BERGER, MORROE, *Equality by Statute:* Legal Controls Over Group Discrimination. Columbia University Press, New York, 1952.

27. BIENSTOCK, GREGORY, SOLOMON M. SCHWARZ, and AARON YUGOW, *Management in Russian Industry and Agriculture*, edited by Arthur Feiler and Jacob Marschak. Cornell University Press, Ithaca, N. Y., 1944.

28. BLAU, PETER M., *Bureaucracy in Modern Society*. Random House, New York, 1956.

29. BLAU, PETER M., *The Dynamics of Bureaucracy*. University of Chicago Press, Chicago, 1955.

30. BLOCH, HERBERT A., and FRANK T. FLYNN, *Delinquency:* The Juvenile Offender in America Today. Random House, New York, 1956.

31. BLOOD, ROBERT O., JR., *Anticipating Your Marriage*. Free Press, Glencoe, Ill., 1955.

32. BLUMER, HERBERT, "Collective Behavior" in *New Outline of the Principles of Sociology*, edited by Alfred M. Lee. Barnes and Noble, New York, 1946, pp. 167–222.

33. BOEKE, JULIUS H., *The Structure of Netherlands Indian Economy*. Institute of Pacific Relations, New York, 1942.

34. BOGUE, DONALD J., "The Geography of Recent Population Trends in the United States," *Annals of the Association of American Geographers*, vol. 44, June, 1954, pp. 124–134.

35. BOGUE, DONALD J., *Population Growth in Standard Metropolitan Areas, 1900–1950*. Housing and Home Finance Agency, Office of the Administrator, Division of Housing Research, Washington, 1953.

36. BOGUE, DONALD J., "Residential Mobility and Migration of Workers" in *Manpower in the United States*, edited by William Haber and others. Harper and Bros., New York, 1954, pp. 143–153.

37. BOGUE, DONALD J., editor, *Needed Urban and Metropolitan Research*. Scripps Foundation for Research in Population Problems, Miami University, Oxford, Ohio, 1953.

38. BOND, FLOYD A., and associates, *Our Needy Aged:* A California Study of a National Problem. Henry Holt and Co., New York, 1954.

39. Bowman, Paul H., and others, *Mobilizing Community Resources for Youth:* Identification and Treatment of Maladjusted, Delinquent, and Gifted Children. Youth Development Series, no. 3, edited by Robert J. Havighurst. Supplementary Educational Monographs, no. 85. University of Chicago Press, Chicago, 1956.

40. Brooks, Robert R. R., *As Steel Goes . . . :* Unionism in a Basic Industry. Yale University Press, New Haven, 1940.

41. Bruno, Frank J., *Trends in Social Work as Reflected in the Proceedings of the National Conference of Social Work, 1874–1946.* Columbia University Press, New York, 1948.

42. Buchanan, Norman S., and Howard S. Ellis, *Approaches to Economic Development.* Twentieth Century Fund, New York, 1955.

43. Buell, Bradley, and others, *Community Planning for Human Services.* Columbia University Press, New York, 1952.

44. Burgess, Ernest W., and Harvey J. Locke, *The Family:* From Institution to Companionship. American Book Co., New York, 1945.

45. Burgess, Ernest W., Joseph D. Lohman, and Clifford R. Shaw, "The Chicago Area Project," *Yearbook of the National Probation Association,* 1937, pp. 8–28.

46. Burns, Eveline M., *The American Social Security System.* Houghton Mifflin Co., Boston, 1949.

47. Burns, Eveline M., "The Financing of Social Welfare" in *New Directions in Social Work,* edited by Cora Kasius. Harper and Bros., New York, 1954, pp. 131–158.

48. Burns, Eveline M., *Social Security and Public Policy.* McGraw-Hill Book Co., New York, 1956.

49. Canadian Department of National Health and Welfare, Research Division, *Social Security Expenditures in Australia. . . . , 1949–50:* A Comparative Study. Ottawa, 1954. Cited in Eveline M. Burns, *Social Security and Public Policy,* p. 5.

50. Caplow, Theodore, *The Sociology of Work.* University of Minnesota Press, Minneapolis, 1954.

51. Caplow, Theodore, "A Theory of Coalitions in the Triad," *American Sociological Review,* vol. 21, August, 1956, pp. 489–493.

52. Carr, Lowell J., and James E. Stermer, *Willow Run:* A Study of Industrialization and Cultural Inadequacy. Harper and Bros., New York, 1952.

53. CARR, ROBERT K., and others, *American Democracy in Theory and Practice:* The National Government. Rev. ed. Rinehart and Co., New York, 1955.

54. CARR, ROBERT K., and others, "Civil Rights in America," *Annals of the American Academy of Political and Social Science*, vol. 275, May, 1951, pp. 1–238.

55. CARRIER, FAITH R., *The Relationship Between the Social Sciences and Social Work, from 1920–1952.* Master's thesis, University of Michigan, Ann Arbor, 1953.

56. CASSIDY, HARRY M., *Social Security and Reconstruction in Canada.* Bruce Humphries, Inc., Boston, 1943.

57. CENTERS, RICHARD, *The Psychology of Social Classes:* A Study of Class Consciousness. Princeton University Press, Princeton, 1949.

58. CHICAGO UNIVERSITY RESEARCH CENTER in Economic Development and Cultural Change, *A Report to the Committee on Economic and Cultural Change.* University of Chicago, Chicago, undated. Hectographed.

59. CHINOY, ELY, *Automobile Workers and the American Dream.* Doubleday and Co., New York, 1955.

60. CHINOY, ELY, "The Tradition of Opportunity and the Aspirations of Automobile Workers," *American Journal of Sociology*, vol. 57, March, 1952, pp. 453–459.

61. CLARK, COLIN, *Conditions of Economic Progress.* 2d ed. Macmillan Co., London, 1951.

62. COHEN, ALBERT K., *Delinquent Boys:* The Culture of the Gang. Free Press, Glencoe, Ill., 1955.

63. COMMUNITY CHESTS AND COUNCILS OF AMERICA, *Boards and Board Members of Health and Welfare Agencies.* Bulletin 179. New York, 1955.

64. COMMUNITY CHESTS AND COUNCILS OF AMERICA, *Budgeting for 1955.* Bulletin 181. New York, undated.

65. CONRAD, ALFRED H., "Redistribution Through Government Budgets in the United States, 1950" in *Income Redistribution and Social Policy*, edited by Alan T. Peacock. Jonathan Cape, London, 1954, pp. 178–267.

66. COTTRELL, WILLIAM FREDERICK, *Energy and Society:* The Relation Between Energy, Social Change, and Economic Development. McGraw-Hill Book Co., New York, 1955.

67. CRAWFORD, PAUL L., DANIEL I. MALAMUD, and JAMES R. DUMP-SON, *Working with Teen-Age Gangs:* A Report on the Central Harlem Street Clubs Project. Welfare Council of New York City, New York, 1950.

68. CREAMER, DANIEL B., and GLADYS V. SWACKHAMER, *Cigar Makers, After the Lay-off:* A Case Study of Effects of Mechanization on Employment of Hand Cigar Makers. Works Progress Administration, National Research Project L-1, Philadelphia, 1937, chap. 4.

69. CREECH, MARGARET, *Three Centuries of Poor Law Administration* (Rhode Island). University of Chicago Press, Chicago, 1936.

70. CUNNINGHAM, JAMES M., HESTER H. WESTERMAN, and JOSEPH FISCHHOFF, "A Follow-up Study of Patients Seen in a Psychiatric Clinic for Children," *American Journal of Orthopsychiatry*, vol. 26, July, 1956, pp. 602–612.

71. DAHL, ROBERT A., and CHARLES E. LINDBLOM, *Politics, Economics, and Welfare.* Harper and Bros., New York, 1953.

72. DALLIN, DAVID J., and BORIS I. NICOLAEVSKY, *Forced Labor in Soviet Russia.* Yale University Press, New Haven, 1947.

73. DAVID, HENRY, *The History of the Haymarket Affair.* Farrar and Rinehart, New York, 1936.

74. DAVIDSON, GEORGE F., "Responsibility to Meet Social Service Needs" in *National Policies for Education, Health and Social Services*, edited by James E. Russell. Doubleday and Co., New York, 1955, pp. 151–172.

75. DAVIS, ALLISON, BURLEIGH B. GARDNER, and MARY R. GARDNER, *Deep South.* University of Chicago Press, Chicago, 1941.

76. DAVIS, ALLISON, and ROBERT J. HAVIGHURST, *Father of the Man.* Houghton Mifflin Co., Boston, 1947.

77. DAVIS, KINGSLEY, "Adolescence and the Social Structure," *Annals of the American Academy of Political and Social Science*, vol. 236, November, 1944, pp. 8–16.

78. DAVIS, KINGSLEY, *Human Society.* Macmillan Co., New York, 1949.

79. DAVIS, KINGSLEY, "Jealousy and Sexual Property," *Social Forces*, vol. 14, March, 1936, pp. 395–405.

80. DAVIS, KINGSLEY, "Mental Hygiene and the Class Structure," in *Mental Health and Mental Disorder:* A Sociological Approach, edited by Arnold M. Rose. W. W. Norton and Co., New York, 1955, pp. 578–598.

81. DAVIS, KINGSLEY, "Small Families Are Still the Fashion," *New York Times Magazine*, July 11, 1954, pp. 17, 35.

82. DAVIS, KINGSLEY, "The Sociology of Parent-Youth Conflict," *American Sociological Review*, vol. 5, August, 1940, pp. 523–535.

83. DAVIS, KINGSLEY, and WILBERT E. MOORE, "Some Principles of Stratification," *American Sociological Review*, vol. 10, April, 1945, pp. 242–249.

84. DAVIS, KINGSLEY, H. C. BREDEMEIER, and MARION J. LEVY, JR., editors, *Modern American Society*. Rinehart and Co., New York, 1949.

85. DENNEY, REUEL, and DAVID RIESMAN, "Leisure in Urbanized America" in *Reader in Urban Sociology*, edited by Paul K. Hatt and Albert J. Reiss, Jr. Free Press, Glencoe, Ill., 1951, pp. 469–480.

86. DETROIT AREA STUDY OF THE UNIVERSITY OF MICHIGAN, *A Social Profile of Detroit, 1953*. Survey Research Center and Department of Sociology, University of Michigan, Ann Arbor, 1953.

87. DEVINE, EDWARD T., *The Spirit of Social Work*. Charities Publication Committee, New York, 1911.

88. DEVINE, EDWARD T., and LILIAN BRANDT, *American Social Work in the Twentieth Century*. Frontier Press, New York, 1921.

89. DEWHURST, J. FREDERIC, and others, *America's Needs and Resources*. Twentieth Century Fund, New York, 1955.

90. DICKS, HENRY V., "Observations on Contemporary Russian Behaviour," *Human Relations*, vol. 5, no. 2, 1952, pp. 111–175.

91. DINKEL, ROBERT M., "Attitudes of Children Toward Supporting Aged Parents," *American Sociological Review*, vol. 9, August, 1944, pp. 370–379.

92. DOLLARD, CHARLES, quoted by Nathan E. Cohen in "An Over-all Look," *National Policies for Education, Health and Social Services*, edited by James E. Russell. Doubleday and Co., New York, 1955, pp. 233–234.

93. DOUGLAS, PAUL H., *Real Wages in the United States, 1890–1926*. Houghton Mifflin Co., Boston, 1930.

94. DUBIN, ROBERT, "Industrial Workers' Worlds: A Study of the 'Central Life Interests' of Industrial Workers," *Social Problems*, vol. 3, January, 1956, pp. 131–142.

95. DUBLIN, LOUIS I., and MORTIMER SPIEGELMAN, *The Facts of Life: From Birth to Death*. Macmillan Co., New York, 1951.

96. DURKHEIM, EMILE, *The Division of Labor in Society*, translated by George Simpson. Free Press, Glencoe, Ill., 1947.

97. EELLS, KENNETH W., ALLISON DAVIS, and others. *Intelligence and Cultural Differences:* A Study of Cultural Learning and Problem-Solving. University of Chicago Press, Chicago, 1951.

98. EGGAN, FREDERICK R., *Social Organization of the Western Pueblos.* University of Chicago Press, Chicago, 1950.

99. ELKIN, FREDERICK, and WILLIAM A. WESTLEY, "The Myth of Adolescent Culture," *American Sociological Review*, vol. 20, December, 1955, pp. 680–684.

100. ENGEL, ROBERT L., *A Study of the Representativeness of the Governing Boards of Seventeen Voluntary Health Associations in the Detroit Metropolitan Area.* Master's thesis, Wayne State University, Detroit, 1954.

101. ENGELS, FRIEDRICH, *The Condition of the Working Classes in England in 1844*, translated by Florence K. Wischnewetzky. George Allen and Unwin, London, 1920.

102. FAURI, FEDELE F., "The Shortage of Social Workers: A Challenge to Social Work Education," *Social Work Journal*, vol. 36, April, 1955, pp. 47–51, 61.

103. FAVA, SYLVIA F., "Suburbanism as a Way of Life," *American Sociological Review*, vol. 21, February, 1956, pp. 34–37.

104. FINK, ARTHUR E., *The Field of Social Work.* Henry Holt and Co., New York, 1942.

105. FLINT CITY-FRINGE SURVEY. Social Science Research Project, University of Michigan, Ann Arbor, 1955.

106. FLORIDA DEPARTMENT OF PUBLIC WELFARE, *1955–1957 Legislative Program for the State of Florida Department of Public Welfare.* Tallahassee, 1955.

107. FOLSOM, JOSEPH K., *The Family and Democratic Society.* John Wiley and Sons, New York, 1943.

108. FOOTE, NELSON N., "Changes in American Marriage Patterns and the Role of Women," *Eugenics Quarterly*, vol. 1, December, 1954, pp. 254–260.

109. FOOTE, NELSON N., "Family Living as Play," *Marriage and Family Living*, vol. 17, November, 1955, pp. 296–301.

110. FOOTE, NELSON N., and LEONARD S. COTTRELL, JR., *Identity and Interpersonal Competence:* A New Direction in Family Research. University of Chicago Press, Chicago, 1955.

111. FORD, LYMAN S., *Spending the Social Welfare Dollar*—What Is Expected of the Planner. Address given at the Forty-second Annual Michigan Welfare Conference, November 28, 1956.

112. FRANCIS, ROY G., and ROBERT C. STONE, *Service and Procedure in Bureaucracy*. University of Minnesota Press, Minneapolis, 1956.

113. FRANK, LAWRENCE K., *Society as the Patient:* Essays on Culture and Personality. Rutgers University Press, New Brunswick, N. J., 1948.

114. FREEDMAN, RONALD, *Recent Migration to Chicago*. University of Chicago Press, Chicago, 1950.

115. FREEDMAN, RONALD, DAVID GOLDBERG, and HARRY SHARP, " 'Ideals' About Family Size in the Detroit Metropolitan Area: 1954," *Milbank Memorial Fund Quarterly*, vol. 33, April, 1955, pp. 187-197.

116. FRENCH, DAVID G., "An Estimate of the Number of Persons Who Will Be Graduated from Schools of Social Work in the United States, 1955 to 1965," *Social Work Education*, vol. 3, June, 1955, p. 43.

117. FREIDSON, ELIOT, "Communications Research and the Concept of the Mass," *American Sociological Review*, vol. 18, June, 1953, pp. 313-317.

118. FRIEDLANDER, WALTER A., *Introduction to Social Welfare*. Prentice-Hall, New York, 1955, p. 4.

119. FURMAN, SYLVAN S., editor, *Reaching the Unreached:* Fundamental Aspects of the Program of the New York City Youth Board. New York City Youth Board, 1952. Mimeographed.

120. GALENSON, WALTER, editor, *Comparative Labor Movements*. Prentice-Hall, New York, 1952.

121. GERTH, HANS H., and C. WRIGHT MILLS, *Character and Social Structure*. Harcourt, Brace and Co., New York, 1953.

122. GOLDHAMER, HERBERT, and ANDREW W. MARSHALL, *Psychosis and Civilization*. Free Press, Glencoe, Ill., 1953.

123. GOLDMAN, ERIC F., "Books That Changed America" in *Saturday Review Reader No. 3*. Bantam Books, New York, 1954, pp. 132-140.

124. GOLDSCHMIDT, WALTER R., *As You Sow*. Harcourt, Brace and Co., New York, 1947.

125. GORDON, LUCILLE, *Studies in the Sociology of Social Workers:* Part 3, Social, Economic, and Political Attitudes and Current Thinking in the Field. Master's thesis, Wayne University, Detroit, 1952.

126. GREENWOOD, ERNEST, *Toward a Sociology of Social Work*. Welfare Council of Metropolitan Los Angeles, 1953.

127. GRENVILLE, WILLIAM W., *Substance of the Speech of the Right Hon. Lord Grenville in the House of Lords, November 30, 1819, on the Marquis of Lansdowne's Motion*. . . . John Murray, London, 1820.

128. GROSS, BERTRAM M., *The Legislative Struggle:* A Study in Social Combat. McGraw-Hill Book Co., New York, 1953.

129. HABER, WILLIAM, and others, editors, *Manpower in the United States*. Harper and Bros., New York, 1954.

130. HACKER, LOUIS M., *The Triumph of American Capitalism*. Simon and Schuster, New York, 1940.

131. HALL, JEROME, *Theft, Law and Society*. 2d ed. Bobbs-Merrill Co., Indianapolis, 1952.

132. HALL, MARY P., *The Social Services of Modern England*. Routledge and Kegan Paul, London, 1953.

133. HALLOWELL, A. IRVING, "The Nature and Function of Property as a Social Institution," *Journal of Legal and Political Sociology*, vol. 1, April, 1943, pp. 115–138.

134. HAMILTON, GORDON, "The Role of Social Casework in Social Policy," *Social Casework*, vol. 33, October, 1952, pp. 315–324.

135. HAMMOND, JOHN L., and BARBARA HAMMOND, *The Rise of Modern Industry*. 2d ed. Methuen and Co., London, 1925.

136. HAMMOND, JOHN L., and BARBARA HAMMOND, *The Town Labourer, 1760–1832*. Longmans, Green and Co., London, 1949. Published for the British Publishers Guild, Ltd., Guild Books, no. 410, 2 vols.

137. HANDLIN, OSCAR, *The Uprooted*. Little, Brown and Co., Boston, 1951.

138. HARRIS, SEYMOUR E., "Comments" in *National Policies for Education, Health and Social Services*, edited by James E. Russell. Doubleday and Co., New York, 1955, pp. 359–371.

139. HART, C. W. M., "Industrial Relations Research and Social Theory," *Canadian Journal of Economics and Political Science*, vol. 15, February, 1949, pp. 53–73.

140. HATT, PAUL K., and ALBERT J. REISS, JR., editors, *Reader in Urban Sociology*. Free Press, Glencoe, Ill., 1951.

141. HAVIGHURST, ROBERT J., and RUTH ALBRECHT, *Older People*. Longmans, Green and Co., New York, 1953.

142. HAVIGHURST, ROBERT J., and others, *A Community Youth Development Program*. Supplementary Educational Monographs, no. 75. University of Chicago Press, Chicago, 1952.

143. HAWLEY, AMOS H., *Human Ecology*. Ronald Press Co., New York, 1950.

144. HAYEK, FRIEDRICH A., editor, *Capitalism and the Historians*. University of Chicago Press, Chicago, 1954.

145. HENDERSON, HARRY, "The Mass-Produced Suburbs: Part 1, How People Live in America's Newest Towns," *Harper's Magazine*, vol. 207, November, 1953, pp. 25–32.

146. HERLING, GUSTAV, *A World Apart*, translated by Joseph Marek. William Heinemann, London, 1951.

147. HEWITT, LESTER E., and RICHARD L. JENKINS, *Fundamental Patterns of Maladjustment:* The Dynamics of Their Origin. State of Illinois, Springfield, 1946.

148. HILL, JOHN G., and RALPH ORMSBY, "The Philadelphia Cost Study," *Social Work Journal*, vol. 34, October, 1953, pp. 165–168, 176–178.

149. HOFFMAN, ISAAC, *Family-Centered Project*. Wilder Foundation, St. Paul, Minn., 1956. Mimeographed.

150. HOFSTADTER, RICHARD, *The American Political Tradition*. Vintage Books, New York, 1954.

151. HOLLINGSHEAD, AUGUST, *Elmtown's Youth:* The Impact of Social Class on Adolescents. John Wiley and Sons, New York, 1949.

152. HOLLIS, ERNEST V., and ALICE L. TAYLOR, *Social Work Education in the United States*. Columbia University Press, New York, 1951.

153. HOMANS, GEORGE C., *The Human Group*. Harcourt, Brace and Co., New York, 1950.

154. HOSELITZ, BERT F., editor, *The Progress of Underdeveloped Areas*. University of Chicago Press, Chicago, 1952.

155. HOWARD, DONALD S., "Social Work and Social Reform" in *New Directions in Social Work*, edited by Cora Kasius. Harper and Bros., New York, 1954, pp. 159–175.

156. HOWE, IRVING, and B. J. WIDICK, *The UAW and Walter Reuther*. Random House, New York, 1949.

157. HUGHES, EVERETT C., "The Knitting of Racial Groups in Industry," *American Sociological Review*, vol. 11, October, 1946, pp. 512–519.

158. HUGHES, EVERETT C., "Mistakes at Work," *Canadian Journal of Economics and Political Science*, vol. 17, August, 1951, pp. 320–327.

159. HUGHES, EVERETT C., "Queries Concerning Industry and Society Growing Out of Study of Ethnic Relations in Industry," *American Sociological Review*, vol. 14, April, 1949, pp. 211–220.

160. HUNTER, FLOYD, *Community Power Structure:* A Study of Decision Makers. University of North Carolina Press, Chapel Hill, 1953.

161. ISARD, WALTER, and VINCENT H. WHITNEY, *Atomic Power:* An Economic and Social Analysis. Blakiston Co., New York, 1952.

162. JACO, E. GARTLY, and IVAN BELKNAP, "Is a New Family Form Emerging in the Urban Fringe?" *American Sociological Review*, vol. 18, October, 1953, pp. 551–557.

163. JAFFEE, ABRAM J., and CHARLES D. STEWART, *Manpower Resources and Utilization.* John Wiley and Sons, New York, 1951.

164. JANOWITZ, MORRIS, *The Community Press in an Urban Setting.* Free Press, Glencoe, Ill., 1952.

165. JANOWITZ, MORRIS, "Public Perspectives on Social Security," *Social Work*, vol. 1, July, 1956, pp. 94–101.

166. JENNINGS, WALTER W., *A History of Economic Progress in the United States.* Thomas Y. Crowell Co., New York, 1926.

167. JOHNSON, ARLIEN, "The Statutory Framework of the Social Services" in *Some Impressions of Social Services in Great Britain.* United States Educational Commission in the United Kingdom, London, 1956.

168. JONES, ALFRED W., *Life, Liberty, and Property.* J. B. Lippincott Co., Philadelphia, 1941.

169. JUNGK, ROBERT, *Tomorrow Is Already Here*, translated by Marguerite Waldman. Simon and Schuster, New York, 1954.

170. KAHL, JOSEPH A., "Educational and Occupational Aspirations of 'Common Man' Boys," *Harvard Educational Review*, vol. 23, Summer, 1953, pp. 186–203.

171. KAHN, ALFRED J., *A Court for Children:* A Study of the New York City Children's Court. Columbia University Press, New York, 1953.

172. KARDINER, ABRAM, *The Psychological Frontiers of Society.* Columbia University Press, New York, 1945.

173. KATZMAN, RUTH M., *A Critical Analysis of Current Fee-Charging Philosophy and Practice in a Family Agency.* Master's thesis, Wayne State University, Detroit, 1955.

174. KENDALL, KATHERINE A., "Orthodoxy and Paradoxes: Dilemmas of Social Work Education," *Social Work*, vol. 1, July, 1956, pp. 43–49.

175. KERR, CLARK, "Industrial Conflict and Its Mediation," *American Journal of Sociology*, vol. 60, November, 1954, pp. 230–245.

176. KERR, CLARK, "What Became of the Independent Spirit?" *Fortune*, vol. 48, July, 1953, pp. 110–111, 134–136.

177. KERR, CLARK, and ABRAHAM SIEGEL, "The Interindustry Propensity to Strike—An International Comparison" in *Industrial Conflict*, edited by Arthur Kornhauser and others. McGraw-Hill Book Co., New York, 1954, pp. 189–212.

178. KERR, CLARK, and others, "The Labour Problem in Economic Development: A Framework for a Reappraisal," *International Labour Review*, vol. 71, March, 1955, pp. 223–235.

179. KESSELMAN, LOUIS C., *The Social Politics of FEPC: A Study in Reform Pressure Movements*. University of North Carolina Press, Chapel Hill, 1948.

180. KEY, VALDIMER O., JR., *Politics, Parties, and Pressure Groups*. 3d ed. Thomas Y. Crowell Co., New York, 1952.

181. KILLIAN, LEWIS M., "The Effects of Southern White Workers on Race Relations in Northern Plants," *American Sociological Review*, vol. 17, June, 1952, pp. 327–331.

182. KILLIAN, LEWIS M., *Southern White Laborers in Chicago's West Side*. Ph.D. thesis, University of Chicago, Chicago, 1949.

183. KINSEY, ALFRED C., WARDELL B. POMEROY, and CLYDE E. MARTIN, *Sexual Behavior in the Human Male*. W. B. Saunders Co., Philadelphia, 1949.

184. KINSEY, ALFRED C., and others, *Sexual Behavior in the Human Female*. W. B. Saunders Co., Philadelphia, 1953.

185. KIRKLAND, EDWARD C., *A History of American Economic Life*. 3d ed. Appleton-Century-Crofts, New York, 1951.

186. KOMAROVSKY, MIRRA, *The Unemployed Man and His Family*. Dryden Press, New York, 1940.

187. KOMAROVSKY, MIRRA, *Women in the Modern World: Their Education and Their Dilemmas*. Little, Brown and Co., Boston, 1953.

188. KORNHAUSER, ARTHUR, ROBIN DUBIN, and ARTHUR M. ROSS, editors, *Industrial Conflict*. McGraw-Hill Book Co., New York, 1954.

189. KORNHAUSER, ARTHUR, HAROLD L. SHEPPARD, and ALBERT J. MAYER, *When Labor Votes*. University Books, New York, 1956.

190. KRAMER, DALE, and MADELINE KARR, *Teen-Age Gangs*. Henry Holt and Co., New York, 1953.

191. KRAUS, HERTHA, *Common Service Resources in a Free Society*. Association for the Study of Community Organization, New York, 1954. Mimeographed.

192. KUZNETS, SIMON, "Economic Growth and Income Inequality," *American Economic Review*, vol. 45, March, 1955, pp. 1–28.

193. KVARACEUS, WILLIAM C., *The Community and the Delinquent*. World Book Co., New York, 1954.

194. KYRK, HAZEL, *Economic Problems of the Family*. Harper and Bros., New York, 1933.

195. KYRK, HAZEL, *The Family in the American Economy*. University of Chicago Press, Chicago, 1953.

196. LANDER, BERNARD, *Towards an Understanding of Juvenile Delinquency*. Columbia University Press, New York, 1954.

197. LANDES, DAVID S., "French Business and the Businessman: A Social and Cultural Analysis" in *Modern France*, edited by Edward M. Earle. Princeton University Press, Princeton, 1951, pp. 334–353.

198. LASSWELL, HAROLD D., *Politics:* Who Gets What, When, How. McGraw-Hill Book Co., New York, 1936.

199. LAZARSFELD, PAUL F., BERNARD BERELSON, and HAZEL GAUDET, *The People's Choice:* How the Voter Makes Up His Mind in a Presidential Campaign. 2d ed. Columbia University Press, New York, 1948.

200. LEBEAUX, CHARLES N., *Some Factors in the Advancement of Professional Social Workers*. Address given at the Fiftieth Annual Meeting of the American Sociological Society, 1955.

201. LEBEAUX, CHARLES N., *A Study of the Detroit Chapter of the American Association of Social Workers*. Unpublished manuscript, Wayne University, Detroit, 1954.

202. LEE, ALFRED M., and ELIZABETH B. LEE, editors, *Social Problems in America*. Henry Holt and Co., New York, 1949.

203. LEE, PORTER R., *Social Work as Cause and Function*. Columbia University Press, New York, 1937.

204. LESTER, RICHARD A., "The Nature and Level of Income Security for a Free Society" in *National Policies for Education, Health and Social Services*, edited by James E. Russell. Doubleday and Co., New York, 1955, pp. 293–320.

205. LESZCZYNSKI, JOHN S., *A Study of the Administrative Reorganization of the United Community Services of Metropolitan Detroit.* Master's thesis, Wayne University, Detroit, 1955.

206. LEVY, MARION J., JR., *The Family Revolution in Modern China.* Harvard University Press, Cambridge, 1949.

207. LEVY, MARION J., JR., "Some Sources of the Vulnerability of the Structures of Relatively Nonindustrialized Societies to Those of Highly Industrialized Societies" in *The Progress of Underdeveloped Areas,* edited by Bert F. Hoselitz. University of Chicago Press, Chicago, 1952, pp. 113–125.

208. LEVY, MARION J., JR., and SHIH KUO-HENG, *The Rise of the Chinese Business Class.* Institute of Pacific Relations, New York, 1949.

209. LEWIS, W. ARTHUR, *The Theory of Economic Growth.* George Allen and Unwin, London, 1955.

210. LIEPMANN, KATE K., *The Journey to Work.* Oxford University Press, New York, 1944.

211. LINTON, RALPH, *The Study of Man.* Appleton Century Co., New York, 1936.

212. LIPPMANN, WALTER, *Public Opinion.* Harcourt, Brace and Co., New York, 1922.

213. LIPSET, SEYMOUR M., and REINHARD BENDIX, "Ideological Equalitarianism and Social Mobility in the United States," *Transactions of the Second World Congress of Sociology,* vol. 2. International Sociological Association, London, 1954, pp. 34–54.

214. LIPSET, SEYMOUR M., and REINHARD BENDIX, "Social Mobility and Occupational Career Patterns: I, Stability of Jobholding," *American Journal of Sociology,* vol. 57, January, 1952, pp. 366–374.

215. LIPSET, SEYMOUR M., and REINHARD BENDIX, "Social Mobility and Occupational Career Patterns: II, Social Mobility," *American Journal of Sociology,* vol. 57, March, 1952, pp. 494–504.

216. LIPSET, SEYMOUR M., and NATALIE ROGOFF, "Class and Opportunity in Europe and the U.S.," *Commentary,* vol. 18, December, 1954, pp. 562–568.

217. MACCOBY, ELEANOR E., PATRICIA K. GIBBS, and the staff of the Laboratory of Human Development, Harvard University, "Methods of Child-Rearing in Two Social Classes" in *Readings in Child Development,* edited by William E. Martin and Celia B. Stendler. Harcourt, Brace and Co., New York, 1954, pp. 380–395.

218. MacCormick, Austin H., "Children in Our Jails," *Annals of the American Academy of Political and Social Science*, vol. 261, January, 1949, pp. 150–157.

219. MacGill, Helen G., "The Oriental Delinquent in the Vancouver Juvenile Court," *Sociology and Social Research*, vol. 22, May-June, 1928, pp. 428–438.

220. McKee, James B., "Status and Power in the Industrial Community: A Comment on Drucker's Thesis," *American Journal of Sociology*, vol. 58, January, 1953, pp. 364–370.

221. Macmahon, Arthur W., John D. Millett, and Gladys Ogden, *The Administration of Federal Work Relief*. Public Administration Service, Chicago, 1941. Published for the Committee on Public Administration of the Social Science Research Council.

222. Maller, Julius B., "Juvenile Delinquency Among the Jews in New York," *Social Forces*, vol. 10, May, 1932, pp. 542–549.

223. Maller, Julius B., "The Trend of Juvenile Delinquency in New York City," *Journal of Juvenile Research*, vol. 17, January, 1933, pp. 10–18.

224. Manis, Jerome G., and Bernard N. Meltzer, "Attitudes of Textile Workers to Class Structure," *American Journal of Sociology*, vol. 60, July, 1954, pp. 30–35.

225. Mannheim, Karl, *Man and Society in an Age of Reconstruction*, translated by Edward A. Shils. Harcourt, Brace and Co., New York, 1940.

226. Mantoux, Paul J., *The Industrial Revolution in the Eighteenth Century*, translated by Marjorie Vernon. 2d ed. Harcourt, Brace and Co., New York, 1927.

227. Marshall, Leon C., *Industrial Society:* Part 1, The Emergence of the Modern Order. University of Chicago Press, Chicago, 1929.

228. Matthews, Donald R., *The Social Background of Political Decision-Makers*. Doubleday and Co., New York, 1954.

229. Mead, Margaret, *And Keep Your Powder Dry!* William Morrow and Co., New York, 1942.

230. Mead, Margaret, editor, *Cultural Patterns and Technical Change*. New American Library, New York, 1955. Originally published by UNESCO, Paris, 1953.

231. Merriam, Ida C., *Social Security Financing*. Social Security Administration, Division of Research and Statistics, Bureau Report 17. Government Printing Office, Washington, 1952.

232. MERRIAM, IDA C., "Social Welfare Expenditures in the United States, 1954–55," *Social Security Bulletin*, vol. 19, October, 1956, pp. 3–10.

233. MERRIAM, IDA C., "Social Welfare in the United States, 1934–54," *Social Security Bulletin*, vol. 18, October, 1955, pp. 3–14, 31.

234. MERRILL, FRANCIS E., and others, *Social Problems*. Alfred A. Knopf, New York, 1950.

235. MERRILL, MAUD A., *Problems of Child Delinquency*. Houghton Mifflin Co., Boston, 1947.

236. MERTON, ROBERT K., *Social Theory and Social Structure:* Toward the Codification of Theory and Research. Free Press, Glencoe, Ill., 1949.

237. MERTON, ROBERT K., and others, editors, *Reader in Bureaucracy*. Free Press, Glencoe, Ill., 1952.

238. MEYER, AGNES E., "No Man Is an Island," *Social Work*, vol. 1, July, 1956, pp. 3–10.

239. MEYERSON, MARTIN, and EDWARD C. BANFIELD, *Politics, Planning, and the Public Interest*: The Case of Public Housing in Chicago. Free Press, Glencoe, Ill., 1955.

240. MICHIGAN JUVENILE COURT REPORTING, 1945–1954: Tenth Anniversary Issue. State Department of Social Welfare in Cooperation with the Michigan Probate Judges' Association, Lansing, 1955.

241. MIERNYK, WILLIAM H., *Inter-Industry Labor Mobility:* The Case of the Displaced Textile Worker. Northeastern University, Bureau of Business and Economic Research, Boston, 1955.

242. MILLER, DANIEL, and GUY E. SWANSON, *The Changing American Parent:* A Study in the Detroit Area. John Wiley and Sons, New York. In preparation.

243. MILLER, HERMAN P., *Income of the American People*. John Wiley and Sons, New York, 1955. Published for the Social Science Research Council in Cooperation with the U.S. Department of Commerce, Bureau of the Census.

244. MILLER, WILLIAM, "The Recruitment of the American Business Elite," *Quarterly Journal of Economics*, vol. 64, May, 1950, pp. 242–253.

245. MILLS, C. WRIGHT, "The American Business Elite," *The Tasks of Economic History*, Supplement 5 to *Journal of Economic History*, December, 1945, pp. 20–44.

246. MILLS, C. WRIGHT, *The Power Elite.* Oxford University Press, London, 1956.

247. MILLS, C. WRIGHT, "The Professional Ideology of Social Pathologists," *American Journal of Sociology*, vol. 49, September, 1943, pp. 165–180.

248. MILLS, C. WRIGHT, *White Collar.* Oxford University Press, New York, 1951.

249. MILLS, C. WRIGHT, CLARENCE SENIOR, and ROSE K. GOLDSEN, *The Puerto Rican Journey.* Harper and Bros., New York, 1950.

250. MILLS, C. WRIGHT, and MELVILLE J. ULMER, *Small Business and Civic Welfare:* Report of the Smaller War Plants Corporation to the Special Committee to Study Problems of American Small Business. U.S. Senate, 79th Congress, 2d Sess., Document 135. Government Printing Office, Washington, 1946.

251. MIRO, ANNELISE, *Industrial Social Work:* Its Principles and Its Practices. Master's thesis, Wayne State University, Detroit, 1956.

252. MOORE, BARRINGTON, JR., *Terror and Progress USSR:* Some Sources of Change and Stability in the Soviet Dictatorship. Harvard University Press, Cambridge, 1954.

253. MOORE, WILBERT E., *Economy and Society.* Doubleday and Co., New York, 1955.

254. MOORE, WILBERT E., "The Emergence of New Property Conceptions in America," *Journal of Legal and Political Sociology*, vol. 1, April, 1943, pp. 34–58.

255. MOORE, WILBERT E., *Industrial Relations and the Social Order.* Rev. ed. Macmillan Co., New York, 1951.

256. MOORE, WILBERT E., *Industrialization and Labor:* Social Aspects of Economic Development. Cornell University Press, Ithaca, N.Y., 1951.

257. MOORE, WILBERT E., "Occupational Structure and Industrial Conflict" in *Industrial Conflict*, edited by Arthur Kornhauser and others. McGraw-Hill Book Co., New York, 1954, pp. 221–231.

258. MUMFORD, LEWIS, *Technics and Civilization.* Harcourt, Brace and Co., New York, 1934.

259. MUSGRAVE, R. A., and others, "Distribution of Tax Payments by Income Groups: A Case Study for 1948," *National Tax Journal*, vol. 4, March, 1951, pp. 1–53.

260. MYERS, CHARLES A., "Patterns of Labor Mobility" in *Manpower in the United States*, edited by William Haber and others. Harper and Bros., New York, 1954, pp. 154–165.

261. NATIONAL ASSOCIATION OF MANUFACTURERS, Economic Principles Commission, *The American Individual Enterprise System:* Its Nature, Evolution, and Future. McGraw-Hill Book Co., New York, 1946, 2 vols.

262. NATIONAL ASSOCIATION OF SOCIAL WORKERS, *Statement re Undergraduate Curriculum in Social Welfare.* Memorandum to Chapters, December 28, 1956. Mimeographed.

263. NATIONAL OPINION RESEARCH CENTER, "Jobs and Occupations: A Popular Estimation" in *Class, Status, and Power*, edited by Reinhard Bendix and Seymour M. Lipset. Free Press, Glencoe, Ill., 1953, pp. 411–426.

264. NEUMANN, FRANZ L., *Behemoth:* The Structure and Practice of National Socialism. Oxford University Press, New York, 1942.

265. *New York Times*, October 12, 1954, p. 13.

266. *New York Times*, October 13, 1954, pp. 1, 14; October 14, 1954, pp. 1, 24.

267. *New York Times*, January 17, 1957, p. 13.

268. NEWCOMER, MABEL, "The Chief Executive of Large Business Corporations," *Explorations in Entrepreneurial History*, vol. 5, 1952–1953, pp. 1–33. Harvard University Research Center in Entrepreneurial History.

269. "1955 SURVEY OF CONSUMER FINANCES," *Federal Reserve Bulletin*, vol. 41, June, 1955, pp. 609–622.

270. OCCUPATIONAL LICENSING LEGISLATION IN THE STATES. Council of State Governments, Chicago, 1952.

271. OGBURN, WILLIAM F., "Implications of the Rising Standard of Living in the United States," *American Journal of Sociology*, vol. 60, May, 1955, pp. 541–546.

272. OGBURN, WILLIAM F., *Social Change:* With Respect to Culture and Original Nature. Viking Press, New York, 1922.

273. OGBURN, WILLIAM F., and MEYER F. NIMKOFF, *Sociology*. 2d ed. Houghton Mifflin Co., Boston, 1950.

274. OGBURN, WILLIAM F., and MEYER F. NIMKOFF, *Technology and the Changing Family*. Houghton Mifflin Co., Boston, 1955.

275. O'HANLON, W. M., *The Operative Classes of Great Britain:* Their Existing State and Its Improvement. Religious Tract Society, London, 1851.

276. OHLIN, LLOYD E., *Sociology and the Field of Corrections.* Russell Sage Foundation, New York, 1956.

277. OHLIN, LLOYD E., HERMAN PIVEN, and DONNELL M. PAPPENFORT, "Major Dilemmas of the Social Worker in Probation and Parole," *National Probation and Parole Association Journal,* vol. 2, July, 1956, pp. 211–225.

278. OVERTON, ALICE, "Casework as a Partnership," *Children,* vol. 3, September-October, 1956, pp. 181–186.

279. PARK, ROBERT E., *The City.* University of Chicago Press, Chicago, 1925.

280. PARSONS, TALCOTT, *Essays in Sociological Theory, Pure and Applied.* Free Press, Glencoe, Ill., 1949.

281. PARSONS, TALCOTT, "H. M. Robertson on Max Weber and His School," *Journal of Political Economy,* vol. 43, October, 1935, pp. 688–696.

282. PARSONS, TALCOTT, *The Social System.* Free Press, Glencoe, Ill., 1951.

283. PEACOCK, ALAN T., and P. R. BROWNING, "The Social Services in Great Britain and the Redistribution of Income" in *Income Redistribution and Social Policy,* edited by Alan T. Peacock. Jonathan Cape, London, 1954, pp. 139–177.

284. PERLMAN, SELIG, *A History of Trade Unionism in the United States.* Macmillan Co., New York, 1922.

285. PERLMAN, SELIG, *A Theory of the Labor Movement.* Macmillan Co., New York, 1928.

286. PETERSEN, WILLIAM, "The 'Scientific' Basis of Our Immigration Policy," *Commentary,* vol. 20, July, 1955, pp. 77–86.

287. PIRENNE, HENRI, "The Stages in the Social History of Capitalism," *American Historical Review,* vol. 19, April, 1914, pp. 494–515. See also *Class, Status, and Power,* edited by Reinhard Bendix and Seymour M. Lipset. Free Press, Glencoe, Ill., 1953, pp. 501–517.

288. POLANSKY, NORMAN, and others, "Social Workers in Society: Results of a Sampling Study," *Social Work Journal,* vol. 34, April, 1953, pp. 74–80.

289. POLLAK, OTTO, "The Culture of Psychiatric Social Work," *Journal of Psychiatric Social Work,* vol. 21, June, 1952, pp. 160–165.

290. POLLAK, OTTO, "Exploring Collaboration Between Casework and Social Science in Practice," *Social Work Journal*, vol. 33, October, 1952, pp. 177–183, 209.

291. POLLAK, OTTO, and collaborators, *Social Science and Psychotherapy for Children*. Russell Sage Foundation, New York, 1952.

292. PORTERFIELD, AUSTIN L., *Youth in Trouble*. Leo Potishman Foundation, Fort Worth, Tex., 1946.

293. PUNEKAR, S. D., *Trade Unionism in India*, edited by C. N. Vakil. New Book Co., Bombay, 1948.

294. QUEEN, STUART A., and JOHN B. ADAMS, *The Family in Various Cultures*. J. B. Lippincott Co., Philadelphia, 1952.

295. REDL, FRITZ, "The Psychology of Gang Formation and the Treatment of Juvenile Delinquents," *Psychoanalytic Study of the Child*, International Universities Press, New York, vol. 1, 1945, pp. 367–377.

296. REED, ELLERY F., "How Effective Are Group-Work Agencies in Preventing Delinquency?" *Social Service Review*, vol. 22, September, 1948, pp. 340–348.

297. REISS, ALBERT J., JR., "Delinquency as the Failure of Personal and Social Controls," *American Sociological Review*, vol. 16, April, 1951, pp. 196–207.

298. REISS, ALBERT J., JR., "Social Correlates of Psychological Types of Delinquency," *American Sociological Review*, vol. 17, December, 1952, pp. 710–718.

299. RICHMOND, MARY E., *The Long View*. Russell Sage Foundation, New York, 1930.

300. RIESMAN, DAVID, *The Lonely Crowd*. Yale University Press, New Haven, 1950.

301. ROBERTSON, HECTOR M., *Aspects of the Rise of Economic Individualism: A Criticism of Max Weber and His School*. Cambridge University Press, Cambridge, England, 1933.

302. ROBINSON, JAMES H., *The Mind in the Making*. Harper and Bros., New York, 1921, p. 165.

303. ROETHLISBERGER, F. J., and WILLIAM J. DICKSON, *Management and the Worker*. Harvard University Press, Cambridge, 1939.

304. ROGERS, CARL R., and ROSELIND F. DYMOND, editors, *Psychotherapy and Personality Change*. University of Chicago Press, Chicago, 1954.

305. Rogoff, Natalie, *Recent Trends in Occupational Mobility*. Free Press, Glencoe, Ill., 1953.

306. Roosevelt, Mrs. Franklin D., "Social Responsibility for Individual Welfare" in *National Policies for Education, Health and Social Services*, edited by James E. Russell. Doubleday and Co., New York, 1955, pp. xxxv–xxxviii.

307. Ross, Aileen D., "Organized Philanthropy in an Urban Community," *Canadian Journal of Economics and Political Science*, vol. 18, November, 1952, pp. 474–486.

308. Ross, Aileen D., "Philanthropic Activity and the Business Career," *Social Forces*, vol. 32, March, 1954, pp. 274–280.

309. Rossi, Peter H., *Why Families Move: A Study in the Social Psychology of Urban Residential Mobility*. Free Press, Glencoe, Ill., 1956.

310. Rubin, Sol, "The Legal Character of Juvenile Delinquency," *Annals of the American Academy of Political and Social Science*, vol. 261, January, 1949, pp. 1–8.

311. Russell, Bertrand, *The Impact of Science on Society*. Columbia University Press, New York, 1951.

312. Samuelson, Paul A., *Economics: An Introductory Analysis*. 2d ed. McGraw-Hill Book Co., New York, 1951.

313. Schattschneider, Elmer E., *Politics, Pressures and the Tariff: A Study of Free Private Enterprise in Pressure Politics, as Shown in the 1929–1930 Revision of the Tariff*. Prentice-Hall, New York, 1935.

314. Schneider, David M., "AASW Members—As Revealed by the 1945 Membership Census," *Compass*, vol. 27, June, 1946, pp. 4–8.

315. Schottland, Charles I., "An Exchange of Views About Social Work Education—Panel Discussion," *Education for Social Work: Proceedings, Annual Program Meeting*. Council on Social Work Education, New York, 1955, pp. 42–44.

316. Schramm, Gustav L., "Philosophy of the Juvenile Court," *Annals of the American Academy of Political and Social Science*, vol. 261, January, 1949, pp. 101–108.

317. Schulze, Robert O., *Economic Dominance and Public Leadership: A Study of the Structure and Process of Power in an Urban Community*. Ph.D. thesis, University of Michigan, Ann Arbor, 1956.

318. SCHWARTZ, EDWARD E., "Statistics of Juvenile Delinquency in the United States," *Annals of the American Academy of Political and Social Science*, vol. 261, January, 1949, pp. 9–20.

319. SÉE, HENRI E., "Commercial, Financial, and Industrial Capitalism" in *Industrial Society:* Part 1, The Emergence of the Modern Order, by Leon C. Marshall. University of Chicago Press, Chicago, 1929, pp. 93–95. Adapted from *Modern Capitalism:* Its Origin and Evolution, Adelphi Co., New York, 1928, pp. 177–182.

320. SELLIN, THORSTEN, *Culture Conflict and Crime*. Social Science Research Council, Bulletin 41, New York, 1938.

321. SELZNICK, PHILIP, *The Organizational Weapon:* A Study of Bolshevik Strategy and Tactics. McGraw-Hill Book Co., New York, 1952.

322. SELZNICK, PHILIP, *TVA and the Grass Roots:* A Study in the Sociology of Formal Organization. University of California Press, Berkeley, 1949.

323. SHANAS, ETHEL, and CATHERINE E. DUNNING, *Recreation and Delinquency*. Chicago Recreation Commission, Chicago, 1942.

324. SHARP, HARRY P., *Migration and Social Participation in the Detroit Area*. Ph.D. thesis, University of Michigan, Ann Arbor, 1954.

325. SHARTLE, CARROLL L., *Occupational Information:* Its Development and Application. 2d ed. Prentice-Hall, New York, 1952.

326. SHAW, CLIFFORD R., and HENRY D. MCKAY, *Juvenile Delinquency and Urban Areas*. University of Chicago Press, Chicago, 1942.

327. SHILS, EDWARD A., *The Torment of Secrecy*. Free Press, Glencoe, Ill., 1956.

328. SHULMAN, HARRY M., "Delinquency Treatment in the Controlled Activity Group," *American Sociological Review*, vol. 10, June, 1945, pp. 405–414.

329. SIMMEL, GEORG, "The Metropolis and Mental Life" in *Reader in Urban Sociology*, edited by Paul K. Hatt and Albert J. Reiss, Jr. Free Press, Glencoe, Ill., 1951, pp. 563–574.

330. SIMON, HERBERT A., and WILLIAM R. DIVINE, "Controlling Human Factors in an Administrative Experiment," *Public Administration Review*, vol. 1, Autumn, 1941, pp. 485–492.

331. SIMON, HERBERT A., DONALD W. SMITHBURG, and VICTOR A. THOMPSON, *Public Administration*. Alfred A. Knopf, New York, 1950.

332. SIPORIN, MAX, "Dual Supervision of Psychiatric Social Workers," *Social Work*, vol. 1, April, 1956, pp. 32–42.

333. SJOBERG, GIDEON, "The Preindustrial City," *American Journal of Sociology*, vol. 60, March, 1955, pp. 438–445.

334. SMITH, ADAM, *The Wealth of Nations*, edited by Edwin Cannan. Modern Library, New York, 1937.

335. SMITH, JOEL, WILLIAM H. FORM, and GREGORY P. STONE, "Local Intimacy in a Middle-Sized City," *American Journal of Sociology*, vol. 60, November, 1954, pp. 276–284.

336. SOCIAL WORK YEAR BOOK 1954. American Association of Social Workers, New York.

337. SOMBART, WERNER, "Capitalism," *Encyclopaedia of the Social Sciences*, vol. 3. Macmillan Co., New York, 1930, pp. 195–208.

338. SOMBART, WERNER, *The Quintessence of Capitalism:* A Study of the History and Psychology of the Modern Business Man, translated and edited by M. Epstein. E. P. Dutton and Co., New York, 1915.

339. SONTHEIMER, MORTON, "The Better Mousetrap," *Journal of Social Casework*, vol. 28, November, 1947, pp. 354–355.

340. SOROKIN, PITIRIM, "American Millionaires and Multi-Millionaires," *Social Forces*, vol. 3, May, 1925, pp. 627–640.

341. SOTTONG, PHILIPP C., "The Dilemma of the Parent as Culture Bearer," *Social Casework*, vol. 36, July, 1955, pp. 302–306.

342. SOULE, GEORGE H., *Time for Living*. Viking Press, New York, 1955.

343. SPAHR, CHARLES B., *An Essay on the Present Distribution of Wealth in the United States*. T. Y. Crowell and Co., New York, 1896.

344. STEVENS, RUTH N., and FRED A. HUTCHINSON, "A New Concept of Supervision Is Tested," *Social Work*, vol. 1, July, 1956, pp. 50–55.

345. STONE, GREGORY P., "City Shoppers and Urban Identification: Observations on the Social Psychology of City Life," *American Journal of Sociology*, vol. 60, July, 1954, pp. 36–45.

346. STOUFFER, SAMUEL A., *Communism, Conformity, and Civil Liberties*. Doubleday and Co., New York, 1955.

347. STUDT, ELLIOT, "Casework in the Correctional Field," *Federal Probation*, vol. 18, September, 1954, pp. 19–26.

348. STUDT, ELLIOT, *Training Personnel for Work with Juvenile Delinquents*. U.S. Department of Health, Education, and Welfare, Children's Bureau Publication 348. Government Printing Office, Washington, 1954.

349. STUDT, ELLIOT, "Treatment of Persons in Conflict with Authority," *Proceedings of the 1956 Social Work Progress Institute.* School of Social Work, University of Michigan, Ann Arbor, 1956, pp. 1–23.

350. SULLENGER, T. EARL, "The Social Significance of Mobility: An Omaha Study." *American Journal of Sociology*, vol. 55, May, 1950, pp. 559–564.

351. SUSSMAN, MARVIN B., "The Help Pattern in the Middle Class Family," *American Sociological Review*, vol. 18, February, 1953, pp. 22–28.

352. SWARD, KEITH T., *The Legend of Henry Ford.* Rinehart and Co., New York, 1948.

353. TAFT, DONALD R., and RICHARD ROBBINS, *International Migrations.* Ronald Press Co., New York, 1955.

354. TAPPAN, PAUL W., "Children and Youth in the Criminal Court," *Annals of the American Academy of Political and Social Science*, vol. 261, January, 1949, pp. 128–136.

355. TAPPAN, PAUL W., *Juvenile Delinquency.* McGraw-Hill Book Co., New York, 1949.

356. TAWNEY, RICHARD H., *Religion and the Rise of Capitalism.* Harcourt, Brace and Co., New York, 1926.

357. TAWNEY, RICHARD H., *The Sickness of an Acquisitive Society.* Fabian Society and George Allen and Unwin, London, 1920.

358. TEETERS, NEGLEY K., and JOHN O. REINEMANN, *The Challenge of Delinquency.* Prentice-Hall, New York, 1950.

359. THOMPSON, LAURA M., and ALICE JOSEPH, *The Hopi Way.* University of Chicago Press, Chicago, 1944.

360. THRASHER, FREDERIC M., "The Boys' Club and Juvenile Delinquency," *American Journal of Sociology*, vol. 42, July, 1936, pp. 66–80.

361. TITMUSS, RICHARD M., *Problems of Social Policy.* H. M. Stationery Office, London, 1950.

362. To SECURE THESE RIGHTS: Report of the President's Committee on Civil Rights. Government Printing Office, Washington, 1947.

363. TREGOE, BENJAMIN, *The Effect of Ethnic Conformity on Dependence and Aggression in Adolescence.* Ph.D. thesis, Harvard University, Cambridge, 1957.

364. TREGOE, BENJAMIN, *Ethnic Analysis:* A Report from the Laboratory of Human Development, Harvard University. Mimeographed. Summarized in a book being prepared by R. Sears, E. Maccoby, and H. Levin, and to be published by Row Peterson and Co., Evanston, Ill.

365. UNITED NATIONS, DEPARTMENT OF SOCIAL AFFAIRS, *Training for Social Work:* An International Survey. Columbia University Press, New York, 1950, p. 13

366. UNESCO, *International Survey of Programs of Social Development.* United Nations, New York, 1955, Document E/CN.5/301.

367. U.S. CONGRESS, JOINT COMMITTEE ON THE ECONOMIC REPORT, *Automation and Technological Change:* Hearings Before the Subcommittee on Economic Stabilization. 84th Congress, 1st Sess. Government Printing Office, Washington, 1955.

368. U.S. CONGRESS, JOINT COMMITTEE ON THE ECONOMIC REPORT, *Characteristics of the Low-Income Population and Related Federal Programs:* Selected Materials Assembled by the Staff of the Subcommittee on Low-Income Families. 84th Congres, 1st Sess. Government Printing Office, Washington, 1955.

369. U.S. CONGRESS, JOINT COMMITTEE ON THE ECONOMIC REPORT, *Making Ends Meet on Less Than $2,000 a Year.* 82d Congress, 1st Sess. Government Printing Office, Washington, 1951.

370. U.S. CONGRESS, SENATE, *Low-Income Families and Economic Stability:* Materials Assembled by the Staff of the Subcommittee on Low-Income Families. 81st Congress, 2d Sess., Senate Document 231. Government Printing Office, Washington, 1950.

371. U.S. DEPARTMENT OF HEALTH, EDUCATION, AND WELFARE, Social Security Administration, *Characteristics of Families Receiving Aid to Dependent Children.* November, 1953.

372. U.S. DEPARTMENT OF HEALTH, EDUCATION, AND WELFARE, Social Security Administration, *Health and Welfare Expenditures of Private Philanthropic Agencies in 1954.* Washington, 1956. Mimeographed.

373. U.S. DEPARTMENT OF HEALTH, EDUCATION, AND WELFARE, Social Security Administration, *Social Security Bulletin*, vol. 19, June, 1956.

374. U.S. DEPARTMENT OF JUSTICE, Federal Bureau of Investigation, *Uniform Crime Reports for the United States*, vol. 26, no. 2, 1955, pp. 111–115.

375. U.S. DEPARTMENT OF LABOR, Bureau of Labor Statistics, *Social Workers in 1950*. American Association of Social Workers, New York, 1951.

376. U.S. DEPARTMENT OF LABOR, Bureau of Labor Statistics, *Employment and Earnings*, vol. 1, May, 1955, Table SB-2; vol. 2, August, 1955, Table B-2.

377. U.S. DEPARTMENT OF LABOR, "Wages in the United States and Europe, 1870 to 1898," *Bulletin of the Department of Labor*, vol. 3, no. 18, September, 1898, pp. 665–693.

378. U.S. EMPLOYMENT SERVICE, Division of Occupational Analysis. *Dictionary of Occupational Titles*. 2d ed. Government Printing Office, Washington, 1949.

379. (U.S.) FEDERAL SECURITY AGENCY, Social Security Administration, *Social Welfare Administration in the United States of America*. Washington, June, 1950.

380. U.S. NEWS AND WORLD REPORT, January 25, 1957, p. 149.

381. VALAORAS, VASILEIOS G., "Patterns of Aging of Human Populations" in *The Social and Biological Challenge of Our Aging Population:* Proceedings of the Eastern States Health Education Conference, 1949. Columbia University Press, New York, 1950, pp. 67–85. Published for the New York Academy of Medicine.

382. VANCE, RUPERT B., and NICHOLAS J. DEMERATH, editors, *The Urban South*. University of North Carolina Press, Chapel Hill, 1954.

383. VINTER, ROBERT D., JR., and WILLIAM F. BUSSIERE, *The Characteristics of Social Agency Board Members*. Springfield College, Springfield, Mass., 1954. Mimeographed.

384. VIRTUE, MAXINE B., *Public Services to Children in Michigan:* A Study of Basic Structure. Michigan pamphlets no. 24, University of Michigan Press, Ann Arbor, 1952.

385. VUCINICH, ALEXANDER S., *Soviet Economic Institutions:* The Social Structure of Production Units. Stanford University Press, Stanford, Calif., 1952.

386. WALKER, CHARLES R., and ROBERT H. GUEST, *The Man on the Assembly Line*. Harvard University Press, Cambridge, 1952.

387. WALLER, WILLARD, *The Family:* A Dynamic Interpretation. Rev. ed. by Reuben L. Hill. Dryden Press, New York, 1951.

388. WALLERSTEIN, JAMES S., and CLEMENT J. WYLE, "Our Law-Abiding Law-Breakers," *Probation*, vol. 25, April, 1947, pp. 107–112, 118.

389. WARDWELL, WALTER I., "The Reduction of Strain in a Marginal Social Role," *American Journal of Sociology*, vol. 61, July, 1955, pp. 16–25.

390. WARNER, W. LLOYD, and JAMES C. ABEGGLEN, *Occupational Mobility in American Business and Industry, 1928–1952*. University of Minnesota Press, Minneapolis, 1955.

391. WARNER, W. LLOYD, ROBERT J. HAVIGHURST, and MARTIN B. LOEB, *Who Shall Be Educated?* The Challenge of Unequal Opportunities. Harper and Bros., New York, 1944.

392. WARNER, W. LLOYD, and JOSEPH O. LOW, *The Social System of the Modern Factory, The Strike:* A Social Analysis. Yale University Press, New Haven, 1947.

393. WATTENBERG, WILLIAM W., "Boys Who Get in Trouble," *Journal of Education*, vol. 131, April, 1948, pp. 117–118.

394. WATTENBERG, WILLIAM W., and JAMES BALISTRIERI, "Automobile Theft: A 'Favored-Group' Delinquency," *American Journal of Sociology*, vol. 57, May, 1952, pp. 575–579.

395. WATTENBERG, WILLIAM W., and JAMES BALISTRIERI, "Gang Membership and Juvenile Misconduct," *American Sociological Review*, vol. 15, December, 1950, pp. 744–752.

396. WEBB, SIDNEY, and BEATRICE WEBB, *English Poor Law History*. Longmans, Green and Co., New York, 1927–1929. Issued in two parts as vol. 7 of *English Local Government*.

397. WEBER, MAX, *General Economic History*, translated by Frank H. Knight. Free Press, Glencoe, Ill., 1950.

398. WEBER, MAX, *The Protestant Ethic and the Spirit of Capitalism*, translated by Talcott Parsons. Charles Scribner's Sons, New York, 1930.

399. WEBER, MAX, *The Theory of Social and Economic Organization*, translated by A. M. Henderson and Talcott Parsons. Oxford University Press, New York, 1947.

400. WELFARE AND HEALTH COUNCIL OF NEW YORK CITY, *New York City, 1955–1965:* A Report to the Community, 1955.

401. WHITE, R. CLYDE, *Administration of Public Welfare*. 2d ed. American Book Co., New York, 1950.

402. WHITE, R. CLYDE, " 'Social Workers in Society': Some Further Evidence," *Social Work Journal*, vol. 34, October, 1953, pp. 161–164.

403. WHITEHEAD, T. N. *Leadership in a Free Society*. Harvard University Press, Cambridge, 1936.

404. WHITNEY, VINCENT H., "Some Sociological Consequences of Atomic Power," *Annals of the American Academy of Political and Social Science*, vol. 290, November, 1953, pp. 67–75.

405. WHYTE, WILLIAM F., *Street Corner Society*. University of Chicago Press, Chicago, 1943.

406. WHYTE, WILLIAM F., editor, *Industry and Society*. McGraw-Hill Book Co., New York, 1946.

407. WHYTE, WILLIAM H., JR., "Budgetism: Opiate of the Middle Class," *Fortune*, vol. 53, May, 1956, pp. 133–137.

408. WHYTE, WILLIAM H., JR., "The Outgoing Life," *Fortune*, vol. 48, July, 1953, pp. 84–88, 156–160.

409. WHYTE, WILLIAM H., JR., "Transients," *Fortune*, vol. 47, 1953: May, pp. 112–117, 221–226; June, pp. 126–131, 186–196; vol. 48, 1953: July, pp. 84–88, 156–160; August, pp. 102–122, 186–190.

410. WILENSKY, HAROLD L., *Intellectuals in Labor Unions:* Organizational Pressures on Professional Roles. Free Press, Glencoe, Ill., 1956.

411. WILLIAMS, ROBIN M., JR., *American Society:* A Sociological Interpretation. Alfred A. Knopf, New York, 1951.

412. WILSON, GERTRUDE, "Social Group Work: Trends and Developments," *Social Work*, vol. 1, October, 1956, pp. 66–75.

413. WILSON, GERTRUDE, and GLADYS RYLAND, *Social Group Work Practice*. Houghton Mifflin Co., Boston, 1949.

414. WILTSE, KERMIT T., "Social Casework Services in the Aid to Dependent Children Program," *Social Service Review*, vol. 28, June, 1954, pp. 173–185.

415. WINCH, ROBERT F., and ROBERT McGINNIS, editors, *Selected Studies in Marriage and the Family*. Henry Holt and Co., New York, 1953.

416. WIRTH, LOUIS, "Consensus and Mass Communication," *American Sociological Review*, vol. 13, February, 1948, pp. 1–15.

417. WIRTH, LOUIS, "Urbanism as a Way of Life," *American Journal of Sociology*, vol. 44, July, 1938, pp. 1–24.

418. WITMER, HELEN L., *Social Work:* An Analysis of a Social Institution. Farrar and Rinehart, New York, 1942.

419. WITMER, HELEN L., and EDITH TUFTS, *The Effectiveness of Delinquency Prevention Programs.* U.S. Department of Health, Education, and Welfare, Children's Bureau Publication 350, Washington, 1954.

420. WITTKE, CARL F., *We Who Built America:* The Saga of the Immigrant. Western Reserve University Press, Cleveland, 1939.

421. WOLFLE, DAEL, *America's Resources of Specialized Talent.* Harper and Bros., New York, 1954.

422. WOYTINSKY, W. S., and others, *Employment and Wages in the United States.* Twentieth Century Fund, New York, 1953.

423. YOUNGDAHL, BENJAMIN, "Social Work at the Crossroads," *Social Work Journal*, vol. 34, July, 1953, pp. 111–113.

424. ZANDER, ALVIN, ARTHUR COHEN, and EZRA STOTLAND, *Role Relations in the Mental Health Profession.* Research Center for Group Dynamics, University of Michigan, Ann Arbor. In preparation.

425. ZIMMER, BASIL E., *Adjustment of Migrants in Urban Areas.* Ph.D. thesis, University of Michigan, Ann Arbor, 1954.

426. ZIMMERMAN, CARLE C., *Family and Civilization.* Harper and Bros., New York, 1947.

Index

383

Sit-down strikes, 106

Sjoberg, Gideon, 117n

Skills: the aged, 78; effective use, 257–259; human relations, 128–129; in large-scale organization, 99, 128–129; managerial, 99; obsolescence, 62–63, 78, 99, 112; retraining, 112; transmission, 340–341; upgrading, 94, 99; women, 74. *See also* Specialization

Slavery, 51

Slum organization, 184–185

Smith, Adam, 28, 59

Social change: technology and, 341–348; urbanism and, 153; value conflicts, 177–180

Social class. *See* Class; Status

Social control: children, 127; consensus and, 129–132; delinquency, 189; internalization of values, 128; mores and, 119; nuclear family, 195–196; power structure and, 265–282; primary group, 122–124; primary vs. secondary values, 118–119; rationalization of, 118–119; rural, 198; and social structure survival, 340–341; in suburbia, 126–127; urban forms, 198; voluntary associations' role, 129–132. *See also* Motivation; Values

Social disorganization and delinquency causation, 183–187

"Social Ethic," 39–41

Social insurance, 42–43; the aged, 77–78, 96f, 143, 151, 156, 159–160; constitutional problems, 150–151; industrialism and, 66; institutionalization, 147; in pre-industrial society, 58, 65; unemployment, 143, 145, 151, 159–160

Social integration, 115–133 *passim;* class factors, 122–129; communications media and, 131–132; consensus and, 129–132; migrants, 123–124; "moral integration," 124n; pluralistic society, 131; residential stability and, 122; slums, 184–185; suburbia, 126–127; theoretical considerations, 340; voluntary associations' role, 130–132

Social isolates. *See* Alienation; Anomie; Anonymity

Social legislation, 89; child labor, 71, 150; contract labor, 53; delinquency, 219–228; expansion, 151; scope, 41–42; Social Security Act, 150; social work supervision, 307

Social movements, 131n. *See also* Labor movement

Social problems, 137–228; the aged, 178; capitalism and, 33, 41–44; child support, 178–179; delinquency, 181–228; deviant behavior, 181–228; industrial

relocation and, 176–177; industrialism and, 41–42; installment-plan living, 174–175; interdependence of, 216–218; leisure, 175–176; mental hygiene education, 179–180; trends, 133; value conflicts, 177–180; working women, 179

Social reform. *See* Reform

Social relations: anonymity, 118–119; atomization, 119–120; control values, 118–119; manipulation of, 119–120; tolerance, 116–133. *See also* Interpersonal relations

Social Security Act, 150

Social status. *See* Status

Social stratification. *See* Class; Stratification; Status

Social structure: conditions for survival, 337–341; definition, 343n; and delinquency causation, 183–187; integration and, 340; "Mass Society," 131n; private interest groups, 119; reform, 216–218; and role conflict, 317–319; and role differentiation, 338–339; routine welfare services, 138–140; slums, 184–185; and welfare clientele, 169–174; and welfare demand, 181. *See also* Class; Family structure; Power; Stratification

Social values. *See* Values

Social welfare: accountability, 141; the aged, 43, 166, 178; auspices, 145–146, 148–167; authority, 150–151; centralization, 149; characteristics, 138–147; charity ideology, 139; child-service, 166; clientele stigmatization, 253–254; community orientation, 164–165; constitutional limitations, 150–151; consumption philosophy, 145–146; continuity, 140n; contractual basis, 143; correctional programs, 154; definition, 17n, 138–140; depression impact, 156; early forms, 54–55; emergency, 104; employment in, 152; English origins, 148; expenditures, 79, 148–167; federal, 150–153; fee-for-service, 143; financing, 152–160; foreign, 157; functional generalization, 144; government role, 145–146, 148–160; immigrant needs, 54–55; and income distribution, 105; "institutional," 138–140; integrative premises, 144; leisure programs, 165; local, 152–153; mutual-aid services, 141; needs orientation, 145–146; new problems, 174–177; occupations in, 291–298; organization, 140–141, 231–334; philosophy, 138–147, 164–165; planning, 263–265, 290–291, 329–330; policy, 233–282; population